Yamaha YZ80/85/125/250 2-Stroke Motocross Bikes Owners Workshop Manual

by Alan Ahlstrand
and John H Haynes
Member of the Guild of Motoring Writers

Models covered:
YZ80, 1986 through 2001
YZ80LW, 1993 through 2001
YZ85, 2002 through 2006
YZ85LW, 2002 through 2006
YZ125, 1986 through 2006
YZ250, 1986 through 2006

(2662 - 8U2)
ABCDE

Haynes Group Limited
Sparkford Nr Yeovil
Somerset BA22 7JJ England

Haynes North America, Inc.
2801 Townsgate Road, Suite 340
Thousand Oaks, CA 91361 USA

www.haynes.com

Disclaimer

There are risks associated with automotive repairs. The ability to make repairs depends on individual skill, experience and proper tools. Individuals should act with due care and acknowledge and assume the risk of making automotive repairs.

The purpose of this manual is to provide comprehensive, useful and accessible automotive repair information, to help you get the best value from your vehicle. However, this manual is not a substitute for a professional certified technician or mechanic. There are risks associated with automotive repairs. The ability to make repairs on a vehicle depends on individual skill, experience, and proper tools. Individuals should act with due care and acknowledge and assume the risk of performing automotive repairs.

This repair manual is produced by a third party and is not associated with an individual car manufacturer. If there is any doubt or discrepancy between this manual and the owner's manual or the factory service manual, please refer to factory service manual or seek assistance from a professional certified technician or mechanic.

Even though we have prepared this manual with extreme care and every attempt is made to ensure that the information in this manual is correct, neither the publisher nor the author can accept responsibility for loss, damage or injury caused by any errors in, or omissions from, the information given.

Acknowledgments

Our thanks to GP Sports, Santa Clara, California, for providing the motorcycles used in these photographs. Thanks also to Mark Zueger, service manager, for arranging the facilities and fitting the mechanical work into his shop's busy schedule. Craig Wardner, the technician who did the mechanical work, deserves special mention both for his extensive knowledge and for his ability to explain things. Wiring Diagrams provided exclusively for Haynes North America, Inc. by Solution Builders.

A book in the Haynes Owners Workshop Manual Series

Printed in India

ISBN-13: 978-1-56392-662-4
ISBN-10: 1-56392-662-8

Library of Congress Control Number: 2007929802

07-208

Contents

2006 YZ125

About this manual

Its purpose

The purpose of this manual is to help you get the best value from your motorcycle. It can do so in several ways. It can help you decide what work must be done, even if you choose to have it done by a dealer service department or a repair shop; it provides information and procedures for routine maintenance and servicing; and it offers diagnostic and repair procedures to follow when trouble occurs.

We hope you use the manual to tackle the work yourself. For many simpler jobs, doing it yourself may be quicker than arranging an appointment to get the vehicle into a shop and making the trips to leave it and pick it up. More importantly, a lot of money can be saved by avoiding the expense the shop must pass on to you to cover its labor and overhead costs. An added benefit is the sense of satisfaction and accomplishment that you feel after doing the job yourself.

Using the manual

The manual is divided into Chapters. Each Chapter is divided into numbered Sections, which are headed in bold type between horizontal lines. Each Section consists of consecutively numbered paragraphs or steps.

At the beginning of each numbered Section you will be referred to any illustrations which apply to the procedures in that Section. The reference numbers used in illustration captions pinpoint the pertinent Section and the Step within that Section. That is, illustration 3.2 means the illustration refers to Section 3 and Step (or paragraph) 2 within that Section.

Procedures, once described in the text, are not normally repeated. When it's necessary to refer to another Chapter, the reference will be given as Chapter and Section number. Cross references given without use of the word 'Chapter' apply to Sections and/or paragraphs in the same Chapter. For example, 'see Section 8' means in the same Chapter.

References to the left or right side of the vehicle assume you are sitting on the seat, facing forward.

Motorcycle manufacturers continually make changes to specifications and recommendations, and these, when notified, are incorporated into our manuals at the earliest opportunity.

Even though we have prepared this manual with extreme care, neither the publisher nor the authors can accept responsibility for any errors in, or omissions from, the information given.

NOTE

A **Note** provides information necessary to properly complete a procedure or information which will make the procedure easier to understand.

CAUTION

A **Caution** provides a special procedure or special steps which must be taken while completing the procedure where the Caution is found. Not heeding a Caution can result in damage to the assembly being worked on.

WARNING

A **Warning** provides a special procedure or special steps which must be taken while completing the procedure where the Warning is found. Not heeding a Warning can result in personal injury.

Introduction to the Yamaha YZ

The YZ80/85 and their taller-wheeled variants, the YZ80/85LW, are highly popular and successful beginner's motocross bikes. The YZ125 and YZ250, with their technically advanced suspension and engine power valve systems, have been seriously competitive machines as long as they have been produced.

The engine on all models is a liquid-cooled two-stroke single. Power is transmitted through a six-speed transmission. All models use a wet multi-plate clutch and chain final drive.

Fuel is delivered to the cylinder by a slide-type carburetor.

The front suspension consists of telescopic forks mounted in upper and lower triple clamps. The rear suspension uses a single shock absorber/coil spring unit and progressive rising rate suspension linkage. A disc brake is used at the front on all models. 1986 through 1992 YZ80 and 1986 and 1987 YZ125/YZ250 models used a drum brake at the rear; all other models use a disc brake.

Identification numbers

The frame serial number is stamped into the front of the frame and printed on a label affixed to the frame. The engine number is stamped into the right side of the crankcase. Both of these numbers should be recorded and kept in a safe place so they can be furnished to law enforcement officials in the event of a theft.

The frame serial number, engine serial number and carburetor identification number should also be kept in a handy place (such as with your driver's license) so they are always available when purchasing or ordering parts for your machine.

The models covered by this manual are as follows:

YZ80, 1986 through 2001
YZ80LW, 1993 through 2001
YZ85, 2002 through 2006
YZ85LW, 2002 through 2006
YZ125, 1986 through 2006
YZ250, 1986 through 2006

The frame serial number is stamped into the steering head

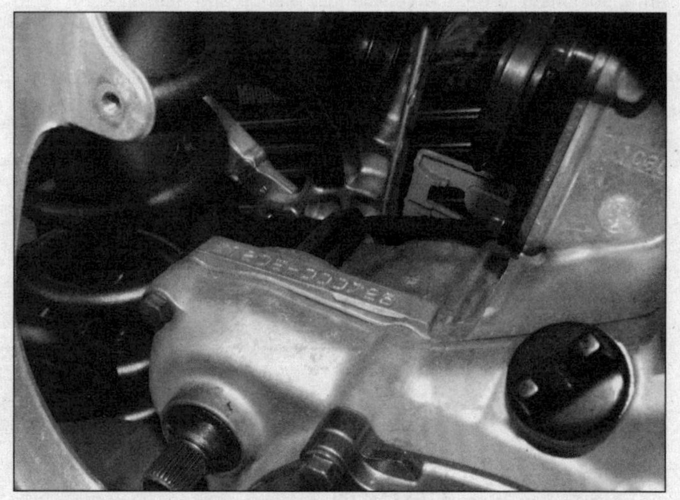

The engine serial number is located on the right side of the crankcase

Buying parts

Once you have found all the identification numbers, record them for reference when buying parts. Since the manufacturers change specifications, parts and vendors (companies that manufacture various components on the machine), providing the ID numbers is the only way to be reasonably sure that you are buying the correct parts.

Whenever possible, take the worn part to the dealer so direct comparison with the new component can be made. Along the trail from the manufacturer to the parts shelf, there are numerous places that the part can end up with the wrong number or be listed incorrectly.

The two places to purchase new parts for your motorcycle - the accessory store and the franchised dealer - differ in the type of parts they carry. While dealers can obtain virtually every part for your motorcycle, the accessory dealer is usually limited to normal high wear items such as shock absorbers, tune-up parts, various engine gaskets, cables, chains, brake parts, etc. Rarely will an accessory outlet have major suspension components, cylinders, transmission gears, or cases.

Used parts can be obtained for roughly half the price of new ones, but you can't always be sure of what you're getting. Once again, take your worn part to the wrecking yard (breaker) for direct comparison.

Whether buying new, used or rebuilt parts, the best course is to deal directly with someone who specializes in parts for your particular make.

General specifications

Bore
- YZ80
  - 1986 through 1992 .... 48.0 mm (1.890 inch)
  - 1993 through 2000
    - US, Canada, Australia, New Zealand: .... 47.0 mm (1.850 inch)
    - All others .... 46.0 mm (1.811 inch)
  - 2001 .... 47.0 mm (1.850 inch)
- YZ85 .... 47.5 mm (1.870 inch)
- YZ125
  - 1986 through 1993 .... 56.0 mm (2.204 inches)
  - 1994 through 2006 .... 54.0 mm 2.126 inch)
- YZ250
  - 1986 through 1998 .... 68.0 mm (2.677 inches)
  - 1999 and later .... 66.4 mm (2.614 inches)

Stroke
- YZ80
  - 1986 .... 47.8 mm (1.880 inch)
  - 1987 through 1992 .... 45.6 mm (1.800 inch)
  - 1993 through 2001 .... 47.8 mm (1.880 inch)
- YZ85 .... 47.8 mm (1.882 inch)
- YZ125
  - 1986 through 1988 .... 50 mm (1.969 inch)
  - 1989 through 1993 .... 50.7 mm (2.000 inch)
  - 1994 and later .... 54.5 mm (2.146 inch)
- YZ250
  - 1986 through 1992 .... 68.0 mm (2.677 inches)
  - 1993 through 1998 .... 68.8 mm (2.709 inches)
  - 1999 and later .... 72 mm (2.835 inches)

Compression ratio
- YZ80
  - 1986 and 1987 .... 8.6 to 1
  - 1988 through 1992 .... 8.3 to 1
  - 1993 through 1996 .... 8.5 to 1
  - 1997
    - 4ES6, 4LC4 .... 8.2 to 1
    - 4GT9, 4LB7 .... 8.25 to 1
  - 1998
    - 4ES7, 4LC5 .... 8.2 to 1
    - 4GTB, 4LB9 .... 8.25 to 1
  - 1999
    - 4ES8, 4LC6 .... 8.2 to 1
    - 4GTD, 4LBB .... 8.25 to 1
  - 2000
    - 4ES9, 4LC7 .... 8.2 to 1
    - 4GTF, 4LBD .... 8.25 to 1
  - 2001 .... 8.2 to 1
- YZ85 .... 8.2 to 1

General specifications (continued)

YZ125	
1986	8.1 to 10.5 to 1
1987 and 1988	8.4 to 10.5 to 1
1989	8.7 to 11.0 to 1
1990	8.9 to 10.3 to 1
1991	9.2 to 10.7 to 1
1992	8.7 to 10.6 to 1
1993	9.1 to 10.3 to 1
1994 and 1995	9.0 to 10.1 to 1
1996 and 1997	8.5 to 10.4 to 1
1998 and 1999	8.9 to 10.9 to 1
2000 through 2002	8.7 to 10.8 to 1
2003 and 2004	8.7 to 11.0 to 1
2005 and later	8.6 to 10.7 to 1
YZ250	
1986	8.22 to 9.72 to 1
1987 and 1988	8.54 to 10.12 to 1
1989	8.7 to 11.0 to 1
1990 through 1992	9.0 to 10.9 to 1
1993 and 1994	9.0 to 10.8 to 1
1995	9.0 to 10.9 to 1
1996	9.0 to 10.4 to 1
1997	8.7 to 10.1 to 1
1998	8.7 to 10.6 to 1
1999 and 2000	8.8 to 10.3 to 1
2001 and 2002	9.1 to 10.6 to 1
2003	
US	9.1 to 10.9 to 1
Canada and Europe	9.1 to 10.6 to 1
2004 and 2005	
Europe	9.1 to 10.6 to 1
All except Europe	9.1 to 10.9 to 1
2006	
Europe	9.1 to 10.6 to 1
All except Europe	9.1 to 10.9 to 1
Wheelbase	
YZ80	
1986 through 1992	1235 mm (48.6 inches)
1993 and 1994	1257 mm (49.5 inches)
1995 through 2001	
YZ80	1257 mm (49.5 inches)
YZ80LW	1283 mm (50.3 inches)
YZ85	1258 mm (49.5 inches)
YZ85LW	1278 mm (35.0 inches)
YZ125	
1986 through 1989	1450 mm (57.1 inches)
1990 through 1992	1470 mm (57.9 inches)
1993	1466 mm (57.7 inches)
1994 and 1995	1452 mm (57.2 inches)
1996	1436 mm (56.5 inches)
1997 through 2001	1444 mm (56.9 inches)
2002 through 2004	1438 mm (56.6 inches)
2005 and later	1443 mm (56.8 inches)
YZ250	
1986 and 1987	1470 mm (57.9 inches)
1988 and 1989	1480 mm (58.3 inches)
1990 through 1992	1495 mm (58.9 inches)
1993 and 1994	1496 mm (58.9 inches)
1995	1492 mm (58.7 inches)
1996 and 1997	1489 mm (58.6 inches)
1998 through 2001	1482 mm (58.3 inches)
2002 through 2005	
US, Australia, New Zealand	1481 mm (58.3 inches)
Canada and Europe	1485 mm (58.5 inches)
2006	1481 mm (58.3 inches)
Overall length	
YZ80	
1986 through 1992	1795 mm (70.7 inches)

1993 through 2001	
YZ80	1803 mm (71.0 inches)
YZ80LW	1891 mm (74.4 inches)
YZ85	1821 mm (71.7 inches)
YZ85LW	
2002	1896 mm (74.4 inches)
2003 and later	1903 mm (74.9 inches)
YZ125	
1986 through 1989	2135 mm (84.1 inches)
1990 through 1992	2165 mm (85.2 inches)
1993	2166 mm (85.3 inches)
1994 through 1996	2149 mm (84.6 inches)
1997	2139 mm (84.2 inches)
1998	
Europe	2136 mm (84.1 inches)
All except Europe	2139 mm (84.2 inches)
1999 through 2001	
Europe	2136 mm (84.1 inches)
All except Europe	2139 mm (84.2 inches)
2002 through 2005	
Europe	2130 mm (83.9 inches)
All except Europe	2134 mm (84.0 inches)
2006	
Europe and Canada	2139 mm (84.2 inches)
All others	2135 mm (84.1 inches)
YZ250	
1986 and 1987	2170 mm (85.4 inches)
1988 and 1989	2180 mm (85.8 inches)
1990 through 1992	2195 mm (58.9 inches)
1993	2193 mm (86.3 inches)
1994 and 1995	2188 mm (86.1 inches)
1996	2187 mm (86.1 inches)
1997	2184 mm (86.0 inches)
1998 through 2001	
Europe	2178 mm (85.7 inches)
All except Europe	2179 mm (85.7 inches)
2002 through 2005	
Europe	2182 mm (85.9 inches)
All except Europe	2183 mm (85.9 inches)
2006	
US, Australia, New Zealand	2178 mm (85.7 inches)
Canada	2183 mm (85.9 inches)
Europe	2184 mm (86.0 inches)
Overall width	
YZ80	
1986 through 1992	765 mm (30.1 inches)
1993 through 2001	735 mm (28.9 inches)
YZ85	758 mm (28.9 inches)
YZ125	
1986 through 1996	850 mm (33.5 inches)
1997 and later	827 mm (32.6 inches)
YZ250	
1986 through 1996	850 mm (33.5 inches)
1997 and later	827 mm (32.6 inches)
Overall height	
YZ80	
1986 through 1992	1060 mm (41.7 inches)
1993 through 2001	
YZ80	1105 mm (43.5 inches)
YZ80LW	1177 mm (46.3 inches)
YZ85	1161 mm (45.7 inches)
YZ85LW	1204 mm (47.4 inches)
YZ125	
1986 through 1988	1240 mm (48.8 inches)
1989	1245 mm (49.0 inches)
1990 and 1991	1225 mm (48.2 inches)
1992	1233 mm (48.5 inches)
1993	1225 mm (48.2 inches)
1994 and 1995	1215 mm (47.8 inches)
1996	1282 mm (50.5 inches)

General specifications (continued)

1997 .... 1314 mm (51.7 inches)
1998 and 1999
Europe .... 1313 mm (51.69 inches)
All except Europe .... 1314 mm (51.73 inches)
2000 and 2001
US and Canada .... 1318 mm (51.9 inches)
Europe .... 1313 mm (51.69 inches)
Australia and New Zealand .... 1314 mm (51.73 inches)
2002 through 2004
US .... 1318 mm (51.9 inches)
Canada, Australia, New Zealand .... 1315 mm (51.8 inches)
Europe .... 1311 mm (51.6 inches)
2005
US, Australia, New Zealand .... 1316 mm (51.8 inches)
Canada, Europe .... 1318 mm (51.9 inches)
2006
US, Australia, New Zealand .... 1315 mm (51.8 inches)
Canada .... 1317 mm (51.9 inches)
Europe .... 1318 mm (51.9 inches)
YZ250
1986 and 1987 .... 1230 mm (48.4 inches)
1988 through 1991 .... 1225 mm (48.2 inches)
1992 .... 1233 mm (48.5 inches)
1993 .... 1225 mm (48.2 inches)
1994 and 1995 .... 1215 mm (47.8 inches)
1996 .... 1269 mm (50.0 inches)
1997 .... 1299 mm (51.1 inches)
1998 and 1999
Europe .... 1302 mm (51.3 inches)
All except Europe .... 1303 mm (51.3 inches)
2000 and 2001
US and Canada .... 1307 mm (51.5 inches)
Europe .... 1302 mm (51.3 inches)
Australia and New Zealand .... 1303 mm (51.3 inches)
2002 through 2005
US .... 1309 mm (51.5 inches)
Canada .... 1307 mm (51.5 inches)
Europe .... 1302 mm (51.3 inches)
Australia, New Zealand .... 1296 mm (51.0 inches)
2006
US .... 1305 mm (31.4 inches)
Canada .... 1308 mm (51.5 inches)
Europe .... 1309 mm (51.5 inches)

Seat height
YZ80
1986 through 1992 .... 800 mm (31.5 inches)
1993 through 2001
YZ80 .... 854 mm (33.6 inches)
YZ80LW .... 890 mm (35.0 inches)
YZ85 .... 864 mm (34.0 inches)
YZ85LW
2002 .... 902 mm (35.0 inches)
2004 and later .... 904 mm (35.6 inches)
YZ125
1986 through 1988 .... 935 mm (36.8 inches)
1989 through 1991 .... 945 mm (37.2 inches)
1992 .... 953 mm (37.5 inches)
1993 through 1995 .... 998 mm (39.3 inches)
1996 and 1997 .... 982 mm (38.7 inches)
1998 and 1999
Europe .... 994 mm (39.1 inches)
All others .... 993 mm (39.1 inches)
2000 and 2001
Europe .... 993 mm (39.1 inches)
All others .... 994 mm (39.1 inches)
2002 through 2004
US, Australia, New Zealand .... 993 mm (39.1 inches)
Canada and Europe .... 992 mm (39.1 inches)

2005 and later
US, Australia, New Zealand .... 992 mm (39.1 inches)
Canada and Europe .... 994 mm (39.1 inches)
YZ250
1986 and 1987 .... 955 mm (37.6 inches)
1988 and 1989 .... 950 mm (37.4 inches)
1990 and 1991 .... 970 mm (38.2 inches)
1992 .... 978 mm (38.5 inches)
1993 .... 998 mm (39.3 inches)
1994 and 1995 .... 992 mm (39.1 inches)
1996 .... 981 mm (38.6 inches)
1997 .... 979 mm (38.5 inches)
1998 through 2001 .... 989 mm (38.9 inches)
2002 through 2005
US, Australia, New Zealand .... 991 mm (39.0 inches)
Canada, Europe .... 990 mm (39.0 inches)
2006
US, Australia, New Zealand .... 994 mm (39.1 inches)
Canada .... 996 mm (39.2 inches)
Europe .... 997 mm (39.3 inches)
Ground clearance
YZ80
1986 through 1992 .... 290 mm (11.4 inches)
1993 through 2001
YZ80 .... 347 mm (13.7 inches)
YZ80LW .... 389 mm (15.3 inches)
YZ85 .... 351 mm (13.8 inches)
YZ85LW
2002 .... 391 mm (15.4 inches)
2003 and later .... 393 mm (15.5 inches)
YZ125
1986 through 1988 .... 350 mm (13.8 inches)
1989 through 1991 .... 355 mm (14.0 inches)
1992 .... 398 mm (15.7 inches)
1993 .... 396 mm (15.6 inches)
1994 and 1995 .... 386 mm (15.2 inches)
1996 .... 398 mm (15.7 inches)
1997 through 2001 .... 400 mm (15.74 inches)
2002 through 2004
US, Australia, New Zealand .... 400 mm (15.74 inches)
Canada and Europe .... 398 mm (15.7 inches)
2005
US .... 387 mm (15.2 inches)
Australia and New Zealand .... 388 mm (15.3 inches)
Canada and Europe .... 389 mm (15.3 inches)
2006
US, Australia, New Zealand .... 386 mm (15.2 inches)
Canada and Europe .... 388 mm (15.3 inches)
YZ250
1986 through 1992 .... 340 mm (13.4 inches)
1993 .... 394 mm (15.5 inches)
1994 and 1995 .... 382 mm (15.0 inches)
1996 .... 393 mm (15.5 inches)
1997 .... 392 mm (15.4 inches)
1998
Europe .... 391 mm (15.4 inches)
All except Europe .... 392 mm (15.4 inches)
1999 through 2001
Europe .... 391 mm (15.4 inches)
All except Europe .... 392 mm (15.4 inches)
2002 through 2005
US, Australia, New Zealand .... 395 mm (15.6 inches)
Canada, Europe .... 393 mm (15.5 inches)
2006
US, Australia, New Zealand .... 382 mm (15.0 inches)
Canada .... 384 mm (15.1 inches)
Europe .... 385 mm (15.2 inches)

General specifications (continued)

Weight	
YZ80	
1986 (net weight)	60.0 kg (132 lbs)
1987 through 1992 (dry)	61.3 kg (135 lbs)
1993 through 2001 (wet, full fuel tank)	
YZ80	71.0 kg (156.5 lbs)
YZ80LW	73.9 kg (162.9 lbs)
YZ85	
2002 through 2004 (wet, full fuel tank)	71 kg (156.5 lbs)
2005 and later (dry)	66 kg (145.5 lbs)
YZ85LW	
2002 through 2004 (wet, full fuel tank)	73.9 kg (162.9 lbs)
2005 and later (dry)	69 kg (152.1 lbs)
YZ125	
1986 (wet, full fuel tank)	94 kg (207 lbs)
1987 and 1988 (wet, full fuel tank)	94.5 kg (208 lbs)
1989 (wet, full fuel tank)	87 kg (192 lbs)
1990 (wet, full fuel tank)	87.5 kg (193 lbs)
1991 through 1997 (wet, full fuel tank)	95 kg (209.5 lbs)
1998 (wet, full fuel tank)	96.5 kg (212.5 lbs)
1999 (wet, full fuel tank)	96 kg (211.4 lbs)
2000 (wet, full fuel tank)	95.5 kg (210.5 lbs)
2001 through 2003 (wet, full fuel tank)	95.0 kg (209.4 lbs)
2004 (dry)	87.0 kg (191.8 lbs)
2005 and later (dry)	86 kg (189.6 lbs)
YZ250	
1986 (wet, full fuel tank)	105 kg (232 lbs)
1987 (wet, full fuel tank)	106 kg (234 lbs)
1988 and 1989 (wet, full fuel tank)	104.5 kg (231 lbs)
1990 through 1997 (wet, full fuel tank)	104 kg (229.3 lbs)
1998 (wet, full fuel tank)	106 kg (234 lbs)
1999 (wet, full fuel tank)	105.5 kg (233 lbs)
2000 (wet, full fuel tank)	105.0 kg (231 lbs)
2001 (wet, full fuel tank)	104.5 kg (230 lbs)
2002 (wet, full fuel tank)	105.0 kg (231 lbs)
2003 (wet, full fuel tank)	104.5 kg (230 lbs)
2004 and 2005 (dry)	97 kg (213.8 lbs)
2006	96.0 kg (211.6 lbs)

Maintenance techniques, tools and working facilities

Basic maintenance techniques

There are a number of techniques involved in maintenance and repair that will be referred to throughout this manual. Application of these techniques will enable the amateur mechanic to be more efficient, better organized and capable of performing the various tasks properly, which will ensure that the repair job is thorough and complete.

Fastening systems

Fasteners, basically, are nuts, bolts and screws used to hold two or more parts together. There are a few things to keep in mind when working with fasteners. Almost all of them use a locking device of some type (either a lock washer, locknut, locking tab or thread adhesive). All threaded fasteners should be clean, straight, have undamaged threads and undamaged corners on the hex head where the wrench fits. Develop the habit of replacing all damaged nuts and bolts with new ones.

Rusted nuts and bolts should be treated with a penetrating oil to ease removal and prevent breakage. Some mechanics use turpentine in a spout type oil can, which works quite well. After applying the rust penetrant, let it -work for a few minutes before trying to loosen the nut or bolt. Badly rusted fasteners may have to be chiseled off or removed with a special nut breaker, available at tool stores.

If a bolt or stud breaks off in an assembly, it can be drilled out and removed with a special tool called an E-Z out (or screw extractor). Most dealer service departments and motorcycle repair shops can perform this task, as well as others (such as the repair of threaded holes that have been stripped out).

Flat washers and lock washers, when removed from an assembly, should always be replaced exactly as removed. Replace any damaged washers with new ones. Always use a flat washer between a lock washer and any soft metal surface (such as aluminum), thin sheet metal or plastic. Special locknuts can only be used once or twice before they lose their locking ability and must be replaced.

Tightening sequences and procedures

When threaded fasteners are tightened, they are often tightened to a specific torque value (torque is basically a twisting force). Over-tightening the fastener can weaken it and cause it to break, while under-tightening can cause it to eventually come loose. Each bolt, depending on the material it's made of, the diameter of its shank and the material it is threaded into, has a specific torque value, which is noted in the Specifications. Be sure to follow the torque recommendations closely.

Fasteners laid out in a pattern (i.e. cylinder head bolts, engine case bolts, etc.) must be loosened or tightened in a sequence to avoid warping the component. Initially, the bolts/nuts should go on finger tight only. Next, they should be tightened one full turn each, in a criss-cross or diagonal pattern. After each one has been tightened one full turn, return to the first one tightened and tighten them all one half turn, following the same pattern. Finally, tighten each of them one quarter turn at a time until each fastener has been tightened to the proper torque. To loosen and remove the fasteners the procedure would be reversed.

Disassembly sequence

Component disassembly should be done with care and purpose to help ensure that the parts go back together properly during reassembly. Always keep track of the sequence in which parts are removed. Take note of special characteristics or marks on parts that can be installed more than one way (such as a grooved thrust washer on a shaft). It's a good idea to lay the disassembled parts out on a clean surface in the order that they were removed. It may also be helpful to make sketches or take instant photos of components before removal.

When removing fasteners from a component, keep track of their locations. Sometimes threading a bolt back in a part, or putting the washers and nut back on a stud, can prevent mix-ups later. If nuts and bolts can't be returned to their original locations, they should be kept in a compartmented box or a series of small boxes. A cupcake or muffin tin is ideal for this purpose, since each cavity can hold the bolts and nuts from a particular area (i.e. engine case bolts, valve cover bolts,

Spark plug gap adjusting tool

Feeler gauge set

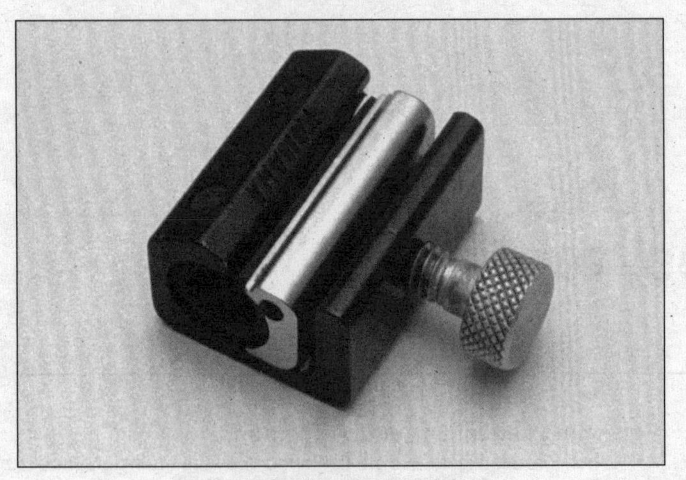
Control cable pressure luber

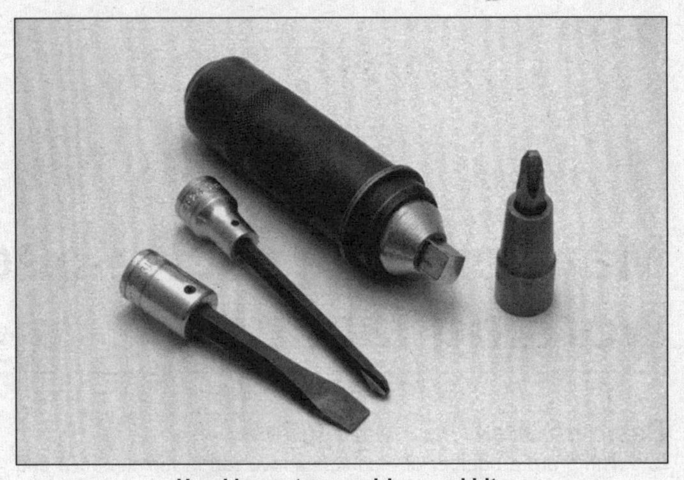
Hand impact screwdriver and bits

engine mount bolts, etc.). A pan of this type is especially helpful when working on assemblies with very small parts (such as the carburetors and the valve train). The cavities can be marked with paint or tape to identify the contents.

Whenever wiring looms, harnesses or connectors are separated, it's a good idea to identify the two halves with numbered pieces of masking tape so they can be easily reconnected.

Gasket sealing surfaces

Throughout any motorcycle, gaskets are used to seal the mating surfaces between components and keep lubricants, fluids, vacuum or pressure contained in an assembly.

Many times these gaskets are coated with a liquid or paste type gasket sealing compound before assembly. Age, heat and pressure can sometimes cause the two parts to stick together so tightly that they are very difficult to separate. In most cases, the part can be loosened by striking it with a soft-faced hammer near the mating surfaces. A regular hammer can be used if a block of wood is placed between the hammer and the part. Do not hammer on cast parts or parts that could be easily damaged. With any particularly stubborn part, always recheck to make sure that every fastener has been removed.

Avoid using a screwdriver or bar to pry apart components, as they can easily mar the gasket sealing surfaces of the parts (which must remain smooth). If prying is absolutely necessary, use a piece of wood, but keep in mind that extra clean-up will be necessary if the wood splinters.

After the parts are separated, the old gasket must be carefully scraped off and the gasket surfaces cleaned. Stubborn gasket material can be soaked with a gasket remover (available in aerosol cans) to soften it so it can be easily scraped off. A scraper can be fashioned from a piece of copper tubing by flattening and sharpening one end. Copper is recommended because it is usually softer than the surfaces to be scraped, which reduces the chance of gouging the part. Some gaskets can be removed with a wire brush, but regardless of the method used, the mating surfaces must be left clean and smooth. If for some reason the gasket surface is gouged, then a gasket sealer thick enough to fill scratches will have to be used during reassembly of the components. For most applications, a non-drying (or semi-drying) gasket sealer is best.

Hose removal tips

Hose removal precautions closely parallel gasket removal precautions. Avoid scratching or gouging the surface that the hose mates against or the connection may leak. Because of various chemical reactions, the rubber in hoses can bond itself to the metal spigot that the hose fits over. To remove a hose, first loosen the hose clamps that secure it to the spigot. Then, with slip joint pliers, grab the hose at the clamp and rotate it around the spigot. Work it back and forth until it is completely free, then pull it off (silicone or other lubricants will ease removal if they can be applied between the hose and the outside of the spigot). Apply the same lubricant to the inside of the hose and the outside of the spigot to simplify installation.

If a hose clamp is broken or damaged, do not reuse it. Also, do not reuse hoses that are cracked, split or torn.

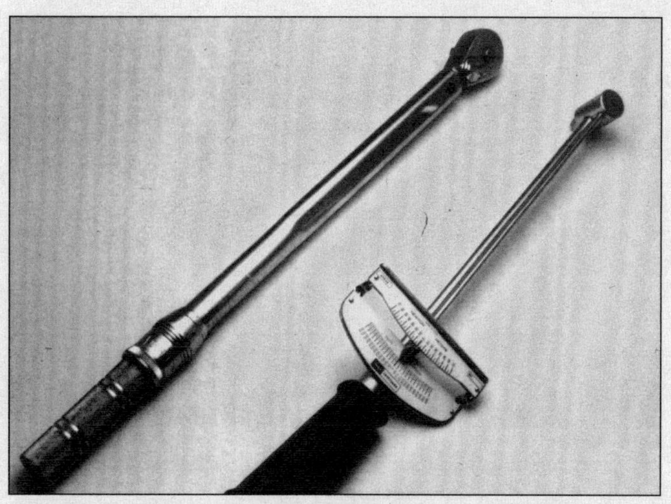

Torque wrenches (left - click; right - beam type)

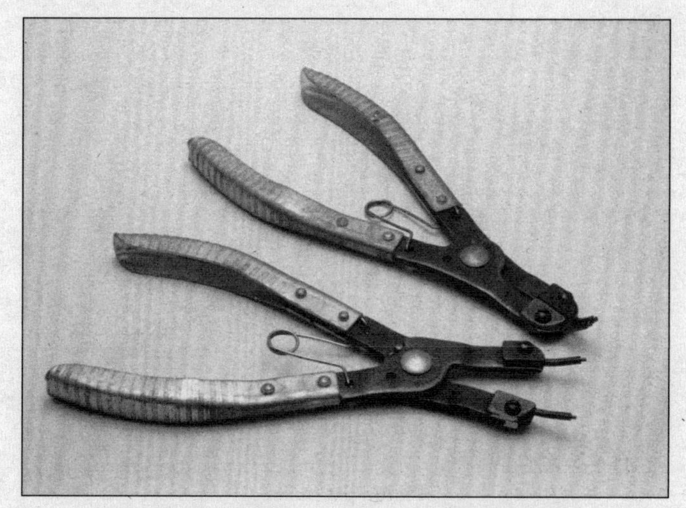

Snap-ring pliers (top - external; bottom - internal)

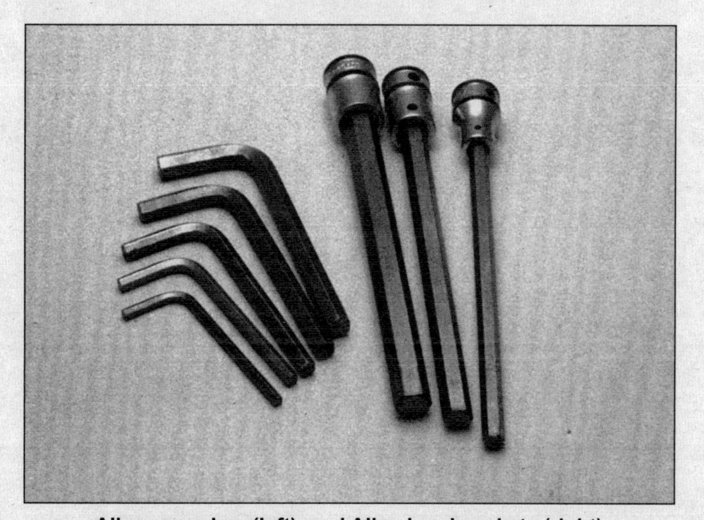

Allen wrenches (left), and Allen head sockets (right)

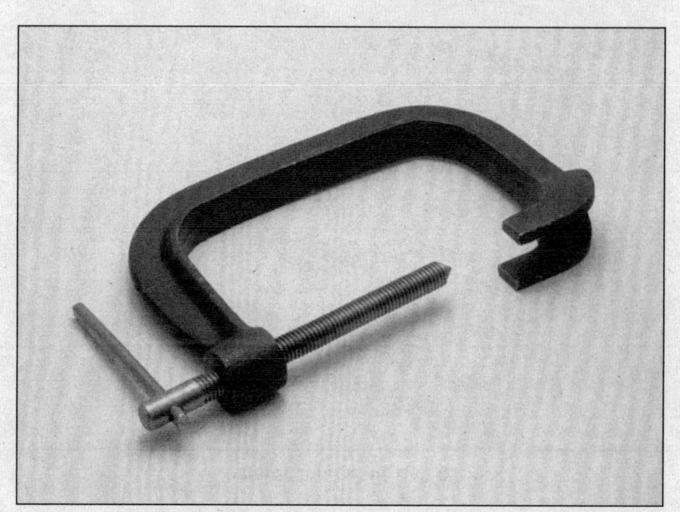

Valve spring compressor

Tools

A selection of good tools is a basic requirement for anyone who plans to maintain and repair a motorcycle. For the owner who has few tools, if any, the initial investment might seem high, but when compared to the spiraling costs of routine maintenance and repair, it is a wise one.

To help the owner decide which tools are needed to perform the tasks detailed in this manual, the following tool lists are offered: *Maintenance and minor repair*, *Repair and overhaul* and *Special*. The newcomer to practical mechanics should start off with the *Maintenance and minor repair* tool kit, which is adequate for the simpler jobs. Then, as confidence and experience grow, the owner can tackle more difficult tasks, buying additional tools as they are needed. Eventually the basic kit will be built into the *Repair and overhaul* tool set. Over a period of time, the experienced do-it-yourselfer will assemble a tool set complete enough for most repair and overhaul procedures and will add tools from the *Special* category when it is felt that the expense is justified by the frequency of use.

Maintenance and minor repair tool kit

The tools in this list should be considered the minimum required for performance of routine maintenance, servicing and minor repair work. We recommend the purchase of combination wrenches (box end and open end combined in one wrench); while more expensive than open-ended ones, they offer the advantages of both types of wrench.

Combination wrench set (6 mm to 22 mm)
Adjustable wrench - 8 in
Spark plug socket (with rubber insert)
Spark plug gap adjusting tool
Feeler gauge set
Standard screwdriver (5/16 in x 6 in)
Phillips screwdriver (No. 2 x 6 in)

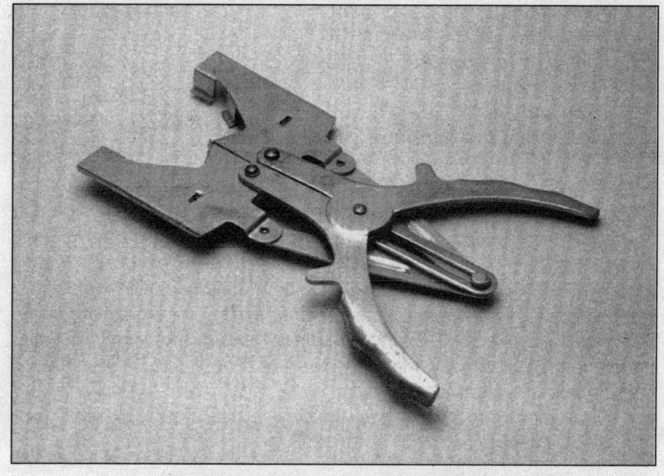

Piston ring removal/installation tool

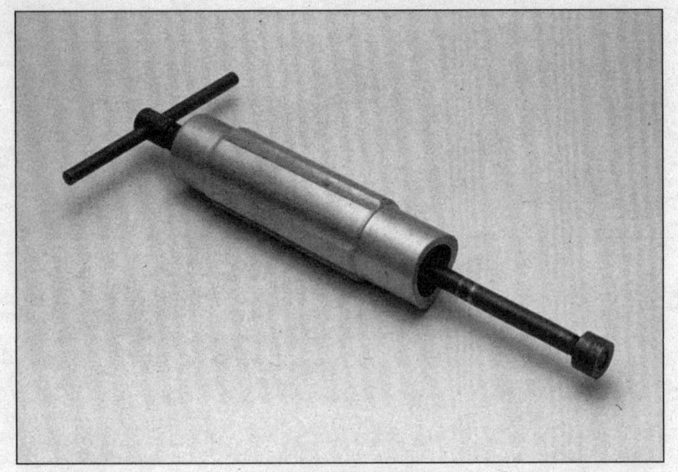

Piston pin puller

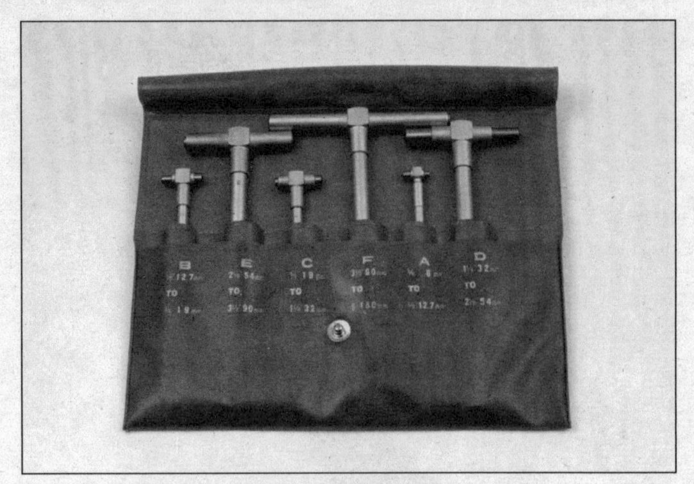

Telescoping gauges

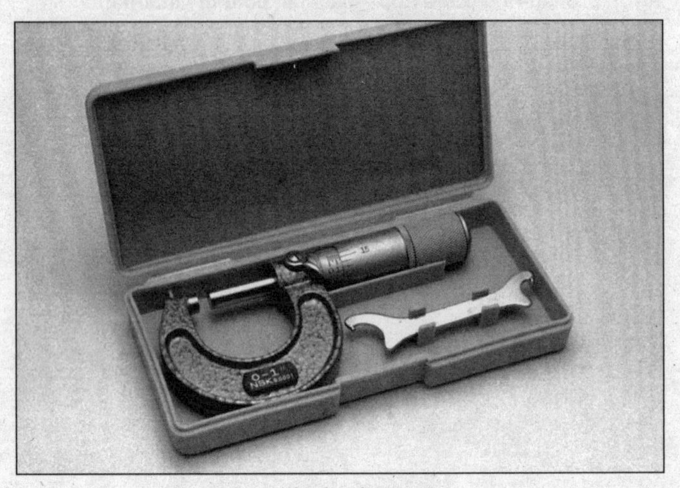

0-to-1 inch micrometer

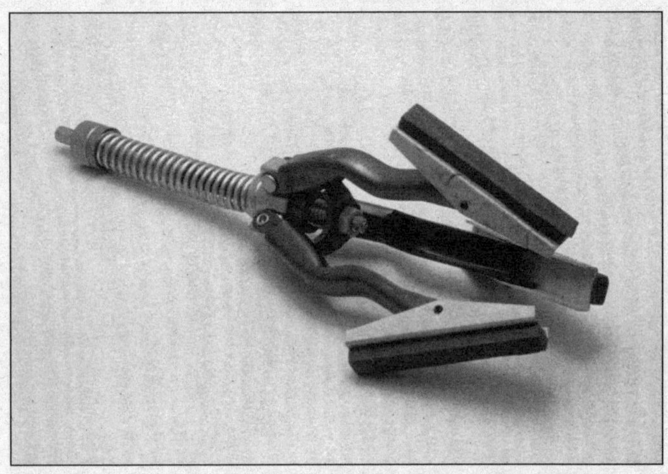

Cylinder surfacing hone

Allen (hex) wrench set (4 mm to 12 mm)
Combination (slip-joint) pliers - 6 in
Hacksaw and assortment of blades
Tire pressure gauge
Control cable pressure luber
Grease gun
Oil can
Fine emery cloth
Wire brush
Hand impact screwdriver and bits
Funnel (medium size)
Safety goggles
Drain pan
Work light with extension cord

Repair and overhaul tool set

These tools are essential for anyone who plans to perform major repairs and are intended to supplement those in the Maintenance and minor repair tool kit. Included is a comprehensive set of sockets which, though expensive, are invaluable because of their versatility (especially when various extensions and drives are available). We recommend the 3/8 inch drive over the 1/2 inch drive for general motorcycle maintenance and repair (ideally, the mechanic would have a 3/8 inch drive set and a 1/2 inch drive set).

Alternator rotor removal tool
Socket set(s)
Reversible ratchet
Extension - 6 in
Universal joint
Torque wrench (same size drive as sockets)
Ball pein hammer - 8 oz
Soft-faced hammer (plastic/rubber)
Standard screwdriver (1/4 in x 6 in)
Standard screwdriver (stubby - 5/16 in)
Phillips screwdriver (No. 3 x 8 in)
Phillips screwdriver (stubby - No. 2)
Pliers - locking
Pliers - lineman's
Pliers - needle nose
Pliers - snap-ring (internal and external)
Cold chisel - 1/2 in
Scriber
Scraper (made from flattened copper tubing)
Center punch
Pin punches (1/16, 1/8, 3/16 in)
Steel rule/straightedge - 12 in
Pin-type spanner wrench
A selection of files
Wire brush (large)

Note: *Another tool which is often useful is an electric drill with a chuck capacity of 3/8 inch (and a set of good quality drill bits).*

Special tools

The tools in this list include those which are not used regularly, are expensive to buy, or which need to be used in accordance with their manufacturer's instructions. Unless these tools will be used frequently,

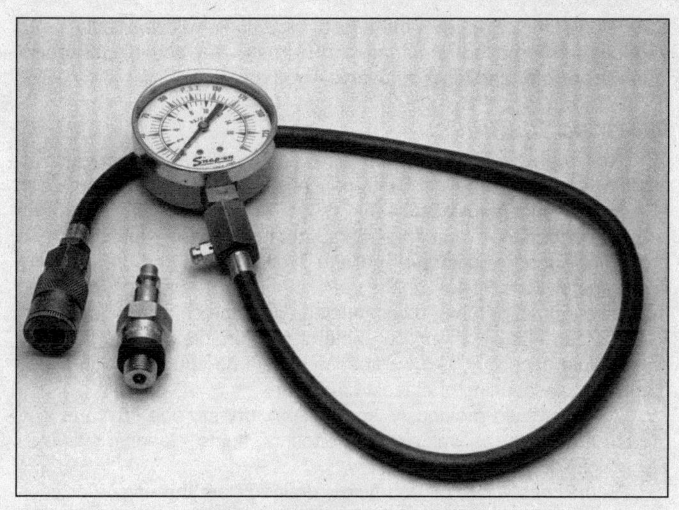
Cylinder compression gauge

Dial indicator set

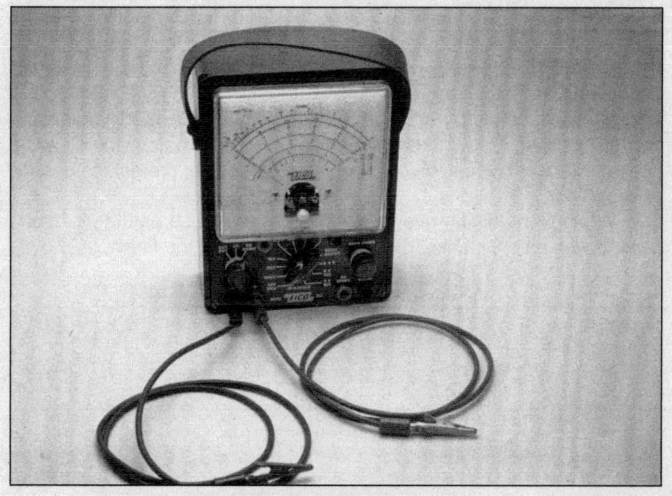
Multimeter (volt/ohm/ammeter)

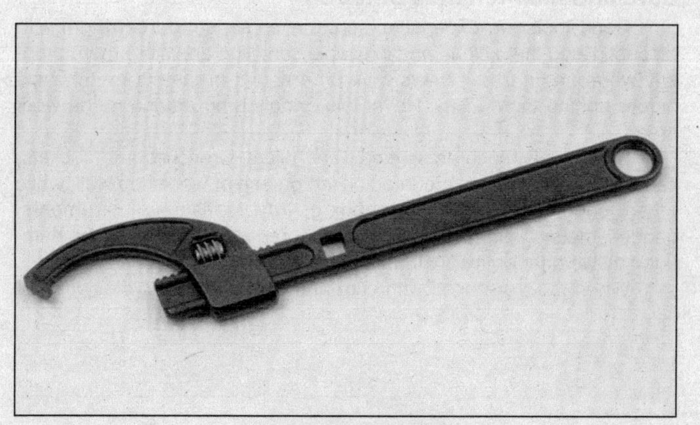
Adjustable spanner

it is not very economical to purchase many of them. A consideration would be to split the cost and use between yourself and a friend or friends (i.e. members of a motorcycle club).

This list primarily contains tools and instruments widely available to the public, as well as some special tools produced by the vehicle manufacturer for distribution to dealer service departments. As a result, references to the manufacturer's special tools are occasionally included in the text of this manual. Generally, an alternative method of doing the job without the special tool is offered. However, sometimes there is no alternative to their use. Where this is the case, and the tool can't be purchased or borrowed, the work should be turned over to the dealer service department or a motorcycle repair shop.

Paddock stand (for models not fitted with a centerstand)
Valve spring compressor
Piston ring removal and installation tool
Piston pin puller
Telescoping gauges
Micrometer(s) and/or dial/Vernier calipers
Cylinder surfacing hone
Cylinder compression gauge
Dial indicator set
Multimeter
Adjustable spanner
Manometer or vacuum gauge set
Small air compressor with blow gun and tire chuck

Alternator rotor puller

Buying tools

For the do-it-yourselfer who is just starting to get involved in motorcycle maintenance and repair, there are a number of options available when purchasing tools. If maintenance and minor repair is the extent of the work to be done, the purchase of individual tools is satisfactory. If, on the other hand, extensive work is planned, it would be a good idea to purchase a modest tool set from one of the large retail chain stores. A set can usually be bought at a substantial savings over the individual tool prices (and they often come with a tool box). As additional tools are needed, add-on sets, individual tools and a larger tool box can be purchased to expand the tool selection. Building a tool set gradually allows the cost of the tools to be spread over a longer period of time and gives the mechanic the freedom to choose only those tools that will actually be used.

Tool stores and motorcycle dealers will often be the only source of some of the special tools that are needed, but regardless of where tools are bought, try to avoid cheap ones (especially when buying screwdrivers and sockets) because they won't last very long. There are plenty of tools around at reasonable prices, but always aim to purchase items which meet the relevant national safety standards. The expense involved in replacing cheap tools will eventually be greater than the initial cost of quality tools.

It is obviously not possible to cover the subject of tools fully here. For those who wish to learn more about tools and their use, there is a book entitled *Motorcycle Workshop Practice Manual* (Book no. 1454) available from the publishers of this manual. It also provides an introduction to basic workshop practice which will be of interest to a home mechanic working on any type of motorcycle.

Care and maintenance of tools

Good tools are expensive, so it makes sense to treat them with respect. Keep them clean and in usable condition and store them properly when not in use. Always wipe off any dirt, grease or metal chips before putting them away. Never leave tools lying around in the work area.

Some tools, such as screwdrivers, pliers, wrenches and sockets, can be hung on a panel mounted on the garage or workshop wall, while others should be kept in a tool box or tray. Measuring instruments, gauges, meters, etc. must be carefully stored where they can't be damaged by weather or impact from other tools.

When tools are used with care and stored properly, they will last a very long time. Even with the best of care, tools will wear out if used frequently. When a tool is damaged or worn out, replace it; subsequent jobs will be safer and more enjoyable if you do.

Working facilities

Not to be overlooked when discussing tools is the workshop. If anything more than routine maintenance is to be carried out, some sort of suitable work area is essential.

It is understood, and appreciated, that many home mechanics do not have a good workshop or garage available and end up removing an engine or doing major repairs outside (it is recommended, however, that the overhaul or repair be completed under the cover of a roof).

A clean, flat workbench or table of comfortable working height is an absolute necessity. The workbench should be equipped with a vise that has a jaw opening of at least four inches.

As mentioned previously, some clean, dry storage space is also required for tools, as well as the lubricants, fluids, cleaning solvents, etc. which soon become necessary.

Sometimes waste oil and fluids, drained from the engine or cooling system during normal maintenance or repairs, present a disposal problem. To avoid pouring them on the ground or into a sewage system, simply pour the used fluids into large containers, seal them with caps and take them to an authorized disposal site or service station. Plastic jugs (such as old antifreeze containers) are ideal for this purpose.

Always keep a supply of old newspapers and clean rags available. Old towels are excellent for mopping up spills. Many mechanics use rolls of paper towels for most work because they are readily available and disposable. To help keep the area under the motorcycle clean, a large cardboard box can be cut open and flattened to protect the garage or shop floor.

Whenever working over a painted surface (such as the fuel tank) cover it with an old blanket or bedspread to protect the finish.

Safety first!

Professional mechanics are trained in safe working procedures. However enthusiastic you may be about getting on with the job at hand, take the time to ensure that your safety is not put at risk. A moment's lack of attention can result in an accident, as can failure to observe simple precautions.

There will always be new ways of having accidents, and the following is not a comprehensive list of all dangers; it is intended rather to make you aware of the risks and to encourage a safe approach to all work you carry out on your bike.

Essential DOs and DON'Ts

DON'T start the engine without first ascertaining that the transmission is in neutral.

DON'T suddenly remove the pressure cap from a hot cooling system - cover it with a cloth and release the pressure gradually first, or you may get scalded by escaping coolant.

DON'T attempt to drain oil until you are sure it has cooled sufficiently to avoid scalding you.

DON'T grasp any part of the engine or exhaust system without first ascertaining that it is cool enough not to burn you.

DON'T allow brake fluid or antifreeze to contact the machine's paint work or plastic components.

DON'T siphon toxic liquids such as fuel, hydraulic fluid or antifreeze by mouth, or allow them to remain on your skin.

DON'T inhale dust - it may be injurious to health (see *Asbestos* heading).

DON'T allow any spilled oil or grease to remain on the floor - wipe it up right away, before someone slips on it.

DON'T use ill fitting wrenches or other tools which may slip and cause injury.

DON'T attempt to lift a heavy component which may be beyond your capability - get assistance.

DON'T rush to finish a job or take unverified short cuts.

DON'T allow children or animals in or around an unattended vehicle.

DON'T inflate a tire to a pressure above the recommended maximum. Apart from over stressing the carcase and wheel rim, in extreme cases the tire may blow off forcibly.

DO ensure that the machine is supported securely at all times. This is especially important when the machine is blocked up to aid wheel or fork removal.

DO take care when attempting to loosen a stubborn nut or bolt. It is generally better to pull on a wrench, rather than push, so that if you slip, you fall away from the machine rather than onto it.

DO wear eye protection when using power tools such as drill, sander, bench grinder etc.

DO use a barrier cream on your hands prior to undertaking dirty jobs - it will protect your skin from infection as well as making the dirt easier to remove afterwards; but make sure your hands aren't left slippery. Note that long-term contact with used engine oil can be a health hazard.

DO keep loose clothing (cuffs, ties etc. and long hair) well out of the way of moving mechanical parts.

DO remove rings, wristwatch etc., before working on the vehicle - especially the electrical system.

DO keep your work area tidy - it is only too easy to fall over articles left lying around.

DO exercise caution when compressing springs for removal or installation. Ensure that the tension is applied and released in a controlled manner, using suitable tools which preclude the possibility of the spring escaping violently.

DO ensure that any lifting tackle used has a safe working load rating adequate for the job.

DO get someone to check periodically that all is well, when working alone on the vehicle.

DO carry out work in a logical sequence and check that everything is correctly assembled and tightened afterwards.

DO remember that your vehicle's safety affects that of yourself and others. If in doubt on any point, get professional advice.

IF, in spite of following these precautions, you are unfortunate enough to injure yourself, seek medical attention as soon as possible.

Asbestos

Certain friction, insulating, sealing and other products - such as brake pads, clutch linings, gaskets, etc. - contain asbestos. *Extreme care must be taken to avoid inhalation of dust from such products since it is hazardous to health*. If in doubt, assume that they *do* contain asbestos.

Fire

Remember at all times that gasoline (petrol) is highly flammable. Never smoke or have any kind of naked flame around, when working on the vehicle. But the risk does not end there - a spark caused by an electrical short-circuit, by two metal surfaces contacting each other, by careless use of tools, or even by static electricity built up in your body under certain conditions, can ignite gasoline (petrol) vapor, which in a confined space is highly explosive. Never use gasoline (petrol) as a cleaning solvent. Use an approved safety solvent.

Always disconnect the battery ground (earth) terminal before working on any part of the fuel or electrical system, and never risk spilling fuel on to a hot engine or exhaust.

It is recommended that a fire extinguisher of a type suitable for fuel and electrical fires is kept handy in the garage or workplace at all times. Never try to extinguish a fuel or electrical fire with water.

Fumes

Certain fumes are highly toxic and can quickly cause unconsciousness and even death if inhaled to any extent. Gasoline (petrol) vapor comes into this category, as do the vapors from certain solvents such as trichloroethylene. Any draining or pouring of such volatile fluids should be done in a well ventilated area.

When using cleaning fluids and solvents, read the instructions carefully. Never use materials from unmarked containers - they may give off poisonous vapors.

Never run the engine of a motor vehicle in an enclosed space such as a garage. Exhaust fumes contain carbon monoxide which is extremely poisonous; if you need to run the engine, always do so in the open air or at least have the rear of the vehicle outside the workplace.

The battery

Never cause a spark, or allow a naked light near the vehicle's battery. It will normally be giving off a certain amount of hydrogen gas, which is highly explosive.

Always disconnect the battery ground (earth) terminal before working on the fuel or electrical systems (except where noted).

If possible, loosen the filler plugs or cover when charging the battery from an external source. Do not charge at an excessive rate or the battery may burst.

Take care when topping up, cleaning or carrying the battery. The acid electrolyte, even when diluted, is very corrosive and should not be allowed to contact the eyes or skin. Always wear rubber gloves and goggles or a face shield. If you ever need to prepare electrolyte yourself, always add the acid slowly to the water; never add the water to the acid.

Electricity

When using an electric power tool, inspection light etc., always ensure that the appliance is correctly connected to its plug and that, where necessary, it is properly grounded (earthed). Do not use such appliances in damp conditions and, again, beware of creating a spark or applying excessive heat in the vicinity of fuel or fuel vapor. Also ensure that the appliances meet national safety standards.

A severe electric shock can result from touching certain parts of the electrical system, such as the spark plug wires (HT leads), when the engine is running or being cranked, particularly if components are damp or the insulation is defective. Where an electronic ignition system is used, the secondary (HT) voltage is much higher and could prove fatal.

Motorcycle chemicals and lubricants

A number of chemicals and lubricants are available for use in motorcycle maintenance and repair. They include a wide variety of products ranging from cleaning solvents and degreasers to lubricants and protective sprays for rubber, plastic and vinyl.

Contact point/spark plug cleaner is a solvent used to clean oily film and dirt from points, grime from electrical connectors and oil deposits from spark plugs. It is oil free and leaves no residue. It can also be used to remove gum and varnish from carburetor jets and other orifices.

Carburetor cleaner is similar to contact point/spark plug cleaner but it usually has a stronger solvent and may leave a slight oily reside. It is not recommended for cleaning electrical components or connections.

Brake system cleaner is used to remove grease or brake fluid from brake system components (where clean surfaces are absolutely necessary and petroleum-based solvents cannot be used); it also leaves no residue.

Silicone-based lubricants are used to protect rubber parts such as hoses and grommets, and are used as lubricants for hinges and locks.

Multi-purpose grease is an all purpose lubricant used wherever grease is more practical than a liquid lubricant such as oil. Some multipurpose grease is colored white and specially formulated to be more resistant to water than ordinary grease.

Gear oil (sometimes called gear lube) is a specially designed oil used in transmissions and final drive units, a s well as other areas where high friction, high temperature lubrication is required. It is available in a number of viscosities (weights) for various applications.

Motor oil, of course, is the lubricant specially formulated for use in the engine. It normally contains a wide variety of additives to prevent corrosion and reduce foaming and wear. Motor oil comes in various weights (viscosity ratings) of from 5 to 80. The recommended weight of the oil depends on the seasonal temperature and the demands on the engine. Light oil is used in cold climates and under light load conditions; heavy oil is used in hot climates and where high loads are encountered. Multi-viscosity oils are designed to have characteristics of both light and heavy oils and are available in a number of weights from 5W-20 to 20W-50.

Gas (petrol) additives perform several functions, depending on their chemical makeup. They usually contain solvents that help dissolve gum and varnish that build up on carburetor and intake parts. They also serve to break down carbon deposits that form on the inside surfaces of the combustion chambers. Some additives contain upper cylinder lubricants for valves and piston rings.

Brake fluid is a specially formulated hydraulic fluid that can withstand the heat and pressure encountered in brake systems. Care must be taken that this fluid does not come in contact with painted surfaces or plastics. An opened container should always be resealed to prevent contamination by water or dirt.

Chain lubricants are formulated especially for use on motorcycle final drive chains. A good chain lube should adhere well and have good penetrating qualities to be effective as a lubricant inside the chain and on the side plates, pins and rollers. Most chain lubes are either the foaming type or quick drying type and are usually marketed as sprays.

Degreasers are heavy duty solvents used to remove grease and grime that may accumulate on engine and frame components. They can be sprayed or brushed on and, depending on the type, are rinsed with either water or solvent.

Solvents are used alone or in combination with degreasers to clean parts and assemblies during repair and overhaul. The home mechanic should use only solvents that are non-flammable and that do not produce irritating fumes.

Gasket sealing compounds may be used in conjunction with gaskets, to improve their sealing capabilities, or alone, to seal metal-to-metal joints. Many gasket sealers can withstand extreme heat, some are impervious to gasoline and lubricants, while others are capable of filling and sealing large cavities. Depending on the intended use, gasket sealers either dry hard or stay relatively soft and pliable. They are usually applied by hand, with a brush, or are sprayed on the gasket sealing surfaces.

Thread cement is an adhesive locking compound that prevents threaded fasteners from loosening because of vibration. It is available in a variety of types for different applications.

Moisture dispersants are usually sprays that can be used to dry out electrical components such as the fuse block and wiring connectors. Some types can also be used as treatment for rubber and as a lubricant for hinges, cables and locks.

Waxes and polishes are used to help protect painted and plated surfaces from the weather. Different types of paint may require the use of different types of wax polish. Some polishes utilize a chemical or abrasive cleaner to help remove the top layer of oxidized (dull) paint on older vehicles. In recent years, many non-wax polishes (that contain a wide variety of chemicals such as polymers and silicones) have been introduced. These non-wax polishes are usually easier to apply and last longer than conventional waxes and polishes.

Troubleshooting

Contents

Engine doesn't start or is difficult to start

1 Kickstarter moves but engine won't start

1 Engine kill switch Off.
2 Wiring open or shorted. Check all wiring connections and harnesses to make sure that they are dry, tight and not corroded. Also check for broken or frayed wires that can cause a short to ground (see wiring diagram, Chapter 5).
3 Engine kill switch defective. Check for wet, dirty or corroded contacts. Clean or replace the switch as necessary (Chapter 5).

2 Kickstarter moves but engine does not turn over

1 Kickstarter mechanism damaged. Inspect and repair or replace (Chapter 2).
2 Damaged kickstarter pinion gears. Inspect and replace the damaged parts (Chapter 2).

3 Kickstarter won't turn engine over (seized)

Seized engine caused by one or more internally damaged components. Failure due to wear, abuse or lack of lubrication. Damage can include seized piston, crankshaft, connecting rod bearings, or transmission gears or bearings. Refer to Chapter 2 for engine disassembly.

4 No fuel flow

1 No fuel in tank.
2 Tank cap air vent obstructed. Usually caused by dirt or water. Remove it and clean the cap vent hole.
3 Clogged strainer in fuel tap. Remove and clean the strainer (Chapter 1).
4 Fuel line clogged. Pull the fuel line loose and carefully blow through it.
5 Inlet needle valve clogged. A very bad batch of fuel with an unusual additive may have been used, or some other foreign material has entered the tank. Many times after a machine has been stored for many months without running, the fuel turns to a varnish-like liquid and forms deposits on the inlet needle valve and jets. The carburetor should be removed and overhauled if draining the float chamber doesn't solve the problem.

5 Engine flooded

1 Float level too high. Check as described in Chapter 4 and replace the float if necessary.
2 Inlet needle valve worn or stuck open. A piece of dirt, rust or other debris can cause the inlet needle to seat improperly, causing excess fuel to be admitted to the float bowl. In this case, the float chamber should be cleaned and the needle and seat inspected. If the needle and seat are worn, then the leaking will persist and the parts should be replaced with new ones (Chapter 4).
3 Starting technique incorrect. Under normal circumstances (i.e., if all the carburetor functions are sound) the machine should start with little or no throttle. When the engine is cold, the choke should be operated and the engine started without opening the throttle. When the engine is at operating temperature, only a very slight amount of throttle should be necessary. If the engine is flooded, turn the fuel tap off and hold the throttle open while cranking the engine. This will allow additional air to reach the cylinder. Remember to turn the fuel tap back on after the engine starts.

6 No spark or weak spark

1 Spark plug dirty, defective or worn out. Locate reason for fouled plug using spark plug condition chart and follow the plug maintenance procedures in Chapter 1.
2 Spark plug cap or secondary wiring faulty. Check condition. Replace either or both components if cracks or deterioration are evident (Chapter 5).
3 Spark plug cap not making good contact. Make sure that the plug cap fits snugly over the plug end.
4 Defective alternator (see Chapter 5).
5 Defective CDI unit (see Chapter 5).
6 Ignition coil defective. Check the coil, referring to Chapter 5.
7 Kill switch shorted. This is usually caused by water, corrosion, damage or excessive wear. The kill switch can be disassembled and cleaned with electrical contact cleaner. If cleaning does not help, replace the switch (Chapter 5).
8 Wiring shorted or broken between:

a) CDI unit and engine kill switch
b) CDI unit and ignition coil
c) CDI unit and alternator
d) Ignition coil and plug

Make sure that all wiring connections are clean, dry and tight. Look for chafed and broken wires (Chapter 5).

7 Compression low

1 Spark plug loose. Remove the plug and inspect the threads. Reinstall and tighten to the specified torque (Chapter 1).
2 Cylinder head not sufficiently tightened down. If the cylinder head is suspected of being loose, then there's a chance that the gasket or head is damaged if the problem has persisted for any length of time. The head nuts and bolts should be tightened to the proper torque in the correct sequence (Chapter 2).
3 Faulty reed valve. Check and replace if necessary (Chapter 2).
4 Cylinder and/or piston worn. Excessive wear will cause compression pressure to leak past the ring. This is usually accompanied by a worn ring as well. A top end overhaul is necessary (Chapter 2).
5 Piston ring worn, weak, broken, or sticking. Broken or sticking piston rings usually indicate a lubrication or carburetion problem that causes excess carbon deposits or seizures to form on the piston and ring. Top end overhaul is necessary (Chapter 2).
6 Piston ring-to-groove clearance excessive. This is caused by excessive wear of the piston ring lands. Piston replacement is necessary (Chapter 2).
7 Cylinder head gasket damaged. If the head is allowed to become loose, or if excessive carbon build-up on a piston crown and combustion chamber causes extremely high compression, the head gasket may leak. Retorquing the head is not always sufficient to restore the seal, so gasket replacement is necessary (Chapter 2).
8 Cylinder head warped. This is caused by overheating or improperly tightened head nuts and bolts. Machine shop resurfacing or head replacement is necessary (Chapter 2).

8 Stalls after starting

1 Improper choke action. Make sure the choke knob is getting a full stroke and staying in the out position.
2 Ignition malfunction. See Chapter 5.
3 Carburetor malfunction. See Chapter 4.
4 Fuel contaminated. The fuel can be contaminated with either dirt or water, or can change chemically if the machine is allowed to sit for more than 24 hours. Drain the tank and float bowl and refill with fresh fuel (Chapter 4).
5 Intake air leak. Check for loose carburetor-to-intake joint connec-

tions or loose carburetor top (Chapter 4).
6 Engine idle speed incorrect. Turn throttle stop screw until the engine idles at the specified rpm (Chapter 1).
7 Crankcase air leak. Refer to Chapter 2 for testing procedure.

9 Rough idle

1 Ignition malfunction. See Chapter 5.
2 Idle speed incorrect. See Chapter 1.
3 Carburetor malfunction. See Chapter 4.
4 Idle fuel/air mixture incorrect. See Chapter 4.
5 Fuel contaminated. The fuel can be contaminated with either dirt or water, or can change chemically if the machine is allowed to sit for several months or more. Drain the tank and float bowls (Chapter 4).
6 Intake air leak. Check for loose carburetor-to-intake joint connections, loose or missing vacuum gauge access port cap or hose, or loose carburetor top (Chapter 4).
7 Air cleaner clogged. Service or replace air cleaner element (Chapter 1).

Poor running at low speed

10 Spark weak

1 Spark plug fouled, defective or worn out. Refer to Chapter 1 for spark plug maintenance.
2 Spark plug cap or secondary wiring defective. Refer to Chapters 1 and 5 for details on the ignition system.
3 Spark plug cap not making contact.
4 Incorrect spark plug. Wrong type, heat range or cap configuration. Check and install correct plug listed in Chapter 1. A cold plug or one with a recessed firing electrode will not operate at low speeds without fouling.
5 CDI unit defective. See Chapter 5.
6 Alternator defective. See Chapter 5.
7 Ignition coil defective. See Chapter 5.

11 Fuel/air mixture incorrect

1 Pilot screw out of adjustment (Chapter 3).
2 Pilot jet or air passage clogged. Remove and overhaul the carburetor (Chapter 4).
3 Air bleed holes clogged. Remove carburetor and blow out all passages (Chapter 4).
4 Air cleaner clogged, poorly sealed or missing.
5 Air cleaner-to-carburetor boot poorly sealed. Look for cracks, holes or loose clamps and replace or repair defective parts.
6 Float level too high or too low. Check and replace the float if necessary (Chapter 4).
7 Fuel tank air vent obstructed. Make sure that the air vent passage in the filler cap is open.
8 Carburetor intake joint loose. Check for cracks, breaks, tears or loose clamps or bolts. Repair or replace the rubber boot and its O-ring.

12 Compression low

1 Spark plug loose. Remove the plug and inspect the threads. Reinstall and tighten to the specified torque (Chapter 1).
2 Cylinder head not sufficiently tightened down. If the cylinder head is suspected of being loose, then there's a chance that the gasket and head are damaged if the problem has persisted for any length of time. The head nuts should be tightened to the proper torque in the correct sequence (Chapter 2).
3 Faulty reed valve. Check and replace if necessary (Chapter 2).
4 Cylinder and/or piston worn. Excessive wear will cause compression pressure to leak past the rings. This is usually accompanied by a worn ring as well. A top end overhaul is necessary (Chapter 2).
5 Piston ring worn, weak, broken, or sticking. Broken or sticking piston rings usually indicate a lubrication or carburetion problem that causes excess carbon deposits or seizures to form on the piston and ring. Top end overhaul is necessary (Chapter 2).
6 Piston ring-to-groove clearance excessive. This is caused by excessive wear of the piston ring lands. Piston replacement is necessary (Chapter 2).
7 Cylinder head gasket damaged. If the head is allowed to become loose, or if excessive carbon build-up on the piston crown and combustion chamber causes extremely high compression, the head gasket may leak. Retorquing the head is not always sufficient to restore the seal, so gasket replacement is necessary (Chapter 2).
8 Cylinder head warped. This is caused by overheating or improperly tightened head nuts and bolts. Machine shop resurfacing or head replacement is necessary (Chapter 2).

13 Poor acceleration

1 Carburetor leaking or dirty. Overhaul the carburetor (Chapter 4).
2 Timing not advancing. The CDI unit may be defective. If so, it must be replaced with a new one, as it can't be repaired.
3 Transmission oil viscosity too high. Using a heavier oil than that recommended in Chapter 1 can cause drag on the engine.
4 Brakes dragging. Usually caused by a sticking caliper piston (disc brakes) or brake cam (drum brakes), by a warped disc or drum or by a bent axle. Repair as necessary (Chapter 7).

Poor running or no power at high speed

14 Firing incorrect

1 Timing not advancing. See Chapter 5.
2 Air cleaner restricted. Clean or replace element (Chapter 1).
3 Spark plug fouled, defective or worn out. See Chapter 1 for spark plug maintenance.
4 Spark plug cap or secondary wiring defective. See Chapters 1 and 5 for details of the ignition system.
5 Spark plug cap not in good contact. See Chapter 5.
6 Incorrect spark plug. Wrong type, heat range or cap configuration. Check and install correct plugs listed in Chapter 1. A cold plug or one with a recessed firing electrode will not operate at low speeds without fouling.
7 CDI unit defective. See Chapter 5.
8 Ignition coil defective. See Chapter 5.

15 Fuel/air mixture incorrect

1 Pilot screw out of adjustment. See Chapter 4 for adjustment procedures.
2 Main jet clogged. Dirt, water or other contaminants can clog the main jet. Clean the fuel tap strainer, the float bowl area, and the jets and carburetor orifices (Chapter 4).
3 Main jet wrong size. See Chapter 4 for jetting details.
4 Throttle shaft-to-carburetor body clearance excessive. Refer to Chapter 4 for inspection and part replacement procedures.
5 Air bleed holes clogged. Remove and overhaul carburetor (Chapter 4).
6 Air cleaner clogged, poorly sealed, or missing.
7 Air cleaner-to-carburetor boot poorly sealed. Look for cracks, holes or loose clamps, and replace or repair defective parts.
8 Float level too high or too low. Check float level and replace the float if necessary (Chapter 4).
9 Fuel tank air vent or vent hose obstructed. Make sure the air vent

passage in the filler cap is open and that the vent hose is not plugged or pinched.
10 Carburetor intake manifold loose. Check for cracks, breaks, tears or loose clamps or bolts. Repair or replace the rubber boots (Chapter 4).
11 Fuel tap clogged. Remove the tap and clean it (Chapter 1).
12 Fuel line clogged. Pull the fuel line loose and carefully blow through it.
13 Crankcase air leak. Refer to Chapter 2 for testing procedures.

16 Compression low

1 Spark plug loose. Remove the plug and inspect the threads. Reinstall and tighten to the specified torque (Chapter 1).
2 Cylinder head not sufficiently tightened down. If the cylinder head is suspected of being loose, then there's a chance that the gasket and head are damaged if the problem has persisted for any length of time. The head nuts and bolts should be tightened to the proper torque in the correct sequence (Chapter 2).
3 Reed valve faulty. Check and replace if necessary (Chapter 2).
4 Cylinder and/or piston worn. Excessive wear will cause compression pressure to leak past the ring. This is usually accompanied by a worn ring as well. A top end overhaul is necessary (Chapter 2).
5 Piston ring worn, weak, broken, or sticking. Broken or sticking piston rings usually indicate a lubrication or carburetion problem that causes excess carbon deposits or seizures to form on the piston and ring. Top end overhaul is necessary (Chapter 2).
6 Piston ring-to-groove clearance excessive. This is caused by excessive wear of the piston ring lands. Piston replacement is necessary (Chapter 2).
7 Cylinder head gasket damaged. If a head is allowed to become loose, or if excessive carbon build-up on the piston crown and combustion chamber causes extremely high compression, the head gasket may leak. Retorquing the head is not always sufficient to restore the seal, so gasket replacement is necessary (Chapter 2).
8 Cylinder head warped. This is caused by overheating or improperly tightened head nuts and bolts. Machine shop resurfacing or head replacement is necessary (Chapter 2).

17 Knocking or pinging

1 Carbon build-up in combustion chamber. Remove and decarbonize the cylinder head (Chapter 2).
2 Incorrect or poor quality fuel. Old or improper grades of fuel can cause detonation. This causes the piston to rattle, thus the knocking or pinging sound. Drain old fuel and always use the recommended fuel grade.
3 Spark plug heat range incorrect. Uncontrolled detonation indicates the plug heat range is too hot. The plug in effect becomes a glow plug, raising cylinder temperatures. Install the proper heat range plug (Chapter 1).
4 Improper air/fuel mixture. This will cause the cylinder to run hot, which leads to detonation. Clogged jets or an air leak can cause this imbalance. See Chapter 4.

18 Miscellaneous causes

1 Throttle valve doesn't open fully. Adjust the cable slack (Chapter 1).
2 Clutch slipping. May be caused by improper adjustment or loose or worn clutch components. Refer to Chapter 1 for adjustment or Chapter 2 for cable replacement and clutch overhaul procedures.
3 Timing not advancing. See Chapter 5.
4 Brakes dragging. Usually caused by debris which has entered the brake piston sealing boot, or from a warped disc or bent axle. Repair as necessary.
5 If the bike has a power valve (Chapter 4) inspect and clean the components. Make sure the exhaust valve or valves open fully at full throttle.

Overheating

19 Engine overheats

1 Coolant level low. Check and add coolant (Chapter 1), then look for leaks (Chapter 3).
2 Air leak at carburetor intake manifold. Check and tighten or replace as necessary (Chapter 4).
3 Incorrect fuel-oil ratio (see Chapter 1). Discard fuel and start with a fresh batch of premix.
4 Carbon build-up in combustion chambers. Remove and decarbonize the cylinder head (Chapter 2).
5 Operation in high ambient temperatures.

20 Firing incorrect

1 Spark plug fouled, defective or worn out. See Chapter 1 for spark plug maintenance.
2 Incorrect spark plug (see Chapter 1).
3 Faulty ignition coil (Chapter 5).

21 Fuel/air mixture incorrect

1 Pilot screw out of adjustment (Chapter 4).
2 Main jet clogged. Dirt, water and other contaminants can clog the main jet. Clean the fuel tap strainer, the float bowl area and the jets and carburetor orifices (Chapter 4).
3 Main jet wrong size. See Chapter 4 for jetting details.
4 Air cleaner poorly sealed or missing.
5 Air cleaner-to-carburetor boot poorly sealed. Look for cracks, holes or loose clamps and replace or repair.
6 Fuel level too low. Check float level and replace the float if necessary (Chapter 4).
7 Fuel tank air vent or hose obstructed. Make sure that the air vent passage in the filler cap is open and the hose is not plugged or kinked.
8 Carburetor intake manifold loose. Check for cracks or loose clamps or bolts. Inspect the gasket and O-ring (Chapter 4).

22 Compression too high

1 Carbon build-up in combustion chamber. Remove and decarbonize the cylinder head (Chapter 2).
2 Improperly machined head surface or installation of incorrect gasket during engine assembly.

23 Engine load excessive

1 Clutch slipping. Can be caused by damaged, loose or worn clutch components. Refer to Chapter 2 for overhaul procedures.
2 Transmission oil viscosity too high. Using a heavier oil than the one recommended in Chapter 1 can cause drag on the engine.
3 Brakes dragging. Usually caused by a sticking caliper piston (disc brakes), brake cam (drum brakes), by a warped disc or drum or by a bent axle. Repair as necessary (Chapter 7).

24 Lubrication inadequate

1 Transmission oil level too low. Friction caused by intermittent lack of lubrication or from oil that is overworked can cause overheating. The oil provides a definite cooling function in the transmission. Check the oil level (Chapter 1).
2 Poor quality or incorrect oil type. Check the Chapter 1 Specifications and change to the correct oil.
3 Incorrect fuel-oil ratio (see Chapter 1). Discard fuel and start with a fresh batch of premix.

25 Miscellaneous causes

Modification to exhaust system. Most aftermarket exhaust systems cause the engine to run leaner, which makes it run hotter. When installing an accessory exhaust system, always rejet the carburetor.

Clutch problems

26 Clutch slipping

1 No clutch lever freeplay. Adjust freeplay (Chapter 1).
2 Friction plates worn or warped. Overhaul the clutch (Chapter 2).
3 Steel plates worn or warped (Chapter 2).
4 Clutch spring(s) broken or weak. Old or heat-damaged spring(s) (from slipping clutch) should be replaced with new ones (Chapter 2).
5 Clutch release mechanism defective. Replace any defective parts (Chapter 2).
6 Clutch center or housing unevenly worn. This causes improper engagement of the plates. Replace the damaged or worn parts (Chapter 2).
7 Clutch inner cable sticking. Caused by a frayed inner cable or kinked outer cable. Replace the clutch cable; repair of a damaged is not advised.

27 Clutch not disengaging completely

1 Clutch improperly adjusted (see Chapter 1).
2 Clutch plates warped or damaged. This will cause clutch drag, which in turn will cause the machine to creep. Overhaul the clutch assembly (Chapter 2).
3 Sagged or broken clutch spring(s). Check and replace the spring(s) (Chapter 2).
4 Transmission oil deteriorated. Old, thin, worn out oil will not provide proper lubrication for the discs, causing the clutch to drag. Replace the oil and filter (Chapter 1).
5 Clutch housing seized on shaft. Lack of lubrication, severe wear or damage can cause the housing to seize on the shaft. Overhaul of the clutch, and perhaps transmission, may be necessary to repair the damage (Chapter 2).
6 Clutch release mechanism defective. Worn or damaged release mechanism parts can stick and fail to apply force to the pressure plate. Overhaul the release mechanism (Chapter 2).
7 Loose clutch center bolt or nut. Causes housing and center misalignment putting a drag on the engine. Engagement adjustment continually varies. Overhaul the clutch assembly (Chapter 2).

Gear shifting problems

28 Doesn't go into gear or lever doesn't return

1 Clutch not disengaging. See Section 27.
2 Shift fork(s) bent or seized. May be caused by lack of lubrication. Overhaul the transmission (Chapter 2).
3 Gear(s) stuck on shaft. Most often caused by a lack of lubrication or excessive wear in transmission bearings and bushings. Overhaul the transmission (Chapter 2).
4 Shift drum binding. Caused by lubrication failure or excessive wear. Replace the drum and bearing (Chapter 2).
5 Shift pedal return spring weak or broken (Chapter 2).
6 Shift pedal broken. Splines stripped out of pedal or shaft, caused by allowing the pedal to get loose. Replace necessary parts (Chapter 2).
7 Shift mechanism pawls broken or worn. Full engagement and rotary movement of shift drum results. Replace shaft assembly (Chapter 2).
8 Pawl spring broken. Allows pawl to float, causing sporadic shift operation. Replace spring (Chapter 2).

29 Jumps out of gear

1 Shift fork(s) worn. Overhaul the transmission (Chapter 2).
2 Gear groove(s) worn. Overhaul the transmission (Chapter 2).
3 Gear dogs or dog slots worn or damaged. The gears should be inspected and replaced. No attempt should be made to service the worn parts.

30 Overshifts

1 Pawl spring weak or broken (Chapter 2).
2 Shift drum stopper lever not functioning (Chapter 2).

Abnormal engine noise

31 Knocking or pinging

1 Carbon build-up in combustion chamber. Remove and decarbonize the cylinder head (Chapter 2).
2 Incorrect fuel-oil ratio, Drain the old fuel (Chapter 4) and always use the recommended grade fuel (Chapter 1).
3 Spark plug heat range incorrect. Uncontrolled detonation indicates that the plug heat range is too hot. The plug in effect becomes a glow plug, raising cylinder temperatures. Install the proper heat range plug (Chapter 1).
4 Improper air/fuel mixture. This will cause the cylinder to run hot and lead to detonation. Clogged jets or an air leak can cause this imbalance. See Chapter 4.
5 Crankcase air leak. See Chapter 2 for testing procedure.
6 Wrong grade of gasoline (octane too low).

32 Piston slap or rattling

1 Cylinder-to-piston clearance excessive. Caused by improper assembly. Inspect and overhaul top end parts (Chapter 2).
2 Connecting rod bent. Caused by over-revving, trying to start a badly flooded engine or from ingesting a foreign object into the combustion chamber. Replace the damaged parts (Chapter 2).
3 Piston pin or piston pin bore worn or seized from wear or lack of lubrication. Replace damaged parts (Chapter 2).
4 Piston ring worn, broken or sticking. Overhaul the top end (Chapter 2).
5 Piston seizure damage. Usually from lack of lubrication or overheating. Replace the pistons and bore the cylinder, as necessary (Chapter 2).
6 Connecting rod upper or lower end clearance excessive. Caused by excessive wear or lack of lubrication. Replace worn parts.

33 Other noise

1 Cylinder head gasket leaking.
2 Exhaust pipe leaking at cylinder head connection. Caused by improper fit of pipe, damaged gasket or loose exhaust flange. All exhaust fasteners should be tightened evenly and carefully. Failure to do this will lead to a leak.
3 Crankshaft runout excessive. Caused by a bent crankshaft (from over-revving) or damage from an upper cylinder component failure.
4 Engine mounting bolts or nuts loose. Tighten all engine mounting bolts and nuts to the specified torque (Chapter 2).
5 Crankshaft bearings worn (Chapter 2).
6 Loose alternator rotor. Tighten the mounting bolt to the specified torque (Chapter 5).

Abnormal driveline noise

34 Clutch noise

1 Clutch housing/friction plate clearance excessive (Chapter 2).
2 Loose or damaged pressure plate and/or bolts (Chapter 2).
3 Broken clutch springs (Chapter 2).

35 Transmission noise

1 Bearings worn. Also includes the possibility that the shafts are worn. Overhaul the transmission (Chapter 2).
2 Gears worn or chipped (Chapter 2).
3 Metal chips jammed in gear teeth. Probably pieces from a broken clutch, gear or shift mechanism that were picked up by the gears. This will cause early bearing failure (Chapter 2).
4 Transmission oil level too low. Causes a howl from transmission. Also affects engine power and clutch operation (Chapter 1).

36 Final drive noise

1 Dry or dirty chain. Inspect, clean and lubricate (see Chapter 1).
2 Chain out of adjustment. Adjust chain slack (see Chapter 1).
3 Chain and sprockets damaged or worn. Inspect the chain and sprockets and replace them as necessary (see Chapter 6).
4 Sprockets loose (see Chapter 6).

Abnormal chassis noise

37 Suspension noise

1 Spring weak or broken. Makes a clicking or scraping sound.
2 Steering head bearings worn or damaged. Clicks when braking. Check and replace as necessary (Chapter 6).
3 Front fork oil level incorrect. Check and correct oil level (see Chapter 6).
4 Front fork(s) assembled incorrectly. Disassemble the fork(s) and check for correct assembly (see Chapter 6).
5 Rear shock absorber fluid level incorrect. Indicates a leak caused by defective seal. Shock will be covered with oil. It may be possible to overhaul the shock and repair the damage; take the shock to a Yamaha dealer or motorcycle repair shop for inspection.
6 Defective shock absorber with internal damage. This is in the body of the shock. It may be possible to overhaul the shock and repair the damage; take the shock to a Yamaha dealer or motorcycle repair shop for inspection.
7 Bent or damaged shock body. Replace the shock with a new one (Chapter 6).

38 Brake noise

1 Squeal caused by pad shim not installed or positioned correctly (Chapter 7).
2 Squeal caused by dust on brake pads. Usually found in combination with glazed pads. Clean using brake cleaning solvent (see Chapter 7). If the pads are glazed, replace them.
3 Contamination of brake pads. Oil, brake fluid or dirt causing pads to chatter or squeal. Clean or replace pads (see Chapter 7).
4 Pads glazed. Caused by excessive heat from prolonged use or from contamination. Do not use sandpaper, emery cloth or carborundum cloth or any other abrasives to roughen pad surface as abrasives will stay in the pad material and damage the disc. A very fine flat file can be used, but pad replacement is suggested as a cure (see Chapter 7).
5 Disc warped. Can cause a chattering, clicking or intermittent squeal. Usually accompanied by a pulsating lever and uneven braking. Replace the disc (see Chapter 7).
6 Drum brake linings worn or contaminated. Can cause scraping or squealing. Replace the shoes (Chapter 7).
7 Drum brake linings warped or worn unevenly. Can cause chattering. Replace the linings (Chapter 7).
8 Brake drum out of round. Can cause chattering. Replace brake drum (Chapter 7).
9 Loose or worn wheel bearings. Check and replace as needed (Chapter 7).

Excessive exhaust smoke

39 White smoke

Oil/fuel mixture too rich. Drain fuel tank and refill with properly-mixed fuel.

40 Black smoke

1 Air cleaner clogged. Clean or replace the element (Chapter 1).
2 Main jet too large or loose. Compare the jet size to the Specifications (Chapter 4).
3 Choke (starter jet) stuck open (Chapter 4).
4 Fuel level too high. Check the float level and replace the float if necessary (Chapter 4).
5 Inlet needle held off needle seat. Clean the float chamber and fuel line and replace the needle and seat if necessary (Chapter 4).

41 Brown smoke

1 Main jet too small or clogged. Lean condition caused by wrong size main jet or by a restricted orifice. Clean float chamber and jets and compare jet size to Specifications (Chapter 4).
2 Fuel flow insufficient. Fuel inlet needle valve stuck closed due to chemical reaction with old fuel. Float level incorrect; check and replace float if necessary. Restricted fuel line. Clean line and float chamber.
3 Carburetor intake tube loose (Chapter 4).
4 Air cleaner poorly sealed or not installed (Chapter 1).

Poor handling or stability

42 Handlebar hard to turn

1 Steering stem adjusting nut too tight (Chapter 6).
2 Steering stem bearings damaged. Roughness can be felt as the

bars are turned from side-to-side. Replace bearings and races (Chapter 6).
3 Races dented or worn. Denting results from wear in only one position (e.g. straight ahead), striking an immovable object or hole or from dropping the machine. Replace races and bearings (Chapter 6).
4 Steering stem bearing lubrication inadequate. Causes are grease getting hard from age or being washed out by high pressure car washes. Remove steering stem, clean and lubricate bearings (Chapter 6).
5 Steering stem bent. Caused by a collision, hitting a pothole or by dropping the machine. Replace damaged part. Don't try to straighten the steering stem (Chapter 6).
6 Front tire air pressure too low (Chapter 1).

43 Handlebar shakes or vibrates excessively

1 Tires worn or out of balance (Chapter 1 or 7).
2 Swingarm bearings worn. Replace worn bearings (Chapter 6).
3 Wheel rim(s) warped or damaged. Inspect wheels (Chapter 7).
4 Wheel bearings worn. Worn front or rear wheel bearings can cause poor tracking. Worn front bearings will cause wobble (Chapter 7).
5 Handlebar clamp bolts loose (Chapter 6).
6 Steering stem or triple clamps loose. Tighten them to the specified torque (Chapters 1 and 6).
7 Engine mounting bolts loose. Will cause excessive vibration with increased engine rpm (Chapter 2).

44 Handlebar pulls to one side

1 Frame bent. Definitely suspect this if the machine has been dropped. May or may not be accompanied by cracking near the bend. Replace the frame (Chapter 8).
2 Front and rear wheels out of alignment. Caused by uneven adjustment of the drive chain adjusters (see Chapter 1). May also be caused by improper location of the axle spacers (see Chapter 6) or from bent steering stem or frame (see Chapter 6).
3 Swingarm bent or twisted. Caused by age (metal fatigue) or impact damage. Replace the swingarm (Chapter 6).
4 Steering stem bent. Caused by impact damage or by dropping the motorcycle. Replace the steering stem (Chapter 6).

45 Poor shock absorbing qualities

1 Too hard:
- *a) Damping adjuster set too hard (see Chapter 6).*
- *b) Fork oil level excessive (see Chapter 6).*
- *c) Fork oil viscosity too high. Use a lighter oil (see the Specifications in Chapter 6).*
- *d) Fork tube bent. Causes a harsh, sticking feeling (see Chapter 6).*
- *e) Fork internal damage (see Chapter 6).*
- *f) Shock internal damage.*
- *g) Tire pressures too high (Chapter 1).*

2 Too soft:
- *a) Damping adjuster set too soft (see Chapter 6).*
- *b) Fork or shock oil insufficient and/or leaking (Chapter 6).*
- *d) Fork oil level too low (see Chapter 6).*
- *d) Fork springs weak or broken (Chapter 6).*

Braking problems

46 Brakes are spongy or weak, don't hold

1 Air in brake line (disc brakes). Caused by inattention to master cylinder fluid level or by leakage. Locate problem and bleed brake (Chapter 7).
2 Pad or disc worn (Chapters 1 and 7).
3 Brake fluid leak. See paragraph 1.
4 Contaminated disc brake pads. Caused by contamination with oil, grease, brake fluid, etc. Clean or replace pads. Clean disc thoroughly with brake cleaner.
5 Brake fluid deteriorated (disc brakes). Fluid is old or contaminated. Drain system, replenish with new fluid and bleed the system (see Chapter 7).
6 Master cylinder internal parts worn or damaged, causing fluid to bypass (see Chapter 7).
7 Master cylinder bore scratched. From ingestion of foreign material or broken spring. Repair or replace master cylinder (see Chapter 7).
8 Disc warped. Replace disc (see Chapter 7).
9 Drum brake linings worn (Chapters 1 and 7).
10 Contaminated drum brake linings. Caused by contamination with oil, grease, etc. Clean or replace linings. Clean drum thoroughly with brake cleaner (Chapter 7).
11 Drum warped. Replace drum (Chapter 7).
12 Drum brake cable out of adjustment or stretched. Adjust or replace the cable (see Chapters 1 and 7).

47 Brake lever or pedal pulsates

1 Disc warped. Replace disc (see Chapter 7).
2 Axle bent. Replace axle (Chapter 6).
3 Brake caliper bolts loose (see Chapter 7).
4 Brake caliper shafts damaged or sticking, causing caliper to bind. Lube the shafts or replace them if they are corroded or bent (see Chapter 7).
5 Wheel warped or otherwise damaged (Chapter 7).
6 Wheel bearings damaged or worn (Chapter 7).
7 Brake drum out of round. Replace brake drum (Chapter 7).

48 Brakes drag

1 Master cylinder piston seized. Caused by wear or damage to piston or cylinder bore (see Chapter 7).
2 Lever or pedal balky or stuck. Check pivot and lubricate (see Chapter 7).
3 Brake caliper binds. Caused by inadequate lubrication or damage to caliper shafts (see Chapter 7).
4 Brake caliper piston seized in bore. Caused by wear or ingestion of dirt past deteriorated seal (see Chapter 7).
5 Brake pad or shoes damaged. Pad or lining material separated from backing plate or shoes. Usually caused by faulty manufacturing process or contact with chemicals. Replace pads (see Chapter 7).
6 Pads or shoes improperly installed (see Chapter 7).
7 Cable sticking. Lubricate or replace cable (see Chapters 1 and 7).
8 Shoes improperly installed (Chapter 7).
9 Brake pedal or lever freeplay insufficient (Chapter 1).
10 Drum brake springs weak. Replace brake springs (Chapter 7).

Notes

Chapter 1
Tune-up and routine maintenance

Contents

Specifications

YZ80/85

Engine

Spark plug type	
1986 and 1987	Champion N-84
1988 through 1992	NGK B9EG
1993 through 1997	
All except Canada and South Africa	NGK B10EG
Canada and South Africa	NGK BR10EG
1998 and 1999	
US	NGK B10EG
All except US	NGK BR10EG
2000 and later	NGK BR10EG
Spark plug gap	0.5 to 0.6 mm (0.020 to 0.024 inch)

Miscellaneous

Brake pad lining thickness limit	
Front	0.8 mm (0.03 inch)
Rear	1.0 mm (0.04 inch)
Rear brake shoe lining limit (drum brakes)	2.0 mm (0.08 inch)
Front brake lever freeplay (1986 through 1996)	
1986	5 to 8 mm (0.2 to 0.3 inch)
1987 and 1988	10 to 20 mm (0.4 to 0.8 inch)
1989 through 1992	2 to 5 mm (0.08 to 0.20 inch)
1993 through 1996	10 to 20 mm (0.4 to 0.8 inch)
Front brake lever distance from handlebar (1997 and later)	
1997	79.5 mm (3.13 inch)
1998 through 2000	82.5 mm (3.25 inches)
2001 and later	95 mm (3.74 inches)
Rear brake pedal freeplay (drum brake models)	20 to 30 mm (3/4 to 1-1/4 inch)

Miscellaneous (continued)

Rear brake pedal height	
1986 and 1987	10 mm (0.4 inches) below top of footpeg
1988 through 1992	Zero (even with top of footpeg)
1993	3 to 8 mm (0.12 to 0.31 inch) below top of footpeg
1994 through 2002	7 mm (0.28 inch) below top of footpeg
2003 and later	4 to 10 mm (0.16 to 0.39 inch) above top of footpeg
Clutch lever freeplay	
1986 through 2001	2 to 3 mm (0.08 to 0.012) at lever gap
2002 and later	10 to 15 mm (039 to 0.59 inch) at lever tip
Throttle grip freeplay	3 to 5 mm (1/8 to 1/4 inch)
Minimum tire tread depth	Not specified
Tire pressures (cold)	
1986 and 1987	Not specified
1988 and later	15 psi (100 kPa)
Tire sizes	
1986	
Front	70/100-17 4PR
Rear	90/100-14 4PR
1987 through 1992	
Front	70/100-17 40M
Rear	90/100-14 49M
1993	Not specified
1994	
Front	70/100-17 40M
Rear	90/100-14 49M
1995 through 2002	Not specified
2003 and later	
YZ85 front	70/100-17 40M
YZ85 rear	90/100-14 49M
YZ85LW front	70/100-19 42M
YZ85LW rear	90/100-16 52M
Drive chain slack	
1986	30 to 35 mm (1-1/4 to 1-1/2 inches)
1987	15 to 20 mm (0.6 to 0.8 inches)
1988 through 1992	30 to 35 mm (1-1/4 to 1-1/2 inches)
1993 through 2000	5 to 15 mm (0.2 to 0.6 inch)
2001 and later	35 to 45 mm ((1.4 to 1.8 inches)
Front fork air pressure	
1986 through 1992	
Standard	Zero psi (zero kPa)
Maximum	17 psi (118 kPa)
Maximum difference between fork legs	1.4 psi (9.8 kPa)
1993 and later	Not applicable

Torque specifications

Transmission oil check bolt	Not specified
Transmission oil drain plug	
1986 through 1992	20 Nm (14 ft-lbs)
1993 and later	10 Nm (86 inch-lbs)
Coolant drain bolt	10 Nm (86 inch-lbs)
Spark plug	
1986 through 1992	25 Nm (18 ft-lbs)
1993 and later	20 Nm (14 ft-lbs)
Wheel spokes	
1986 through 1999	6 Nm (52 inch-lbs)
2000 and later	3 Nm (26 inch-lbs)
Rim lock locknut	Not specified
Steering stem adjusting nut*	
1986 and 1987	
Initial torque	Not specified
Final torque	8 Nm (70 inch-lbs)
1988 through 1992	
Initial torque	38 Nm (27 ft-lbs)
Final torque	8 Nm (70 inch-lbs)
1993 and later	
Initial torque	38 Nm (27 ft-lbs)
Final torque	4 Nm (35 inch-lbs)

**Torque setting requires a Yamaha ring nut wrench, placed on the torque wrench at a right angle.*

Recommended lubricants and fluids

Fuel	
1986 through 1992	
With Yamalube R	24:1 mix of gasoline (90 Research octane or higher) to oil
With Castrol R30, A545 or A547	20:1 mix of gasoline (90 Research octane or higher) to oil
1993 except Australia	
With Yamalube R	24:1 mix of gasoline (premium unleaded, 95 Research octane or higher) to oil
With Castrol R30, A545 or A547	20:1 mix of gasoline (premium unleaded, 95 Research octane or higher) to oil
1993 Australia	
With Yamalube R	24:1 mix of gasoline (unleaded only) to oil
With Castrol R30, A545 or A547	20:1 mix of gasoline (unleaded only) to oil
1994 through 1997 except Australia	30:1 mix of gasoline (premium unleaded, 95 Research octane or higher) and Yamalube R, Castrol R30 or Castrol A747
1994 through 1997 Australia	30:1 mix of gasoline (unleaded only) and Yamalube R, Castrol R30 or Castrol A747
1998 through 2000 except Australia	30:1 mix of gasoline (premium unleaded, 95 or higher Research octane) and Yamalube 2-R or Castrol A747
1998 through 2000 Australia	30:1 mix of gasoline (unleaded only) and Yamalube 2-R or Castrol A747
2001 through 2004 except Australia	30:1 mix of gasoline (premium unleaded, 95 or higher Research octane) and Yamalube 2-R
2001 through 2004 Australia	30:1 mix of gasoline (unleaded only) and Yamalube 2-R
2005 and later	30:1 mix of gasoline (premium unleaded, 95 or higher Research octane) and Yamalube 2-R
Transmission oil	
Type	Yamalube 4-stroke oil or API grade SE multigrade four-stroke oil manufactured for use in motorcycles
Viscosity	10W-30
Capacity at oil change	
1986 through 1992	650 cc (0.69 US qt, 1.04 Imp pt)
1993 and later	500 cc (0.52 US qt, 0.88 Imp pt)
Capacity after overhaul	
1986 through 1992	700 cc (0.74 US qt, 1.34 Imp pt)
1993 and later	550 cc (0.58 US qt, 0.96 Imp pt)
Air cleaner element oil	Foam filter oil or SAE 10W-30 engine oil
Coolant	
Type	Ethylene glycol antifreeze compatible with aluminum engines, mixed 50/50 with water
Capacity	
1986 through 2001	500 cc (0.52 US qt, 0.88 Imp pt)
2002 and later	540 cc (0.57 US qt, 0.96 Imp pt)
Brake fluid	
1986 and 1987	DOT 3
1998 through 1993	DOT 4 (DOT 3 acceptable)
1994 and later	DOT 4
Drive chain lubricant	
1986 through 1992	Racing chain lube
1993 and later	Chain lube or 10W-30 engine oil
Fork oil	See Chapter 6
Miscellaneous	
Wheel bearings	Medium weight, lithium-based multi-purpose grease
Swingarm pivot bushings	Molybdenum disulfide
Cables and lever pivots	Yamaha cable lube or WD-40
Throttle grip, cable ends	Lightweight, lithium-based multi-purpose grease

YZ125

Engine

Spark plug type	
1986 and 1987	Champion N-84, N84G or N59G
1988 through 1989	NGK B9EG or B9EGV
1990	NGK B9EG
1991	
All except Canada and South Africa	NGK B9EG
Canada and South Africa	NGK BR9EG
1992 through 1995	NGK BR9EG

Engine (continued)

1996	
All except Canada and South Africa	NGK B9EG
Canada and South Africa	NGK BR9EG
1997	
All except Europe, Canada and South Africa	NGK B9EG
Europe, Canada and South Africa	NGK BR9EG
1998 through 2005	NGK BR9EG
1996	NGK BR9EVX
Spark plug gap	
1986 through 2005	0.5 to 0.6 mm (0.020 to 0.024 inch)
2006	0.6 to 0.7 mm (0024 to 0.028 inch)

Miscellaneous

Brake pad lining thickness limit	
1986 through 1989 (front and rear)	0.8 m (0.03 inch)
1990 through 1993	
Front	1.6 mm (0.06 inch)
Rear	1.0 mm (0.04 inch)
1994 and later (front and rear)	1.0 mm (0.04 inch)
Rear brake shoe lining limit (drum brakes)	2.0 mm (0.08 inch)
Front brake lever freeplay (1986 through 1995)	
1986 through 1993	10 to 20 mm (0.4 to 0.8 inch)
1994 and 1995	2 to 5 mm (0.08 to 0.20 inch)
Front brake lever distance from handlebar (1996 and later)	
1996	79.5 mm (3.13 inches)
1997 through 2000	82.5 mm (3.25 inches)
2001 and later	95 mm (3.74 inches)
Rear brake pedal freeplay (drum brake models)	20 to 30 mm (3/4 to 1-1/4 inch)
Rear brake pedal height	
1986	Even with top of footpeg, +/- 10 mm (0.4 inches)
1987 through 1995	Zero (even with top of footpeg)
1996 through 2001	5 mm (0.20 inch) below top of footpeg
2002 and later	Zero (even with top of footpeg)
Clutch lever freeplay	
1986 through 1993	2 to 3 mm (0.08 to 0.012) at lever gap
1994 through 2001	2 to 4 mm (0.08 to 0.16 inch at lever gap
2002 and later	8 to 13 mm (0.31 to 0.51 inch) at lever tip
Throttle grip freeplay	3 to 5 mm (1/8 to 1/4 inch)
Minimum tire tread depth	Not specified
Tire pressures (cold)	
1986	Not specified
1987 and later	15 psi (100 kPa)
Tire sizes	
1986	
Front	80/100-21 4PR
Rear	100/100-18 4PR
1987	
Front	80/100-21 M23
Rear	100/100-18 M22
1988 and 1989	
Front	80/100-21 51M
Rear	100/100-18 59M
1990 and later	
Front	80/100-21 51M
Rear	100/90-19 57M
Drive chain slack	
1986	30 to 50 mm (1.2 to 2.0 inches)
1987 through 1991	15 to 20 mm (0.6 to 0.8 inches)
1992 through 1995	30 to 35 mm (1-1/4 to 1-1/2 inches)
1996	45 to 50 mm (1.8 to 2.0 inches)
1997 through 2004	40 to 50 mm (1.6 to 2.0 inches)
2005 and later	48 to 58 mm (1.9 to 2.3 inches)
Front fork air pressure	
1986	
Standard	Zero psi (zero kPa)
Maximum	36 psi (245 kPa)
1987	
Standard	Zero psi (zero kPa)
Maximum	17 psi (120 kPa)

1988	
Standard	Zero psi (zero kPa)
Maximum	15 psi (100 kPa)
1989 and later	Not applicable

Torque specifications

Transmission oil check bolt	
1986 through 1990	Not specified
1991 and later	10 Nm (86 inch-lbs)
Transmission oil drain plug	20 Nm (14 ft-lbs)
Coolant drain bolt	10 Nm (86 inch-lbs)
Spark plug	
1986 through 1988	20 Nm (14 ft-lbs)
1989 through 1993	25 Nm (18 ft-lbs)
1994 and later	20 Nm (14 ft-lbs)
Wheel spokes	
1986 through 1988	Not specified
1989 through 1998	6 Nm (52 inch-lbs)
1999 and later	3 Nm (26 inch-lbs)
Rim lock locknut	Not specified
Steering stem adjusting nut*	
1986 and 1987 (final torque)	10 Nm (86 inch-lbs)
1989 through 1992	
Initial torque	38 Nm (27 ft-lbs)
Final torque	8 Nm (70 inch-lbs)
1993	
Initial torque	38 Nm (27 ft-lbs)
Final torque	4 Nm (35 inch-lbs)
1994	
Initial torque	38 Nm (27 ft-lbs)
Final torque	6.5 Nm (78 inch-lbs)
1995 and later	
Initial torque	38 Nm (27 ft-lbs)
Final torque	7 Nm (84 inch-lbs)

**Torque setting requires a Yamaha ring nut wrench, placed on the torque wrench at a right angle.*

Recommended lubricants and fluids

Fuel	
1986 through 1989	
With Yamalube R	24:1 mix of gasoline (90 Research octane or higher) to oil
With Castrol R30, A545 or A547	20:1 mix of gasoline (90 Research octane or higher) to oil
1990	
With Yamalube R	24:1 mix of gasoline (90 Research octane or higher) to oil
With Castrol R30 or A547	20:1 mix of gasoline (90 Research octane or higher) to oil
1991 through 1995 except Australia	
With Yamalube R	24:1 mix of gasoline (premium unleaded, 95 Research octane or higher) to oil
With Castrol R30 or A547	20:1 mix of gasoline (premium unleaded, 95 Research octane or higher) to oil
1991 through 1995 Australia	
With Yamalube R	24:1 mix of gasoline (unleaded only) to oil
With Castrol R30 or A547	20:1 mix of gasoline (unleaded only) to oil
1996 and 1997 except Australia	
With Yamalube R	24:1 mix of gasoline (premium unleaded, 95 Research octane or higher) to oil
With Castrol R30 or A747	20:1 mix of gasoline (premium unleaded, 95 Research octane or higher) to oil
1996 and 1997 Australia	
With Yamalube R	24:1 mix of gasoline (unleaded only) to oil
With Castrol R30 or A747	20:1 mix of gasoline (unleaded only) to oil
1998 and 1999 except Australia	30:1 mix of gasoline (premium unleaded, 95 Research octane or higher) and Yamalube 2-R or Castrol A747
1998 and 1999 Australia	30:1 mix of gasoline (unleaded only) and Yamalube 2-R or Castrol A747
2000 and 2001 except Australia	30:1 mix of gasoline (premium unleaded, 95 or higher Research octane) and Yamalube 2-R
2000 and 2001 Australia	30:1 mix of gasoline (unleaded only) and Yamalube 2-R
2002 through 2004 except South Africa	30:1 mix of gasoline (premium unleaded, 95 or higher Research octane) and Yamalube 2-R

Recommended lubricants and fluids (continued)

2002 through 2004 South Africa	30:1 mix of gasoline (unleaded only) and Yamalube 2-R
2005 and later	30:1 mix of gasoline (premium unleaded, 95 or higher Research octane) and Yamalube 2-R
Transmission oil	
Type	Yamalube 4-stroke oil or API grade SE multigrade four-stroke oil manufactured for use in motorcycles
Viscosity	10W-30
Capacity at oil change*	
1986 through 1989	600 cc (0.63 US qt, 1.06 Imp pt)
1990 through 2004	650 cc (0.65 US qt, 1.14 Imp pt)
2005 and later	660 cc (0.69 US qt, 1.16 Imp pt)
Capacity after overhaul*	
1986 through 1989	650 cc (0.65 US qt, 1.314 Imp pt)
1990 and later	700 c (0.74 US qt, 0.1.24 Imp pt)
Air cleaner element oil	
1986 through 1988	Foam filter oil
1989 and later	Foam filter oil or SAE 10W-30 engine oil
Coolant	
Type	Ethylene glycol antifreeze compatible with aluminum engines, mixed 50/50 with water
Capacity	
1986 through 1988	600 cc (0.63 US qt, 1.06 Imp pt)
1989 though 1992	900 cc (0.95 US qt, 1.58 Imp pt)
1993 through 1996	1.0 liter (1.06 US qt, 1.76 Imp pt)
1997 through 2000	1.03 liter (1.09 US qt, 1.82 Imp pt)
2001	1.0 liter (1.06 US qt, 1.76 Imp pt)
2002 through 2004	0.95 liter (1.0 US qt, 1.68 Imp pt)
2005 and later	0.9 liter (0.95 US qt, 1.58 Imp pt)
Brake fluid	
1986 and 1987	DOT 3
1988 through 1991	DOT 4 (DOT 3 acceptable)
1992 and later	DOT 4
Drive chain lubricant	
1986 through 1992	Yamaha chain lube or equivalent
1993 and later	Chain lube or 10W-30 engine oil
Fork oil	See Chapter 6
Miscellaneous	
Wheel bearings	Medium weight, lithium-based multi-purpose grease
Swingarm pivot bushings	Molybdenum disulfide
Cables and lever pivots	Yamaha cable lube or WD-40
Throttle grip, cable ends	Lightweight, lithium-based multi-purpose grease

**Approximate capacity; use oil check bolt to determine exact amount (see text).*

YZ250

Engine

Spark plug type	
1986	Champion N-86, N86G, N-2G or N-2C
1987	Champion N-86, N86G, N-2G or N-2C or NGK B8EG, B8EGV
1988	NGK B8EG, B8EGV
1989	Champion N-86, N-86G, NGK B8EG, B8EGV
1990	NGK B8EG
1991 through 1995	
All except Canada and South Africa	NGK B8EG
Canada and South Africa	NGK BR8EG
1996 and later	NGK B8EG
Spark plug gap	0.5 to 0.6 mm (0.020 to 0.024 inch)

Miscellaneous

Brake pad lining thickness limit	
1986 through 1989 (front and rear)	0.8 mm (0.03 inch)
1990 through 1993	
Front	1.6 mm (0.06 inch)
Rear	1.0 mm (0.04 inch)
1994 and later (front and rear)	1.0 mm (0.04 inch)
Rear brake shoe lining limit (drum brakes)	2.0 mm (0.08 inch)

Front brake lever freeplay (1986 through 1995)	
1986 through 1993	10 to 20 mm (0.4 to 0.8 inch)
1994 and 1995	2 to 5 mm (0.08 to 0.20 inch)
Front brake lever distance from handlebar (1996 and later)	
1996	79.5 mm (3.13 inches)
1997 through 2000	82.5 mm (3.25 inches)
2001 and later	95 mm (3.74 inches)
Rear brake pedal freeplay (1986 through 1992)	10 to 20 mm (0.4 to 0.8 inch)
Rear brake pedal height	
1986	Even with top of footpeg, +/- 10 mm (0.4 inches)
1987 through 1995	Zero (even with top of footpeg)
1996 through 2001	5 mm (0.20 inch) below top of footpeg
2002 and later	Zero (even with top of footpeg)
Clutch lever freeplay	
1986 through 1993	2 to 3 mm (0.08 to 0.012) at lever gap
1994 through 2001	2 to 4 mm (0.08 to 0.16 inch at lever gap
2002 and later	8 to 13 mm (0.31 to 0.51 inch) at lever tip
Throttle grip freeplay	
1986	Not specified
1987 and later	3 to 5 mm (1/8 to 1/4 inch)
Minimum tire tread depth	Not specified
Tire pressures (cold)	
1986	Not specified
1987	98 kPa (14 psi)
1988 and later	15 psi (100 kPa)
Tire sizes	
1986	
Front	80/100-21 4PR
Rear	100/100-18 4PR
1987	
Front	80/100-21
Rear	100/100-18
1988	
Front	80/100-21 51M
Rear	110/100-18 64M
1989	
Front	80/100-21 51M
Rear	110/90-19 59M
1990 and later	
Front	80/100-21 51M
Rear	100/90-19 62M
Drive chain slack	
1986	20 to 30 mm (0.8 to 1.2 inches)
1987 through 1989	15 to 20 mm (0.6 to 0.8 inches)
1990 through 1995	30 to 35 mm (1.2 to 1.4 inches)
1996	45 to 50 mm (1.8 to 2.0 inches)
1997 through 2004	40 to 50 mm (1.6 to 2.0 inches)
2005	Not available
2006	48 to 58 mm (1.9 to 2.3 inches)
Front fork air pressure	
1986	
Standard	Zero psi (zero kPa)
Maximum	36 psi (245 kPa)
1987	
Standard	Zero psi (zero kPa)
Maximum	14 psi (98 kPa)
1988	
Standard	Zero psi (zero kPa)
Maximum	15 psi (100 kPa)
1989 and later	Not applicable

Torque specifications

Transmission oil check bolt	
1986 through 1990	Not specified
1991 and later	10 Nm (86 inch-lbs)
Transmission oil drain plug	
1986 through 2004	20 Nm (14 ft-lbs)
2005	Not available
2006	23 Nm 17 ft-lbs)

Torque specifications (continued)

Coolant drain bolt
- 1986 through 1989 .... 10 Nm (86 inch-lbs)
- 1990 through 1994 .... 12 Nm (104 inch-lbs)
- 1995 and later .... 10 Nm (86 inch-lbs)

Spark plug
- 1986 and 1987 .... 20 Nm (14 ft-lbs)
- 1988 through 1994 .... 25 Nm (18 ft-lbs)
- 1995 and later .... 20 Nm (14 ft-lbs)

Wheel spokes
- 1986 through 1997 .... 6 Nm (52 inch-lbs)
- 1998 and later .... 3 Nm (26 inch-lbs)

Rim lock locknut .... Not specified

Steering stem adjusting nut*
- 1986 and 1987 (final torque) .... 10 Nm (86 inch-lbs)
- 1988 and 1989
  - Initial torque .... 38 Nm (27 ft-lbs)
  - Final torque .... 10 Nm (84 inch-lbs)
- 1990 through 1993
  - Initial torque .... 38 Nm (27 ft-lbs)
  - Final torque .... 4 Nm (35 inch-lbs)
- 1994
  - Initial torque .... 38 Nm (27 ft-lbs)
  - Final torque .... 6.5 Nm (78 inch-lbs)
- 1995 and later
  - Initial torque .... 38 Nm (27 ft-lbs)
  - Final torque .... 7 Nm (84 inch-lbs)

Torque setting requires a Yamaha ring nut wrench, placed on the torque wrench at a right angle.

Recommended lubricants and fluids

Fuel
- 1986 through 1988
  - With Yamalube R .... 24:1 mix of gasoline (90 Research octane or higher) to oil
  - With Castrol R30, A545 or A747 .... 20:1 mix of gasoline (90 Research octane or higher) to oil
- 1989 except Australia
  - With Yamalube R .... 24:1 mix of gasoline (90 Research octane or higher) to oil
  - With Castrol R30, A545 or A747 .... 20:1 mix of gasoline (90 Research octane or higher) to oil
- 1989 Australia
  - With Yamalube R .... 24:1 mix of gasoline (unleaded only) to oil
  - With Castrol R30, A545 or A747 .... 20:1 mix of gasoline (unleaded only) to oil
- 1990
  - With Yamalube R .... 24:1 mix of gasoline (90 Research octane or higher) to oil
  - With Castrol R30 or A747 .... 20:1 mix of gasoline (90 Research octane or higher) to oil
- 1991 through 1995 except Australia
  - With Yamalube R .... 24:1 mix of gasoline (premium unleaded, 95 Research octane or higher) to oil
  - With Castrol R30 or A747 .... 20:1 mix of gasoline (premium unleaded, 95 Research octane or higher) to oil
- 1991 through 1995 Australia
  - With Yamalube R .... 24:1 mix of gasoline (unleaded only) to oil
  - With Castrol R30 or 747 .... 20:1 mix of gasoline (unleaded only) to oil
- 1996 through 2000 except Australia .... 30:1 mix of gasoline (premium unleaded, 95 Research octane or higher) and Yamalube 2-R or Castrol A747
- 1996 through 2000 Australia .... 30:1 mix of gasoline (unleaded only) and Yamalube 2-R or Castrol A747
- 2001 and 2002 except Australia .... 30:1 mix of gasoline (premium unleaded, 95 or higher Research octane) and Yamalube 2-R
- 2001 and 2002 Australia .... 30:1 mix of gasoline (unleaded only) and Yamalube 2-R
- 2003 and 2004 except South Africa .... 30:1 mix of gasoline (premium unleaded, 95 or higher Research octane) and Yamalube 2-R
- 2003 and 2004 South Africa .... 30:1 mix of gasoline (unleaded only) and Yamalube 2-R
- 2005 .... Not available
- 2006 .... 30:1 mix of gasoline (premium unleaded, 95 or higher Research octane) and Yamalube 2-R

Transmission oil
- Type .... Yamalube 4-stroke oil or API grade SE multigrade four-stroke oil manufactured for use in motorcycles
- Viscosity 10W-30

Capacity at oil change*	
1986 and 1987	850 cc (0.9 US qt, 1.5 Imp pt)
1988 and later	750 cc (0.79 US qt, 1.32 Imp pt)
Capacity after overhaul*	
1986 and 1987	900 cc (0.95 US qt, 1.58 Imp pt)
1988 and later	800 cc (0.85 qt, 1.4 Imp pt)
Air cleaner element oil	
1986 through 1992	Foam filter oil
1993 and later	Foam filter oil or 2-stroke engine oil
Coolant	
Type	Ethylene glycol antifreeze compatible with aluminum engines, mixed 50/50 with water
Capacity	
1986 through 1992	1.0 liter (1.06 US qt, 1.76 Imp pt)
1993 through 1995	1.2 liter (1.27 US qt, 2.12 Imp pt)
1996	1.13 liter (1.19 US qt, 1.98 Imp pt)
1997 and 1998	1.14 liter (1.2 US qt, 2.0 Imp pt)
1999 and later	1.2 liter (1.27 US qt, 2.12 Imp pt)
Brake fluid	
1986 and 1987	DOT 3
1988 through 1993	DOT 4 (DOT 3 acceptable)
1994 and later	DOT 4
Drive chain lubricant	
1986 through 1992	Yamaha chain lube or equivalent
1993 and later	Chain lube or 10W-30 engine oil
Fork oil	See Chapter 6
Miscellaneous	
Wheel bearings	Medium weight, lithium-based multi-purpose grease
Swingarm pivot bushings	Molybdenum disulfide
Cables and lever pivots	Yamaha cable lube or WD-40
Throttle grip, cable ends	Lightweight, lithium-based multi-purpose grease

**Approximate capacity; use oil check bolt to determine exact amount (see text).*

1 Yamaha YZ Routine maintenance intervals

Note: *This schedule was developed for your motorcycle's intended purpose, motocross competition. It's based on numbers of races. The intervals listed below are the shortest intervals recommended by the manufacturer for each particular operation during the model years covered in this manual. Your owner's manual may have different intervals for your model.*

Before each race

Make sure the engine kill switch works properly (see Section 3)
Check the throttle for smooth operation and correct freeplay (See Section 4)
Check clutch operation and freeplay (See Section 5)
Inspect and lubricate the control cables (See Section 6)
Check brake fluid level (hydraulic brakes) (See Section 7)
Check the brake pads and shoes for wear (See Section 8)
Check the operation of both brakes - check the front brake lever and rear brake pedal for correct freeplay (See Section 9)
Check the tires for damage, the presence of foreign objects and correct air pressure (see Section 10)
Lubricate and inspect the drive chain, sprockets and sliders (see Section 11)
Check all fasteners, including axle nuts, for tightness (see Section 12)
Check and adjust the steering head bearings (See Section 13)
Inspect the front and rear suspensions (see Section 14)
Lubricate the swingarm bearings and rear shock linkage pivot points (see Chapter 6)
Check the coolant level and inspect the cooling system (see Section 15)
Clean the air filter element (see Section 16)
Clean and gap the spark plug (see Section 17)
Clean and inspect the power valve (if equipped) (see Chapter 2)
Inspect and tighten the expansion chamber and muffler (see Section 18)
Inspect and clean the cylinder head and cylinder (see Chapter 2)
Inspect and clean the piston, pin and rings (see Chapter 2)
Check and adjust the carburetor; clean if necessary (see Section 19 and Chapter 4)
Clean and inspect the frame (see Chapter 8)

Before every third race

Replace the piston rings (see Chapter 2)
Inspect the fuel tank and supply valve (see Chapter 4)
Inspect and lubricate the wheel bearings (see Chapter 7)

Before every fifth race

Clean the muffler (see Section 18)
Change the transmission oil (see Section 20)
Replace the piston and rings (see Chapter 2)
Tighten the alternator rotor nut (see Chapter 5)
Inspect and clean the crankshaft (see Chapter 2)
Change the fork oil (see Section 21)
Clean and lubricate the steering head bearings (see Chapter 6)

Every year

Change the brake fluid (see Chapter 7)
Replace the rear shock absorber spring seat (see Chapter 6)

Every two years

Change the coolant (see Section 15)

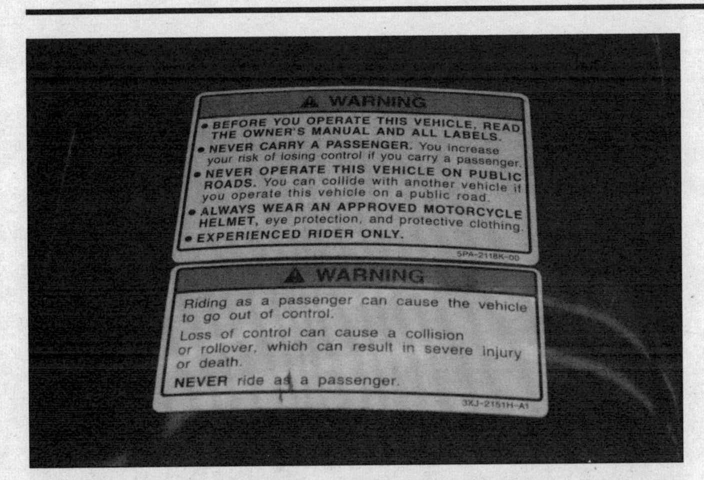

2.1 Decals on the motorcycle include maintenance and safety information

2 Introduction to tune-up and routine maintenance

Refer to illustration 2.1

This Chapter covers in detail the checks and procedures necessary for the tune-up and routine maintenance of your motorcycle. Section 1 includes the routine maintenance schedule, which is designed to keep the machine in proper running condition and prevent possible problems. The remaining Sections contain detailed procedures for carrying out the items listed on the maintenance schedule, as well as additional maintenance information designed to increase reliability. Maintenance and safety information is also printed on decals, which are mounted in various locations on the motorcycle **(see illustration)**. Where information on the decals differs from that presented in this Chapter, use the decal information.

Since routine maintenance plays such an important role in the safe and efficient operation of your motorcycle, it is presented here as a comprehensive check list. For the rider who does all of the bike's maintenance, these lists outline the procedures and checks that should be done on a routine basis.

Deciding where to start or plug into the routine maintenance schedule depends on several factors. If you have owned the bike for some time but have never performed any maintenance on it, then you may want to start at the nearest interval and include some additional procedures to ensure that nothing important is overlooked. If you have just had a major engine overhaul, then you may want to start the maintenance routine from the beginning. If you have a used machine and have no knowledge of its history or maintenance record, you may desire to combine all the checks into one large service initially and then settle into the maintenance schedule prescribed.

The Sections which outline the inspection and maintenance procedures are written as step-by-step comprehensive guides to the actual performance of the work. They explain in detail each of the routine inspections and maintenance procedures on the check list. References to additional information in applicable Chapters are also included and should not be overlooked.

Before beginning any actual maintenance or repair, the machine should be cleaned thoroughly, especially around the oil filler plug, radiator cap, air filter cover, carburetor, etc. Cleaning will help ensure that dirt does not contaminate the engine and will allow you to detect wear and damage that could otherwise easily go unnoticed.

3 Engine kill switch - check

Start the engine, then use the kill switch to shut it off. If it doesn't shut off or if the engine doesn't start, refer to Chapter 5 and the wiring diagrams at the end of the book to test the switch.

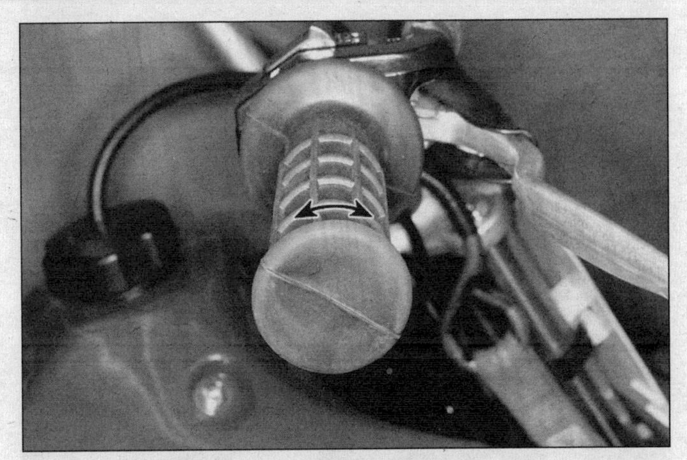

4.2 Measure throttle freeplay at the grip

4 Throttle and choke operation/grip freeplay - check and adjustment

Throttle check

Refer to illustration 4.2

1 Make sure the throttle twistgrip moves easily from fully closed to fully open with the front wheel turned at various angles. The grip should return automatically from fully open to fully closed when released. If the throttle sticks, check the throttle cable for cracks or kinks in the housings. Also, make sure the inner cable is clean and well-lubricated.

2 Check for a small amount of freeplay at the twistgrip **(see illustration)** and compare the freeplay to the value listed in this Chapter's Specifications.

Throttle adjustment

1986 through 1992 YZ80

Refer to illustration 4.5

3 Locate both adjusters, one at the carburetor and one partway along the cable.

4 Loosen the locknut on the mid-cable adjuster. Turn the adjuster all the way in, then tighten the locknut.

5 Loosen the locknut at the carburetor **(see illustration)**. Turn the adjuster to obtain the freeplay listed in this Chapter's Specifications, then tighten the locknut.

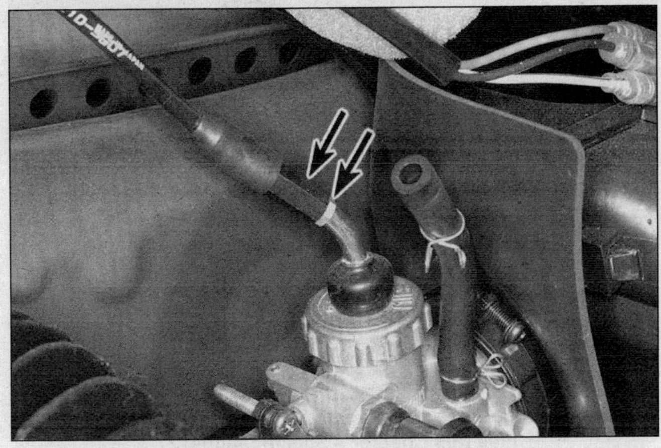

4.5 Loosen the locknut (right arrow) and turn the adjuster (left arrow) to obtain the specified freeplay

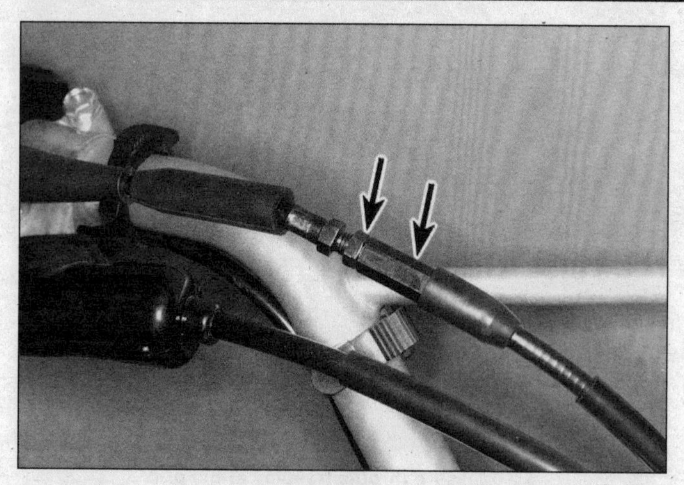

4.9 Loosen the locknut (left arrow) and turn the adjuster right arrow) to adjust freeplay

4.10 The choke knob (arrow) should operate smoothly

1986 and 1987 YZ125/250

6 On these models, minor adjustments are made at the twistgrip end of the accelerator cable and major adjustments are made at the carburetor end of the cable.

7 Pull back the rubber cover from the adjuster and loosen the locknut or lockwheel on the cable. Turn the adjuster until the specified freeplay is obtained, then retighten the lockwheel.

8 If freeplay can't be adjusted at the grip end, loosen the locknut at the carburetor end of the cable **(see illustration 4.5)**. Turn the adjuster to set freeplay, then tighten the locknut securely.

All other models

Refer to illustration 4.9

9 Throttle cable adjustments are made at the throttle grip end of the cable. Pull back the rubber cover from the adjuster and loosen the locknut or lockwheel on the cable **(see illustration)**. Turn the adjuster until the specified freeplay is obtained, then retighten the locknut or lockwheel.

Choke - operation check

Refer to illustration 4.10

10 Check that the choke knob moves smoothly **(see illustration)**. If not, refer to Chapter 4 and remove the choke plunger for inspection.

5 Clutch - check and freeplay adjustment

Refer to illustrations 5.1, 5.2, 5.4a, 5.4b, 5.4c and 5.4d

1 Operate the clutch lever and measure freeplay at the tip of the lever or in the gap between the lever and bracket, depending on model (refer to this Chapter's Specifications for the gap and measurement point) **(see illustration)**. If it's not within the range listed in this Chapter's Specifications, adjust it as follows.

2 On all YZ80/85 models and early YZ125/250 models, pull back the rubber cover from the adjuster at the handlebar **(see illustration)**. Loosen the lockwheel or locknut and turn the adjuster to change freeplay.

3 Some models are equipped with a mid-cable adjuster, which is several inches farther down the cable **(see illustration 5.2)**. If freeplay can't be brought within specifications by using the handlebar adjuster, make adjustments at the mid-cable adjuster.

4 Later YZ125/250 models have a fine adjuster under the cap **(see illustrations)**. This can be used to make very small adjustments after the freeplay has been set using the locknut and adjuster.

5 If freeplay can't be adjusted to within the specified range, the cable is probably stretched and should be replaced with a new one (see Chapter 2).

5.1 On some models, clutch freeplay is measured at the lever gap (see this Chapter's Specifications) . . .

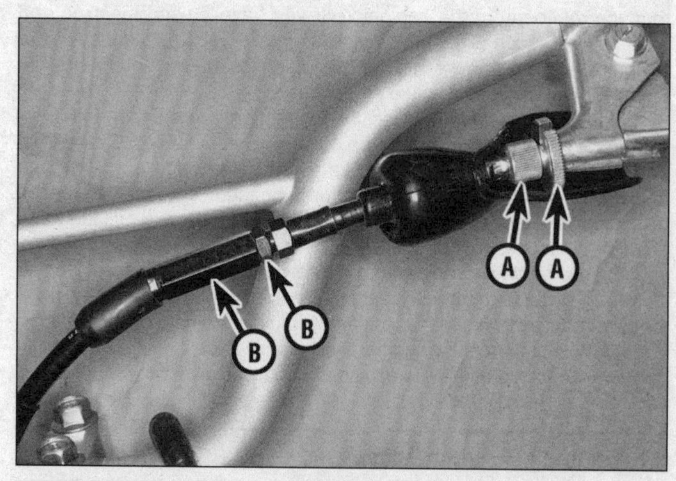

5.2 . . . to adjust it, loosen the locknut and turn the adjuster first at the handlebar adjuster (A), then at the mid-cable adjuster (if equipped) (B)

5.4a On later YZ125/250 models, measure freeplay at the lever tip; the adjusters are inside the boot (left arrow) and cap (right arrow) . . .

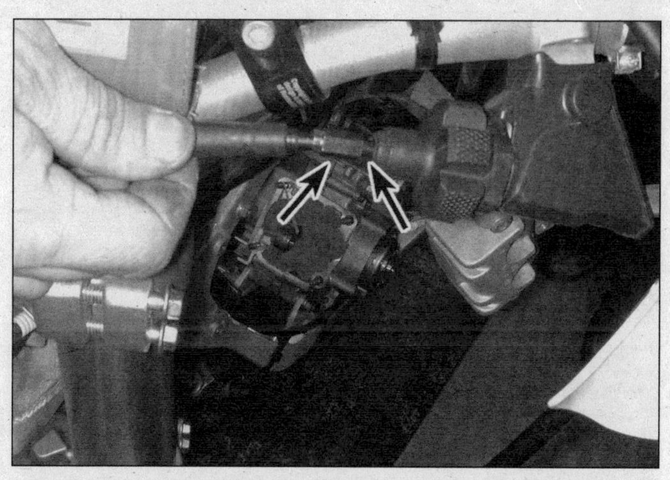

5.4b . . . to make initial adjustments, pull back the boot, loosen the locknut (right arrow) and turn the adjuster (left arrow) . . .

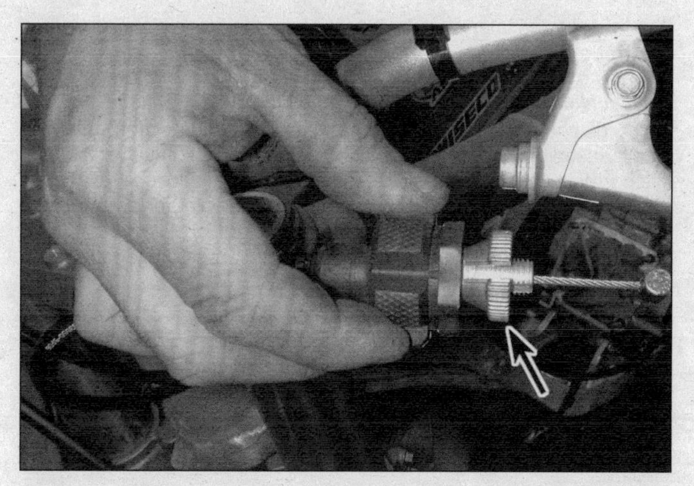

5.4c . . . and if necessary, pull back the cap and turn this adjuster to make fine adjustments

5.4d Align the tab inside the cap (arrow) with the adjuster groove when you install the cap

6 Lubrication - general

Refer to illustration 6.3

1 Since the controls, cables and various other components of a motorcycle are exposed to the elements, they should be lubricated periodically to ensure safe and trouble-free operation.

2 The throttle twistgrip, brake lever, brake pedal and kickstarter pedal pivot should be lubricated frequently. In order for the lubricant to be applied where it will do the most good, the component should be disassembled. However, if chain and cable lubricant is being used, it can be applied to the pivot joint gaps and will usually work its way into the areas where friction occurs. If motor oil or light grease is being used, apply it sparingly as it may attract dirt (which could cause the controls to bind or wear at an accelerated rate). **Note:** *One of the best lubricants for the control lever pivots is a dry-film lubricant (available from many sources by different names).*

3 The throttle and clutch cables should be removed and treated with a commercially available cable lubricant which is specially formulated for use on motorcycle control cables. Small adapters for pressure lubricating the cables with spray can lubricants are available and ensure that the cable is lubricated along its entire length **(see illustration)**. When attaching the cable to the lever, be sure to lubricate the barrel-shaped fitting at the end with multi-purpose grease.

4 To lubricate the cables, disconnect them at the upper end, then lubricate the cable with a pressure lube adapter **(see illustration 6.3)**. See Chapter 4 (throttle cable) or Chapter 2 (clutch cable).

5 Lubrication of the swingarm and rear suspension linkage pivots requires removal of the components.

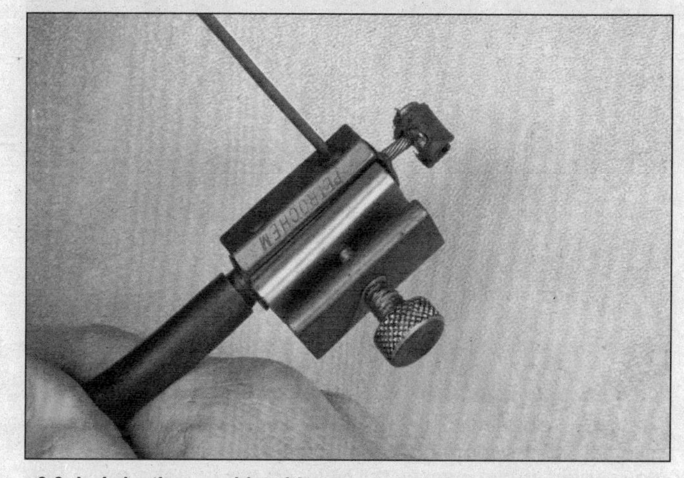

6.3 Lubricating a cable with a pressure lube adapter (make sure the tool seats around the inner cable)

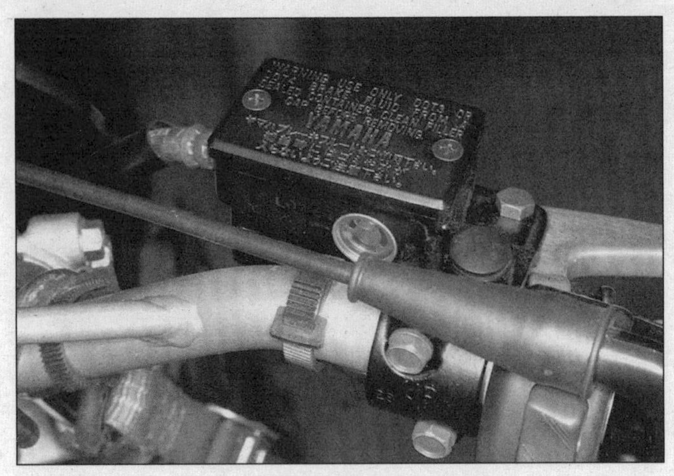

7.3a The front brake fluid level is visible in the window; make sure it's above the LOWER mark

7.3b The rear brake fluid level on early models is visible through the translucent reservoir

6 Refer to Chapter 6 for the following lubrication procedures:

a) *Swingarm bearings, dust seals and rear suspension linkage pivots*

b) *Steering head bearings*

7 Refer to Chapter 7 for the following lubrication procedures:

a) *Front and rear wheel bearings*

b) *Brake pedal pivot*

7 Brake fluid - check

Refer to illustrations 7.3a, 7.3b, 7.3c and 7.4

1 To ensure proper operation of the hydraulic disc brakes, the fluid level in the master cylinder reservoirs must be maintained within a safe range.

2 With the motorcycle supported in an upright position, turn the handlebars until the top of the front brake master cylinder is as level as possible.

3 The front brake fluid level is visible in the window on the reservoir **(see illustration)**. Make sure the fluid level is above the Lower mark cast on the master cylinder body next to the reservoir. The rear brake fluid level on early models is visible through the plastic reservoir **(see illustration)**. On later models, it's visible in the reservoir window **(see illustration)**.

4 If the fluid level is low, clean the area around the reservoir cover. On reservoirs with windows, remove the cover screws and take off the cover, diaphragm retainer and diaphragm **(see illustration)**. On rear plastic reservoirs, unscrew the cover. Add new brake fluid of the type listed in this Chapter's Specifications until the fluid level is even with the line cast inside the reservoir (aluminum reservoirs) or even with the upper level line (plastic reservoirs).

5 Install the diaphragm, retainer and cover, then tighten the cover screws securely.

8 Brake system - general check

1 A routine general check of the brakes will ensure that any problems are discovered and remedied before the rider's safety is jeopardized.

2 Check the brake lever and pedal for loose connections, excessive play, bends, and other damage. Replace any damaged parts with new ones (see Chapter 7).

3 Make sure all brake fasteners are tight. Check the brakes for wear as described below.

7.3c On later models, the rear brake fluid level is visible in the reservoir window (lower left arrow); if it's below the LOWER mark (lower right arrow), remove the cover screws (upper arrows) and lift off the cap to add fluid

7.4 Lift off the cover and diaphragm to add fluid

8.4a On early models, remove the inspection plug (arrow) to inspect the pads . . .

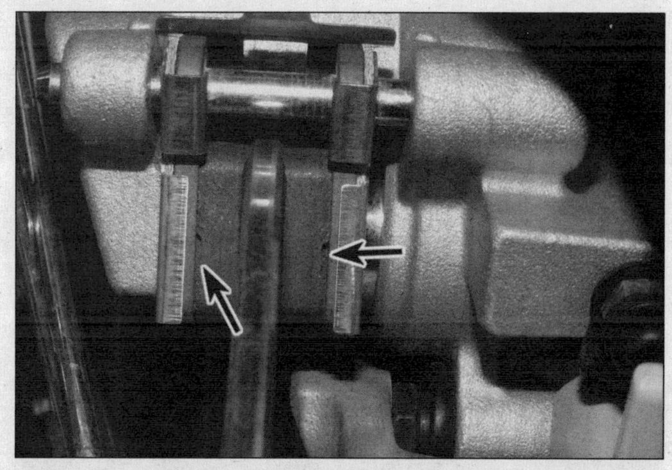

8.4b . . . on later models, the back of the caliper is open - when the pad material is worn to the wear indicator notches (arrows), it's time for new pads

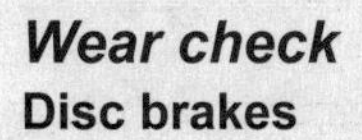

Wear check

Disc brakes

Refer to illustrations 8.4a and 8.4b

4 There's a groove on the inside of each pad next to the metal backing **(see illustrations)**. When the friction material is nearly worn down to the groove, it's time to replace the pads (even if only one pad is worn that far).

Rear drum brakes

Refer to illustration 8.6

5 Operate the brake pedal. If operation is rough or sticky, refer to Section 6 and lubricate the cable.

6 With the rear brake lever and pedal freeplay properly adjusted (see Section 9), check the wear indicator triangular mark on the brake panel **(see illustration)**. If the slot in the brake arm lines up with the mark when the pedal is pressed, refer to Chapter 7 and replace the brake shoes.

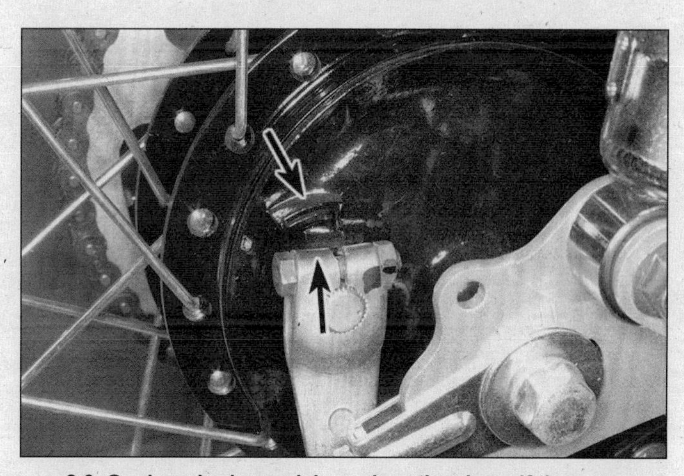

8.6 On drum brake models, replace the shoes if the wear indicator on the brake arm lines up with the limit line on the brake panel (arrows)

9 Brake lever and pedal - check and adjustment

Front brake lever

Refer to illustration 9.1, 9.2a and 9.2b

1 Check either brake lever freeplay or the distance from the lever tip to the handlebar, depending on model (see this Chapter's Specifications for the measurement that applies to your bike). If you're measuring freeplay, squeeze the front brake lever and note how far the lever travels before you feel resistance **(see illustration)**. If it exceeds the limit listed in this Chapter's Specifications, adjust the front brake.

2 Loosen the locknut and turn the adjusting screw or adjusting bolt **(see illustrations)**. Tighten the locknut after making the adjustment.

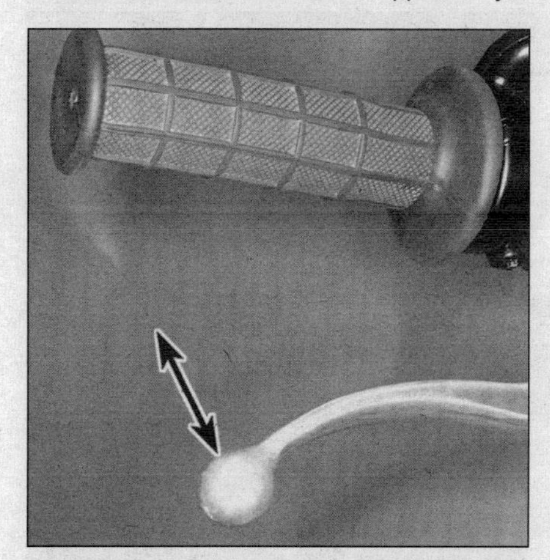

9.1 On early models, measure front brake freeplay at the lever tip; on later models, measure lever position

9.2a Make adjustments by loosening the locknut and turning the screw (early models) . . .

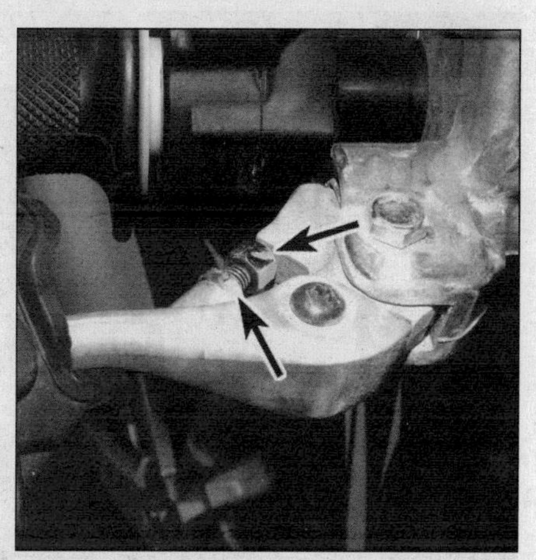

9.2b . . . or by loosening the locknut and turning the adjusting bolt (later models)

9.6 To adjust rear brake pedal freeplay on drum brake models, turn the adjuster nut at the rear end of the brake rod (arrow)

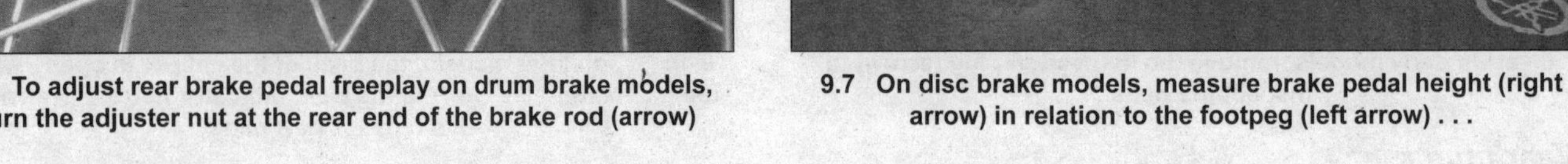

9.7 On disc brake models, measure brake pedal height (right arrow) in relation to the footpeg (left arrow) . . .

3 Recheck lever travel (see Step 1). If it's still not within the Specifications, refer to Chapter 7 and bleed the brakes.

Rear brake pedal

Drum brake models

Refer to illustration 9.6

4 Measure brake pedal height above the footpeg and compare it with the value listed in this Chapter's Specifications. Adjust if necessary.

5 To adjust brake pedal height, loosen the locknut and turn the adjusting bolt (they're mounted on the right side of the frame above and behind the brake pedal).

6 Check the play of the brake pedal. If it exceeds the limit listed in this Chapter's Specifications, adjust it with the nut at the rear end of the brake rod **(see illustration)**.

Disc brake models

Refer to illustrations 9.7 and 9.8

7 Measure brake pedal height in relation to the footpeg and compare it with the value listed in this Chapter's Specifications **(see illustration)**. Adjust if necessary.

8 To adjust pedal height, loosen the locknut and turn the pushrod on the rear master cylinder **(see illustration)**. Be sure there is enough thread showing on the pushrod after the adjustment. If you have to use up all the threads to get the adjustment within Specifications, bleed the brakes or overhaul the master cylinder and caliper (see Chapter 7). Also do this if the end of the pushrod comes closer than 2 mm (0.080 inch) to the brake pedal.

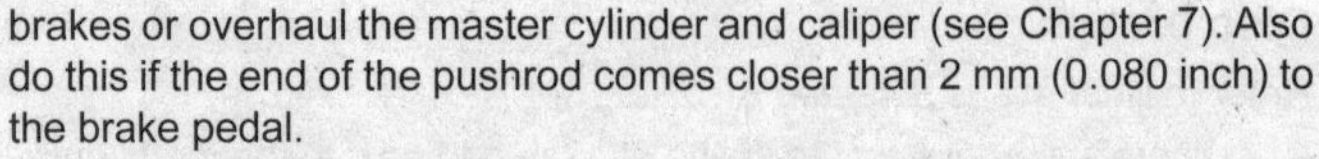

9 Pedal freeplay on disc brake models is automatic and no means of manual adjustment is provided.

10 Tires/wheels - general check

Refer to illustrations 10.4, 10.5 and 10.7

1 Routine tire and wheel checks should be made with the realization that your safety depends to a great extent on their condition.

2 Check the tires carefully for cuts, tears, embedded nails or other sharp objects and excessive wear. Operation of the motorcycle with excessively worn tires is extremely hazardous, as traction and handling are directly affected. Check the tread depth at the center of the tire and compare it to the value listed in this Chapter's Specifications. Yamaha doesn't specify a minimum tread depth for some models, but as a general rule, tires should be replaced with new ones when the tread knobs are worn to 8 mm (5/16 inch) or less.

3 Repair or replace punctured tires as soon as damage is noted. Do not try to patch a torn tire, as wheel balance and tire reliability may be impaired.

4 Check the tire pressures when the tires are cold and keep them properly inflated **(see illustration)**. Proper air pressure will increase

9.8 . . . to adjust it, loosen the locknut (lower arrow) and turn the adjusting nut (upper arrow) - do not over-adjust it (see text)

10.4 Check tire pressure with a gauge

10.5 Make sure the spokes are tight, but don't overtighten them

10.7 Tighten the locknut on the rim lock securely

tire life and provide maximum stability and ride comfort. Keep in mind that low tire pressures may cause the tire to slip on the rim or come off, while high tire pressures will cause abnormal tread wear and unsafe handling.

5 The wheels should be kept clean and checked periodically for cracks, bending, loose spokes and rust. Never attempt to repair damaged wheels; they must be replaced with new ones. Loose spokes can be tightened with a spoke wrench **(see illustration)**, but be careful not to overtighten and distort the wheel rim.

6 Check the valve stem locknuts to make sure they're tight. Also, make sure the valve stem cap is in place and tight. If it is missing, install a new one made of metal or hard plastic.

7 Check the tightness of the locknut on the rim lock **(see illustration)**. If it's loose, tighten it securely.

11 Drive chain and sprockets - check, adjustment and lubrication

Refer to illustrations 11.3, 11.5, 11.6a, 11.6b and 11.6c

1 A neglected drive chain won't last long and can quickly damage the sprockets. Routine chain adjustment isn't difficult and will ensure maximum chain and sprocket life. **Note:** *The chain should be routinely replaced at the interval listed in Section 1.*

2 To check the chain, support the bike securely with the rear wheel off the ground. Place the transmission in neutral.

3 Push down and pull up on the bottom run of the chain (YZ80/85 models) or the top run of the chain (YZ125/250 models) and measure the slack midway between the two sprockets **(see illustration)**. Compare the measurements to the value listed in this Chapter's Specifications. As wear occurs, the chain will actually stretch, which means adjustment by removing some slack from the chain. In some cases where lubrication has been neglected, corrosion and galling may cause the links to bind and kink, which effectively shortens the chain's length. If the chain is tight between the sprockets, rusty or kinked, it's time to replace it with a new one. **Note:** *Repeat the chain slack measurement along the length of the chain - ideally, every inch or so. If you find a tight area, mark it with a felt pen or paint and repeat the measurement after the bike has been ridden. If the chain's still tight in the same areas, it may be damaged or worn. Because a tight or kinked chain can damage the transmission countershaft bearing, it's a good idea to replace it.*

4 Check the entire length of the chain for damaged rollers, loose links and loose pins.

5 Check the teeth on the engine sprocket **(see illustration)** and the rear sprocket for wear (see Chapter 6). Refer to Chapter 6 for the sprocket replacement procedure if the sprockets appear to be worn excessively.

11.3 On 125 and 250 models, measure drive chain slack along the upper chain run (on 80/85 models, measure at the lower chain run)

11.5 Check the engine sprocket for excessive wear - if it's worn, replace both sprockets and the drive chain as a set

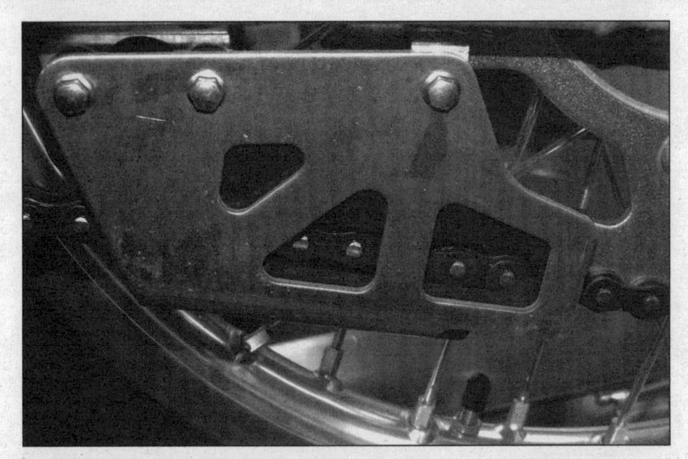

11.6a Check the chain sliders for wear; typical locations are below the swingarm . . .

11.6b . . . wrapped around the swingarm . . .

11.6c . . . and attached to the frame above the swingarm

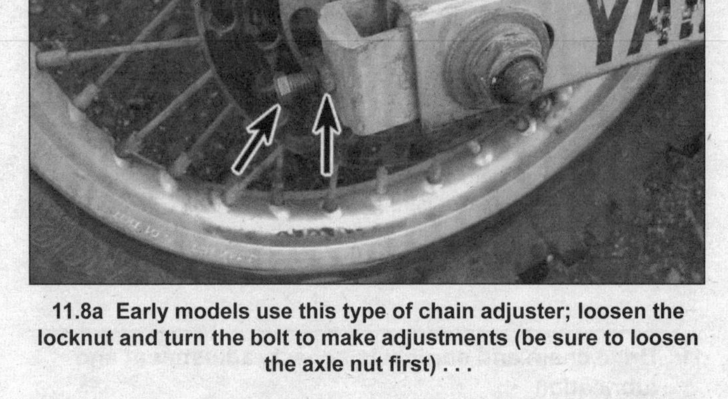

11.8a Early models use this type of chain adjuster; loosen the locknut and turn the bolt to make adjustments (be sure to loosen the axle nut first) . . .

6 Check the chain sliders and roller(s) **(see illustrations)**. If a slider is worn, measure its thickness. If it's less than the value listed in the Chapter 6 Specifications, replace it (see Chapter 6).

Adjustment

Refer to illustrations 11.8a, 11.8b and 11.8c

7 Rotate the rear wheel until the chain is positioned with the least amount of slack present.

8 Loosen the rear axle nut (see Chapter 7). Loosen the locknut and turn the adjuster on each side of the swingarm evenly until the proper chain tension is obtained (get the adjuster on the chain side close, then set the adjuster on the opposite side) **(see illustrations)**. Be sure to turn the adjusters evenly to keep the wheel in alignment. If the adjusters reach the end of their travel, the chain is excessively worn and should be replaced with a new one (see Chapter 6).

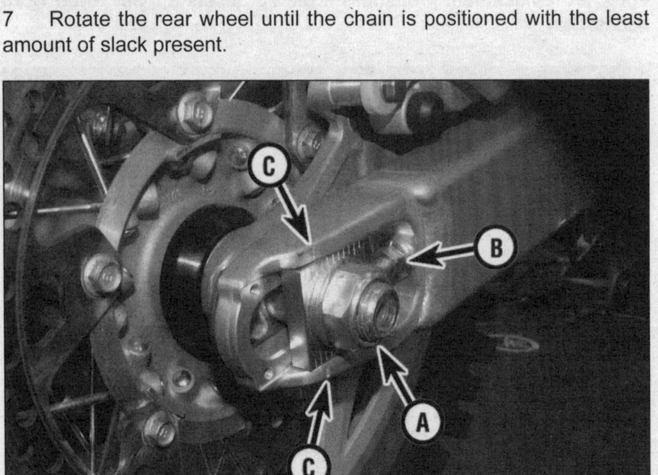

11.8b . . . later models use this design . . .

A Axle nut
B Locknut and adjusting bolt
C Indicator marks

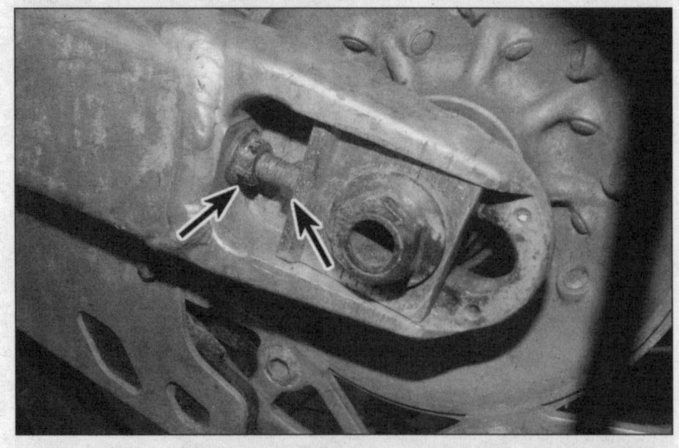

11.8c . . . loosen the locknut (left arrow) and turn the adjusting bolt (right arrow) to make adjustments

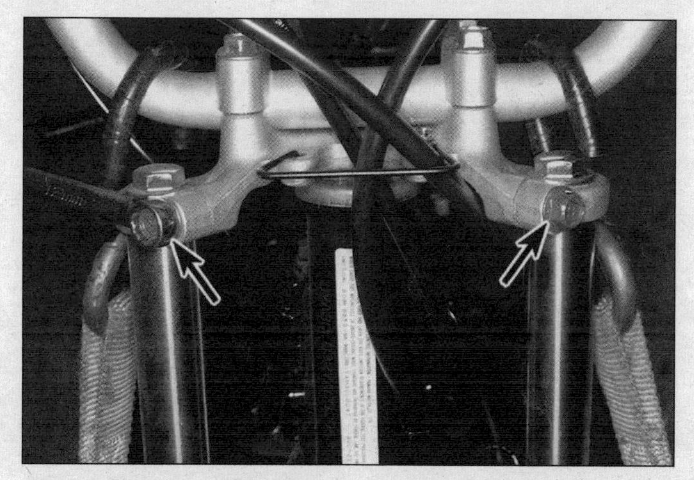

13.5a Loosen the upper triple clamp pinch bolts . . .

13.5b . . . and the steering stem bolt

9 When the chain has the correct amount of slack, make sure the marks on the adjusters correspond to the same relative marks on each side of the swingarm **(see illustration 11.8b)**. Tighten the axle nut to the torque listed in the Chapter 7 Specifications.

Lubrication

Note: *If the chain is dirty, it should be removed and cleaned before it's lubricated (see Chapter 6).*

10 Use a good quality chain lubricant of the type listed in this Chapter's Specifications. Apply the lubricant along the top of the lower chain run, so that when the bike is ridden centrifugal force will move the lubricant into the chain, rather than throwing it off.

11 After applying the lubricant, let it soak in a few minutes before wiping off any excess.

12 Fasteners - check

1 Since vibration of the machine tends to loosen fasteners, all nuts, bolts, screws, etc. should be periodically checked for proper tightness. Also make sure all cotter pins or other safety fasteners are correctly installed.

2 Pay particular attention to the following:

Spark plug
Transmission oil drain plug and check bolt
Gearshift pedal
Brake lever and pedal
Kickstarter pedal
Footpegs
Engine mounting bolts
Steering stem locknut
Front axle nut
Rear axle nut
Skid plate bolts

3 If a torque wrench is available, use it along with the torque specifications at the beginning of this, or other, Chapters.

13 Steering head bearings - check and adjustment

Inspection

1 These motorcycles are equipped with ball-and-cone or roller-and-cone type steering head bearings, which can become dented, rough or loose during normal use of the machine. In extreme cases, worn or loose steering head bearings can cause steering wobble that is potentially dangerous.

2 To check the bearings, lift up the front end of the motorcycle and place a secure support beneath the engine so the front wheel is off the ground.

3 Point the wheel straight ahead and slowly move the handlebars from side-to-side. Dents or roughness in the bearing will be felt and the bars will not move smoothly. **Note:** *Make sure any hesitation in movement is not being caused by the cables and wiring harnesses that run to the handlebars.*

4 Next, grasp the fork legs and try to move the wheel forward and backward. Any looseness in the steering head bearing s will be felt. If play is felt in the bearings, adjust the steering head as follows.

Adjustment

1986 through 1992 YZ80, 1986 through 1989 YZ125, 1986 through 1989 YZ250

Refer to illustrations 13.5a, 13.5b and 13.6

5 Loosen the upper triple clamp pinch bolts and the steering stem bolt **(see illustrations)**.

6 Tighten the ring nut with a Yamaha ring nut wrench (YU-33975) or a suitable substitute **(see illustration)**. Don't torque the nut, just tighten it until you feel resistance.

7 If you have the Yamaha special tool, attach a torque wrench to it so they form a right angle. Tighten the ring nut to the initial torque listed in this Chapter's Specifications.

8 Loosen the ring nut one turn, then tighten it to the final torque listed in this Chapter's Specifications.

9 Recheck the adjustment by turning the handlebars lock-to-lock. If it feels a little tight, loosen the ring nut a little bit and recheck. If it feels loose, repeat the adjustment (see Steps 6 through 8).

10 When the steering head feels like all freeplay has been removed,

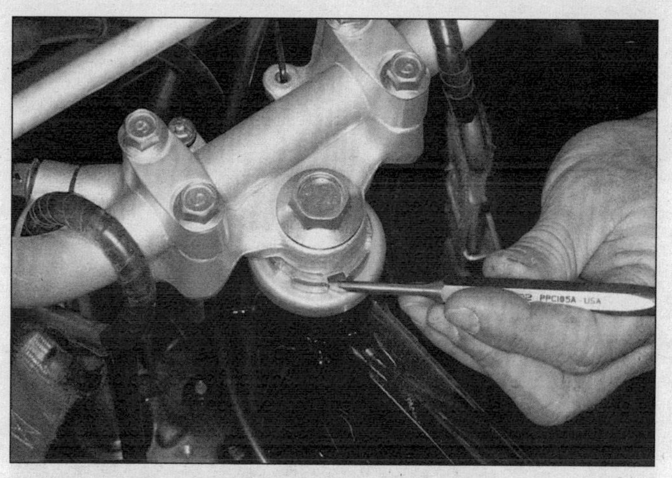

13.6 Tighten the ring nut with a Yamaha ring nut wrench or a suitable substitute, such as this punch, until you feel resistance

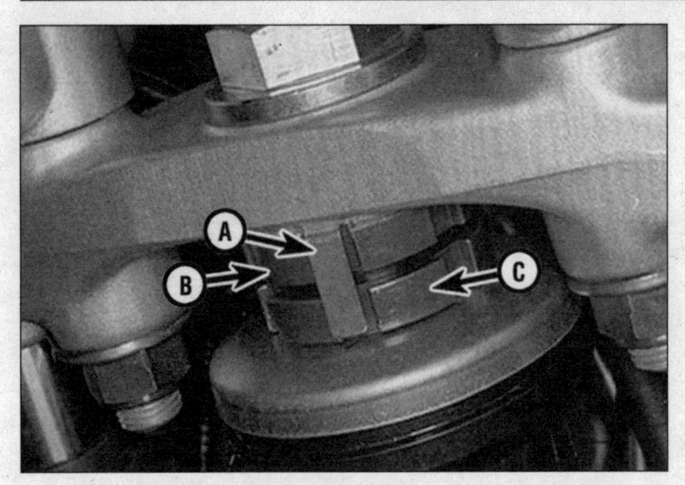

13.13 With the upper triple clamp removed, remove the lockwasher (A) and upper ring nut (B); adjust with the lower ring nut (C)

but it's not binding or loose, tighten the steering stem bolt and the upper triple clamp pinch bolts to the torque listed in the Chapter 6 Specifications.

1990 through 1992 YZ125/250

Refer to illustration 13.13

11 These models use two ring nuts on the steering stem. They're held in position by a lockwasher with long tabs that fit into the slots in the nuts.
12 Remove the handlebar and upper triple clamp (see Chapter 6).
13 Remove the lockwasher and the upper ring nut **(see illustration)**.
14 If you have the Yamaha special tool, attach a torque wrench to it so they form a right angle. Tighten the lower ring nut to the initial torque listed in this Chapter's Specifications.
15 Loosen the lower ring nut one turn, then tighten it to the final torque listed in this Chapter's Specifications.
16 Recheck the adjustment by turning the steering stem lock-to-lock. If it feels a little tight, loosen the lower ring nut a little bit and recheck. If it feels loose, repeat the adjustment (see Steps 14 and 15).
17 When the steering head feels like all freeplay has been removed, but it's not binding or loose, install the upper ring nut. Hold the lower ring nut so it won't turn and tighten the upper ring nut against it to line up the slots in the upper and lower nuts.
18 Install the lockwasher, engaging its tabs with the slots.
19 Install the upper triple clamp and handlebar (see Chapter 6).

14.4 Remove the air valve cap to check fork pressure

13.21 Loosen the ring nut with an adjustable spanner wrench such as this one

1993 and later models

Refer to illustration 13.21

20 Remove the handlebar and upper triple clamp (see Chapter 6). If you're working on a YZ125/250, remove the washer that's installed under the triple clamp on the steering stem.
21 Loosen the ring nut, then retighten it to the initial torque listed in this Chapter's Specifications **(see illustration)**.
22 Loosen the ring nut one full turn, then tighten it to the final torque listed in this Chapter's Specifications.
23 Recheck the adjustment by turning the steering stem lock-to-lock. If it feels a little tight, loosen the lower ring nut a little bit and recheck. If it feels loose, repeat the adjustment (see Steps 21 and 22).
24 Install the upper triple clamp and handlebar (see Chapter 6).

14 Suspension - check

Refer to illustrations 14.4, 14.5a, 14.5b and 14.5c

1 The suspension components must be maintained in top operating condition to ensure rider safety. Loose, worn or damaged suspension parts decrease the motorcycle's stability and control.
2 Lock the front brake and push on the handlebars to compress the front forks several times. See if they move up-and-down smoothly without binding. If binding is felt, the forks should be disassembled and inspected as described in Chapter 6.
3 Check the tightness of all front suspension nuts and bolts to be sure none have worked loose.
4 On 1986 and 1987 models, with the front forks cold and fully extended (bike jacked up so the front wheel is off the ground), remove the air valve caps (if equipped) from the forks and check air pressure with a pressure gauge **(see illustration)**. Compare with the reading listed in this Chapter's Specifications. **Note:** *Air will heat up and expand during a race, stiffening the forks.*
5 Check for oil leaking from the fork seals **(see illustration)**. As part of this inspection, check for foreign material at the bases of the fork legs and for built-up dirt behind the fork protectors **(see illustrations)**. Either of these will wear out the fork seals prematurely when the fork leg compresses, causing the seals to leak.
6 Inspect the rear shock absorber for fluid leakage and tightness of the mounting nuts and bolts. If leakage is found, the shock should be replaced.
7 Check the rear suspension linkage for loose fasteners, leaking grease and damaged components. Tighten loose fasteners to the torques listed in the Chapter 6 Specifications. If grease has been leaking, disassemble the linkage, clean and lubricate it and replace the

14.5a Oil leakage from the fork seals (arrow) . . .

14.5b . . . can be caused by sand or dirt at the bottom of the fork leg . . .

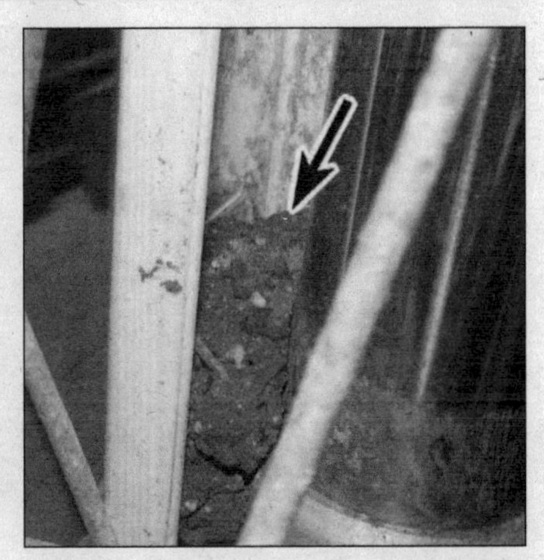

14.5c . . . and built-up dirt between the fork leg and protector (arrow) can cause the same problem

seals (see Chapter 6). Replace any damaged components with new ones. The rear shock linkage bearings should be lubricated before each race if the bike is used in competition (see Chapter 6).

8 Support the motorcycle securely upright with its rear wheel off the ground. Grab the swingarm on each side, just ahead of the axle. Rock the swingarm from side to side - there should be no discernible movement at the rear. If there's a little movement or a slight clicking can be heard, make sure the swingarm pivot shaft is tight. If the pivot shaft is tight but movement is still noticeable, the swingarm will have to be removed and the bearings replaced as described in Chapter 6.

9 Inspect the tightness of the rear suspension nuts and bolts.

15 Cooling system - level check, inspection and coolant change

Level check

Refer to illustration 15.1

Warning: *Checking the coolant level on these bikes requires removal of the radiator cap. Always be sure the engine is cool before removing the radiator cap; otherwise, scalding coolant may spray out of the radiator opening, causing serious burns.*

1 With the engine cool, unscrew the radiator cap **(see illustration)**. Coolant should be up to the bottom of the filler neck.

2 If the coolant level is low, top up with the mixture of antifreeze and water listed in this Chapter's Specifications.

System inspection

Refer to illustration 15.7

3 Refer to Chapter 3 and remove the radiator shrouds. Clean mud, leaves or other obstructions out of the radiator fins with low-pressure water or compressed air.

4 If any fins are bent, carefully straighten them with a small screwdriver, taking care not to puncture the coolant tubes in the radiator.

5 If more than 20 percent of the radiator's surface area is blocked, replace the radiator.

6 Check the coolant hoses for swelling, cracks, burns, cuts or other defects. Replace the hoses if their condition is doubtful. Make sure the hose clamps are tight and free of corrosion. Tighten loose clamps and replace corroded or damaged ones.

7 Check for leaks at the water pump weep hole **(see illustration)** and gaskets. Also check for leaks at the coolant drain plug(s). Replace water pump or drain plug gaskets if they've been leaking. If coolant has been leaking from the weep hole, it's time for a new water pump seal (see Chapter 3).

Coolant change

Refer to illustration 15.9

Warning 1: *Do not allow antifreeze to come in contact with your skin or painted surfaces of the vehicle. Rinse off spills immediately with plenty of water. Antifreeze is highly toxic if ingested. Never leave antifreeze lying around in an open container or in puddles on the floor; children and pets are attracted by its sweet smell and may drink it. Check with local authorities about disposing of used antifreeze. Many communities have collection centers which will see that antifreeze is disposed of safely.*

15.1 Follow safety precautions when removing the radiator cap

15.7 Check for coolant leakage from the weep hole (lower arrow); remove the drain plug (upper arrow) to drain the coolant

15.9 Coolant will spurt out of the drain hole when the radiator cap is removed, so have a container ready

Warning 2: *Don't remove the radiator cap or the drain bolt when the engine and radiator are hot. Scalding coolant and steam will be blown out under pressure, which could cause serious injury. To open the radiator cap or the drain bolt, place a thick rag, like a towel, over the radiator cap; slowly rotate the cap counterclockwise to the first stop. This procedure allows any residual pressure to escape. When the steam has stopped escaping, press down on the cap while turning it counterclockwise and remove it.*

8 Place a drain pan beneath the water pump drain bolt **(see illustration 15.7)**.

9 Remove the drain bolt. Coolant will dribble out until the radiator cap is removed, then it will flow **(see illustration)**.

10 Once the coolant has drained completely, place a new gasket on the drain bolt and install it in the engine. Fill the cooling system with the antifreeze and water mixture listed in this Chapter's Specifications.

11 Lean the bike about twenty-degrees to one side, then the other, several times. This will allow air trapped in the coolant passages to make its way to the top of the coolant.

12 Check coolant level. It should be up to the bottom of the radiator filler neck. Add more antifreeze/water mixture if necessary.

13 Start the engine and check for leaks. Warm up the engine, then let it cool completely and recheck the coolant level.

16 Air cleaner element - servicing

Refer to illustrations 16.2 and 16.3

1 On 1986 through 1988 YZ80 models, remove the right side cover.

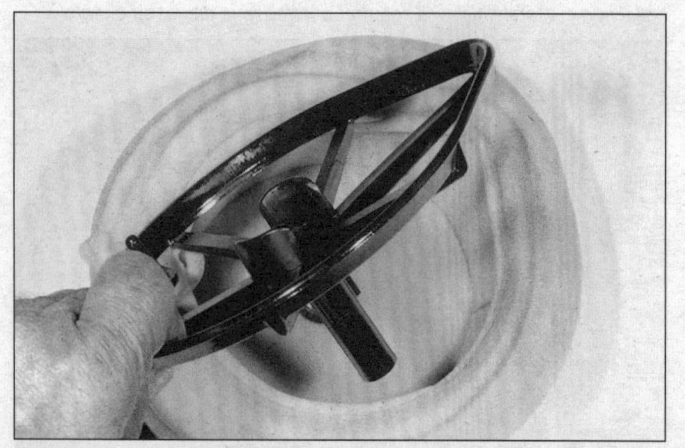

16.3 Separate the foam element from the holder for cleaning and re-oiling

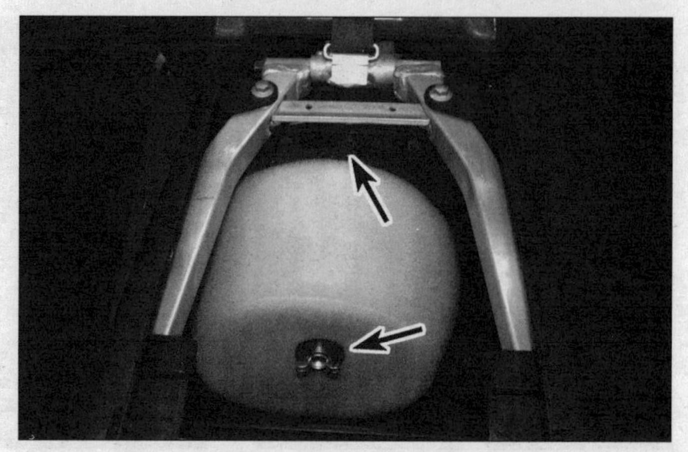

16.2 Unscrew the element bolt (lower arrow) and lift out the element; the tab (upper arrow) should be up when the element is installed

On 1986 through 1988 YZ125/250 models, remove the left side cover. On all later models, remove the seat (see Chapter 8).

2 Unscrew the filter element bolt or nut **(see illustration)**. Lift out the element and pull the bolt out of it.

3 Separate the element holder from the foam element **(see illustration)**.

4 Thoroughly clean the element in high-flash point or non-flammable safety solvent. Do not use gasoline. After cleaning, squeeze out the solvent and allow the element to dry completely.

5 Coat the element with foam filter oil recommended in this Chapter's Specifications, then squeeze the element to work the oil through the foam. Once the element is soaked with oil, squeeze out the excess.

6 Place the holder on the element. On some models, there's an inner tab on the end foam piece; align this with the groove in the element holder.

7 Install the element in the case with its locating tab up (1989 and later models) **(see illustration 16.2)**.

8 The remainder of installation is the reverse of the removal steps.

17 Spark plug - check and replacement

Refer to illustrations 17.1, 17.6a and 17.6b

1 Twist the spark plug cap to break it free from the plug, then pull it off **(see illustration)**.

2 If available, use compressed air to blow any accumulated debris

17.1 Pull the rubber cap off the spark plug and unscrew it with a socket; on some models, there's an arrow to indicate which side of the cap faces the plug

17.6a Spark plug manufacturers recommend using a wire type gauge when checking the gap - if the wire doesn't slide between the electrodes with a slight drag, adjustment is required

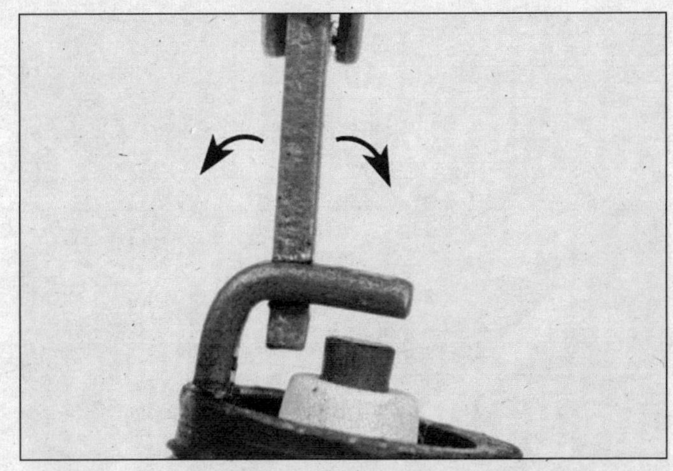

17.6b To change the gap, bend the side electrode only, as indicated by the arrows, and be very careful not to crack or chip the ceramic insulator surrounding the center electrode

from around the spark plug. Remove the plug with a spark plug socket.

3 Inspect the electrodes for wear. Both the center and side electrodes should have square edges and the side electrode should be of uniform thickness. Look for excessive deposits (especially oil fouling) and evidence of a cracked or chipped insulator around the center electrode. Check the threads, the washer and the ceramic insulator body for cracks and other damage.

4 If the electrodes are not excessively worn, and if the deposits can be easily removed with a wire brush, the plug can be regapped and reused (if no cracks or chips are visible in the insulator). If in doubt concerning the condition of the plug, replace it with a new one, as the expense is minimal. The plug should be replaced at the interval listed in the maintenance schedule.

5 Cleaning the spark plug by sandblasting is permitted, provided you clean the plug with a high flash-point solvent afterwards.

6 Before installing a new plug, make sure it is the correct type and heat range. Check the gap between the electrodes, as it is not preset. For best results, use a wire-type gauge rather than a flat gauge to check the gap **(see illustration)**. If the gap must be adjusted, bend the side electrode only and be very careful not to chip or crack the insulator nose **(see illustration)**. Make sure the washer is in place before installing the plug.

7 Since the cylinder head is made of aluminum, which is soft and easily damaged, thread the plug into the head by hand. Slip a short length of hose over the end of the plug to use as a tool to thread it into place. The hose will grip the plug well enough to turn it, but will start to slip if the plug begins to cross-thread in the hole - this will prevent damaged threads and the accompanying repair costs.

8 Once the plug is finger tight, tighten the plug to the torque listed in this Chapter's Specifications.

9 Reconnect the spark plug cap.

18 Exhaust system - inspection and glass wool replacement

Refer to illustrations 18.5a and 18.5b

Warning: *Make sure the exhaust system is cool before doing this procedure.*

1 Periodically check the exhaust system for leaks and loose fasteners (see Chapter 4).

2 Check the expansion chamber springs at the cylinder to make sure they're unbroken and securely attached. Replace broken springs.

3 Check the expansion chamber for cracks or dents. The shape of the chamber has an important effect on engine performance, so dents should not be ignored. Small dents can be removed or large dented areas replaced using body shop sheet metal repair techniques.

4 At the specified interval, remove the muffler (see Chapter 4), clean the inner pipe and replace the glass wool in the muffler as described below.

5 Place the muffler bracket in a padded vise. Remove the bolts from the muffler casing, then pull out the inner pipe and glass wool insert. Pull the inner pipe out of the glass wool **(see illustrations)**.

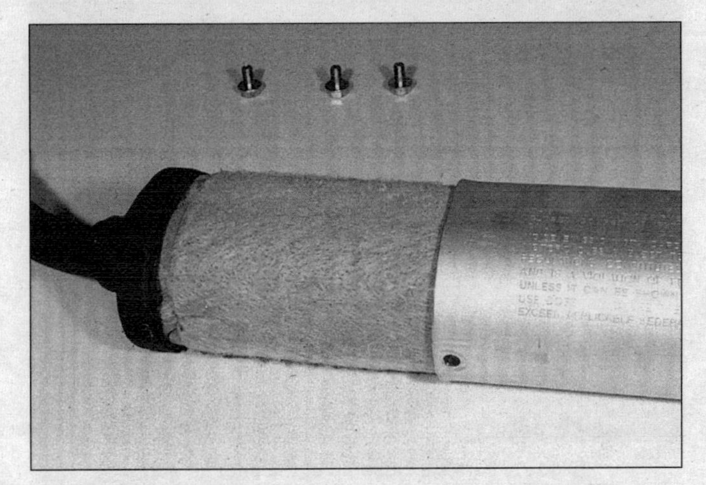

18.5a Pull the inner pipe and glass wool out of the muffler . . .

18.5b . . . and separate the inner pipe from the glass wool

19.3a Throttle stop screw (left arrow) and pilot air screw (right arrow) (1986 through 2001 YZ80)

19.3b Throttle stop screw (upper arrow) and pilot air screw (lower arrow) on a 2004 YZ250

6 Clean the small holes in the inner pipe with a wire brush.

7 Apply muffler sealant to the front and rear ends of the inner pipe where it contacts the muffler case. Install a new glass wool insert and the inner pipe in the case. Tighten the bolts securely, but don't over-tighten them and strip the threads.

19 Carburetor - check and adjustment

Check

1 Check around the carburetor for signs of fuel leakage. If the float chamber gasket or jet plug O-ring has been leaking, replace them (see Chapter 4).

2 Make sure the intake tubes are securely connected and in good condition. Tighten the clamps if they're loose. If the rubber has deteriorated or is damaged, remove the carburetor and replace the tubes with new ones (see Chapter 4).

Adjustment

Refer to illustrations 19.3a, 19.3b, 19.3c and 19.3d

3 Warm the engine to normal operating temperature (ten minutes of stop-and-go riding should be enough). Locate the throttle stop screw and pilot air screw on the carburetor. The throttle stop screw protrudes from the carburetor and, on some models, is secured by a locknut (on other models there's a spring under the screw head). The pilot air screw does not have a locknut. On 1986 YZ125 models, as well as 1986 through 1988 YZ250 models, the throttle stop and pilot air screws are on opposite sides of the carburetor. On later models, they're on the same side **(see illustrations)**.

4 With the engine off, turn the pilot air screw in until it bottoms *lightly*. Back the screw out the number of turns listed in this Chapter's Specifications.

5 Loosen the locknut on the throttle stop screw. Start the engine and let it idle. Turn the throttle stop screw to set the idle at its lowest smooth speed.

6 Turn the air screw (adjust the fuel/air mixture) to raise the idle speed as high as possible, then lower it to the lowest smooth speed with the throttle stop screw.

7 Rev the engine sharply with the transmission in Neutral. Engine speed should rise quickly and smoothly. If not, adjust the air screw in 1/8 turn increments until it does. **Note:** *If you can't get smooth acceleration, check for other problems such as a fouled spark plug.*

8 With the idle speed set correctly, tighten locknut on the throttle stop screw.

19.3c Here is the throttle stop screw (upper arrow) and pilot air screw (lower arrow) on a 2006 YZ125 (YZ80 models similar) . . .

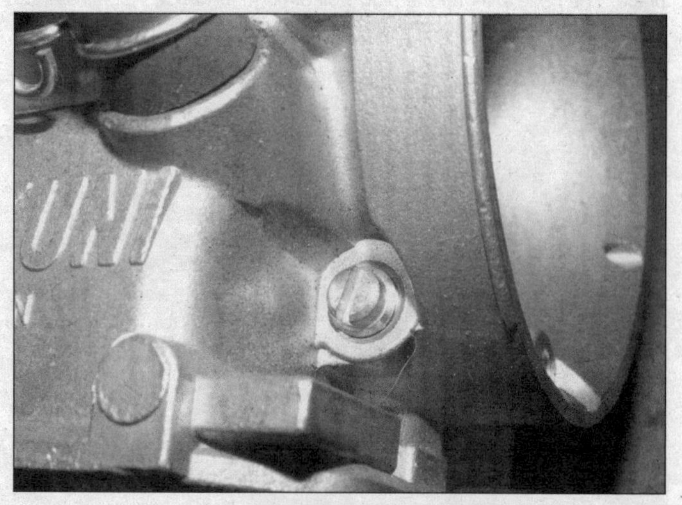

19.3d . . . here's a close-up of the pilot air screw

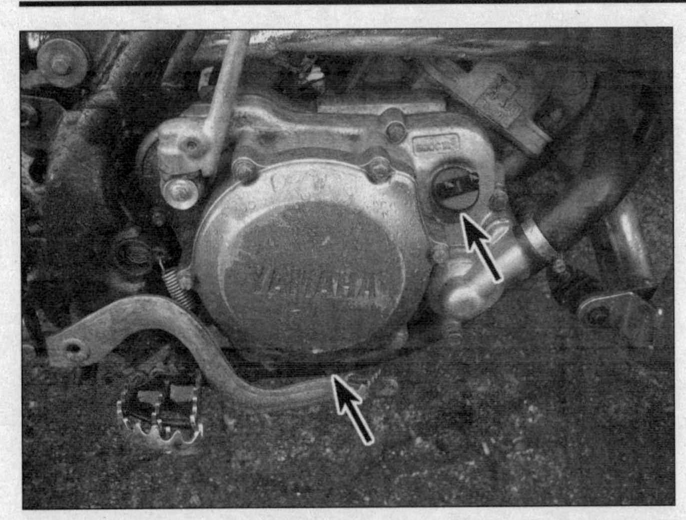

20.3a Here are the transmission oil filler cap and check bolt on a 1996 YZ125 . . .

20.3b . . . and here's the 2006 YZ125 (other models similar)

20 Transmission oil - level check and change

Level check

Refer to illustrations 20.3a, 20.3b and 20.3c

1 **Warning:** *Let the engine cool before performing this procedure. If the level check is performed just after running the engine, hot oil may spurt out.* Perform this check with the engine off. On all except 1993 and later YZ80/YZ85 models, the oil level is checked by removing the check bolt or screw. On 1993 and later YZ80/85 models, there isn't any way to check the level except by draining the oil and measuring the quantity that comes out.

2 Support the bike in an upright position.

3 With the engine off, unscrew the oil check bolt (if equipped) **(see illustrations)**. A small amount of oil should flow out of the hole.

4 If no oil flows out of the hole, remove the oil filler cap **(see illustration 20.3a or 20.3b)**. Add oil through the filler cap hole until it starts to flow from the check bolt hole. Let any excess drain, then reinstall the check bolt and filler cap.

Change

Refer to illustration 20.9

5 Consistent routine oil changes are the single most important maintenance procedure you can perform on these models. The oil not only lubricates the internal parts of the transmission and clutch, but it also acts as a coolant, a cleaner, a sealant, and a protectant. Because of these demands, the oil takes a terrific amount of abuse and should be replaced often with new oil of the recommended grade and type. Saving a little money on the difference in cost between a good oil and a cheap oil won't pay off if the engine is damaged. **Caution:** *Yamaha recommends against using oil additives. The transmission oil also lubricates the clutch plates, and additives may cause the clutch to slip.*

6 Before changing the oil, warm up the engine by running it for three minutes so the oil will drain easily. Be careful when draining the oil, as the exhaust pipe, the engine and the oil itself can cause severe burns.

7 Park the motorcycle over a clean drain pan.

8 Remove the oil filler cap to vent the crankcase and act as a reminder that there is no oil in the engine. Also remove the oil check bolt **(see illustrations 20.3a, 20.3b and 20.3c)**.

9 Next, remove the drain plug from the crankcase **(see illustration)** and allow the oil to drain into the pan. Do not lose the sealing washer on the drain plug.

10 Check the condition of the drain plug threads. Replace the plug if the threads are damaged.

11 Slip a new sealing washer over the drain plug, then install and tighten the plug to the torque listed in this Chapter's Specifications. Avoid overtightening, as damage to the threads or engine case will result.

20.3c The oil level check bolt or screw (arrow) has a sealing washer

20.9 The transmission oil drain plug on all except 1993 and later YZ80/85 models is in the bottom of the crankcase (arrow)

12 Before refilling the engine, check the old oil carefully. If the oil was drained into a clean pan, small pieces of metal or other material can be easily detected. If the oil is very metallic colored, then the engine is experiencing wear from break-in (new engine) or from insufficient lubrication. If there are flakes or chips of metal in the oil, then something is drastically wrong internally and the engine will have to be disassembled for inspection and repair.
13 If there are pieces of fiber-like material in the oil, the clutch is experiencing excessive wear and should be checked.
14 If the inspection of the oil turns up nothing unusual, refill the engine as described below.
15 With the bike supported in an upright position, fill the crankcase until oil begins to flow from the check bolt hole. The specified capacity is only a guide; use the check bolt to determine the exact amount of oil to use.
16 Allow excess oil to flow from the check bolt hole, then install the check bolt with a new sealing washer and tighten it to the torque listed in this Chapter's Specifications. Install the filler cap.
17 Check around the drain plug and check bolt for leaks.
18 The old oil drained from the transmission cannot be reused in its present state and should be disposed of. Check with your local refuse disposal company, disposal facility or environmental agency to see whether they will accept the oil for recycling. Don't pour used oil into drains or onto the ground. After the oil has cooled, it can be drained into a suitable container (capped plastic jugs, topped bottles, milk cartons, etc.) for transport to one of these disposal sites.

21 Front fork oil change

Refer to illustration 21.6

1 The following steps apply to the damper rod forks used on 1986 and 1987 models. On other models, which are equipped with cartridge forks, you'll need to disassemble the forks part-way to drain the oil (see Chapter 6).
2 Support the motorcycle securely upright.
3 Remove the handlebars (see Chapter 6).
4 Remove the fork cap bolts.
5 Wrap a rag around the top of the fork to catch dripping oil, the lift out the fork spring from each fork.
6 Place a pan under the fork drain bolt and remove the drain bolt and gasket **(see illustration)**. **Warning:** *Do not allow the fork oil to drip onto the tire or brake disc. If it does, wash it off with soap and water before riding the motorcycle.*

21.6 Early models have a fork oil drain bolt (arrow)

7 After most of the oil has drained, slowly compress and release the forks to pump out the rest of the oil. An assistant may be needed to do this.
8 Check the drain bolt gasket for damage and replace it if necessary. Clean the threads of the drain bolt with solvent and let it dry, then reinstall the bolt and gasket, tightening it securely.
9 Pour the type and amount of fork oil listed in the Chapter 6 Specifications into the fork tube through the opening at the top. Slowly pump the forks a few times to purge air from the upper and lower chambers.
10 Fully compress the front forks (you may need an assistant to do this). Insert a stiff tape measure into the fork tube and measure the distance from the oil to the top of the fork tube (see Chapter 6). Compare your measurement to the value listed in the Chapter 6 Specifications, drain or add oil as necessary until the level is correct.
11 Check the O-ring on the fork cap bolt and replace it with a new one if it's deteriorated, broken or otherwise damaged. Install the fork spring. Install the cap bolt and tighten it to the Chapter 6 Specifications.
12 Repeat the procedure for the other fork. It is essential that the oil quantity and level are identical in each fork.
13 Install the handlebar, being sure to locate it correctly in the brackets, and tighten the handlebar bracket bolts to the torque listed in the Chapter 6 Specifications.

Chapter 2
Engine, clutch and transmission

Contents

Specifications

YZ80/85

Cylinder head warpage limit .... 0.03 mm (0.0012 inch)

Cylinder

Bore	
YZ80	
1986 through 1992	
Standard	48.00 (1.894 inches)
Limit	48.10 mm (1.894 inches)
1993 (4ES1)*	
Standard	47.000 to 47.014 mm (1.8504 to 1.8509 inches)
Limit	47.10 mm (1.850 inches)
1993 (4GT1)*	
Standard	46.000 to 46.014 mm (1.8110 to 1.8116 inches)
Limit	46.10 mm (1.815 inches)
1994 (4ES3)*	
Standard	47.000 to 47.014 mm (1.8504 to 1.8509 inches)
Limit	47.10 mm (1.850 inches)
1994 (4GT3)*	
Standard	46.000 to 46.014 mm (1.8110 to 1.8116 inches)
Limit	46.10 mm (1.815 inches)
1995 (4ES4)*	
Standard	47.000 to 47.014 mm (1.8504 to 1.8509 inches)
Limit	47.10 mm (1.850 inches)
Bore	
YZ80	
1995 (4LB3)*	
Standard	46.000 to 46.014 mm (1.8110 to 1.8116 inches)
Limit	46.10 mm (1.815 inches)
1996 (4ES5, 4LC3)*	
Standard	47.000 to 47.014 mm (1.8504 to 1.8509 inches)
Limit	47.10 mm (1.850 inches)
1996 (4GT7, 4LB5)*	
Standard	46.000 to 46.014 mm (1.8110 to 1.8116 inches)
Limit	46.10 mm (1.815 inches)
1997 (4ES6, 4LC4)*	
Standard	47.000 to 47.014 mm (1.8504 to 1.8509 inches)
Limit	47.10 mm (1.850 inches)
1997 (4GT9, 4LB7)*	
Standard	46.000 to 46.014 mm (1.8110 to 1.8116 inches)
Limit	46.10 mm (1.815 inches)

Cylinder (continued)

1998 (4ES7, 4LC5)*	
Standard	47.000 to 47.014 mm (1.8504 to 1.8509 inches)
Limit	47.10 mm (1.850 inches)
1998 (4GTB, 4LB9)*	
Standard	46.000 to 46.014 mm (1.8110 to 1.8116 inches)
Limit	46.10 mm (1.815 inches)
1999 (4ES8, 4LC6)*	
Standard	47.000 to 47.014 mm (1.8504 to 1.8509 inches)
Limit	47.10 mm (1.850 inches)
1999 (4GTD, 4LBB)*	
Standard	46.000 to 46.014 mm (1.8110 to 1.8116 inches)
Limit	46.10 mm (1.815 inches)
2000 (4ES9, 4LC7)*	
Standard	47.000 to 47.014 mm (1.8504 to 1.8509 inches)
Limit	47.10 mm (1.850 inches)
2000 (4GTF, 4LBD)*	
Standard	46.000 to 46.014 mm (1.8110 to 1.8116 inches)
Limit	46.10 mm (1.815 inches)
2001	
Standard	47.000 to 47.014 mm (1.8504 to 1.8509 inches)
Limit	47.10 mm (1.850 inches)
YZ85	
Standard	47.500 to 47.514 mm (1.874 to 1.8706 inches)
Limit	47.6 mm (1.874 inches)
Taper limit	0.05 mm (0.002 inch)
Out-of-round limit	0.10 mm (0.004 inch)

**Initial digits of model code.*

Piston

Piston diameter (YZ80)	
1986 through 1992	
Standard	47.94 48.00 mm (1.87 to 1.890 inches)
Limit	46.90 mm (1.846 inch)
First oversize	48.25 mm (1.900 inch)
Second oversize	48.50 mm (1.909 inch)
1993 (4ES1)*	
Standard	46.957 to 46.972 mm (1.8487 to 1.8493 inches)
Limit	47.10 mm (1.850 inches)
1993 (4GT1)*	
Standard	46.000 to 46.014 mm (1.8110 to 1.8116 inches)
Limit	46.10 mm (1.815 inches)
1994 (4ES3)*	
Standard	46.957 to 46.972 mm (1.8487 to 1.8493 inches)
Limit	47.10 mm (1.850 inches)
1994 (4GT3)*	
Standard	46.000 to 46.014 mm (1.8110 to 1.8116 inches)
Limit	46.10 mm (1.815 inches)
1995 (4ES3)*	
Standard	46.957 to 46.972 mm (1.8487 to 1.8493 inches)
Limit	47.10 mm (1.850 inches)
1995 (4GT3)*	
Standard	46.000 to 46.014 mm (1.8110 to 1.8116 inches)
Limit	46.10 mm (1.815 inches)
1996 (4ES5, 4LC3)*	
Standard	46.957 to 46.972 mm (1.8487 to 1.8493 inches)
Limit	47.10 mm (1.850 inches)
1996 (4GT7, 4LB5)*	
Standard	46.000 to 46.014 mm (1.8110 to 1.8116 inches)
Limit	46.10 mm (1.815 inches)
1997 (4ES6, 4LC4)*	
Standard	46.957 to 46.972 mm (1.8487 to 1.8493 inches)
Limit	47.10 mm (1.850 inches)
1997 (4GT9, 4LB7)*	
Standard	46.000 to 46.014 mm (1.8110 to 1.8116 inches)
Limit	46.10 mm (1.815 inches)
1998 (4ES7, 4LC5)*	
Standard	46.957 to 46.972 mm (1.8487 to 1.8493 inches)
Limit	47.10 mm (1.850 inches)

1998 (4GTB, 4LB9)*	
Standard	46.000 to 46.014 mm (1.8110 to 1.8116 inches)
Limit	46.10 mm (1.815 inches)
1999 (4ES8, 4LC6)*	
Standard	46.957 to 46.972 mm (1.8487 to 1.8493 inches)
Limit	47.10 mm (1.850 inches)
1999 (4GTD, 4LBB)*	
Standard	46.000 to 46.014 mm (1.8110 to 1.8116 inches)
Limit	46.10 mm (1.815 inches)
2000 (4ES9, 4LC7)*	
Standard	46.957 to 46.972 mm (1.8487 to 1.8493 inches)
Limit	47.10 mm (1.850 inches)
2000 (4GTF, 4LBD)*	
Standard	46.000 to 46.014 mm (1.8110 to 1.8116 inches)
Limit	46.10 mm (1.815 inches)
2001	
Standard	46.000 to 46.014 mm (1.8110 to 1.8116 inches)
Limit	46.10 mm (1.815 inches)
Piston diameter (YZ85)	
Standard	47.457 to 47.472 mm (1.8684 to 1.8690 inches)
Limit	Not specified
Piston diameter measuring point (above bottom of piston)	
YZ80	
1980 through 1992	15 mm (0.60 inch)
1993 through 1995	5 mm (0.20 inch)
1996 through 2001	20 mm (0.79 inch)
YZ85	20 mm (0.79 inch)
Piston-to-cylinder clearance	
1986 through 1992	
Standard	0.060 to 0.065 mm (0.0024 to 0.0026 inch)
Limit	0.10 mm (0.004 inch)
1993 on	
Standard	0.040 to 0.045 mm (0.0016 to 0.0018 inch)
Limit	0.10 mm (0.004 inch)
Piston pin bore in piston	
YZ80	Not specified
YZ85	14.004 to 14.015 mm (0.5513 to 0.518 inch)
Standard	14.002 to 14.008 mm (0.5513 to 0.5515 inch)
Limit	14.02 mm (0.552 inch)
Piston pin outer diameter	
1986 through 1992	Not specified
1993 through 2002	
Standard	13.996 to 14.000 mm (0.5510 to 0.5512 inch)
Limit	13.975 mm (0.5502 inch)
2003 and later	
Standard	14.000 to 14.015 mm (0.5513 to 0.5518 inch)
Limit	14.040 mm (0.5528 inch)
Ring end gap	
1986 and later	
Standard	0.30 to 0.45 mm (0.012 to 0.018 inch)
Limit	0.8 mm (0.031 inch)
Ring side clearance	
1986 through 1995	
Standard	0.03 to 0.07 mm (0.0012 to 0.0028 inch)
Limit	0.1 mm (0.04 inch)
1996 and later	
Standard	0.030 to 0.065 mm (0.0012 to 0.0025 inch)
Limit	0.1 mm (0.04 inch)

Reed valve

Bending limit	
1986 through 1991	0.3 mm (0.012 inch)
1992 and later	0.2 mm (0.08 inch)
Stopper height	
1986 through 1992	8.3 to 8.7 mm (0.33 to 0.34 inch)
1993 through 1995	6.8 to 7.2 mm (0.268 to 0.283 inch)
1996 and later	7.4 to 7.8 mm (0.291 to 0.307 inch)

Clutch

Spring free length	
1986	
Standard	32.0 mm (1.26 inches)
Limit	31.0 mm (1.22 inches)
1987 through 1992	
Standard	33.0 mm (1.30 inches)
Limit	31.0 mm (1.22 inches)
1993 and 1994	
Standard	36.0 mm (1.42 inches)
Limit	34.0 mm (1.34 inches)
1995 through 2004	
Standard	34.0 mm (1.34 inches)
Limit	31.0 mm (1.22 inches)
2005 and later	
Standard	33.0 mm (1.30 inches)
Limit	31.0 mm (1.22 inches)
Friction plate thickness	
Standard	2.9 to 3.1 mm (0.114 to 0.122 inch)
Limit	2.7 mm (0.106 inch)
Metal plate warpage limit	
1986 through 1992	0.05 mm (0.002 inch)
1993 and later	0.10 mm (0.004 inch)

Kickstarter

Clip rotation force	
1986 through 1991	0.8 to 1.2 kg (1.8 to 2.6 lbs)
1992	0.8 to 1.5 kg (1.8 to 3.3 lbs)
1993 through 1998	0.9 to 1.5 kg (2.0 to 3.3 lbs)
1999 and later	0.6 to 1.5 kg (1.3 to 3.3 lbs)

Shift drum and forks

Fork shaft bending limit	
1986 through 1992	No visible bending
1993 and later	0.05 mm (0.002 inch)

Transmission

Mainshaft and countershaft bending limit	
1986 through 1991	0.08 mm (0.003 inch)
1992 through 2001	0.10 mm (0.04 inch)
2002 and later	Not specified

Crankshaft

Connecting rod side clearance	0.2 to 0.7 mm (0.008 to 0.028 inch)
Connecting rod small end side play	0.5 to 1.2 mm (0.020 to 0.047 inch)
Crankshaft bend limit	0.03 mm (0.0012 inch)
Crankshaft width (crank throw to crank throw)	44.90 to 4.95 mm (1.768 to 1.770 inches)

Torque specifications

Engine mounting bolts	
1986 through 1991	40 Nm (29 ft-lbs)
1992 and later	69 Nm (50 ft-lbs)
Cylinder head nuts	
1986 through 1992	25 Nm (18 ft-lbs)
1993 and later	30 Nm (22 ft-lbs)
Cylinder nuts	
1986 through 1992	Not applicable
1993 and later	28 Nm (20 ft-lbs)
Carburetor intake tube bolts	
1986	Not specified
1987 through 1992	10 Nm (86 inch-lbs)
1993 and later	8 Nm (70 inch-lbs)
Right crankcase cover bolts	10 Nm (86 inch-lbs)
Clutch spring bolts	6 Nm (52 inch-lbs)
Clutch center nut	
1986 through 1992	55 Nm (40 ft-lbs)
1993 and later	70 Nm (50 ft-lbs)
Primary drive gear bolt or nut	
1986 through 1992	68 Nm (49 ft-lbs)
1993 through 2001	80 Nm (58 ft-lbs)
2002 and later	79 Nm (57 ft-lbs)

Shift cam plate to shift drum bolt	Not applicable
Shift drum stopper arm bolt	Not applicable
Shift pedal pinch bolt	10 Nm (86 inch-lbs)
Crankcase bolts	
1986	12 Nm (104 inch-lbs)
1987 through 1991	10 Nm (86 inch-lbs)
1992	7 Nm (61 inch-lbs)
1993 and later	8 Nm (70 inch-lbs)

YZ125

Cylinder head warpage limit	0.03 mm (0.0012 inch)

Cylinder

Bore	
1986 through 1993	56.000 to 56.002 mm (2.2047 to 2.2055 inches)
1993 and later	
Standard	54.000 to 54.014 mm (2.1259 to 2.1266 inch)
Limit	54.10 mm (2.129 inches)
Taper limit	0.05 mm (0.002 inch)
Out-of-round limit	0.10 mm (0.004 inch)

Piston

Piston diameter	
1986 through 1993	
Standard	55.94 to 56.00 mm (2.203 to 2.205 inches)
First oversize	56.25 mm (2.215 inches)
Second oversize	56.50 mm (2.224 inches)
Third oversize	56.75 mm (2.234 inches)
1994 through 1998	
All except Europe and Australia	46.957 to 46.972 mm (1.8487 to 1.8493 inch)
Europe and Australia	45.957 to 45.92 mm (1.8093 to 1.8099 inch)
1999	
All except Europe, Australia and UK (4ES8, 4LC6)	46.957 to 46.972 mm (1.8487 to 1.8493 inch)
Europe, Australia and UK (4ES8, 4LC6)	45.957 to 45.92 mm (1.8093 to 1.8099 inch)
2000	
4ES9, 4LC7	46.957 to 46.972 mm (1.8487 to 1.8493 inch)
4GTF, 4LBD	45.957 to 45.92 mm (1.8093 to 1.8099 inch)
2001	46.957 to 46.972 mm (1.8487 to 1.8493 inch)
2002 and later	47.457 to 47.472 mm (1.8684 to 1.8690 inch)
Piston diameter measuring point (above bottom of piston)	
1986 and 1987	19 mm (0.75 inch)
1988	15 mm (0.60 inch)
1989 and 1990	19 mm (0.75 inch)
1991 through 1993	15 mm (0.60 inch)
1994 through 1998	10 mm (0.40 inch)
1999 and later	17.5 mm (0.69 inch)
Piston-to-cylinder clearance	
1986 through 1988	
Standard	0.055 to 0.060 mm (0.0022 to 0.0024 inch)
Limit	0.10 mm (0.004 inch)
1989	
Standard	0.050 to 0.055 mm (0.0020 to 0.0022 inch)
Limit	0.10 mm (0.004 inch)
1990 and later	
Standard	0.040 to 0.045 mm (0.0016 to 0.0018 inch)
Limit	0.10 mm (0.004 inch)
Piston pin bore in piston	Not specified
Piston pin outer diameter	
1986 through 1989	Not specified
1990 through 1996	
Standard	15.995 to 16.000 mm (0.6297 to 0.6300 inch)
Limit	15.975 mm (0.6289 inch)
1997 and later	
Standard	14.995 to 15.000mm (0.5904 to 0.5906 inch)
Limit	14.975 mm (0.5896 inch)
Ring end gap	
1986 through 1990	
Standard	0.35 to 0.50 mm (0.012 to 0.018 inch)
Limit	0.8 mm (0.031 inch)

Piston (continued)

1991 through 1994	
Standard	0.50 to 0.65 mm (0.020 to 0.026 inch)
Limit	0.8 mm (0.031 inch)
1995 and later	
Standard	0.50 to 0.70 mm (0.020 to 0.028 inch)
Limit	1.2 mm (0.047 inch)
Ring side clearance	
1986 through 1994	
Standard	0.03 to 0.07 mm (0.0012 to 0.0028 inch)
Limit	0.1 mm (0.04 inch)
1995 and later	
Standard	0.035 to 0.070 mm (0.0014 to 0.0028 inch)
Limit	0.1 mm (0.04 inch)

Reed valve

Bending limit	
1986	1.5 mm (0.059 inch)
1987	0.6 mm (0.024 inch)
1989 and 1990	1.5 mm (0.059 inch)
1991 through 1993	0.2 mm (0.008 inch)
1994	1.5 mm (0.059 inch)
1995 and later	0.2 mm (0.008 inch)
Stopper height	
1986	9.0 +/- 0.2 mm (0.345 +/- 0.08 inch)
1987 through 1990	9.0 mm (0.345 inch)
1991 and 1992	8.5 to 8.9 mm (0.335 to 0.350 inch)
1993	9.1 to 9.5 mm (0.358 to 0.374 inch)
1994	7.6 mm (0.299 inch)
1995 through 2000	7.4 to 7.8 mm (0.291 to 0.307 inch)
2001 and later	8.2 to 8.6 mm (0.323 to 0.339 inch)

Clutch

Spring free length	
1986	
Standard	35.0 mm (1.38 inches)
Limit	33.0 mm (1.30 inches)
1987 through 1990	
Standard	36.2 mm (1.43 inches)
Limit	34.2 mm (1.35 inches)
1991 and later	
Standard	40.1 mm (1.579 inches)
Limit	38.1 mm (1.500 inches)
Friction plate thickness	
Standard	2.9 to 3.1 mm (0.114 to 0.122 inch)
Limit	2.7 mm (0.106 inch)
Metal plate warpage limit	0.05 mm (0.002 inch)

Kickstarter

Clip rotation force	0.8 to 1.2 kg (1.8 to 2.6 lbs)

Shift drum and forks

Fork shaft bending limit	
1986	No visible bending
1987 and later	0.05 mm (0.002 inch)

Transmission

Mainshaft and countershaft bending limit	
1986	Not specified
1987 and later	0.10 mm (0.04 inch)

Crankshaft

Connecting rod side clearance	
1986 through 2004	0.2 to 0.7 mm (0.008 to 0.028 inch)
2005 and later	0.06 to 0.64 mm (0.002 to 0.025 inch)
Connecting rod small end side play	0.8 to 1.0 mm (0.031 to 0.039 inch)
Crankshaft bend limit	0.03 mm (0.0012 inch)
Crankshaft width (crank throw to crank throw)	55.90 to 55.95 mm (2.201 to 2.203 inches)

Torque specifications

Engine mounting bolts	
1986	32 Nm (23 ft-lbs)
1987	30 Nm (22 ft-lbs)
1988 through 1992	32 Nm (23 ft-lbs)
1993 and 1994	34 Nm (24 ft-lbs)
1995	
Upper bracket	34 Nm (24 ft-lbs)
Forward through-bolt	34 Nm (24 ft-lbs)
Rear through-bolt	69 Nm (50 ft-lbs)
1996	
Upper bracket	34 Nm (24 ft-lbs)
Forward through-bolt	37 Nm (27 ft-lbs)
Rear through-bolt	69 Nm (50 ft-lbs)
1997 through 2003	
Upper bracket bolts	34 Nm (24 ft-lbs)
Through-bolts	69 Nm (50 ft-lbs)
2004 and later	
Upper bracket bolts	34 Nm (24 ft-lbs)
Through-bolts	64 Nm (46 ft-lbs)
Cylinder head nuts	
1986 through 1993	30 Nm (22 ft-lbs)
1994 and later	28 Nm (20 ft-lbs)
Cylinder nuts	
1986 through 1993	25 Nm (18 ft-lbs)
1994 through 1997	28 Nm (20 ft-lbs)
1998 and later	30 Nm (22 ft-lbs)
Carburetor intake tube bolts	
1986	Not specified
1987 and 1988	10 Nm (86 inch-lbs)
1989	12 Nm (104 inch-lbs)
1990 and later	10 Nm (86 inch-lbs)
Right crankcase cover bolts	10 Nm (86 inch-lbs)
Clutch spring bolts	
1986 through 1989	6 Nm (52 inch-lbs)
1990 and later	10 Nm (86 inch-lbs)
Clutch center nut	80 Nm (58 ft-lbs)
Primary drive gear bolt or nut	
1986 through 1990	80 Nm (58 ft-lbs)
1991 through 2004	55 Nm (40 ft-lbs)
2005 and later	48 Nm (35 ft-lbs)
Shift cam plate to shift drum bolt	Not specified
Shift drum stopper arm bolt	
1986	14 Nm (120 inch-lbs)
1987 and later	10 Nm (86 inch-lbs)
Shift pedal pinch bolt	
1986 through 2002	10 Nm (86 inch-lbs)
2003 and later	12 Nm (86 inch-lbs)
Shift guide bolts	
1986 through 1992	Not specified
1993 and later	10 Nm (86 inch-lbs)
Crankcase bolts	
1986 through 1993	12 Nm (104 inch-lbs)
1994 and later	14 Nm (120 inch-lbs)

YZ250

Cylinder head warpage limit	0.03 mm (0.0012 inch)

Cylinder

Bore	
1986 through 1990	68.00 to 68.02 mm (2.6772 to 2.6780 inches)
1991	Not available
1992 and 1993	
Standard	68.000 to 68.014 mm (2.6772 to 2.6777 inch)
Limit	68.10 mm (2.681 inches)
1994	
Standard	68.00 to 68.02 mm (2.6772 to 2.6780 inches)
Limit	68.10 mm (2.681 inches)

Cylinder (continued)

1995 through 1998	
Standard	68.000 to 68.014 mm (2.6772 to 2.6777 inch)
Limit	68.10 mm (2.681 inches)
1999 and later	
Standard	66.400 to 66.414 mm (2.6142 to 2.6147 inch)
Limit	66.5 mm (2.618 inches)
Taper limit	0.05 mm (0.002 inch)
Out-of-round limit	0.10 mm (0.004 inch)

Piston

Piston diameter	
1986 through 1988	
Standard	67.94 to 68.00 mm (2.675 to 2.677 inches)
First oversize	68.25 mm (2.69 inches)
Second oversize	68.50 mm (2.70 inches)
Third oversize	68.75 mm (2.71 inches)
1989 and 1990	67.94 to 67.98 mm (2.675 to 2.676 inches)
1991	Not available
1992 through 1998	67.952 to 67.967 mm (2.6753 to 2.6759 inches)
1999 and later	66.352 to 66.367 mm (2.6120 to 2.6129 inches)
Piston diameter measuring point (above bottom of piston)	
1986 through 1990	31 mm (0.75 inch)
1991	Not available
1992 through 1995	5 to 10 mm (0.20 to 0.39 inch)
1996 through 1998	25 mm (0.98 inch)
1999 and later	17.5 mm (0.69 inch)
Piston-to-cylinder clearance	
1986 through 1988	
Standard	0.070 to 0.075 mm (0.0028 to 0.0030 inch)
Limit	0.10 mm (0.004 inch)
1989	
Standard	0.060 to 0.065 mm (0.0020 to 0.0022 inch)
Limit	0.10 mm (0.004 inch)
1991	Not available
1992 and later	
Standard	0.045 to 0.050 mm (0.0018 to 0.0020 inch)
Limit	0.10 mm (0.004 inch)
Piston pin bore in piston	Not specified
Piston pin outer diameter	
1986 through 1989	Not specified
1990 and later	
Standard	17.995 to 18.000 mm (0.7085 to 0.7087 inch)
Limit	17.975 mm (0.7077 inch)
Ring end gap	
1986	
Standard	0.45 to 0.60 mm (0.018 to 0.024 inch)
Limit	0.8 mm (0.031 inch)
1987 through 1994	
Standard	0.55 to 0.70 mm (0.022 to 0.028 inch)
Limit	
1987 and 1998	0.9 mm (0.035 inch)
1989 through 1994	1.0 mm (0.004 inch)
1995 through 1998	
Standard	0.55 to 0.75 mm (0.022 to 0.030 inch)
Limit	1.3 mm (0.051 inch)
1999 and later	
Standard	0.40 to 0.575 mm (0.016 to 0.022 inch)
Limit	0.95 mm (0.037 inch)
Ring side clearance	
1986 and 1987	
Standard	0.04 to 0.08 mm (0.0016 to 0.0031 inch)
Limit	0.1 mm (0.04 inch)
1988 through 1990 (top ring)	
Standard	0.04 to 0.08 mm (0.0016 to 0.0031 inch)
Limit	0.1 mm (0.04 inch)
1988 through 1990 (second ring)	
Standard	0.03 to 0.07 mm (0.001 to 0.003 inch)
Limit	0.1 mm (0.04 inch)

1991	Not available
1992 and 1993 (top ring)	
Standard	0.45 to 0.80 mm (0.0018 to 0.0031 inch)
Limit	0.1 mm (0.04 inch)
1992 and 1993 (second ring)	
Standard	0.35 to 0.70 mm (0.0014 to 0.0028 inch)
Limit	0.1 mm (0.04 inch)
1994 through 1998	
Standard	0.030 to 0.070 mm (0.0012 to 0.0028 inch)
Limit	0.1 mm (0.04 inch)
1999 and later	
Standard	0.030 to 0.065 mm (0.0012 to 0.0026 inch)
Limit	0.1 mm (0.04 inch)

Reed valve

Bending limit	
1986	1.5 mm (0.059 inch)
1987 and 1988	0.6 mm (0.024 inch)
1989	1.5 mm (0.059 inch)
1990	0.3 mm (0.012 inch)
1991 through 1993	0.2 mm (0.008 inch)
1994	0.3 mm (0.012 inch)
1995 and later	0.2 mm (0.008 inch)
Stopper height	
1986 through 1989	8.4 to 8.8 mm (0.33 to 0.35 inch)
1990 through 1992	10.4 to 10.8 mm (0.409 to 0.425 inch)
1993	10.3 to 10.7 mm (0.406 to 0.421 inch)
1994	10.4 to 10.8 mm (0.409 to 0.425 inch)
1995 and later	10.3 to 10.7 mm (0.406 to 0.421 inch)

Clutch

Spring free length	
1986	
Standard	36.4 mm (1.43 inches)
Limit	35.4 mm (1.39 inches)
1987	
Standard	38.3 mm (1.51 inches)
Limit	36.3 mm (1.43 inches)
1988 through 1994	
Standard	40.1 mm (1.579 inches)
Limit	37.1 mm (1.460 inches)
1995	
Standard	40.1 mm (1.579 inches)
Limit	38.1 mm (1.500 inches)
1996 and 1997	
Standard	41.2 mm (1.622 inches)
Limit	39.2 mm (1.543 inches)
1998 and 1999	
Standard	40.1 mm (1.579 inches)
Limit	38.1 mm (1.500 inches)
2000 and 2001	
Standard	44.0 mm (1.732 inches)
Limit	42.0 mm (1.654 inches)
2002 and later	
Standard	50.0 mm (1.969 inches)
Limit	48.0 mm (1.890 inches)
Friction plate thickness	
Standard	2.9 to 3.1 mm (0.114 to 0.122 inch)
Limit	2.7 mm (0.106 inch)
Metal plate warpage limit	
1986 through 1990	0.05 (0.002 inch)
1991	Not available
1992	0.1 mm (0.004 inch)
1993 and later	0.2 mm (0.008 inch)

Shift drum and forks

Fork shaft bending limit	0.05 mm (0.002 inch)

Transmission

Mainshaft and countershaft bending limit	0.10 mm (0.04 inch)

Crankshaft

Connecting rod side clearance	0.25 to 0.75 mm (0.010 to 0.030 inch)
Connecting rod small end side play	
Standard	0.4 to 1.0 mm (0.016 to 0.039 inch)
Limit	2.0 mm (0.08 inch)
Crankshaft bend limit	
1986 through 1995	0.03 mm (0.0012 inch)
1996	0.05 mm (0.002 inch)
Crankshaft width (crank throw to crank throw)	
1986 through 1998	61.95 to 62.0 mm (2.439 to 2.441 inches)
1999 and later	59.95 to 60.00 mm (2.60 to 2.362 inches)

Torque specifications

Engine mounting bolts	
1986 and 1987	32 Nm (23 ft-lbs)
1988	
Lower front brackets to engine and frame	32 Nm (23 ft-lbs)
Lower through-bolt	65 Nm (47 ft-lbs)
Upper bracket to engine	65 Nm (47 ft-lbs)
Upper bracket to frame	32 Nm (23 ft-lbs)
1989	32 Nm (23 ft-lbs)
1990 through 1992	
Lower through-bolt	64 Nm (46 ft-lbs)
All other bolts	32 Nm (23 ft-lbs)
1993 and 1994	
Upper bracket to frame	34 Nm (24 ft-lbs)
Upper bracket to engine	69 Nm (50 ft-lbs)
Lower front bracket to engine	41 Nm (30 ft-lbs)
Lower front bracket to frame	34 Nm (24 ft-lbs)
Lower through-bolt	69 Nm (50 ft-lbs)
1995	
Upper bracket to frame	34 Nm (24 ft-lbs)
Upper bracket to engine	69 Nm (50 ft-lbs)
Lower front bracket to engine	34 Nm (24 ft-lbs)
Lower front bracket to frame	41 Nm (30 ft-lbs)
Lower through-bolt	69 Nm (50 ft-lbs)
1996	
Upper bracket to frame	34 Nm (24 ft-lbs)
Upper bracket to engine	69 Nm (50 ft-lbs)
Forward through-bolt	37 Nm (27 ft-lbs)
Rear through-bolt	69 Nm (50 ft-lbs)
1997 through 2004	
Upper bracket to frame	34 Nm (24 ft-lbs)
Upper bracket to engine	69 Nm (50 ft-lbs)
Through-bolts	69 Nm (50 ft-lbs)
2004 and later	
Upper bracket to frame	34 Nm (24 ft-lbs)
Upper bracket to engine	64 Nm (46 ft-lbs)
Through-bolts	64 Nm (46 ft-lbs)
Cylinder head nuts	
1986 through 1994	30 Nm (22 ft-lbs)
1995 through 2000	28 Nm (20 ft-lbs)
2001 and later	25 Nm (18 ft-lbs)
Cylinder nuts	
1986 through 2003	35 Nm (25 ft-lbs)
2004 and later	42 Nm (30 ft-lbs)
Carburetor intake tube bolts	
1986 through 1988	Not specified
1989 through 1994	12 Nm (104 inch-lbs)
1995 and later	10 Nm (86 inch-lbs)
Right crankcase cover bolts	10 Nm (86 inch-lbs)
Clutch spring bolts	10 Nm (86 inch-lbs)
Clutch center nut	75 Nm (54 ft-lbs)
Primary drive gear bolt or nut	
1986 through 1988	115 Nm (85 ft-lbs)
1989	85 Nm (63 ft-lbs)
1990	115 Nm (85 ft-lbs)
1991	Not available
1992 through 1998	75 Nm (54 ft-lbs)
1999 and later	55 Nm (40 ft-lbs)

Shift cam plate to shift drum bolt	
1986 through 1991	Not specified
1992 and later	30 Nm (22 ft-lbs)
Shift drum stopper arm bolt	
1986 through 1989	15 Nm (132 inch-lbs)
1990 through 1994	14 Nm (120 inch-lbs)
1995 and later	10 Nm (86 inch-lbs)
Shift pedal pinch bolt	10 Nm (86 inch-lbs)
Shift guide bolts	
1986 through 1991	Not specified
1992 and later	10 Nm (86 inch-lbs)
Crankcase bolts	
1986 through 1994	12 Nm (104 inch-lbs)
1995 and later	14 Nm (120 inch-lbs)

1 General information

The engine/transmission unit is of the liquid-cooled, single-cylinder two-stroke design. The engine/transmission assembly is constructed from aluminum alloy. The crankcase is divided vertically.

The cylinder, piston, crankshaft bearings and connecting rod lower end bearing are lubricated by the fuel, which is a mixture of gasoline and two-stroke oil (see Chapter 1 for fuel specifications). The transmission and clutch are lubricated by four-stroke engine oil, which is contained in a sump within the crankcase. Power from the crankshaft is routed to the transmission via a wet, multi-plate type clutch. The transmission on YZ80, YZ85 and YZ125 models has six forward gears. On YZ250 models it has five forward gears.

2 Operations possible with the engine in the frame

The components and assemblies listed below can be removed without having to remove the engine from the frame. If, however, a number of areas require attention at the same time, removal of the engine is recommended.

Cylinder and piston
External shift mechanism
Clutch and primary drive gear
Kickstarter

3 Operations requiring engine removal

It is necessary to remove the engine/transmission assembly from the frame and separate the crankcase halves to gain access to the following components:

Crankshaft and connecting rod
Transmission shafts
Internal shift mechanism (gearshift spindle, shift drum and forks)
Crankcase bearings

4 Major engine repair - general note

1 It is not always easy to determine when or if an engine should be completely overhauled, as a number of factors must be considered.

2 High mileage is not necessarily an indication that an overhaul is needed, while low mileage, on the other hand, does not preclude the need for an overhaul. Regular maintenance is probably the single most important consideration. This is especially true if the bike is used in competition. An engine that has been maintained properly will most likely give many hours of reliable service. Conversely, a neglected engine, or one which has not been broken in properly, may require an overhaul very early in its life.

3 Poor running that can't be accounted for by seemingly obvious causes (fouled spark plug, leaking head or cylinder base gasket, worn piston ring, carburetor problems) may be due to leaking crankshaft seals. In two-stroke engines, the crankcase acts as a suction pump to draw in fuel mixture and as a compressor to force it into the cylinder. If the crankcase seals are leaking, the pressure drop will cause a loss of performance.

4 If the engine is making obvious knocking or rumbling noises, the connecting rod and/or main bearings are probably at fault. The upper connecting rod bearing should be replaced at the maintenance interval listed in Chapter 1.

5 A top-end overhaul, part of regularly scheduled maintenance on these machines, consists of replacing the piston and ring and inspecting the cylinder bore. The cylinder on some models can be bored for an oversize piston if necessary; on others, the cylinder and piston must be replaced with new ones if they're worn.

6 A lower-end engine overhaul generally involves inspecting the crankshaft, transmission and crankcase bearings and seals. Unlike four-stroke engines equipped with plain main and connecting rod bearings, there isn't much in the way of machine work that can be done to refurbish existing parts. Worn bearings, gears, seals and shift mechanism parts should be replaced with new ones. The crankshaft and connecting rod are permanently assembled, so if one of these components (or the connecting rod lower end bearing) needs to be replaced, both must be. While the engine is being overhauled, other components such as the carburetor can be rebuilt also. The end result should be a like-new engine that will give as many trouble-free hours as the original.

7 Before beginning the engine overhaul, read through all of the related procedures to familiarize yourself with the scope and requirements of the job. Overhauling an engine is not all that difficult, but it is time consuming. Check on the availability of parts and make sure that any necessary special tools, equipment and supplies are obtained in advance.

8 Most work can be done with typical shop hand tools, although a number of precision measuring tools are required for inspecting parts to determine if they must be replaced. Often a dealer service department or repair shop will handle the inspection of parts and offer advice concerning reconditioning and replacement. As a general rule, time is the primary cost of an overhaul so it doesn't pay to install worn or substandard parts.

9 As a final note, to ensure maximum life and minimum trouble from a rebuilt engine, everything must be assembled with care in a spotlessly clean environment.

5 Crankcase pressure and vacuum - check

This test can pinpoint the cause of otherwise unexplained poor running. It can also prevent piston seizures by detecting air leaks that can cause a lean mixture. It requires special equipment, but can easily be done by a Yamaha dealer or other motorcycle shop. If you regularly work on two-stroke engines, you might want to consider purchasing the tester for yourself (or with a group of other riders). You may also be able to fabricate the tester.

6.11 On YZ125/250 models, remove the upper mounting bracket . . .

6.12 . . . and on all models, the two through-bolts under the engine (arrows)

The test involves sealing off the intake and exhaust ports (and the power valve openings on models so equipped), then applying vacuum and pressure to the spark plug hole with a hand vacuum/pressure pump, similar to the type used for brake bleeding and automotive vacuum testing.

First, remove the carburetor and exhaust system. Block off the carburetor opening with a rubber plug, clamped securely in position. Place a rubber sheet (cut from a tire tube or similar material) over the exhaust port and secure it with a metal plate. If the bike has a power valve, you'll need to seal these openings as well, using rubber gaskets and special adapters.

Apply air pressure to the spark plug hole with the vacuum/pressure pump. Check for leaks at the crankcase gasket, intake manifold, reed valve gasket, cylinder base gasket and head gasket. If the crankcase gasket leaks between the transmission sump and the crankcase (the area where the crankshaft spins), transmission oil will be sucked into the crankcase, causing the fuel mixture to be oil-rich. Also check the seal at the alternator end of the crankshaft. If the leaks are large, air will hiss as it passes through them. Small leaks can be detected by pouring soapy water over the suspected area and looking for bubbles.

After checking for air leaks, apply vacuum with the pump. If vacuum leaks down quickly, the crankshaft seals are leaking.

6 Engine - removal and installation

Note: *Engine removal and installation should be done with the aid of an assistant to avoid damage or injury that could occur if the engine is dropped.*

Removal

Refer to illustrations 6.11, 6.12 and 6.13

1 Drain the transmission oil and coolant (see Chapter 1).

2 Remove the seat and side covers (see Chapter 8).

3 Where necessary for access, remove the brake pedal (see Chapter 7).

4 Remove the fuel tank, exhaust system and carburetor (see Chapter 4).

5 Disconnect the spark plug wire (see Chapter 1).

6 Disconnect the coolant hoses from the engine (see Chapter 3). If you're working on a 1993 or later YZ125 or a 1990 or later YZ250, remove the radiators (see Chapter 3).

7 Disconnect the CDI magneto wires (refer to Chapter 5 for component location if necessary). Detach the wires from their retainers.

8 Remove the drive chain and sprocket (see Chapter 6).

9 Disconnect the clutch cable (see Section 12).

10 Support the bike securely upright so it can't fall over during the remainder of this procedure. Support the engine with a jack, if necessary, using a block of wood between the jack and the engine to protect the crankcase.

11 If you're working on a YZ125 or YZ250, remove the upper engine mount **(see illustration)**.

12 Remove the engine mounting bolts and nuts at the front and bottom **(see illustration)**.

13 Remove the swingarm pivot bolt nut (see Chapter 6). The pivot bolt passes through the rear of the crankcase to act as an engine support **(see illustration)**, so it needs to be pulled out of the crankcase. On 2002 and later YZ250 models, you'll need to remove the shaft completely, so the swingarm must be supported to keep it from dropping when the shaft is removed. On all other models, to avoid removing the swingarm completely, pull the bolt only until it clears the engine. Leave the bolt in the right swingarm pivot while you lift the engine out.

14 Have an assistant help you lift the engine out of the frame, if necessary.

15 Slowly lower the engine to a suitable work surface.

Installation

16 Have an assistant help lift the engine into the frame, then align the mounting bolt holes and install the bolts, nuts and brackets. Tighten them to the torques listed in this Chapter's Specifications. Refer to the Chapter 6 Specifications for the swingarm pivot bolt torque.

17 The remainder of installation is the reverse of the removal steps, with the following additions:

6.13 Pull the swingarm pivot bolt partway out (all the way out on 2002 and later YZ250 models) and remove the engine - put the bolt back to support the swingarm after the engine is removed, and don't forget to reinstall the collars (arrows) on reassembly

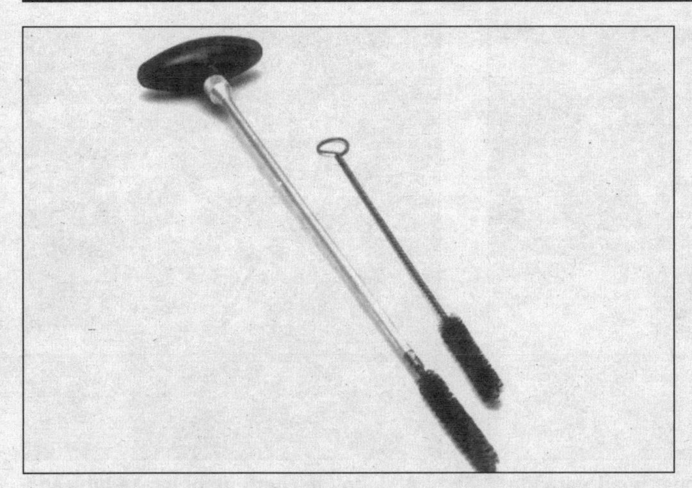

7.2 A selection of brushes is required for cleaning holes and passages in the engine components

7.3 An engine stand can be made from short lengths of lumber and lag bolts or nails

a) *Use a new exhaust pipe gasket.*
b) *Adjust the throttle cable and clutch cable following the procedures in Chapter 1.*
c) *Fill the engine with coolant and the transmission with oil, also following the procedures in Chapter 1.*
d) *Run the engine and check for oil, coolant or exhaust leaks.*

7 Engine disassembly and reassembly - general information

Refer to illustrations 7.2 and 7.3

1 Before disassembling the engine, clean the exterior with a degreaser and rinse it with water. A clean engine will make the job easier and prevent the possibility of getting dirt into the internal areas of the engine.

2 In addition to the precision measuring tools mentioned earlier, you will need a torque wrench and oil gallery brushes **(see illustration)**. Some new, clean engine oil of the correct grade and type (two-stroke oil, four-stroke oil or both, depending on whether it's a top-end or bottom-end overhaul), some engine assembly lube (or moly-based grease) and a tube of RTV (silicone) sealant will also be required.

3 An engine support stand made from short lengths of 2 x 4's bolted together will facilitate the disassembly and reassembly procedures **(see illustration)**. If you have an automotive-type engine stand, an adapter plate can be made from a piece of plate, some angle iron and some nuts and bolts.

4 When disassembling the engine, keep "mated" parts together (including gears, shift forks and shafts, etc.) that have been in contact with each other during engine operation. These "mated" parts must be reused or replaced as an assembly.

5 Engine/transmission disassembly should be done in the following general order with reference to the appropriate Sections.

Remove the cylinder head
Remove the cylinder
Remove the piston
Remove the water pump
Remove the clutch
Remove the primary drive gear
Remove the kickstarter
Remove the external shift mechanism
Remove the CDI magneto
Separate the crankcase halves
Remove the internal shift mechanism
Remove the transmission shafts and gears
Remove the crankshaft and connecting rod

6 Reassembly is accomplished by reversing the general disassembly sequence.

8.4 The YZ80/85 cylinder head is secured by four nuts; YZ125 models (shown) use five; YZ250 models use six

8 Cylinder head - removal, inspection and installation

Caution: *The engine must be completely cool before beginning this procedure, or the cylinder head may become warped.*

Note: *This procedure is described with the engine in the frame. If the engine has been removed, ignore the steps which don't apply.*

Removal

Refer to illustrations 8.4 and 8.6

1 Drain the cooling system (see Chapter 1) and disconnect the radiator hose(s) from the cylinder head (see Chapter 3).

2 Disconnect the spark plug wire (see Chapter 1).

3 Where necessary for access, remove the seat, side covers and fuel tank (see Chapters 8 and 4).

4 Loosen the cylinder head nuts in two or three stages, in a criss-cross pattern **(see illustration)**. Remove the nuts once they're all loose.

5 Lift the cylinder head off the cylinder. If the head is stuck, use a wooden dowel inserted into the spark plug hole to lever the head off. Don't attempt to pry the head off by inserting a screwdriver between the head and the cylinder - you'll damage the sealing surfaces. Locate the cylinder head dowel(s) - they may have come off with the head or remained in the cylinder.

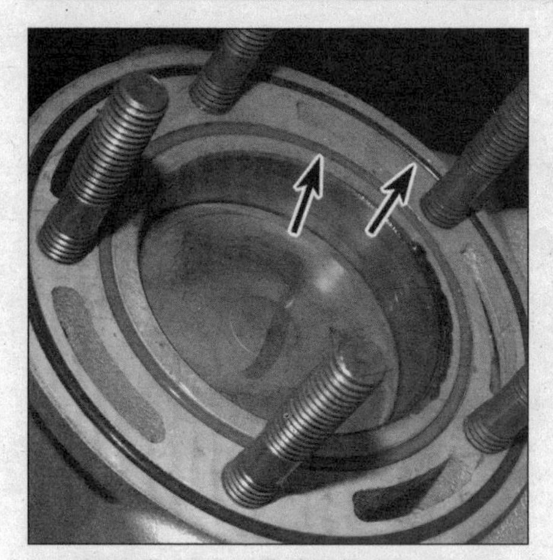

8.6 Remove the O-rings from the grooves

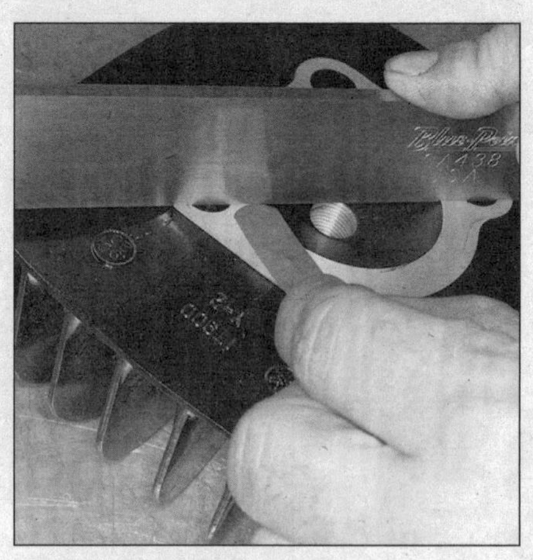

8.10 Check for cylinder head warpage with a straightedge and feeler gauge

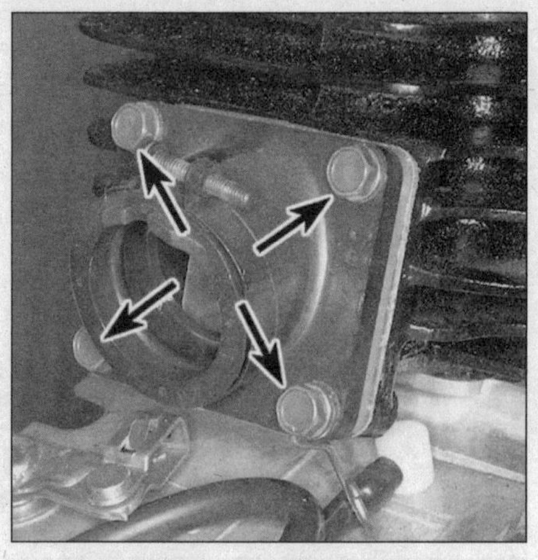

9.2 Unbolt the carburetor intake tube and remove it from the cylinder with its O-ring . . .

6 Rotate the piston to the top of the cylinder or stuff a clean rag into the cylinder to prevent the entry of debris. Once this is done, remove the O-rings from the cylinder **(see illustration)**.

Inspection

Refer to illustration 8.10

7 Check the O-rings and the mating surfaces on the cylinder head and cylinder for leakage, which could indicate warpage.

8 Clean all traces of old O-ring from the cylinder head and cylinder. Be careful not to let any of the material fall into the cylinder or coolant passages.

9 Inspect the head very carefully for cracks and other damage. If cracks are found, a new head will be required

10 Using a precision straightedge and a feeler gauge, check the head gasket mating surface for warpage. Lay the straightedge across the head, intersecting the head bolt holes, and try to slip a feeler gauge under it, on either side of the combustion chamber **(see illustration)**. The feeler gauge thickness should be the same as the cylinder head warpage limit listed in this Chapter's Specifications. If the feeler gauge can be inserted between the head and the straightedge, the head is warped and must either be machined or, if warpage is excessive, replaced with a new one.

Installation

11 Install new O-rings in place on the cylinder **(see illustration 8.6)**. Never reuse the old O-rings and don't use any type of gasket sealant.

12 Carefully lower the cylinder head over the studs.

13 Install the cylinder head nuts and tighten them evenly, in a criss-cross pattern, to the torque listed in this Chapter's Specifications.

14 The remainder of installation is the reverse of the removal steps. Be sure to refill the cooling system (see Chapter 1).

9 Reed valve - removal, inspection and installation

Removal

Refer to illustrations 9.2, 9.3a and 9.3b

1 Remove the carburetor (see Chapter 4).

2 Unbolt the carburetor intake tube from the cylinder **(see illustration)**. Take off the intake tube and its O-ring.

3 Remove the insert, then pull the reed valve out of the cylinder and remove the gasket **(see illustrations)**.

Inspection

Refer to illustrations 9.5 and 9.6

4 Check the reed valve for obvious damage, such as cracked or broken reeds or stoppers. Also make sure there's no clearance between the reeds and the edges where they make contact with the seats.

5 Measure the gap between the reed valves and the valve body (this is the "bending limit"), and the reed valve stopper height **(see illustration)**. If either is not within the limits listed in this Chapter's Specifications, replace the reed valves or stoppers.

9.3a Pull out the insert . . .

9.3b . . . then pull out the reed valve and remove the gasket

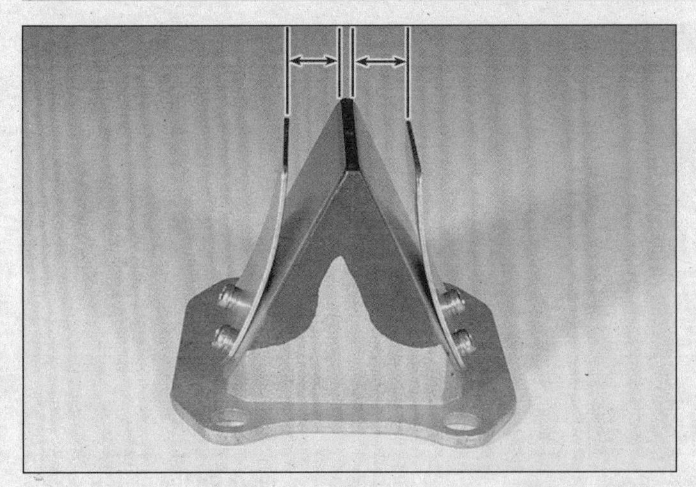

9.5 Measure the gap between the reed stoppers and reeds (this is the "stopper height," shown here) as well as between the reeds and valve body (bending limit)

9.6 Remove the screws to detach the reed stoppers from the reed valve; on installation, align the diagonally cut corners of the reed and stopper

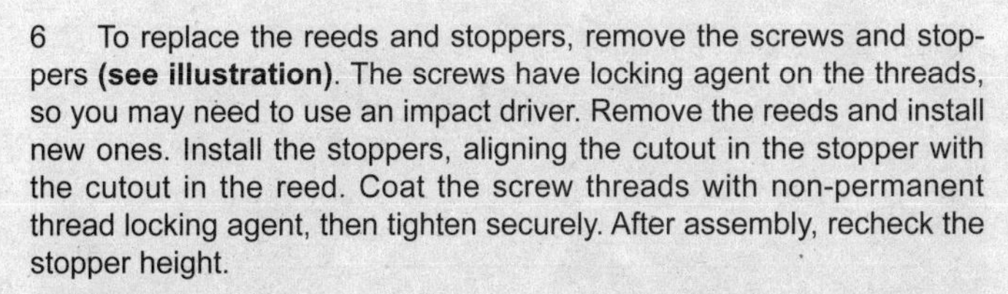

6 To replace the reeds and stoppers, remove the screws and stoppers **(see illustration)**. The screws have locking agent on the threads, so you may need to use an impact driver. Remove the reeds and install new ones. Install the stoppers, aligning the cutout in the stopper with the cutout in the reed. Coat the screw threads with non-permanent thread locking agent, then tighten securely. After assembly, recheck the stopper height.

Installation

7 Installation is the reverse of the removal steps, with the following additions:

a) Use a new gasket between the reed valve assembly and cylinder.
b) Use a new O-ring between the carburetor intake tube and the reed valve assembly.
c) Tighten the intake tube bolts in a criss-cross pattern to the torque listed in this Chapter's Specifications.

10 Cylinder - removal, inspection and installation

Removal

Refer to illustrations 10.2a, 10.2b and 10.3

1 Remove the cylinder head (see Section 8). Make sure the crankshaft is positioned at top dead center (TDC). If you're working on a YZ125 or YZ250, disconnect the power valve governor (see Chapter 4).

2 On all except 1986 through 1992 YZ80 models, remove four nuts securing the cylinder to the crankcase **(see illustrations)**. The cylinder on early YZ80 models is secured by the same nuts and studs that secure the cylinder head.

3 Lift the cylinder straight up off the piston **(see illustration)**. If it's stuck, tap around its perimeter with a soft-faced hammer. Don't attempt to pry between the cylinder and the crankcase, as you'll ruin the sealing surfaces.

4 Locate the dowel pins (they may have come off with the cylinder or still be in the crankcase) **(see illustration 10.3)**. Be careful not to let these drop into the engine. Stuff clean shop rags around the piston and remove the gasket and all traces of old gasket material from the surfaces of the cylinder and the crankcase.

Inspection

Refer to illustrations 10.7 and 10.8

Caution: *Don't attempt to separate the liner from the cylinder.*

5 Check the top surface of the cylinder for warpage. Measure along the sides, alongside the studs or across the stud holes. Yamaha doesn't specify a warpage limit, but if the surfaces are warped the cylinder should be replaced.

6 If you're working on a 1993 or later YZ80/85 or a 1991 or later YZ125/250, look for the bore size code on the base of the cylinder **(see illustration 10.2b)**. This should match the code on the piston crown.

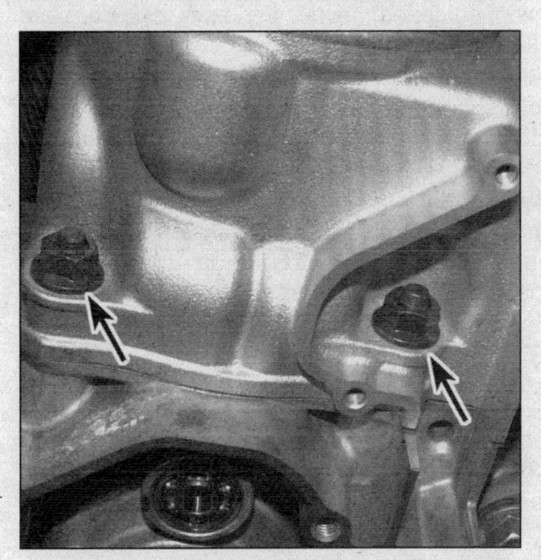

10.2a All except 1992 and earlier YZ80 models, remove two nuts from the right side of the cylinder (arrows) . . .

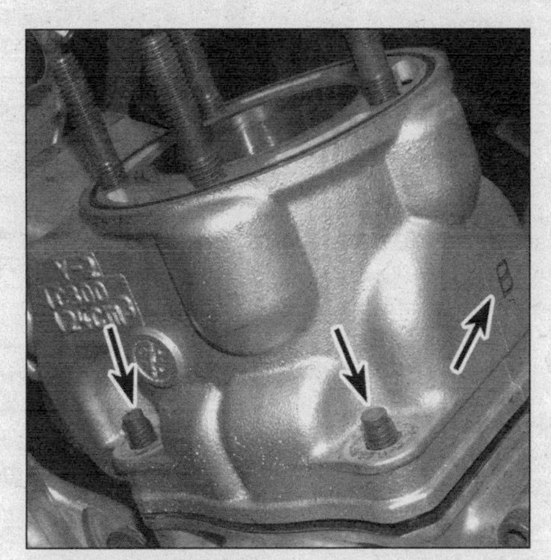

10.2b . . . and two nuts from the left side (left arrows); the letter code on later models (right arrow) indicates bore grade

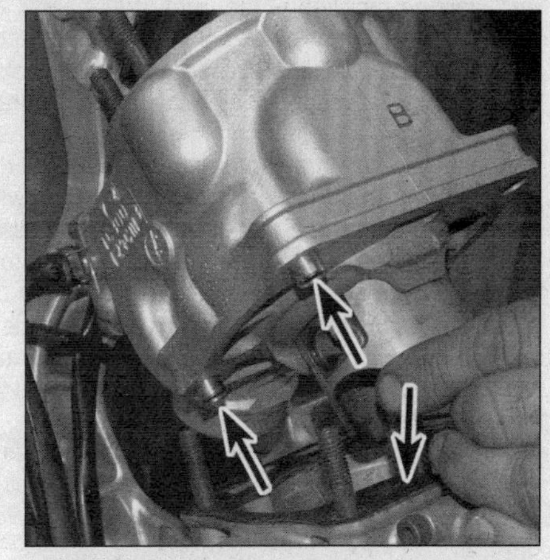

10.3 Lift the cylinder off, locate the dowels (upper arrows) and remove the gasket (lower arrow)

10.7 This cylinder was damaged (arrows) when the ring ends rotated away from the dowel and snagged on the port

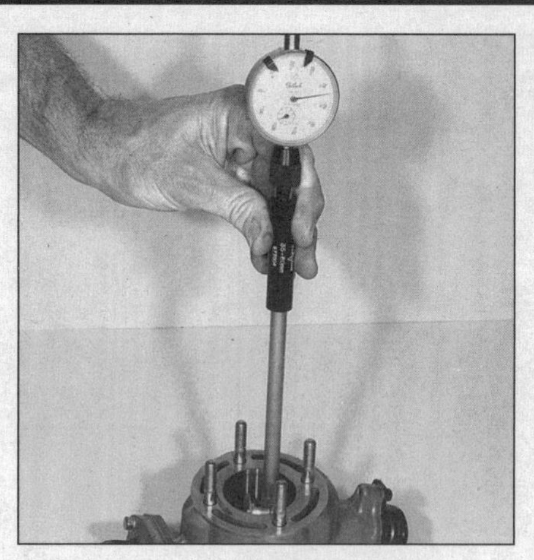

10.8 Measure bore diameter with a bore gauge

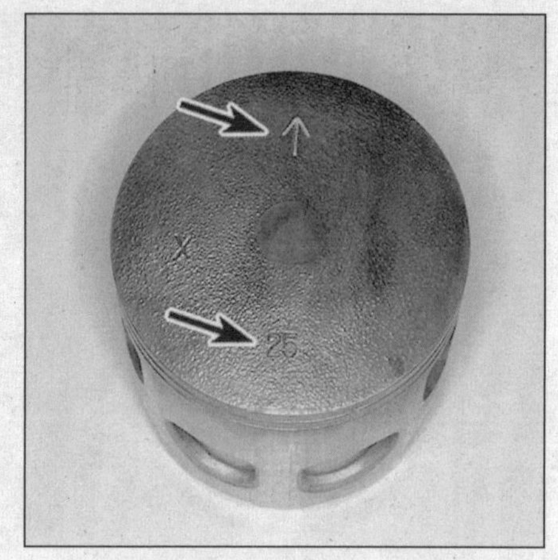

11.3a The arrow mark on the piston points to the front of the engine - the "25" mark indicates that the piston is an oversize (early models only)

7 Check the cylinder walls carefully for scratches and score marks. Major damage, such as that caused by a ring gap out of position, is cause for cylinder replacement **(see illustration)**.

8 Using the appropriate precision measuring tools, check the cylinder's diameter at the top, center and bottom of the cylinder bore, parallel to the crankshaft axis **(see illustration)**. Next, measure the cylinder's diameter at the same three locations across the crankshaft axis. Compare the results to this Chapter's Specifications.

9 If you're working on a 1986 through 1992 YZ80 or a 1986 through 1988 YZ125/250 and the cylinder walls are tapered, out-of-round, worn beyond the specified limits, or badly scuffed or scored, you can have the cylinder rebored and honed by a dealer service department or a motorcycle repair shop. If a rebore is done, oversize pistons and rings will be required as well.

10 If you're working on a 1993 or later YZ80/85 or a 1989 or later YZ125/250, the cylinder will have to be replaced if the conditions described in Step 9 are found.

11 As an alternative, if the precision measuring tools are not available, a dealer service department or repair shop will make the measurements and offer advice concerning servicing of the cylinder.

12 If it's in reasonably good condition and not worn to the outside of the limits, and if the piston-to-cylinder clearance can be maintained properly, then the cylinder does not have to be rebored; honing is all that is necessary.

13 To perform the honing operation you will need the proper size flexible hone with fine stones as shown in *Maintenance techniques, tools and working facilities* at the front of this book, or a "bottle brush" type hone, plenty of light oil or honing oil, some shop towels and an electric drill motor. Hold the cylinder in a vise (cushioned with soft jaws or wood blocks) when performing the honing operation. Mount the hone in the drill motor, compress the stones and slip the hone into the cylinder. Lubricate the cylinder thoroughly, turn on the drill and move the hone up and down in the cylinder at a pace which will produce a fine crosshatch pattern on the cylinder wall with the crosshatch lines intersecting at approximately a 60-degree angle. Be sure to use plenty of lubricant and do not take off any more material than is absolutely necessary to produce the desired effect. Do not withdraw the hone from the cylinder while it is running. Instead, shut off the drill and continue moving the hone up and down in the cylinder until it comes to a complete stop, then compress the stones and withdraw the hone. Wipe the oil out of the cylinder. Remember, do not remove too much material from the cylinder wall. If you do not have the tools, or do not desire to perform the honing operation, a dealer service department or motorcycle repair shop will generally do it for a reasonable fee.

14 Next, the cylinder must be thoroughly washed with warm soapy water to remove all traces of the abrasive grit produced during the honing operation. Be sure to run a brush through the bolt holes and flush them with running water. After rinsing, dry the cylinder thoroughly and apply a coat of light, rust-preventative oil to all machined surfaces.

11.3b Wear eye projection and remove the circlip with a pointed tool or needle-nosed pliers

Installation

15 Lubricate the piston with plenty of clean two-stroke engine oil.

16 Install the dowel pins (if equipped), then lower a new cylinder base gasket over them **(see illustration 10.3)**.

17 Install the cylinder over the studs and carefully lower it down until the piston crown fits into the cylinder liner. Push down on the cylinder, making sure the piston doesn't get cocked sideways, until the bottom of the cylinder liner slides down past the piston ring. Be sure not to rotate the cylinder, as this may snag the piston ring on the exhaust port. A wood or plastic hammer handle can be used to gently tap the cylinder down, but don't use too much force or the piston will be damaged.

18 The remainder of installation is the reverse of the removal steps.

11 Piston and ring - removal, inspection and installation

Note: *For bikes used in competition, periodic replacement of the piston and ring is a routine maintenance procedure that should be done at the intervals listed in Chapter 1.*

1 The piston is attached to the connecting rod with a piston pin that is a slip fit in the piston and connecting rod needle bearing.

2 Before removing the piston from the rod, stuff a clean shop towel into the crankcase hole, around the connecting rod. This will prevent the circlips from falling into the crankcase if they are inadvertently dropped.

11.4a Push the piston pin partway out, then pull it the rest of the way

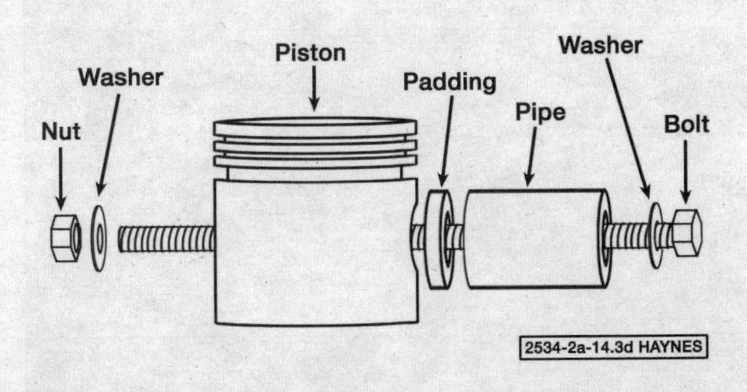

11.4b The piston pin should come out by hand - if it doesn't, this removal tool can be fabricated from readily available parts

Removal

Refer to illustrations 11.3a, 11.3b, 11.4a, 11.4b and 11.4c

3 The piston should have an arrow on its crown that goes toward the exhaust (front) side of the engine. If this mark is not visible due to carbon buildup, scribe an arrow into the piston crown before removal. Support the piston and pry the circlip out with a pointed tool or needle-nosed pliers **(see illustration)**.

4 Push the piston pin out from the opposite end to free the piston from the rod **(see illustration)**. You may have to deburr the area around the groove to enable the pin to slide out (use a triangular file for this procedure). If the pin won't come out, you can fabricate a piston pin removal tool from a long bolt, a nut, a piece of tubing and washers **(see illustration)**. Once you've removed the pin, remove the needle bearing **(see illustration)**.

Inspection

Refer to illustrations 11.6, 11.13, 11.14, 11.15a, 11.15b, 11.16 and 11.17

5 Before the inspection process can be carried out, the piston must be cleaned and the old piston ring removed.

6 Carefully remove the ring(s) from the piston **(see illustration)**. Do not nick or gouge the pistons in the process. A ring removal and installation tool will make this easier, but you can use your fingers if you don't have one - just be sure not to cut yourself.

7 Scrape all traces of carbon from the top of the piston. A hand-held wire brush or a piece of fine emery cloth can be used once most of the deposits have been scraped away. Do not, under any circumstances, use a wire brush mounted in a drill motor to remove deposits from the piston; the piston material is soft and will be eroded away by the wire brush.

8 Use a piston ring groove cleaning tool to remove any carbon deposits from the ring groove. If a tool is not available, a piece broken off the old ring will do the job. Be very careful to remove only the carbon deposits. Do not remove any metal and do not nick or gouge the sides of the ring grooves.

9 Once the deposits have been removed, clean the piston with solvent and dry it thoroughly.

10 Normal piston wear appears as even, vertical wear on the thrust surfaces of the piston and slight looseness of the ring(s) in the groove(s).

11 Carefully inspect each piston for cracks around the skirt, at the pin bosses and at the ring lands.

12 Look for scoring and scuffing on the thrust faces of the skirt, holes in the piston crown and burned areas at the edge of the crown. If the skirt is scored or scuffed, the engine may have been suffering from overheating and/or abnormal combustion, which caused excessively high operating temperatures. A hole in the piston crown, an extreme to be sure, is an indication that abnormal combustion (pre-ignition) was occurring. Burned areas at the edge of the piston crown are usually evidence of spark knock (detonation). If any of the above problems exist, the causes must be corrected or the damage will occur again.

13 Measure the piston ring-to-groove clearance (side clearance) by

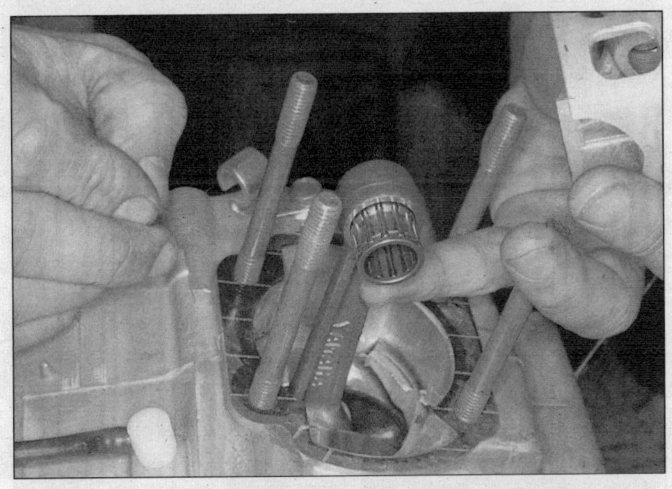

11.4c Slide the small-end bearing out of the connecting rod

11.6 Remove the piston ring(s) with a ring removal and installation tool if you have one; you can use fingers instead if you're careful

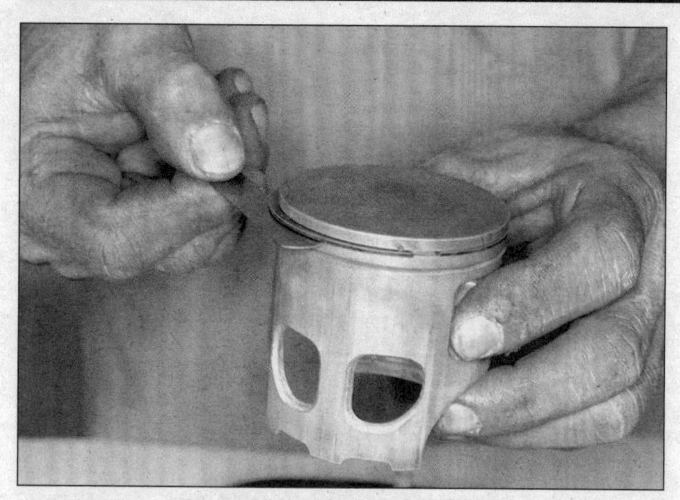

11.13 Measure side clearance between the piston and ring(s) with a feeler gauge

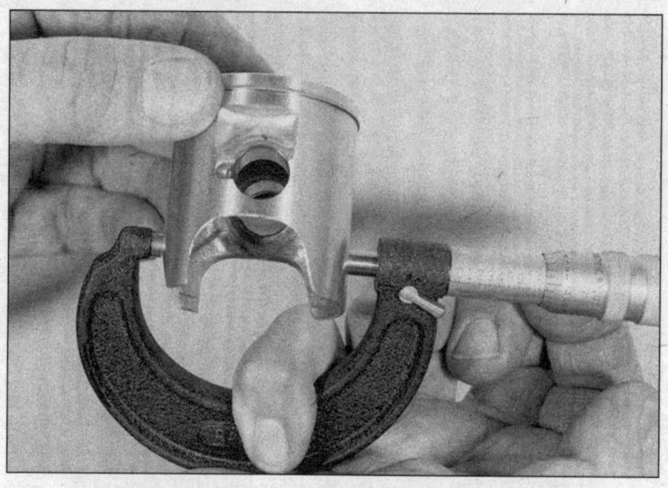

11.14 Measure the piston diameter with a micrometer

laying a new piston ring in the ring groove and slipping a feeler gauge in beside it **(see illustration)**. Check the clearance at three or four locations around the groove. If the clearance is greater than specified, a new piston will have to be used when the engine is reassembled.

14 Check the piston-to-bore clearance by measuring the bore (see Section 10) and the piston diameter **(see illustration)**. Measure the piston across the skirt on the thrust faces at a 90-degree angle to the piston pin, at the specified distance up from the bottom of the skirt. Subtract the piston diameter from the bore diameter to obtain the clearance. If it is greater than specified, the cylinder will have to be rebored and a new oversized piston and ring installed (1986 through 1992 YZ80 and 1986 through 1988 YZ125/250) or the cylinder and piston will have to be replaced (all other models). If the appropriate precision measuring tools are not available, the piston-to-cylinder clearance can be obtained, though not quite as accurately, using feeler gauge stock. Feeler gauge stock comes in 12-inch lengths and various thickness and is generally available at auto parts stores. To check the clearance, slip a piece of feeler gauge stock of the same thickness as the specified piston clearance into the cylinder along with appropriate piston. The cylinder should be upside down and the piston must be positioned exactly as it normally would be. Place the feeler gauge between the piston and cylinder on one of the thrust faces (90-degrees to the piston pin bore). The piston should slip through the cylinder (with the feeler gauge in place) with moderate pressure. If it falls through, or slides through easily, the clearance is excessive and a new piston will be required. If the piston binds at the lower end of the cylinder and is loose toward the top, the cylinder is tapered, and if tight spots are encountered as the piston/feeler gauge is rotated in the cylinder, the cylinder is out-of-round. Be sure to have the cylinder and piston checked by a dealer service department or a repair shop to confirm your findings before purchasing new parts.

15 Measure the ring end gap. Push the piston ring into the cylinder from the top, down to the bottom of the ring travel area inside the cylinder. Square the ring in the bore by tapping it with the piston crown **(see illustration)**. Measure the gap between the ends of the ring with a feeler gauge **(see illustration)**. On two-ring pistons, measure both rings; if either has a gap greater than the value listed in this Chapter's Specifications, replace both rings with new ones.

16 Apply clean two-stroke oil to the pin, insert it into the piston and check for freeplay by rocking the pin back-and-forth **(see illustration)**. If the pin is loose, a new piston and possibly new pin must be installed. To determine which, measure the pin diameter and compare it with the value listed in this Chapter's Specifications (or have this done by a dealer or repair shop) **(see illustration)**.

17 Repeat Step 16, this time inserting the piston pin into the connecting rod needle bearing **(see illustration)**. If it wobbles and the pin diameter is within specifications, replace the needle bearing.

Installation

Refer to illustrations 11.19a and 11.19b

18 Install the piston with its arrow toward the exhaust side (front) of the engine. Lubricate the pin and the rod needle bearing with two-stroke oil of the type listed in the Chapter 1 Specifications.

19 Install a new circlip in the groove in one side of the piston (don't

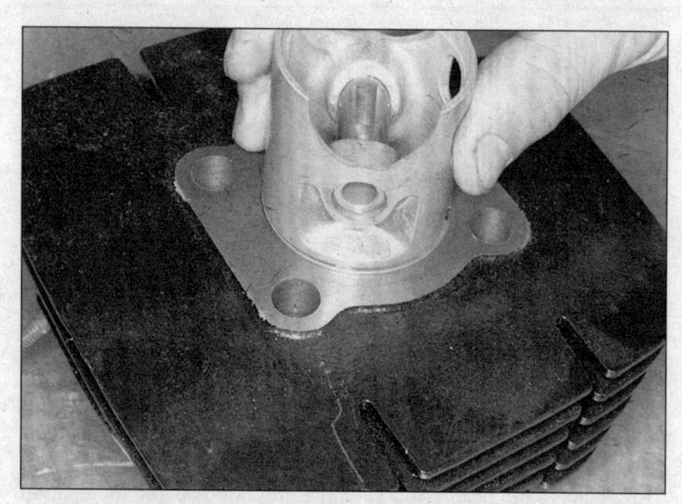

11.15a Use the piston to push the ring squarely into the bore . . .

11.15b . . . then measure the ring end gap with a feeler gauge

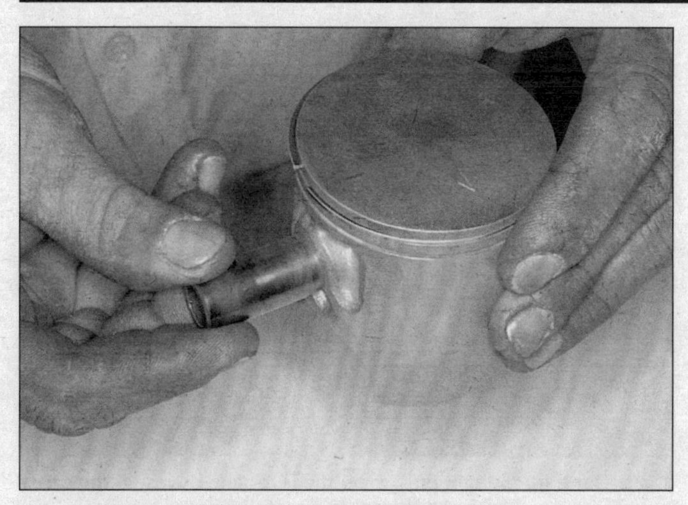

11.16 Slip the pin into the piston and try to wiggle it back-and-forth; if it's loose, replace the piston and pin; the needle bearing in the rod should be replaced if its condition is in doubt

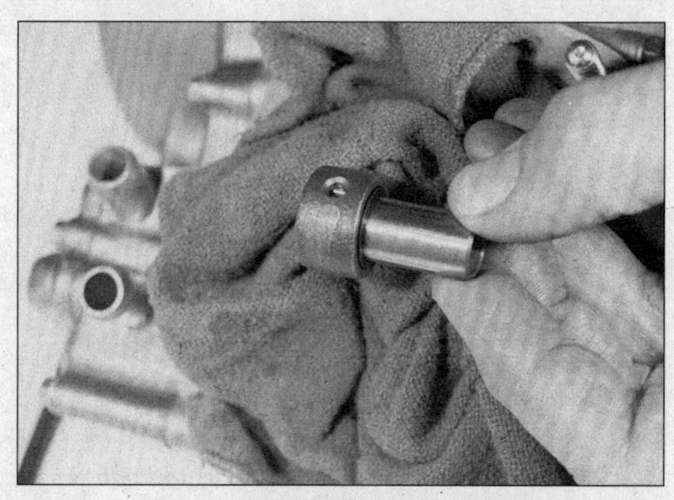

11.17 The needle bearing should be replaced if the pin wobbles inside it

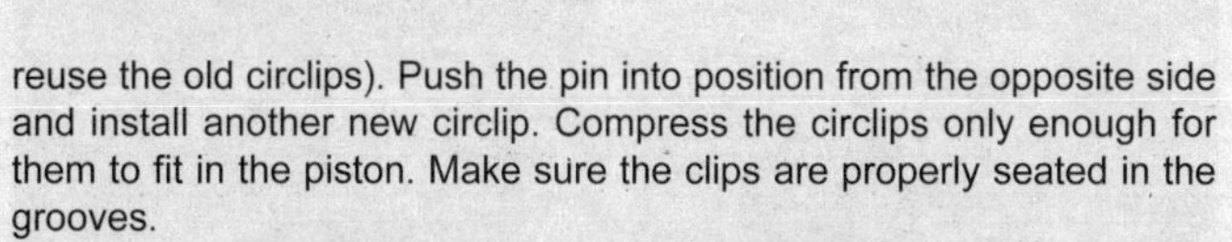

reuse the old circlips). Push the pin into position from the opposite side and install another new circlip. Compress the circlips only enough for them to fit in the piston. Make sure the clips are properly seated in the grooves.

19 Locate the manufacturer's mark on the piston ring near one of the ends **(see illustration)**. Turn the ring so this mark is upward, then carefully spread it and install it in the ring groove. Make sure the end gap is positioned over the dowel pin in the ring groove **(see illustration)**. **Caution:** *If the ring gap is not placed over the dowel, the ring may spin in the bore and cause severe cylinder wall damage.*

12 Clutch - removal, inspection and installation

Cable

Removal

Refer to illustrations 12.2, 12.3a, 12.3b and 12.3c

1 Loosen the cable adjuster at the handlebar grip all the way (see Chapter 1). Rotate the cable so the inner cable aligns with the slot in the lever, then slip the cable end fitting out of the lever.

2 If the bike has an external lifter lever, free the cable from the engine bracket **(see illustration)**. Disengage the cable from the lifter lever, then pull the outer cable out of the bracket and slip the inner cable through the slot in the bracket.

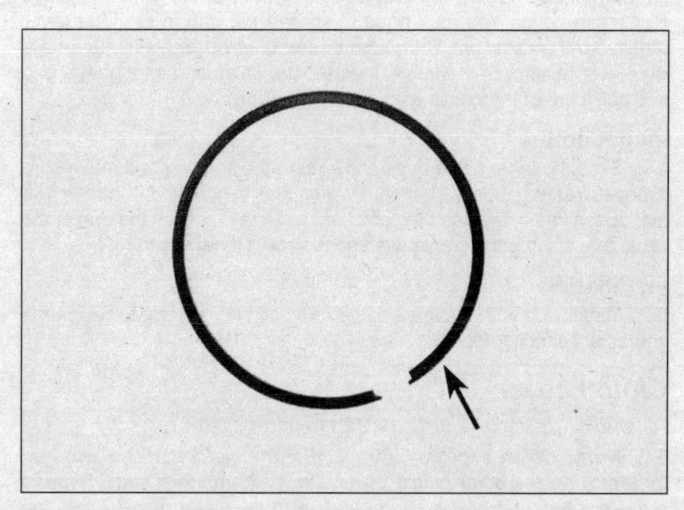

11.19a The manufacturer's mark near the ring gap (arrow) should be facing up when the ring is installed

11.19b Position the ring ends on either side of the dowel pin in the ring groove (arrow) (two-ring piston shown

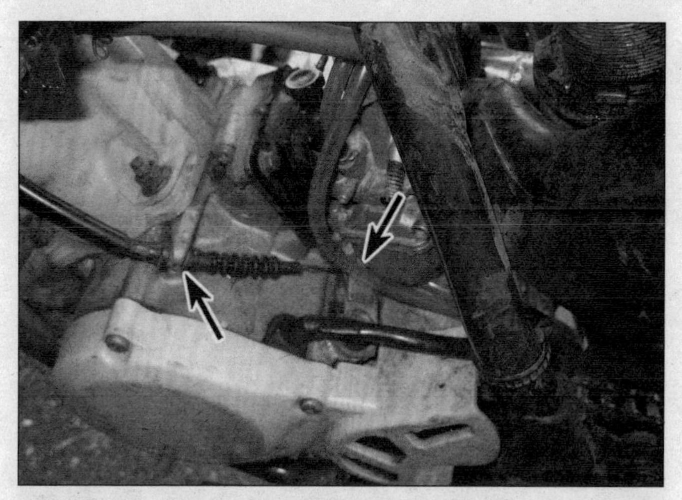

12.2 Disengage the cable from the bracket (left arrow), then rotate the lever arm against spring tension and slip the cable out of its slot (external lifter lever)

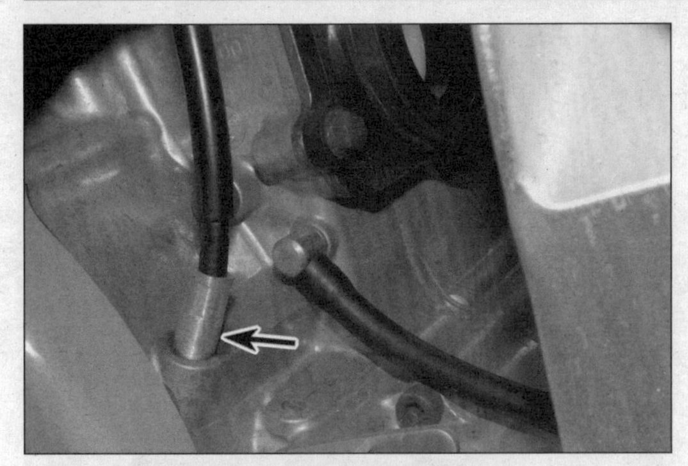

12.3a If the cable enters the engine like this (arrow) the bike has an internal lifter lever

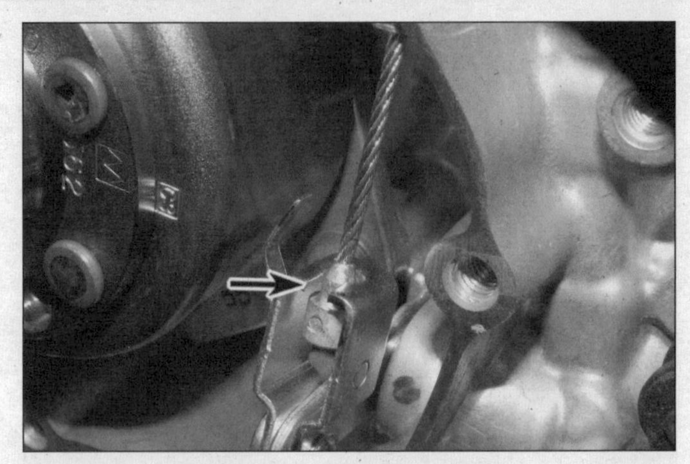

12.3b Bend up the tab, pull up on the lever and down on the cable and slip the cable out of the slot

3 If the cable passes through a hole in the crankcase, the bike has an internal lifter lever **(see illustration)**. In this case, remove the left crankcase cover. You may need to spread the gap in the lifter lever slightly so the cable will fit through it **(see illustration)**. Pull up on the lifter lever to slacken the cable, then slip the cable end through the gap and pull it out of the crankcase **(see illustration)**.

Inspection

4 Slide the inner cable back and forth in the housing and make sure it moves freely. If it doesn't, try lubricating it as described in Chapter 1. If that doesn't help, replace the cable. Inspect the O-ring on the end of the cable that fits into the crankcase and replace it if necessary.

Installation

5 Installation is the reverse of the removal steps. Refer to Chapter 1 and adjust clutch freeplay.

Clutch cover

Refer to illustrations 12.9, 12.10, 12.11a and 12.11b

6 **Note:** *On all except YZ80 models, the clutch can be serviced by removing the outer clutch cover. On YZ80 models, you'll need to remove the right crankcase over, including the water pump.* Drain the transmission oil (see Chapter 1). If you're working on a YZ80, drain the coolant and disconnect the hose from the water pump (see Chapter 3).

7 Where necessary for removal access, remove the brake pedal and kickstarter pedal (see Chapter 7 and Section 15).

8 On models with an external lifter lever, disconnect the clutch cable

12.3c Pull the cable out of the engine - use a new O-ring on installation

from the lifter lever as described above.

9 Remove the cover bolts and pull the cover off the engine **(see illustration)**. Tap gently with a rubber mallet if necessary to break the gasket seal. Don't pry against the mating surfaces of the cover and crankcase.

10 Once the cover is off, locate the dowels **(see illustration)**; they may have stayed in the crankcase or come off with the cover.

11 If necessary, unbolt the right crankcase cover and remove it

12.9 On models with an outer clutch cover, remove the cover bolts (arrows) . . .

12.10 . . . then take off the cover and locate the dowels

A Dowels
B Pressure plate bolts

12.11a To remove the right crankcase cover, remove its bolts (arrows) . . .

12.11b . . . then remove the cover and locate the dowels (arrows) (late model YZ125 shown)

together with the water pump **(see illustration)**. Once the cover is off, locate the dowels **(see illustration)**; they may have stayed in the crankcase or come off with the cover.

Lifter lever

Refer to illustration 12.13

12 Disconnect the cable and remove the right crankcase cover as described above.

13 On YZ125 and YZ250 models with an external lifter lever, unscrew the lever retaining bolt. Note how the spring is installed (if equipped) , then pull the lifter lever out of the crankcase **(see illustration)**.

14 Check for visible wear or damage at the contact points of the lifter lever and pushrod. Replace any parts that show problems.

15 Inspect the lifter shaft seal **(see illustration 12.13)**. If it has been leaking, pry it out. If the needle bearing (used on models with an external lifter lever) is worn or damaged, remove it and install a new one. Pack the needle bearing with grease and press in a new seal.

16 Installation is the reverse of the removal steps.

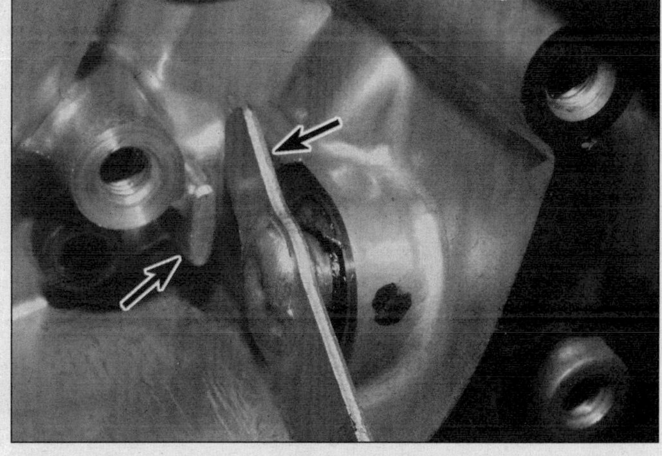

12.13 Turn the lifter lever so its end clears the stop (arrow), then pull it out of the crankcase

Clutch

Removal

Refer to illustrations 12.19a through 12.19h

17 Remove the clutch cover as described above.

18 Remove the pressure plate **(see illustration 12.10)**.

19 Refer to the accompanying illustrations to remove the clutch **(see illustrations)**.

12.19a Note how the lockwasher tabs engage the clutch housing (arrows, on models so equipped), then bend the lockwasher away from the nut

12.19b Hold the clutch center from turning using a tool like this (or equivalent), then unscrew the nut

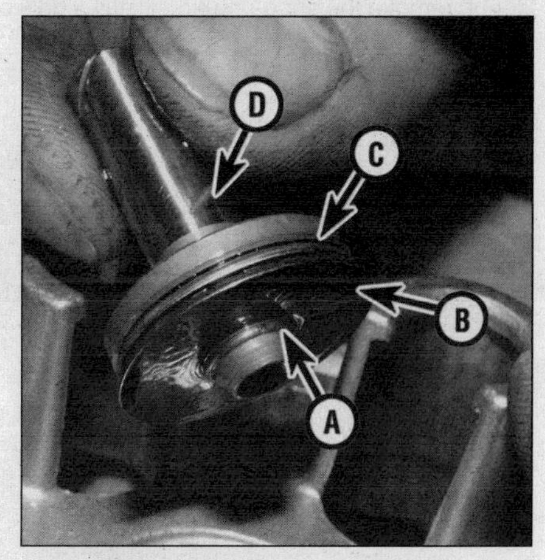

12.19c Check the outer pushrod for wear and damage (2006 YZ125 shown)

A Circlip
B Washer
C Bearing
D Outer pushrod

12.19d Remove the clutch center, together with the clutch plates, then remove the thrust washer

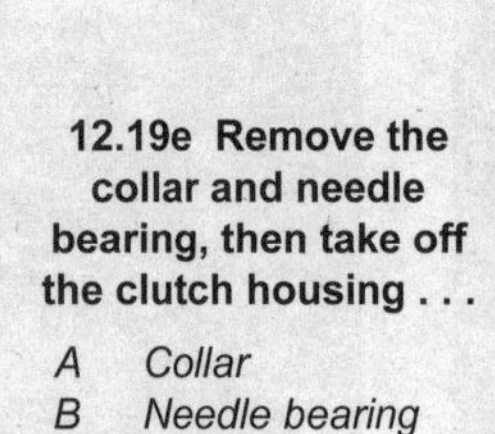

12.19e Remove the collar and needle bearing, then take off the clutch housing . . .

A Collar
B Needle bearing
C Clutch housing

12.19f . . . and remove the thrust washer from behind the clutch housing

12.19g Remove the ball from the transmission shaft . . .

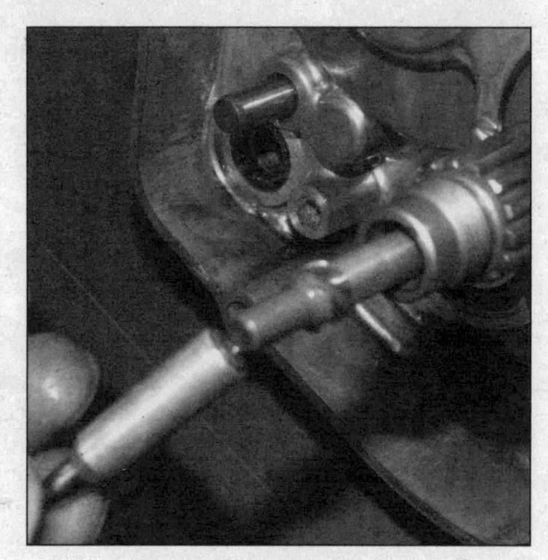

12.19h . . . then pull out the pushrod with a magnet

Inspection

Refer to illustrations 12.21

20 Rotate the release bearing and check it for rough, loose or noisy operation **(see illustration 12.19c).** If the bearing's condition is in doubt, remove the snap-ring and install a new one.

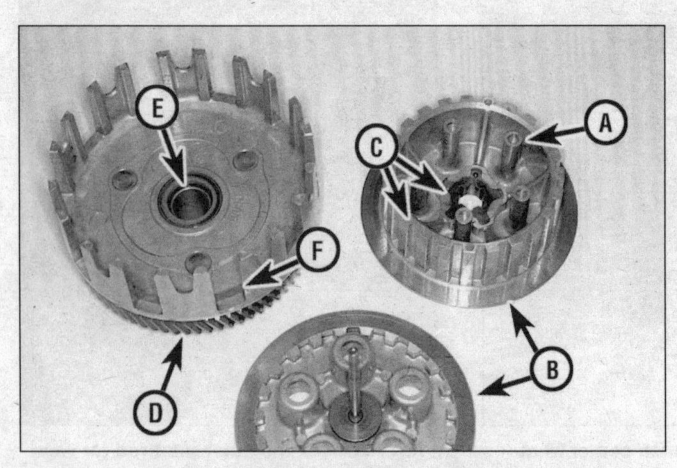

12.21 Clutch inspection points

A Spring posts
B Friction surfaces
C Splines
D Primary driven gear
E Clutch housing bushing
F Clutch housing slots

21 Check the friction surface on the pressure plate for scoring or wear **(see illustration)**. Replace the pressure plate if any defects are found.

22 Check the edges of the slots in the clutch housing for indentations made by the friction plate tabs. If the indentations are deep they can prevent clutch release, so the housing should be replaced with a new one. If the indentations can be removed easily with a file, the life of the housing can be prolonged to an extent. Also, check the driven

12.22 Hold the clutch housing so it won't turn and try to rotate the primary driven gear; if there's any play, replace the clutch housing

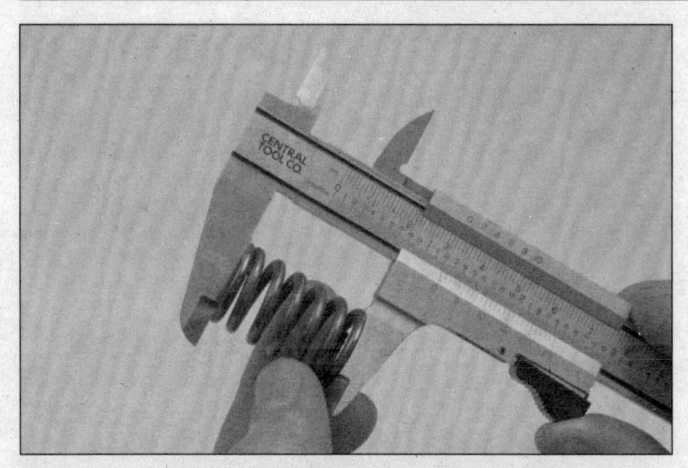

12.25 Measure the clutch spring free length

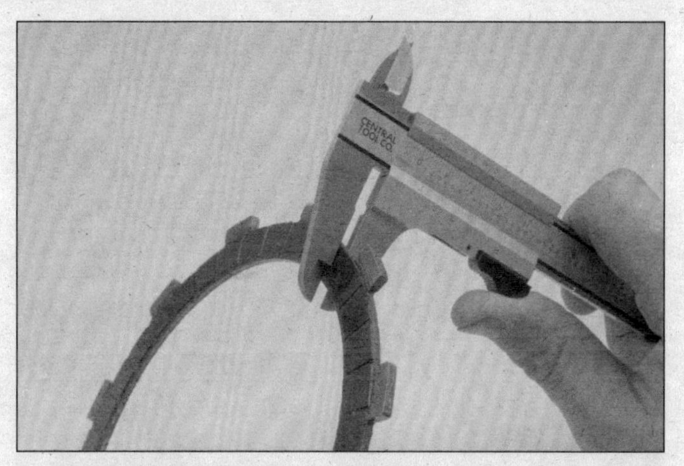

12.26 Measure the thickness of the friction plates

gear teeth for cracks, chips and excessive wear and the springs on the back side (if equipped) for breakage **(see illustration)**. If the gear is worn or damaged or the springs are broken, the clutch housing must be replaced with a new one.

23 Check the bearing surface in the center of the clutch housing for score marks, scratches and excessive wear. Also check the inside and outside diameters of the clutch housing bushing and the thrust washers. Replace any worn parts.

24 Check the clutch center's friction surface and slots for scoring, wear and indentations **(see illustration 12.21)**. Also check the splines in the middle of the clutch center. Replace the clutch center if problems are found.

25 Measure the free length of the clutch springs **(see illustration)** and compare the results to this Chapter's Specifications. If the springs have sagged, or if cracks are noted, replace them with new ones as a set.

26 If the lining material of the friction plates smells burnt or if it is glazed, new parts are required. If the metal clutch plates are scored or discolored, they must be replaced with new ones. Measure the thickness of the friction plates **(see illustration)** and replace with new parts any friction plates that are worn (it's best to replace them as a set).

27 Lay the metal plates, one at a time, on a perfectly flat surface (such as a piece of plate glass) and check for warpage by trying to slip a feeler gauge between the flat surface and the plate **(see illustration)**. The feeler gauge should be the same thickness as the maximum warp listed in this Chapter's Specifications. Do this at several places around the plate's circumference. If the feeler gauge can be slipped under the plate, it is warped and should be replaced with a new one.

28 Check the tabs on the friction plates for excessive wear and mushroomed edges. They can be cleaned up with a file if the deformation is not severe. Check the friction plates for warpage as described in Step 27.

Installation

29 Installation is the reverse of the removal steps, with the following additions:

a) *If you're working on a YZ125 or YZ250, install a new lockwasher and position its tabs between the ribs of the clutch center. Tighten the clutch nut to the torque listed in this Chapter's Specifications, then bend the lockwasher against two of the flats on the nut.*

b) *If you're working on a YZ80 or YZ85, install the conical washer with its concave side toward the engine.*

c) *Coat the friction plates with clean transmission oil of the proper type (see Chapter 1) before you install them.*

d) *Install a friction plate, then alternate the remaining metal and friction plates until they're all installed. Friction plates go on first and last, so the friction material contacts the metal surfaces of the clutch center and the pressure plate.*

e) *Apply grease to the ends of the clutch pushrod and the pushrod's steel ball.*

13 Primary drive gear - removal, inspection and installation

Removal

Refer to illustrations 13.2 and 13.4

1 Remove the right crankcase cover (see Section 12).

2 Wedge a copper washer or penny between the teeth of the primary drive gear and the primary driven gear on the clutch housing. Unscrew the primary drive gear locknut or bolt and remove the lockwasher (if equipped) **(see illustration)**.

3 Remove the clutch (Section 12).

12.27 Check the metal plates for warpage

13.2 Remove the bolt or nut from the primary drive gear . . .

13.4 . . . take it off the crankshaft and remove the collar (if equipped)

4 Slide the primary drive gear off the crankshaft **(see illustration)**. Remove the collar or thrust plate from behind the gear (all except 1986 through 1990 YZ125 models).

Inspection

5 Check the drive gear(s) for obvious damage such as chipped or broken teeth. Replace it if any of these problems are found.

Installation

6 Installation is the reverse of the removal steps. Wedge the underside of the gear using the same method used for removal, then tighten the locknut or bolt to the torque listed in this Chapter's Specifications. On later YZ125 models, use thread locking agent on the bolt threads.

14 External shift mechanism - removal, inspection and installation

Shift pedal

Removal

Refer to illustration 14.1

1 Look for alignment marks on the end of the shift pedal and gearshift spindle **(see illustration)**. If they aren't visible, make your own marks with a sharp punch.

2 Remove the shift pedal pinch bolt and slide the pedal off the shaft.

14.1 If you don't see a punch mark on the pedal and the end of the spindle, make your own marks - a felt pen will work

Inspection

3 Check the shift pedal for wear or damage such as bending. Check the splines on the shift pedal and gearshift spindle for stripping or step wear. Replace the pedal or spindle if these problems are found.

4 Check the gearshift spindle seal for signs of oil leakage. If it has been leaking, remove the gearshift spindle as described below. Pry the seal out of the cover and install a new one. You may be able to push the seal in with your thumbs; if not, tap it in with a hammer and block of wood or a socket the same diameter as the seal.

Installation

5 Line up the punch marks, install the shift pedal and tighten the pinch bolt.

External shift linkage

Removal

All YZ80/85 and 1986 through 1990 YZ125/250 models

6 Remove the shift pedal as described above.

7 Remove the clutch (Section 12).

8 Note how the gearshift spindle's return spring fits over its pin and how the gearshift spindle's pawls engage the shift drum pins. Pull the gearshift spindle out of the crankcase.

1991 and later YZ125/250 models

Refer to illustrations 14.9a through 14.9l

9 Refer to the accompanying illustrations to remove the linkage **(see illustrations)**.

14.9a 1991 and later YZ125/250 models use a pawl-type shift linkage (YZ125 shown; YZ250 similar); note how the return spring fits over the pin (arrow) . . .

14.9b . . . then disengage the shift shaft and pull it out of the engine . . .

14.9c ... along with the thrust washer

14.9d Note how the roller (arrow) is installed (on 1998 and later YZ250 models, it contacts the upper side of the shift drum cam) ...

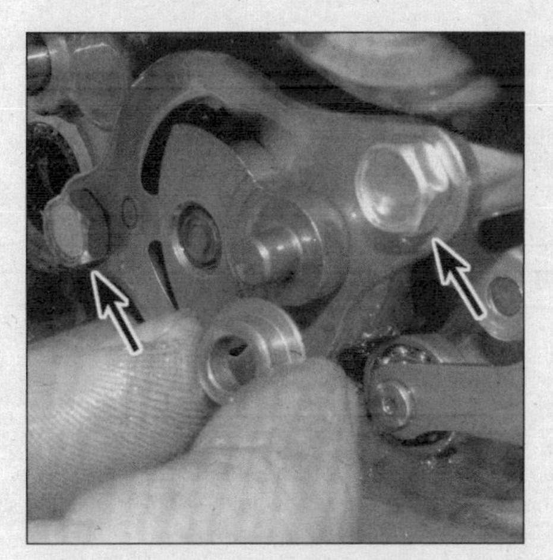

14.9e ... then take it off and remove the shift guide bolts (arrows) ...

14.9f ... and remove the shift guide together with the pawl assembly

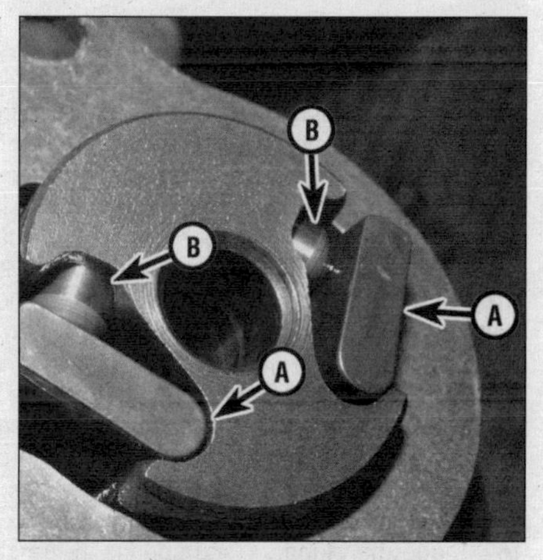

14.9g Note which way the rounded ends of the pawls and plungers face ...

A Pawls B Plungers

Inspection

10 Check the gearshift spindle return spring and splines for damage. The return spring can be replaced separately, but if the splines are damaged the complete shaft must be replaced.

11 Check the condition of the stopper arm and spring. Replace the stopper arm if it's worn where it contacts the shift cam. Replace the spring if it's bent.

12 On models so equipped, inspect the shifter pawls and the shift cam for wear on their contact surfaces. If they're worn or damaged, replace the cam and both pawls. Replace the pawl springs if there's any doubt about their condition.

14.9h ... than separate the pawl assembly from the shift guide ...

14.9i ... and remove the springs and plungers

14.9j On YZ125 and early YZ250 models, note how the stopper lever spring hooks around the lever (1999 and later YZ250 models use a spring attached to the opposite end of the lever from the roller)

Installation

13 If you're working on a YZ80/85 or a 1986 through 1990 YZ125/250, reverse the removal steps to install the gearshift spindle.

14 Install the stopper arm and spring on the crankcase. If you're working on a YZ125 or a 1998 and earlier YZ250, place the straight end of the spring against the cast boss on the crankcase and the hooked end over the stopper arm. If you're working on a 1999 or later YZ250, hook one end of the spring to the arm and the other to the engine. Tighten the stopper arm bolt securely, but don't overtighten it and strip the threads.

15 Pull the stopper arm down and position the shift drum cam on the shift drum, aligning the hole in the back of the cam with the pin on the shift drum. Apply non-permanent thread locking agent to the threads of the bolt, then tighten it to the torque listed in this Chapter's Specifications. Engage the roller end of the stopper arm with the neutral notch in the shift drum cam.

16 Place the plungers and springs in the shifter. Install the pawls, making sure the rounded ends point in the proper direction **(see illustration 14.9g)**. Place the assembly in the guide plate so the guide plate holds it together.

17 Place the drum shifter assembly in the crankcase, engaging the ratchet pawls with the shift drum cam **(see illustration 14.9d).** Tighten the guide plate bolts securely, but don't overtighten them and strip the threads.

18 Place the shifter collar on the drum shifter **(see illustration 14.9e)**.

14.9k Pry the stopper lever down and unbolt the shift cam – on assembly, align its notch with the shift drum pin (arrows)

19 Make sure the thrust washer is in place on the gearshift spindle, then carefully slide the spindle into the crankcase, taking care not to damage the seal on the other side.

20 The remainder of installation is the reverse of the removal steps.

21 Check the transmission oil level and add some, if necessary (see Chapter 1).

15 Kickstarter - removal, inspection and installation

Removal

Pedal

Refer to illustration 15.2

1 The kickstarter pedal is accessible from outside the engine. The kickstarter mechanism can be reached by removing the right crankcase cover (see Section 12).

2 Look for a punch mark on the end of the kickstarter spindle. If you can't see one, make your own to align with the slit in the pedal shaft. Remove the bolt, pinch bolt or nut and slide the pedal off the spindle **(see illustration)**.

Kickstarter mechanism

Refer to illustrations 15.6, 15.7, 15.8, 15.9a and 15.9b

3 Remove the kickstarter pedal (see Step 2).

4 Remove the right crankcase cover (see Section 12).

5 Remove the clutch (see Section 12).

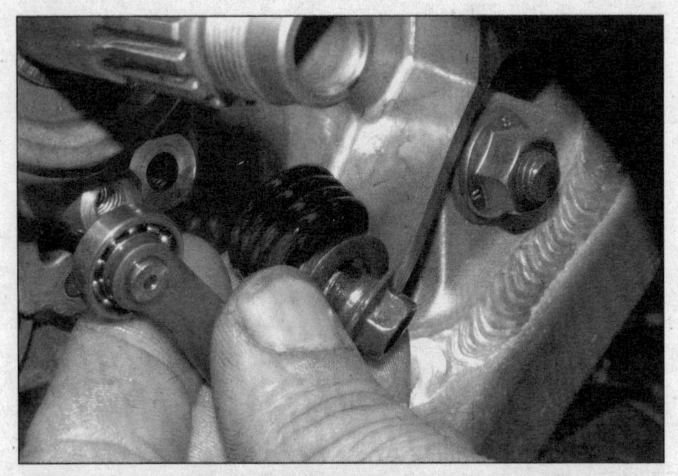

14.9l Unbolt the stopper lever and remove it, together with the spring (YZ125 shown)

15.2 Remove the nut, pinch bolt or bolt (shown) and take the kickstarter pedal off the spindle

15.6 Remove the snap-ring (upper arrow) and washer (if equipped) (lower arrow), then slide the idler gear off its shaft

15.7 Disengage the kickstarter spring from the crankcase and take the assembly off

15.8 Disengage the collar from the kickstarter spring, then remove the collar and spring . . .

6 Remove the snap-ring and washer and slip the idler gear off its shaft **(see illustration)**. If you're working on a 1993 or later YZ80/85 model, remove the thrust washer that's behind the idler gear.

7 Unhook the spring from the crankcase and pull the kickstarter out of the engine **(see illustration)**.

8 Disengage the return spring from the hole in the shaft **(see illustration)**.

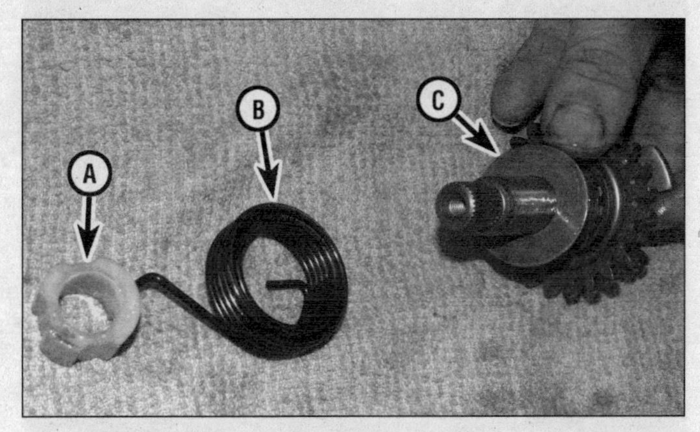

15.9a On YZ125 models, remove the thrust washer . . .

A Collar
B Return spring
C Thrust washer

9 If you're working on a YZ80/85, YZ125 or 1986 through 1998 YZ250, slide off the return spring, collar, and thrust washer, then remove the pinion gear and ratchet spring **(see illustrations)**.

10 If you're working on a 1999 or later YZ250, remove the snap-ring, thrust washer, ratchet spring, ratchet wheel, snap-ring, thrust washer and ratchet gear from the shaft.

Inspection

11 Check all parts for wear or damage, paying special attention to the teeth on the ratchet and the matching teeth on the pinion gear. Replace worn or damaged parts.

Installation

12 Installation is the reverse of the removal steps, with the following addition: Replace any snap-rings that were removed with new ones.

13 Slip the pedal onto the kickstarter spindle, aligning the marks. Install the pinch bolt and tighten it securely.

16 Crankcase - disassembly and reassembly

1 To examine and repair or replace the crankshaft, connecting rod, bearings and transmission components, the crankcase must be split into two parts.

Disassembly

Refer to illustrations 16.10, 16.11a, 16.11b, 16.11c and 16.12

2 Remove the engine from the motorcycle (see Section 6).

15.9b . . . pinion gear and clip (arrow)

16.10 Remove the crankcase bolts (arrows) (YZ125 shown)

16.11a Place the crankcase on a support such as wooden blocks

16.11b Attach a puller so it pushes against the crankshaft and tighten it to push the case halves apart . . .

16.11c . . . watch the case seam (arrow) as the case halves separate to make sure the upper half is not tilting

3 Remove the carburetor, if not already done (see Chapter 3).
4 Remove the alternator rotor (see Chapter 5).
5 Remove the clutch (see Section 12).
6 Remove the external shift mechanism (see Section 14).
7 Remove the cylinder head, cylinder and piston (see Sections 8, 10 and 11).
8 Remove the kickstarter (see Section 15).
9 Check carefully to make sure there aren't any remaining components that attach the halves of the crankcase together.
10 Loosen the crankcase bolts evenly in two or three stages, then remove them **(see illustration)**.
11 Place the crankcase with one side down on a support such as wooden blocks **(see illustration)**. Attach a puller to the crankcase **(see illustration)**. As you slowly tighten the puller, carefully tap the crankcase apart and lift the upper half off the lower half **(see illustration)**. Don't pry against the mating surfaces or they'll develop leaks.
12 Locate the crankcase dowels **(see illustration)**.
13 Refer to Sections 17 through 20 for information on the internal components of the crankcase.

Reassembly

Refer to illustration 16.15

14 Remove all traces of old gasket and sealant from the crankcase mating surfaces with a sharpening stone or similar tool. Be careful not to let any fall into the case as this is done and be careful not to damage the mating surfaces.

16.12 Lift the upper case half off and locate the dowels (arrows)

16.15 Use a new O-ring (arrow) on the large dowel during assembly

17.3a Some bearing retainers are secured with Torx screws (arrows) - you'll need a Torx bit to remove these

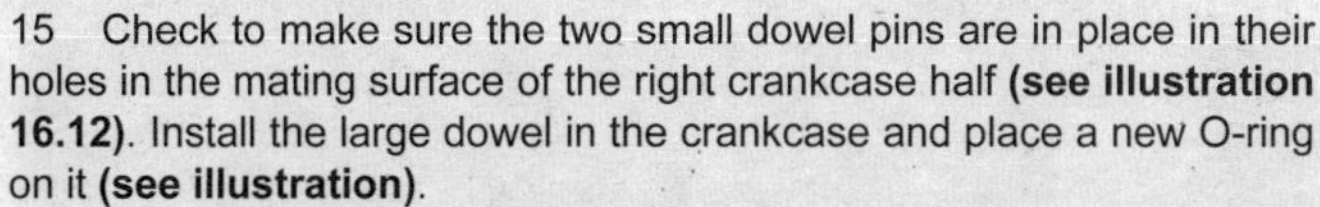

15 Check to make sure the two small dowel pins are in place in their holes in the mating surface of the right crankcase half **(see illustration 16.12)**. Install the large dowel in the crankcase and place a new O-ring on it **(see illustration)**.

16 Pour some transmission oil over the transmission gears. Don't get any oil in the crankshaft cavity or on the crankcase mating surface.

17 Coat the crankcase mating surface with a thin layer of Yamabond or equivalent sealant.

18 Carefully place the upper crankcase half onto the lower crankcase half. While doing this, make sure the transmission shafts, shift drum and crankshaft fit into their bearings in the right crankcase half.

19 Install the crankcase bolts and tighten them so they are just snug. Then tighten them evenly in two or three stages to the torque listed in this Chapter's Specifications.

20 Turn the transmission mainshaft to make sure it turns freely. Also make sure the crankshaft turns freely.

21 The remainder of assembly is the reverse of disassembly.

17 Crankcase components - inspection and servicing

Refer to illustration 17.3a and 17.3b

1 Separate the crankcase and remove the following:

a) *Shift drum and forks (see Section 18).*
b) *Transmission shafts and gears (see Section 19).*
c) *Crankshaft (see Section 20).*

2 Clean the crankcase halves thoroughly with new solvent and dry them with compressed air. All oil passages should be blown out with compressed air and all traces of old gasket should be removed from the mating surfaces. **Caution:** *Be very careful not to nick or gouge the crankcase mating surfaces or leaks will result. Check both crankcase halves very carefully for cracks and other damage.*

3 Check the bearings in the case halves **(see illustrations)**. If the bearings don't turn smoothly, replace them. For bearings which aren't accessible from the outside, a blind hole puller will be needed for removal. Drive the remaining bearings out with a bearing driver or a socket having an outside diameter slightly smaller than that of the bearing outer race. Before installing the bearings, allow them to sit in the freezer overnight, and about fifteen-minutes before installation, place the case half in an oven, set to about 200-degrees F, and allow it to heat up. The bearings are an interference fit, and this will ease installation. **Warning:** *Before heating the case, wash it thoroughly with soap and water so no explosive fumes are present. Also, don't use a flame to heat the case.* Install the ball bearings with a socket or bearing driver that bears against the bearing outer race.

17.3b . . . you'll need a blind hole puller to remove bearings that are not accessible from both sides of the case (arrow)

4 Replace the oil seals whenever the crankcase is disassembled. The crankshaft seals are critical to the performance of two-stroke engines, so they should be replaced whenever the crankcase is disassembled, even if they look perfectly alright.

5 If any damage is found that can't be repaired, replace the crankcase halves as a set.

6 Assemble the case halves (see Section 16) and check to make sure the crankshaft and the transmission shafts turn freely.

18 Shift drum and forks - removal, inspection and installation

1 Refer to Section 16 and separate the crankcase halves.

Removal

Refer to illustrations 18.2a through 18.2f

2 Pull up on each shift rod until it clears the case, then move the

18.2a Note how the shift forks engage the shift drum . . .

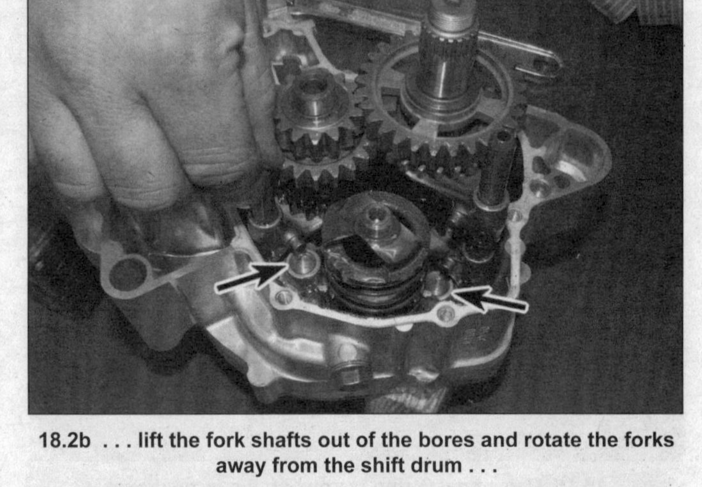

18.2b . . . lift the fork shafts out of the bores and rotate the forks away from the shift drum . . .

18.2c Lift the shift drum out of the crankcase

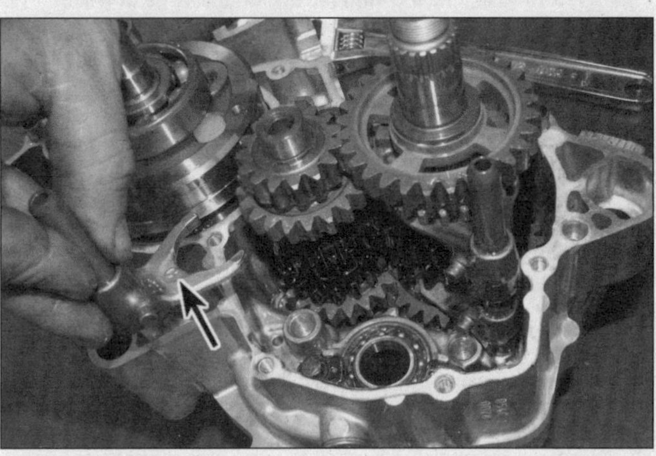

18.2d Lift out the center fork and shaft, noting the letter C on the fork (arrow) . . .

rods and forks away from the gears and shift drum **(see illustrations)**.

3 Lift the shift drum out of the case.

Inspection

Refer to illustrations 18.6a, 18.6b and 18.8

4 Wash all of the components in clean solvent and dry them off.

5 Inspect the shift fork grooves in the gears. If a groove is worn or scored, replace the affected gear (see Section 19) and inspect its corresponding shift fork.

6 Check the shift forks for distortion and wear, especially at the fork fingers **(see illustrations)**. If they are discolored or severely worn they are probably bent. Inspect the guide pins for excessive wear and distortion and replace any defective parts with new ones.

7 Check the shift fork shaft for evidence of wear, galling and other damage. Make sure the shift forks move smoothly on the shaft. If the shaft is worn or bent, replace it with a new one **(see illustration 18.6b)**.

8 Check the edges of the grooves in the drum for signs of excessive wear **(see illustration)**.

18.2e . . . and remove the left fork and shaft, noting the letter L (arrow) . . .

18.2f . . . you may have to remove the transmission shafts to get the right shift fork out of the case

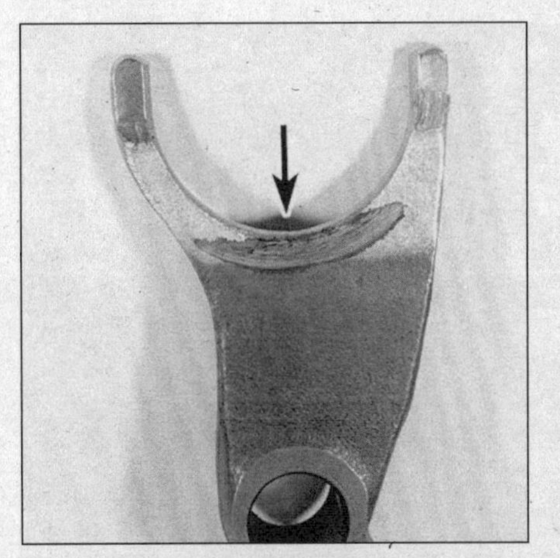

18.6a An arc-shaped burn mark like this means the fork was rubbing against a gear, probably due to bending or worn fork fingers

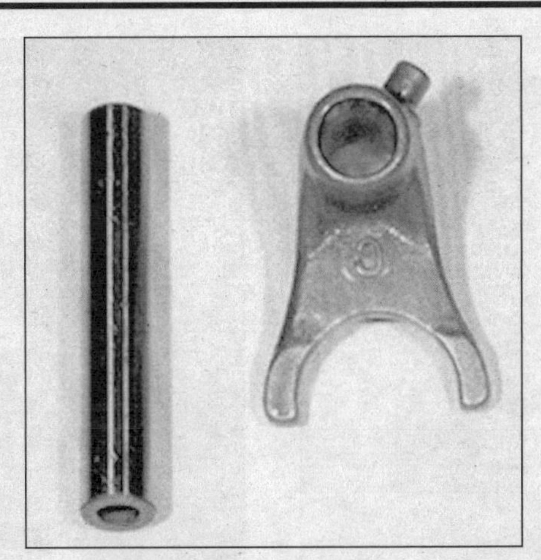

18.6b Inspect the shift fork pins and fingers and inspect the fork shafts

18.8 Check the shift drum grooves for wear, especially at the points; this is where the most friction occurs

9 Spin the shift drum bearing with fingers and replace it if it's rough, loose or noisy.

Installation

10 Installation is the reverse of the removal steps. Refer to the identifying letters (R, C and L) on the forks and make sure they're installed in the correct positions, with the letters facing in the proper direction. Engage the fork fingers with the gear grooves.

19 Transmission shafts - removal, disassembly, inspection, assembly and installation

Note: *When disassembling the transmission shafts, place the parts on a long rod or thread a wire through them to keep them in order and facing the proper direction.*

Removal

Refer to illustration 19.4

1 Remove the engine, then separate the case halves (see Sections 6 and 16).

2 The transmission components remain in the lower case half when the case is separated **(see illustration 18.2a).**

3 Refer to Section 18 and remove the shift drum and forks.

4 Lift the transmission shafts out of the case together, then remove any components that remained in the case **(see illustration)**.

5 Separate the shafts once they're lifted out. If you're not planning to disassemble them right away, reinstall the thrust washers and place a large rubber band over both ends of each shaft so the gears won't slide off.

19.4 Lift the shafts out of the case together

Disassembly

Refer to illustrations 19.6a and 19.6b

6 To disassemble the shafts, remove the snap-rings and slide the gears, bushings and thrust washers off **(see illustrations)**.

19.6a Countershaft details (YZ125 shown; others similar)

19.6b Mainshaft details (YZ125 shown; others similar)

19.10 Inspect the slots (left arrow) and dogs (right arrow) and replace the gears if the corners are rounded off

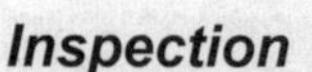

Inspection

Refer to illustration 19.10

7 Wash all of the components in clean solvent and dry them off.

8 Inspect the shift fork grooves in gears so equipped. If a groove is worn or scored, replace the affected gear and inspect its corresponding shift fork.

9 Check the gear teeth for cracking and other obvious damage. Check the bushing or surface in the inner diameter of the freewheeling gears for scoring or heat discoloration. Replace parts that are damaged or worn beyond the limits.

10 Inspect the engagement dogs and dog holes on gears so equipped for excessive wear or rounding off **(see illustration)**. Replace the paired gears as a set if necessary.

11 Check the transmission shafts for wear. If they're visibly worn, replace the shaft(s).

12 Check the gear bushings for wear and replace any that are worn.

13 Inspect the thrust washers. They should be replaced if they show any visible wear or scoring. It's a good idea to replace them whenever the transmission is disassembled.

14 Check the transmission shaft bearings in the crankcase for roughness, looseness or noise and replace them if necessary.

15 Discard the snap-rings and use new ones on reassembly.

19.17 The gears should mesh like this when the shafts are installed in the case (2006 YZ125 shown)

19.16 The snap-ring ends (upper arrows) should be centered on a spline groove (lower arrow)

Assembly and installation

Refer to illustrations 19.16 and 19.17

16 Assembly and installation are the reverse of the removal procedure, but take note of the following points:

- a) *Make sure the snap-rings are securely seated in their grooves, with their rounded sides facing the direction of thrust (toward the gears they hold on the shafts). The ends of the snap rings must fit in raised splines, so the gap in the snap-ring aligns with a spline groove* **(see illustration)**.
- b) *Lubricate the components with engine oil before assembling them.*

17 After assembly, check the gears to make sure they're installed correctly **(see illustration)**.

20 Crankshaft and connecting rod - removal, inspection and installation

Removal

Refer to illustrations 20.1a and 20.1b

Note: *Removal and installation of the crankshaft requires some special tools. If you don't have the necessary equipment or suitable substitutes, have the crankshaft removed and installed by a dealer service department or other qualified shop.*

1 Place the right crankcase half on blocks and remove it with a puller **(see illustration)**. The ball bearing may remain in the crankcase or come out with the crankshaft. If it stays on the crankshaft, remove it with a press and bearing splitter **(see illustration)**. Discard the bearing, no matter what its apparent condition, and use a new one on installation.

Inspection

Refer to illustration 20.2

2 Measure the side clearance between connecting rod and crankshaft with a feeler gauge **(see illustration)**. If it's more than the limit listed in this Chapter's Specifications, replace the crankshaft and connecting rod as an assembly.

3 Check the crankshaft and splines for visible wear or damage, such as step wear of the splines or scoring. If any of these conditions are found, replace the crankshaft and connecting rod as an assembly.

4 Set the crankshaft in a pair of V-blocks, with a dial indicator contacting each end. Rotate the crankshaft and note the runout. If the run-

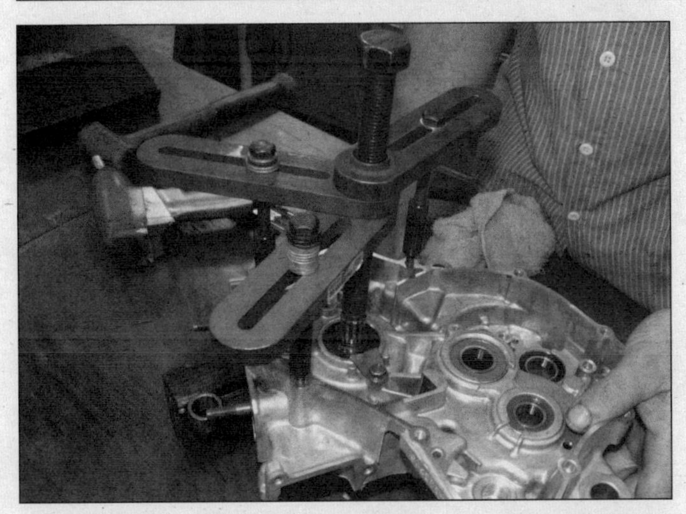

20.1a Set up a puller like this and push the crankshaft out of the crankcase . . .

20.1b If the bearing stays on the crankshaft, remove it with a bearing splitter and a puller

20.2 Check the connecting rod side clearance with a feeler gauge

20.7 Thread the adapter into the end of the crankshaft . . .

20.8 . . . and attach the puller to the adapter

out at either end is beyond the limit listed in this Chapter's Specifications, replace the crankshaft and connecting rod as an assembly.

5 Measure the width from the outside of one crank throw to the outside of the other crank throw. If it's not within the range listed in this Chapter's Specifications, replace the crankshaft and connecting rod as an assembly.

Installation

Refer to illustrations 20.7 and 20.8

6 Pry out the crankshaft seals, then install new ones with a seal driver or a socket the same diameter as the seal.

7 Thread a puller adapter into the end of the crankshaft **(see illustration)**.

8 Install the crankshaft puller and collar on the end of the crankshaft **(see illustration)**.

9 Hold the puller shaft with one wrench and turn the nut with another wrench to pull the crankshaft into the center race of the ball bearing.

10 Remove the special tools from the crankshaft.

11 Installation is the reverse of the removal steps.

21 Recommended start-up and break-in procedure

1 This procedure should be followed each time the piston and ring, cylinder, crankshaft or crankshaft bearings are replaced. Make sure the transmission and controls, especially the brakes, function properly before riding the machine.
2 Place pieces of tape on the throttle twist grip and the handlebar next to it to indicate the half throttle and three-quarter throttle positions.
3 Make sure there is fuel in the tank, then operate the choke.
4 Start the engine and ride for ten minutes, using no more than half throttle. Use the transmission to keep from lugging or over-revving the engine.
5 Shut the engine off and let it cool completely. Once the engine has cooled, ride for another ten minutes, again using no more than half throttle, without lugging or over-revving the engine.
6 Let the engine cool again, then ride for 10 minutes using no more than three-quarters throttle. Again, do not lug or over-rev the engine.
7 Let the engine cool, then ride for three more ten-minute periods, again using no more than three-quarters throttle, letting the engine cool completely between each period.
8 Check carefully for transmission oil and coolant leaks.
9 Upon completion of the break-in rides, and after the engine has cooled down completely, recheck the transmission oil and coolant level (see Chapter 1).

COMMON ENGINE OVERHAUL TERMS

B

Backlash - The amount of play between two parts. Usually refers to how much one gear can be moved back and forth without moving gear with which it's meshed.

Bearing knock - The noise created by movement of a part in a loose or worn bearing.

Blueprinting - Dismantling an engine and reassembling it to EXACT specifications.

Bore - An engine cylinder, or any cylindrical hole; also used to describe the process of enlarging or accurately refinishing a hole with a cutting tool, as to bore an engine cylinder. The bore size is the diameter of the hole.

Boring - Renewing the cylinders by cutting them out to a specified size. A boring bar is used to make the cut.

Bottom end - A term which refers collectively to the engine block, crankshaft, main bearings and the big ends of the connecting rods.

Break-in - The period of operation between installation of new or rebuilt parts and time in which parts are worn to the correct fit. Riding at reduced and varying speed for a specified time to permit parts to wear to the correct fit.

Bushing - A one-piece sleeve placed in a bore to serve as a bearing surface for shaft, piston pin, etc. Usually replaceable.

C

Carbon - Hard, or soft, black deposits found in combustion chamber, on plugs, under rings, on and under valve heads.

Chamfer - To bevel across (or a bevel on) the sharp edge of an object.

Chase - To repair damaged threads with a tap or die.

Combustion chamber - The space between the piston and the cylinder head, with the piston at top dead center, in which air-fuel mixture is burned.

Compression ratio - The relationship between cylinder volume (clearance volume) when the piston is at top dead center and cylinder volume when the piston is at bottom dead center.

Connecting rod - The rod that connects the crank on the crankshaft with the piston. Sometimes called a con rod.

Crankcase - The lower part of the engine in which the crankshaft rotates; includes the transmission.

Crank kit - A reconditioned crankshaft and new main and connecting rod bearings.

Crankpin - The part of a crankshaft to which a connecting rod is attached.

Crankshaft - The main rotating member, or shaft, running the length of the crankcase, with an offset throw to which the connecting rod is attached; changes the reciprocating motion of the piston into rotating motion.

Cylinder sleeve - A replaceable sleeve, or liner, pressed into the cylinder block to form the cylinder bore.

D

Deburring - Removing the burrs (rough edges or areas) from a bearing.

Deglazer - A tool, rotated by an electric motor, used to remove glaze from cylinder walls so a new set of rings will seat.

E

Endplay - The amount of lengthwise movement between two parts. As applied to a crankshaft, the distance that the crankshaft can move forward and back in the cylinder block.

F

Face - A machinist's term that refers to removing metal from the end of a shaft or the face of a larger part, such as a flywheel.

Fatigue - A breakdown of material through a large number of loading and unloading cycles. The first signs are cracks followed shortly by breaks.

Feeler gauge - A thin strip of hardened steel, ground to an exact thickness, used to check clearances between parts.

Free height - The unloaded length or height of a spring.

Freeplay - The looseness in a linkage, or an assembly of parts, between the initial application of force and actual movement. Usually perceived as slop or slight delay.

Freeze plug - See Core plug.

G

Gallery - A large passage in the block that forms a reservoir for engine oil pressure.

Glaze - The very smooth, glassy finish that develops on cylinder walls while an engine is in service.

H

Heli-Coil - A rethreading device used when threads are worn or damaged. The device is installed in a retapped hole to reduce the thread size to the original size.

J

Journal - The surface of a rotating shaft which turns in a bearing.

K

Key - A small piece of metal inserted into matching grooves machined into two parts fitted together - such as a gear pressed onto a shaft - which prevents slippage between the two parts.

Knock - The heavy metallic engine sound, produced in the combustion chamber as a result of abnormal combustion - usually detonation. Knock is usually caused by a loose or worn bearing. Also referred to as detonation, pinging and spark knock. Connecting rod or main bearing knocks are created by too much oil clearance or insufficient lubrication.

L

Lands - The portions of metal between the piston ring grooves.

Lash - The amount of free motion in a gear train, between gears, or in a mechanical assembly, that occurs before movement can begin. Usually refers to the lash in a valve train.

M

Machining - The process of using a machine to remove metal from a metal part.

Main bearings - The bearings that support the crankshaft.

O

O.D. - Outside diameter.

Oil gallery - A pipe or drilled passageway in the engine used to carry engine oil from one area to another.

Oil seal - A seal which keeps oil from leaking out of a compartment. Usually refers to a dynamic seal around a rotating shaft or other moving part.

O-ring - A type of sealing ring made of a special rubberlike material; in use, the O-ring is compressed into a groove to provide the sealing action.

Overhaul - To completely disassemble a unit, clean and inspect all parts, reassemble it with the original or new parts and make all adjustments necessary for proper operation.

P

Pip mark - A little dot or indentation which indicates the top side of a compression ring.

Piston - The cylindrical part, attached to the connecting rod, that moves up and down in the cylinder as the crankshaft rotates. When the fuel charge is fired, the piston transfers the force of the explosion to the connecting rod, then to the crankshaft.

Piston pin (or wrist pin) - The cylindrical and usually hollow steel pin that passes through the piston. The piston pin fastens the piston to the upper end of the connecting rod.

Piston ring - The split ring fitted to the groove in a piston. The ring contacts the sides of the ring groove and also rubs against the cylinder wall, thus sealing space between piston and wall.

Piston ring groove - The slots or grooves cut in piston heads to hold piston rings in position.

Piston skirt - The portion of the piston below the rings and the piston pin hole.

Press-fit - A tight fit between two parts that requires pressure to force the parts together. Also referred to as drive, or force, fit.

Prussian blue - A blue pigment; in solution, useful in determining the area of contact between two surfaces.

R

Race (bearing) - The inner or outer ring that provides a contact surface for balls or rollers in bearing.

Ream - To size, enlarge or smooth a hole by using a round cutting tool with fluted edges.

Ring job - The process of reconditioning the cylinders and installing new rings.

Runout - Wobble. The amount a shaft rotates out-of-true.

S

Scored - Scratched or grooved, as a cylinder wall may be scored by abrasive particles moved up and down by the piston rings.

Scuffing - A type of wear in which there's a transfer of material between parts moving against each other; shows up as pits or grooves in the mating surfaces.

Seat - The surface upon which another part rests or seats. For example, the valve seat is the matched surface upon which the valve face rests. Also used to refer to wearing into a good fit; for example, piston rings seat after a few miles of driving.

Static balance - The balance of an object while it's stationary.

Step - The wear on the lower portion of a ring land caused by excessive side and back-clearance. The height of the step indicates the ring's extra side clearance and the length of the step projecting from the back wall of the groove represents the ring's back clearance.

Stroke - The distance the piston moves when traveling from top dead center to bottom dead center, or from bottom dead center to top dead center.

Stud - A metal rod with threads on both ends.

T

Tang - A lip on the end of a plain bearing used to align the bearing during assembly.

Tap - To cut threads in a hole. Also refers to the fluted tool used to cut threads.

Taper - A gradual reduction in the width of a shaft or hole; in an engine cylinder, taper usually takes the form of uneven wear, more pronounced at the top than at the bottom.

Throw - The offset portion of the crankshaft to which the connecting rod is affixed.

Thrust washer - A bronze or hardened steel washer placed between two moving parts. The washer prevents longitudinal movement and provides a bearing surface for thrust surfaces of parts.

Tolerance - The amount of variation permitted from an exact size of measurement. Actual amount from smallest acceptable dimension to largest acceptable dimension.

U

Undercut - A machined groove below the normal surface.

W

Water jacket - The spaces around the cylinders, between the inner and outer shells of the cylinder block or head, through which coolant circulates.

Web - A supporting structure across a cavity.

Woodruff key - A key with a radiused backside (viewed from the side).

Chapter 3
Cooling system

Contents

Specifications

General

Radiator cap relief pressure	
YZ80/85	
1986	108 kPa (16 psi)
1987 and later	95 to 125 kPa (14 to 18 psi)
YZ125/250	
1986 through 1989	108 kPa (16 psi)
1990 and later	95 to 125 kPa (14 to 18 psi)

Torque specifications

Water pump impeller (removable impeller only)	14 Nm (120 inch-lbs)
Water pump bolts	10 Nm (86 inch-lbs)

1 General information

The motorcycles covered by this manual are equipped with a liquid cooling system which utilizes a water/antifreeze mixture to carry away excess heat produced during combustion. The combustion chamber and cylinder are surrounded by a water jacket, through which the coolant is circulated by the water pump. The pump is mounted to the right side of the crankcase near the front and is driven by a gear. YZ80/85 models use a single radiator; all other models have two radiators. The coolant is pumped through the radiator(s) where it is cooled, then out of the radiator(s) and through the cylinder head and cylinder.

Because these bikes are intended for motocross competition, the cooling system is a very basic one, without a temperature gauge or light, fan, coolant reservoir or thermostat.

2 Radiator cap - check

If problems such as overheating or loss of coolant occur, check the entire system as described in Chapter 1. The radiator cap opening pressure should be checked by a dealer service department or service station equipped with the special tester required to do the job. If the cap is defective, replace it with a new one.

3 Coolant hoses - removal and installation

Refer to illustrations 3.2a, 3.2b and 3.2c

Warning: *The engine must be completely cool before beginning this procedure.*

1 The coolant hoses are all secured by screw-type clamps to fittings on the engine and radiator. On early YZ125/250 models, the hose from the water pump runs to a Y-fitting that branches to the bottoms of both radiators. The hose from the engine runs to a Y-fitting that branches to the tops of both radiators. On later models, the water pump hose runs to the bottom of the right radiator, a connecting hose joins the bottoms of both radiators to each other, and a hose runs from the top of the left radiator back to the engine.

2 To remove a hose, loosen its clamp and carefully pry it off the fitting **(see illustrations)**.

3 If the hose is stuck, pry the edge up slightly with a pointed tool and spray brake or electrical contact cleaner into the gap. Work the tool

3.2a The water pump-to-radiator hose is on the right side (late YZ125 shown)

3.2b The radiators are connected at the bottom by a hose (shown) or by a Y-fitting on early models

around the fitting, lifting the edge of the hose and spraying into the gap until the hose comes free of the fitting.

4 In extreme cases, you may have to slit the hose and cut it off the fitting with a knife. Make sure you can get a replacement hose before doing this.

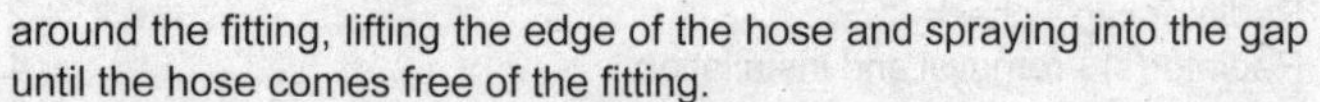

4 Radiator(s) - removal and installation

Warning: *The engine must be completely cool before beginning this procedure.*

Removal

Refer to illustrations 4.2 and 4.4

1 Support the bike securely upright. Remove the radiator shroud(s) (see Chapter 8) and drain the cooling system (see Chapter 1).

2 Remove the grille bolts and separate the grille from the radiator **(see illustration)**.

3 Disconnect the radiator hoses (see Section 3). Note:

4 Remove the radiator mounting bolts **(see illustration 4.2 and the accompanying illustration)**.

5 Lift the radiator away from the frame. Inspect the mounting bolt grommets and replace them if they're worn or deteriorated.

6 Installation is the reverse of the removal steps, with the following additions:

3.2c The radiator-to-engine hose is on the left side

a) *Tighten the mounting bolts securely, but don't overtighten them and distort the grommets.*
b) *Fill the cooling system (see Chapter 1).*
c) *Run the engine and check for coolant leaks.*

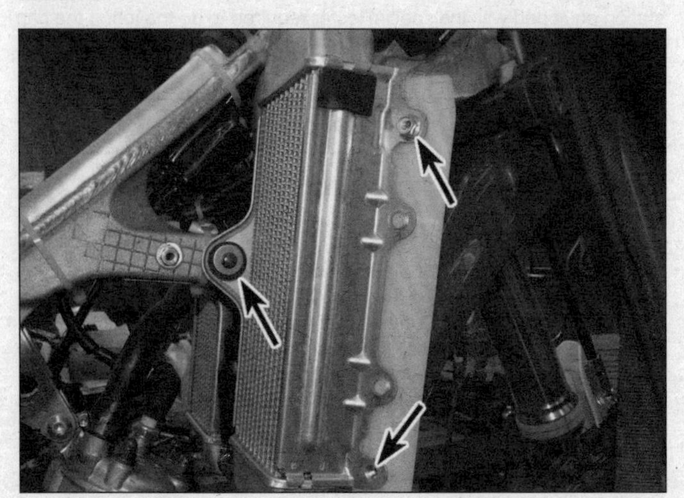
4.2 Remove the grille bolts (right arrows) and the rear mounting bolt (left arrow) . . .

4.4 . . . then detach the grille and remove the front mounting bolts

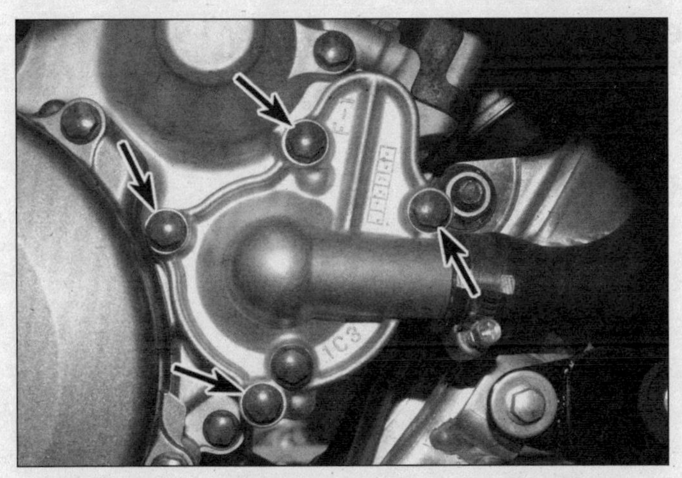

5.3a The water pump is bolted to the lower right part of the engine (this is a YZ125) . . .

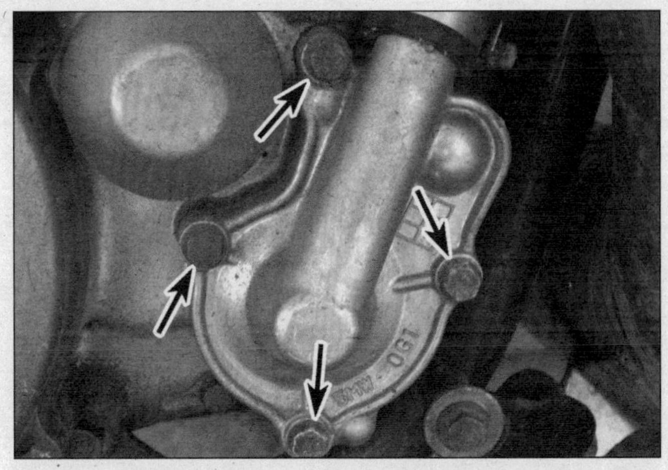

5.3b . . . on later YZ250 models, the lower mounting bolt is also the drain bolt

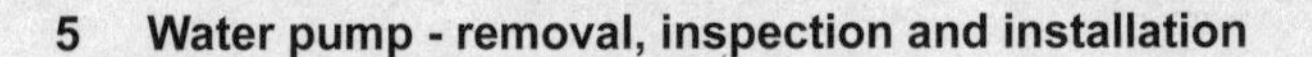

5 Water pump - removal, inspection and installation

Warning: *The engine must be completely cool before beginning this procedure.*

Removal

Refer to illustrations 5.3a, 5.3b and 5.7

1 Drain the cooling system (see Chapter 1).

2 Disconnect the hoses from the water pump.

3 Remove the pump cover bolts **(see illustrations)**. The bolts are different lengths, so tag them for reinstallation.

4 Take off the pump cover and gasket.

5 If you're working on a 2002 or later YZ80/85, or a 1998 or later YZ125/250, unscrew the impeller from its shaft and remove the copper washer. On all other models, the impeller is permanently attached to its shaft, so you'll need to remove the right crankcase cover to remove the impeller.

6 To remove the pump shaft, remove the right crankcase cover together with the shaft (see Chapter 2, Section 12).

7 On models with a permanently attached impeller, remove the circlip, washer, spacer (if equipped) and gear **(see illustration)**. Remove the washer from behind the gear and push the retaining pin out of the impeller shaft.

5.7 On models with a fixed impeller, you'll need to remove the gear from the back side to get the impeller shaft out

A Circlip
B Washer
C Spacer (integral with the gear on some models)
D Water pump gear
E Power valve governor gear (YZ125/250)

8 On all models, pull the impeller shat out of the pump body, twisting it as you remove it to prevent damage to the seal.

Inspection

9 Check the impeller seal for wear or damage. This seal separates the coolant from the oil supply used by the transmission and clutch. If the transmission oil is milky or foamy, coolant may have been leaking into it past the seal. Refer to Section 6 and replace it.

10 To inspect the bearings and impeller driven gear, you'll need to remove the right crankcase cover (see Chapter 2). Wiggle the impeller shaft and check for play. If it can be wiggled from side to side, the bearings need to be replaced. Lift the impeller shaft out of the bearing(s) in the cover. Spin the bearing and check it for roughness, looseness or noise and replace it if any problems are found.

Installation

11 Installation is the reverse of the removal steps, with the following additions:

- a) *Use a new gasket.*
- b) *Engage the water pump gear (and the power valve governor gear on YZ125/250 models) with the primary drive gear* **(see illustration 5.7)**.
- c) *Tighten the water pump bolts to the torque listed in this Chapter's Specifications.*
- d) *Fill the cooling system (see Chapter 1). If the right crankcase cover was removed, fill the transmission with the proper type of oil (see Chapter 1).*
- e) *Run the engine and check for coolant leaks.*

6 Water pump seal and bearings - replacement

1 If coolant has been leaking from the weep hole (see Chapter 1), the water pump seal(s) needs to be replaced.

2 Remove the right crankcase cover (Chapter 2) and the water pump impeller shaft (see Section 5).

3 Some models are equipped with a ball bearing, mounted in the right crankcase cover. Remove the bearing with a slide hammer and bearing puller attachment. Drive in a new bearing with a bearing driver or socket that bears against the bearing outer race.

4 Pry the seal out of its bore. Install a new one with a bearing driver or a socket the same diameter as the seal. The WATER SIDE mark (if equipped) faces outward (away from the engine when the crankcase cover is mounted on the engine).

5 The remainder of installation is the reverse of removal. Refill the cooling system with the proper type of antifreeze, and the transmission with the proper type of oil (see Chapter 1).

Notes

Chapter 4
Fuel and exhaust systems

Contents

Specifications

General

Fuel type .... See Chapter 1

Carburetor (YZ80)

1986 through 1992

Type	Mikuni VM26SS
ID mark	1LR00
Main jet	280
Air jet	1.0
Needle/clip position	5H22-3
Needle jet	Q-2
Pilot jet	35
Standard air screw setting	1-3/4 turns out
Starter jet	40
Float height	20 to 22 mm (0.79 +/- 0.87 inch)

1993

Type	Mikuni VM26SS
ID mark	4ES00
Main jet	270
Air jet	1.0
Needle/clip position	5H22-3
Needle jet	Q-2
Pilot jet	35
Standard air screw setting	1-3/4 turns out
Starter jet	40
Float height	20 to 22 mm (0.79 +/- 0.87 inch)

Carburetor (YZ80) (continued)

1994 through 1996

Type	Mikuni VM26SS
ID mark	4ES01
Main jet	290
Air jet	1.0
Needle/clip position	5H22-4
Needle jet	Q-2
Pilot jet	35
Standard air screw setting	1-3/4 turns out
Starter jet	40
Float height	20 to 22 mm (0.79 +/- 0.87 inch)

1997 through 2001

Type	Mikuni VM26SS
ID mark	4ES10
Main jet	300
Air jet	1.0
Needle/clip position	5H22-3
Needle jet	Q-2
Pilot jet	32.5
Standard air screw setting	1-3/4 turns out
Starter jet	40
Float height	20 to 22 mm (0.79 +/- 0.87 inch)

Carburetor (PW85)

2002 and later

Type	Keihin PWK28
ID mark	5PA 00
Main jet	128
Needle/clip position	NBKF-2
Pilot jet	45
Standard air screw setting	2 turns out
Starter jet	62
Float height	18 to 20 mm (0.71 +/- 0.79 inch)

Carburetor (YZ125)

1986

Type	Mikuni TM34SS
ID mark	1LX00
Main jet	270
Needle/clip position	7DJ1-3
Needle jet	P-8
Pilot jet	40
Standard air screw setting	1-3/4 turns out
Starter jet	80
Float height	9.5 +/- 1.0 mm (0.374 +/- 0.04 inch)

1987

Type	Mikuni TM34SS
ID mark	2HG00
Main jet	270
Needle/clip position	7DJ1-2
Needle jet	Q-2
Pilot jet	50
Standard air screw setting	1-3/4 turns out
Starter jet	80
Float height	11 to 13 mm (0.374 +/- 0.04 inch)
Fuel level	1.5 to 2.5 mm (0.06 to 0.10 inch)

1988

Type	Mikuni TM34SS
ID mark	2VN00
Main jet	270
Needle/clip position	7DJ1-2
Needle jet	Q-2
Pilot jet	50
Standard air screw setting	1-3/4 turns out
Starter jet	80
Float height	11 to 13 mm (0.374 +/- 0.04 inch)
Fuel level	1.5 to 2.5 mm (0.06 to 0.10 inch)

1989

Type	Mikuni TM35SS

ID mark	3JD00
Main jet	280
Needle/clip position	6EN15-55-2
Needle jet	R-1
Pilot jet	20
Standard air screw setting	1 turn out
Starter jet	80
Float arm height	15.2 to 17.2 mm (0.60 +/- 0.68 inch)
1990	
Type	Mikuni TM35SS
ID mark	3SR00
Main jet	310
Needle/clip position	6EN15-56-3
Needle jet	R-1
Pilot jet	20
Standard air screw setting	1-1/2 turns out
Starter jet	80
Float arm height	15.2 to 17.2 mm (0.60 +/- 0.68 inch)
1991	
Type	Mikuni TM35SS
ID mark	
All except Europe	3XJ00
Europe	3XJ10
Main jet	330
Needle/clip position	
All except Europe	6EN15-55-3
Europe	6EN15-54-4
Needle jet	R-1
Pilot jet	20
Standard air screw setting	
All except Europe	1-1/2 +/- 1/4 turns out
Europe	1-3/4 +/- 1/4 turns out
Starter jet	80
Float arm height	15.2 to 17.2 mm (0.60 +/- 0.68 inch)
1992	
Type	Mikuni TM35SS
ID mark	
All except Europe	4DB00
Europe	4DB10
Main jet	330
Needle/clip position	6EN15-56-3
Needle jet	R-1
Pilot jet	20
Standard air screw setting	
All except Europe	1-1/2 +/- 1/4 turns out
Europe	1-3/4 +/- 1/4 turns out
Starter jet	80
Float arm height	15.2 to 17.2 mm (0.60 +/- 0.68 inch)
1993	
Type	Mikuni TM35SS
ID mark	4EX10
Main jet	330
Needle/clip position	6EN15-56-3
Needle jet	R-1
Pilot jet	20
Standard air screw setting	
All except Europe	1-1/2 +/- 1/4 turns out
Europe	1-3/4 +/- 1/4 turns out
Starter jet	80
Float arm height	15.2 to 17.2 mm (0.60 +/- 0.68 inch)
1994	
Type	Mikuni TM35SS
ID mark	4JY10
Main jet	320
Needle/clip position	6EJ35-59-3
Needle jet	R-1
Pilot jet	15
Standard air screw setting	1-7/8 +/- 1/4 turns out
Starter jet	80
Float arm height	15.2 to 17.2 mm (0.60 +/- 0.68 inch)

Carburetor (YZ125) (continued)

1995	
Type	Mikuni TMX36SS
ID mark	
All except Europe	4PE00
Europe	4PE10
Main jet	
All except Europe	360
Europe	370
Needle/clip position	6EG36-63-3
Needle jet	
All except Europe	Q-9
Europe	R-0
Pilot jet	
All except Europe	55
Europe	50
Standard air screw setting	
All except Europe	2 turns out
Europe	1-3/4 turns out
Starter jet	80
Float arm height	14.5 to 15.5 mm (0.60 +/- 0.68 inch)
1996	
Type	Mikuni TMX36SS
ID mark	4SS00
Main jet	350
Needle/clip position	6BRG9-69-3
Needle jet	S-9
Pilot jet	55
Standard air screw setting	1-3/4 turns out
Starter jet	80
Float arm height	14.5 to 15.5 mm (0.60 +/- 0.68 inch)
1997	
Type	Mikuni TMX36SS
ID mark	
All except Europe	XM400
Europe	XM410
Main jet	350
Needle/clip position	
All except Europe	6BEG9-69-2
Europe	6BEG9-69-3
Needle jet	S-9
Pilot jet	
All except Europe	50
Europe	55
Standard air screw setting	
All except Europe	1-1/2 turns out
Europe	1-3/4 turns out
Starter jet	80
Fuel level	3.5 to 4.5 mm (0.14 +/- 0.18 inch)
1998	
Type	Mikuni TMX36SS
ID mark	5HD10
Main jet	350
Needle/clip position	6BEF16-69-4
Needle jet	S-9
Pilot jet	45
Standard air screw setting	2-1/4 turns out
Starter jet	80
Fuel level	3.5 to 4.5 mm (0.14 +/- 0.18 inch)
1999	
Type	Mikuni TMXX36SS
ID mark	
All except Europe	5ET00
Europe	5ET10
Main jet	350
Needle/clip position	
All except Europe	6DHY53-76-3
Europe	6DHD52-76-4

Pilot jet	
All except Europe	45
Europe	50
Standard air screw setting	
All except Europe	1-3/4 turns out
Europe	1-1/4 turns out
Starter jet	80
Fuel level	11.5 to 12.5 mm (0.14 +/- 0.18 inch)
2000	
Type	Mikuni TMXX36SS
ID mark	
All except Europe	5HD00
Europe	5HD10
Main jet	
All except Europe	350
Europe	380
Needle/clip position	
All except Europe	6DHY53-75-3
Europe	6DHD56-75-3
Pilot jet	35
Standard air screw setting	
All except Europe	1-1/2 turns out
Europe	1-3/4 turns out
Starter jet	80
Fuel level	12.5 to 13.5 mm (0.49 +/- 0.53 inch)
2001	
Type	Mikuni TMXX38SS
ID mark	
All except Europe	5MV1 00
Europe	5MV2 10
Main jet	
All except Europe	460
Europe	450
Needle/clip position	
All except Europe	6BGK79-75-3
Europe	6BHY1-75-3
Pilot jet	
All except Europe	25
Europe	30
Standard air screw setting	
All except Europe	1-1/4 turns out
Europe	1-1/2 turns out
Starter jet	80
Fuel level	13.5 to 14.5 mm (0.53 +/- 0.57 inch)
2002	
Type	Mikuni TMXX38SS
ID mark	
All except Europe	5NY1 00
Europe	5NY2 10
Main jet	
All except Europe	420
Europe	430
Needle/clip position	
All except Europe	6CHY5-79-3
Europe	6CHY5-77-3
Pilot jet	30
Standard air screw setting	
All except Europe	2-1/2 turns out
Europe	1-3/4 turns out
Starter jet	80
Fuel level	
All except Europe	9.5 to 10.5 mm (0.37 +/- 0.41 inch)
Europe	11.5 to 12.5 mm (0.45 +/- 0.49 inch)
2003	
Type	Mikuni TMXX38SS
ID mark	
All except Europe	5UN1 00
Europe	5UN2 10
Main jet	410

Carburetor (YZ125) (continued)

Needle/clip position	
All except Europe	6CHY6-82-3
Europe	6CHY6-82-4
Pilot jet	40
Standard air screw setting	
All except Europe	2 turns out
Europe	1-1/2 turns out
Starter jet	80
Fuel level	9.5 to 10.5 mm (0.37 +/- 0.41 inch)
2004	
Type	Mikuni TMXX38SS
ID mark	
All except Europe	5XE1 00
Europe	5XE2 10
Main jet	410
Needle/clip position	
All except Europe	6CHY6-81-3
Europe	6CHY6-80-3
Pilot jet	
All except Europe	40
Europe	37.5
Standard air screw setting	
All except Europe	2 turns out
Europe	1-1/2 turns out
Starter jet	80
Fuel level	9.5 to 10.5 mm (0.37 +/- 0.41 inch)
2005	
Type	Mikuni TMXX38SS
ID mark	
All except Europe	1C31 00
Europe	1C32 10
Main jet	410
Needle/clip position	6CHY5-80-4
Pilot jet	40
Standard air screw setting	2-1/4 turns out
Starter jet	80
Fuel level	9.5 to 10.5 mm (0.37 +/- 0.41 inch)
2006	
Type	Mikuni TMXX38SS
ID mark	
US and Canada	1 C35 30
Europe	1 C36 40
Australia, New Zealand, South Africa	1 C37 50
Main jet	
US and Canada	410
All except US and Canada	430
Needle/clip position	
US and Canada	6BFY42-74-3
All except US and Canada	6BFY43-74-3
Pilot jet	
All except Europe	40
Europe	45
Standard air screw setting	2-1/4 turns out
Starter jet	80
Fuel level	9.5 to 10.5 mm (0.37 +/- 0.41 inch)

Carburetor (YZ250)

1986	
Type	Mikuni VM38SS
ID mark	1LU00
Main jet	340
Needle/clip position	6F16-2
Needle jet	Q-4
Pilot jet	40
Standard air screw setting	2-1/4 turns out
Starter jet	90
Float height	26.0 to 28.0 mm (1.02 +/- 1.10 inch)

1987	
Type	Mikuni VM38SS
ID mark	52HH00
Main jet	350
Needle/clip position	6F16-2
Needle jet	Q-4
Pilot jet	30
Standard air screw setting	2 turns out
Starter jet	90
Float height	26.0 to 28.0 mm (1.02 +/- 1.10 inch)
1988	
Type	Mikuni VM38SS
ID mark	2VM00
Main jet	370
Needle/clip position	6F62-2
Needle jet	R-4
Pilot jet	45
Standard air screw setting	1-1/2 turns out
Starter jet	90
Float height	26.0 to 28.0 mm (1.02 +/- 1.10 inch)
1989	
Type	Mikuni TM38SS
ID mark	3JE00
Main jet	340
Needle/clip position	6DJ8-63-3
Needle jet	R-1
Pilot jet	60
Standard air screw setting	1-1/2 turns out
Starter jet	80
Float arm height	15.2 to 17.2 mm (0.60 +/- 0.68 inch)
1990	
Type	Mikuni TM38SS
ID mark	3SP10
Main jet	370
Needle/clip position	6DJ8-60-3
Needle jet	R-1
Pilot jet	40
Standard air screw setting	1-3/4 turns out
Starter jet	80
Float arm height	15.2 to 17.2 mm (0.60 +/- 0.68 inch)
1991	
Type	Mikuni TM38SS
ID mark	
All except Europe	3XK00
Europe	3XK10
Main jet	
All except Europe	330
Europe	340
Needle/clip position	
All except Europe	6DJ8-61-4
Europe	6DJ8-60-4
Needle jet	R-1
Pilot jet	45
Standard air screw setting	
All except Europe	1-3/4 turns out
Europe	1-1/2 turns out
Starter jet	80
Float arm height	15.2 to 17.2 mm (0.60 to 0.68 inch)
1992	
Type	Mikuni TM38SS
ID mark	
All except Europe	4DA00
Europe	4DA10
Main jet	350
Needle/clip position	
All except Europe	6EJ33-31-3
Europe	6DJ8-57-4
Needle jet	R-1
Pilot jet	45

Carburetor (YZ250) (continued)

Standard air screw setting	
All except Europe	1-1/2 turns out
Europe	1 turn out
Starter jet	80
Float arm height	15.2 to 17.2 mm (0.60 +/- 0.68 inch)
1993	
Type	Mikuni TM38SS
ID mark	
All except Europe, Australia, New Zealand	4EW00
Europe, Australia, New Zealand	4EW10
Main jet	
All except Europe, Australia, New Zealand	350
Europe, Australia, New Zealand	370
Needle/clip position	
All except Europe, Australia, New Zealand	6EJ33-61-3
Europe, Australia, New Zealand	6EJ33-61-4
Needle jet	R-1
Pilot jet	50
Standard air screw setting	1-3/4 +/- 1/4 turns out
Starter jet	80
Float arm height	15.2 to 17.2 mm (0.60 +/- 0.68 inch)
1994	
Type	Mikuni TM38SS
ID mark	
All except Europe	4JX00
Europe	4EW10
Main jet	
All except Europe	350
Europe	370
Needle/clip position	6EJ33-61-4
Needle jet	R-1
Pilot jet	
All except Europe	40
Europe	45
Standard air screw setting	
All except Europe	1-3/4 +/- 1/4 turns out
Europe	1-1/4 +/- 1/4 turns out
Starter jet	80
Float arm height	15.2 to 17.2 mm (0.60 +/- 0.68 inch)
1995	
Type	Keihin PWK38
ID mark	
All except Europe	4MX00
Europe	4MX10
Main jet	
All except Europe	175
Europe	180
Needle/clip position	
All except Europe	R1367K-3
Europe	R1367K-4
Needle jet	2.9
Pilot jet	48
Standard air screw setting	1-1/4 turns out
Starter jet	85
Float arm height	15 to 17 mm (0.59 +/- 0.69 inch)
1996	
Type	Keihin PWM38
ID mark	4SR00
Main jet	175
Needle/clip position	N3CD-3
Needle jet	2.9
Pilot jet	42
Standard air screw setting	1-1/2 turns out
Starter jet	85
Float arm height	5.5 to 7.5 mm (0.22 +/- 0.30 inch)
1997	
Type	Keihin PWM38

ID mark	
All except Europe, Australia, New Zealand	4XL10
Europe, Australia, New Zealand	4XL00
Main jet	170
Main air jet	200
Needle/clip position	
All except Europe, Australia, New Zealand	N3VG-3
Europe, Australia, New Zealand	N4DG-3
Needle jet	2.9
Pilot jet	
All except Europe, Australia, New Zealand	50
Europe, Australia, New Zealand	48
Standard air screw setting	1-3/4 turns out
Starter jet	85
Float arm height	5.5 to 7.5 mm (0.22 +/- 0.30 inch)
1998	
Type	Keihin PWM38
ID mark	
All except Europe	5JD00
Europe	5JD10
Main jet	172
Main air jet	200
Needle/clip position	
All except Europe	N3VF-3
Europe	N4AF-3
Needle jet	2.9
Pilot jet	
All except Europe	48
Europe	52
Standard air screw setting	
All except Europe	1-3/4 turns out
Europe	1-1/4 turns out
Starter jet	85
Float arm height	5.5 to 7.5 mm (0.22 +/- 0.30 inch)
1999	
Type	Keihin PWM38
ID mark	
All except Europe	5CU00
Europe	5CU10
Main jet	172
Main air jet	200
Needle/clip position	
All except Europe	N3VF-2
Europe	N4DE-3
Needle jet	2.9
Pilot jet	
All except Europe	50
Europe	52
Standard air screw setting	1 turn out
Starter jet	85
Power jet	80
Float arm height	5.5 to 7.5 mm (0.22 +/- 0.30 inch)
2000	
Type	Keihin PWM38
ID mark	
All except Europe	5HC00
Europe	5HC10
Main jet	175
Main air jet	200
Needle/clip position	N3CW-3
Needle jet	2.9
Pilot jet	
All except Europe	50
Europe	55
Standard air screw setting	1 turn out
Starter jet	85
Power jet	55
Float arm height	5.5 to 7.5 mm (0.22 +/- 0.30 inch)

Carburetor (YZ250) (continued)

2001	
Type	Keihin PWM38
ID mark	
All except Europe	5MW00
Europe	5MW10
Main jet	
All except Europe	178
Europe	180
Main air jet	200
Needle/clip position	
All except Europe	N3EJ-2
Europe	N3CW-3
Needle jet	2.9
Pilot jet	
All except Europe	50
Europe	55
Standard air screw setting	
All except Europe	1 turn out
Europe	1-3/4 turn out
Starter jet	85
Power jet	
All except Europe	55
Europe	50
Float arm height	5.5 to 7.5 mm (0.22 +/- 0.30 inch)
2002	
Type	Keihin PWK38S
ID mark	
All except Europe	5NX1 00
Europe	5NX2 10
Main jet	
All except Europe	178
Europe	175
Needle/clip position	
All except Europe	N3EJ-2
Europe	N3CW-3
Pilot jet	
All except Europe	50
Europe	52
Standard air screw setting	
All except Europe	1 turn out
Europe	1-3/8 turns out
Starter jet	85
Power jet	50
Float arm height	5.5 to 7.5 mm (0.22 +/- 0.30 inch)
2003	
Type	Keihin PWK38S
ID mark	
All except Europe	5NX1 00
Europe	5UP2 10
Main jet	
All except Europe	178
Europe	180
Needle/clip position	
All except Europe	N3EJ-2
Europe	N3EW-3
Pilot jet	
All except Europe	50
Europe	52
Standard air screw setting	
All except Europe	1 turn out
Europe	7/8 turn out
Starter jet	85
Power jet	50
Float arm height	5.5 to 7.5 mm (0.22 +/- 0.30 inch)
2004	
Type	Keihin PWK38S

ID mark	
All except Europe	5NX1 00
Europe	5UP2 10
Main jet	
All except Europe	178
Europe	180
Needle/clip position	
All except Europe	N3EJ-2
Europe	N3EW-3
Pilot jet	
All except Europe	50
Europe	52
Standard air screw setting	
All except Europe	1 turn out
Europe	7/8 turn out
Starter jet	85
Power jet	50
Float arm height	5.5 to 7.5 mm (0.22 +/- 0.30 inch)
2005	
Type	Keihin PWK38S
ID mark	
All except Europe	1P81 00
Europe	1P82 10
Main jet	
All except Europe	178
Europe	180
Needle/clip position	
All except Europe	N3EJ-2
Europe	N3EW-3
Pilot jet	
All except Europe	50
Europe	52
Standard air screw setting	
All except Europe	1 turn out
Europe	7/8 turn out
Starter jet	85
Power jet	50
Float arm height	5.5 to 7.5 mm (0.22 +/- 0.30 inch)
2006	
Type	Keihin PWK38S
ID mark	
US and Canada	1P85 30
Australia, New Zealand, South Africa	1P86 40
Europe	1P87 50
Main jet	
All except Europe	178
Europe	180
Needle/clip position	
US and Canada	N3EJ-2
Australia, New Zealand, South Africa	N3EW-3
Europe	N3EW-2
Pilot jet	
All except Europe	50
Europe	52
Standard air screw setting	
US and Canada	1 turn out
Australia, New Zealand, South Africa	1-1/4 turns out
Europe	2-1/ turns out
Starter jet	85
Power jet	50
Float arm height	5.5 to 7.5 mm (0.22 +/- 0.30 inch)

2.2 Squeeze the ends of the clamp together, slide it down the hose, then disconnect the fuel line from the tap

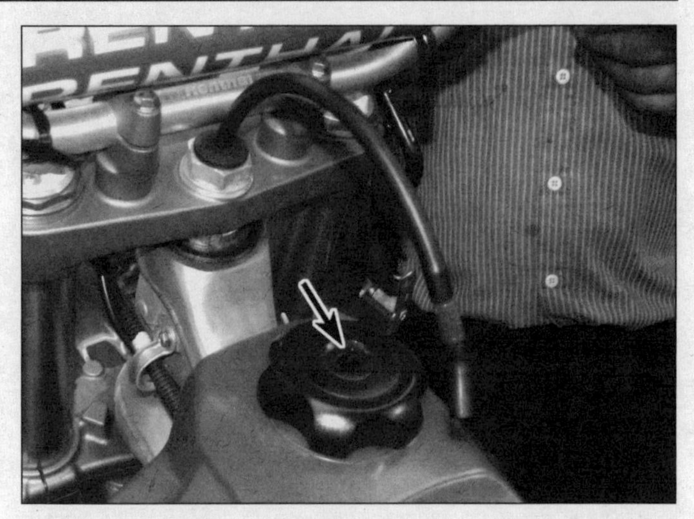

2.3a Pull the vent hose off of the tank fitting or out of the steering stem nut

1 General information

All models use the slide carburetor design, in which the slide acts as the throttle valve. Early YZ80 and YZ250 models use a round slide; all others use a flat slide or modified flat slide. For cold starting on all models, a choke plunger is actuated by a knob.

The exhaust system consists of an expansion chamber and muffler with a replaceable core. All YZ125/250 models have a power valve, which is a means of varying the effective exhaust port timing to provide the ideal amount of exhaust flow at each end of the powerband. Early bikes use a rotary valve mounted in an integral cast housing at the front of the cylinder. Later models use one or two sliding gates in the exhaust port. The power valve on all models so equipped is actuated by a centrifugal governor.

2 Fuel tank - removal and installation

Warning: *Gasoline is extremely flammable, so take extra precautions when you work on any part of the fuel system. Don't smoke or allow open flames or bare light bulbs near the work area, and don't work in a garage where a gas-type appliance (such as a water heater or clothes dryer) is present. Since gasoline is carcinogenic, wear nitrile gloves when there's a possibility of being exposed to fuel, and, if you spill any fuel on your skin, rinse it off immediately with soap and water. Mop up any spills immediately and do not store fuel-soaked rags where they could ignite. When you perform any kind of work on the fuel system, wear safety glasses and have an extinguisher suitable for a class B type fire (flammable liquids) on hand.*

Removal

Refer to illustrations 2.2, 2.3a, 2.3b and 2.4

1 Remove the seat and side covers (see Chapter 8).

2 Turn the fuel tap to Off and disconnect the fuel line.

3 Pull the fuel tank vent hose off the fitting on the filler cap **(see illustration)**. Unhook the strap from the rear of the tank **(see illustration)**.

4 Unbolt the front end of the fuel tank **(see illustration)**. Lift the fuel tank off the bike together with the fuel tap.

Installation

Refer to illustration 2.6a, 2.6b, 2.7a and 2.7b

6 Before installing the tank, check the condition of the rubber mounting bushings at the front, the isolators on the frame and the rubber strap at the rear - if they're hardened, cracked, or show any other signs of

2.3b Note how the ends of the tank strap are shaped (one is designed for the button on the tank and the other for the hook on the frame), then unhook the strap . . .

2.4 Remove the mounting bolt(s) at the front of the tank

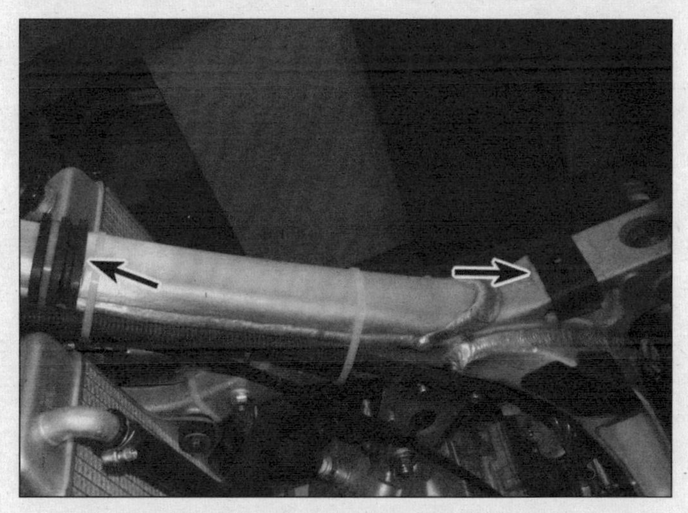

2.6a Check for deteriorated or damaged isolators on the frame (arrows) . . .

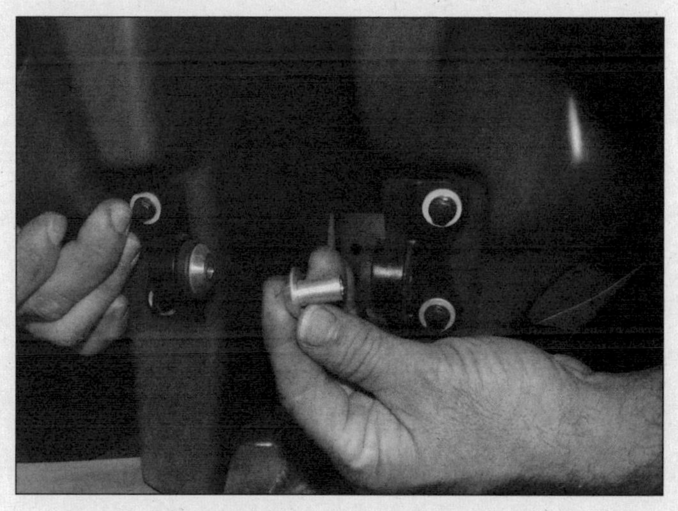

2.6b . . . and inspect the tank bushings

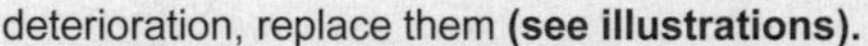

deterioration, replace them **(see illustrations).**

7 When installing the tank, reverse the removal procedure. The rubber tab on the retaining strap goes under the tank **(see illustration)**. The arrow on the one-way valve in the vent hose points toward the tank **(see illustration)**. Make sure the tank does not pinch any wires. Tighten the tank mounting bolts securely, but don't overtighten them and strip the threads.

3 Carburetor overhaul - general information

1 Poor engine performance, hesitation, hard starting, stalling, flooding and backfiring are all signs that major carburetor maintenance may be required.

2 Keep in mind that many so-called carburetor problems are really not carburetor problems at all, but mechanical problems within the engine or ignition system malfunctions. Try to establish for certain that the carburetor is in need of maintenance before beginning a major overhaul.

3 Check the fuel tap and its strainer screen, the fuel lines, the intake manifold clamps, the O-ring between the intake manifold and cylinder head, the vacuum hoses, the air filter element, the cylinder compression, crankcase vacuum and compression, the spark plug and the ignition timing before assuming that a carburetor overhaul is required. If the bike has been unused for more than 24 hours, drain the float chamber and refill the tank with fresh fuel.

4 Most carburetor problems are caused by dirt particles, varnish and other deposits which build up in and block the fuel and air passages. Also, in time, gaskets and O-rings shrink or deteriorate and cause fuel and air leaks which lead to poor performance.

5 When the carburetor is overhauled, it is generally disassembled completely and the parts are cleaned thoroughly with a carburetor cleaning solvent and dried with filtered, unlubricated compressed air. The fuel and air passages are also blown through with compressed air to force out any dirt that may have been loosened but not removed by the solvent. Once the cleaning process is complete, the carburetor is reassembled using new gaskets, O-rings and, generally, a new inlet needle valve and seat.

6 Before disassembling the carburetor, make sure you have the necessary gasket, O-rings and other parts, some carburetor cleaner, a supply of rags, some means of blowing out the carburetor passages and a clean place to work.

4 Carburetor - removal and installation

Warning: *Gasoline is extremely flammable, so take extra precautions when you work on any part of the fuel system. See the* **Warning** *in Section 2.*

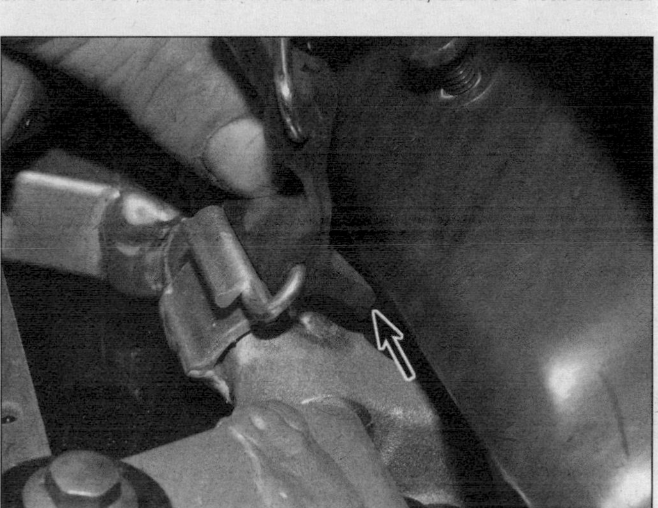

2.7a The tab on the retaining strap goes between the tank and frame (arrow)

2.7b The arrow on the one-way valve points toward the tank

4.4a Loosen the clamps (arrows); then free the carburetor from the air cleaner housing . . .

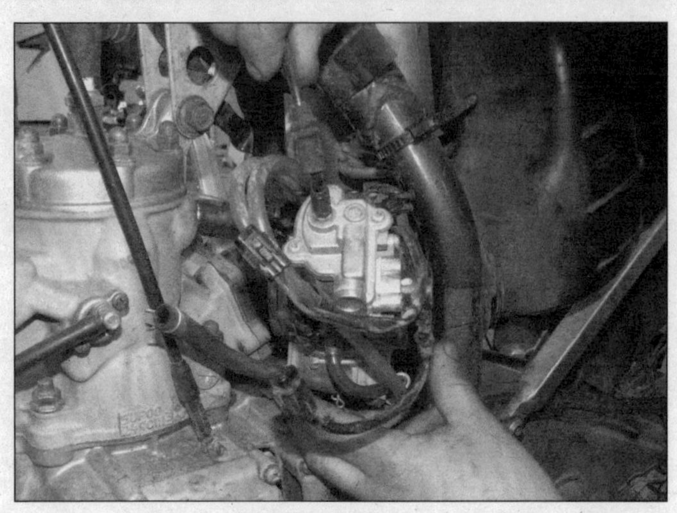

4.4b . . . and pull it out with the throttle cable still connected

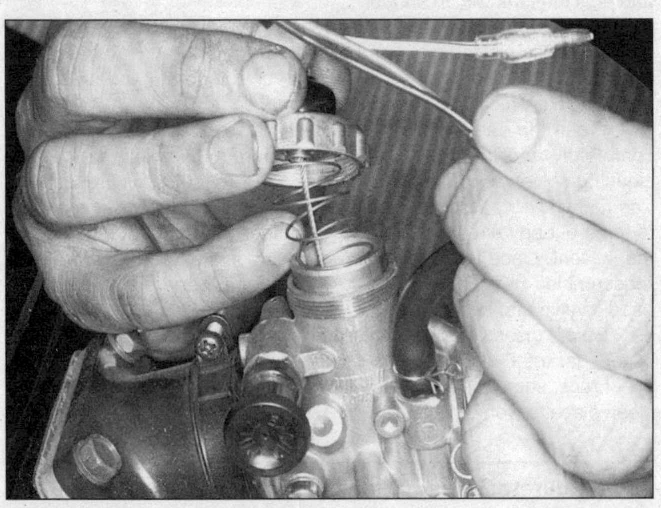

4.5 If the carburetor has a round cap, unscrew it and pull out the jet needle, spring and throttle valve

Removal

Refer to illustrations 4.4a, 4.4b, 4.5, 4.6a, 4.6b and 4.7

1 Remove the seat and both side covers (see Chapter 8).

2 Where necessary for access, remove the fuel tank. If there's room to remove the carburetor with the fuel tank installed, disconnect the fuel line from the tap (see Section 2).

3 On models equipped with a throttle position sensor, disconnect the electrical connector(s).

4 Loosen the carburetor clamps and work the rear end of the carburetor out of the air cleaner housing **(see illustration)**. Free the carburetor from the intake tube and take it out of the bike, with the throttle cable still attached **(see illustration)**.

5 If the carburetor has a round cap, unscrew it and lift it off, together with the spring, jet needle and throttle piston **(see illustration)**.

6 If the carburetor has a flat cap, remove the screws and lift the cap off the carburetor, together with the spring, jet needle and throttle piston **(see illustrations)**.

7 Compress the spring and spring seat against the carburetor cap with your hand. While holding the spring in this position, slip the end of the throttle cable out of the groove in the throttle piston or cable holder **(see illustrations)**.

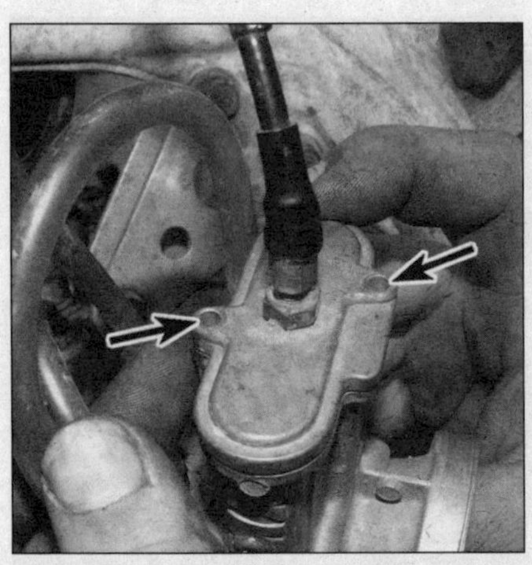

4.6a Remove the cover screws (arrows) (this is a TMX36SS Mikuni) . . .

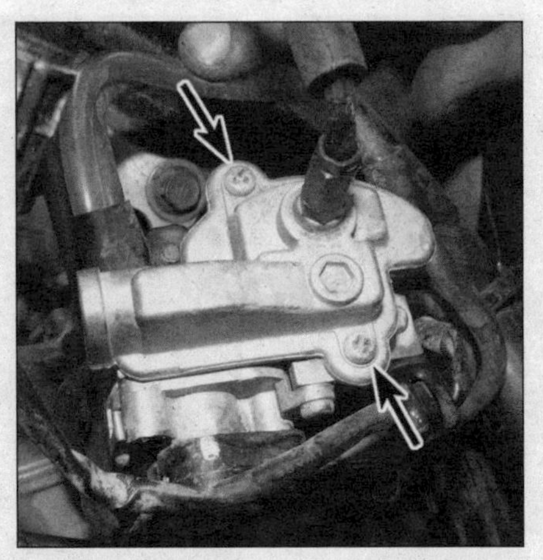

4.6b . . . and this is a PWK38S Keihin (other models similar)

4.7 Slip the cable end out of the slot in the holder

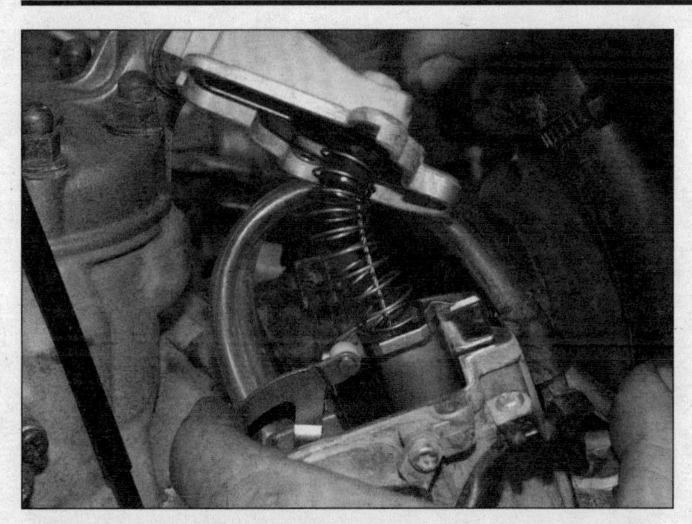

4.8 When reinstalling a PWK38S Keihin, pull back the throttle roller and make sure it fits correctly in the cap

Installation

Refer to illustration 4.8

8 Installation is the reverse of the removal steps, with the following additions:

a) *If you're working on a TMXX38SS Mikuni, pull back the throttle roller so it fits inside the cap* **(see illustration)**.

b) *Adjust the throttle freeplay (see Chapter 1).*

c) *Adjust the idle speed and fuel/air mixture (see Chapter 1).*

5 Carburetor - disassembly, cleaning and inspection

Warning: *Gasoline is extremely flammable, so take extra precautions when you work on any part of the fuel system. See the* **Warning** *in Section 2.*

Note: *these procedures are grouped by carburetor design. To see which carburetor your bike has, refer to this Chapter's Specifications.*

Disassembly

1 Remove the carburetor from the machine as described in Section 6.

2 Set the carburetor on a clean working surface. Take note of how the vent hoses are routed, including locations of hose retainers.

Mikuni VM26SS and TM34SS

Refer to illustrations 5.3a through 5.3m

3 To disassemble the carburetor, refer to the accompanying illustrations **(see illustrations)**.

Mikuni TM35SS and TM38SS

4 These carburetors are basically the same as the carburetors described in Step 3, but are equipped with a flat slide instead of a round slide. In addition, they have a baffle in the float chamber which must be lifted out for access to the main jet and pilot jet. Refer to Step 3 for disassembly procedures.

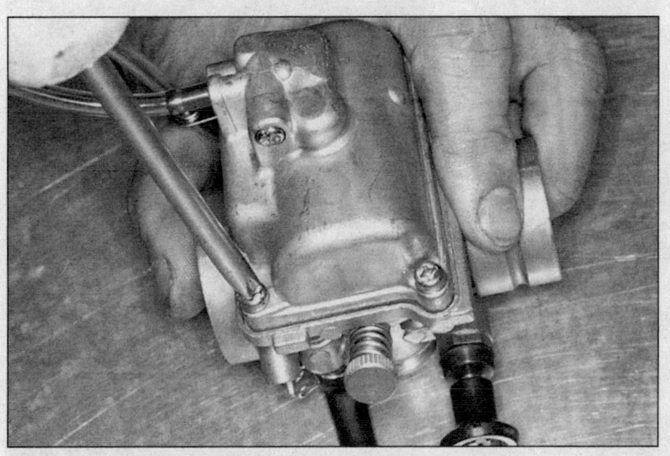

5.3a Remove the float chamber screws . . .

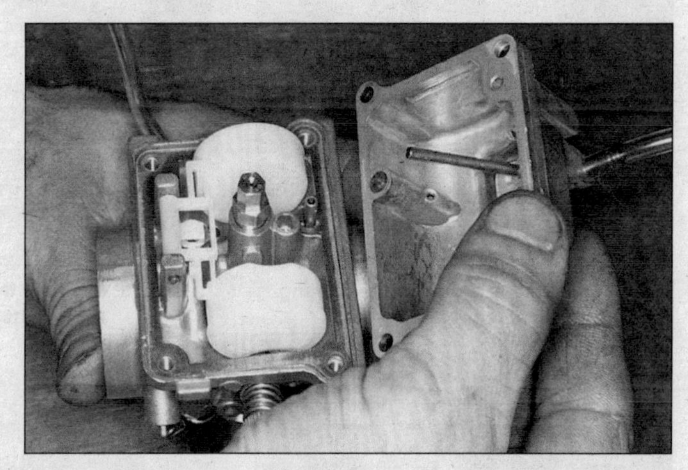

5.3b . . . remove the float chamber and gasket . . .

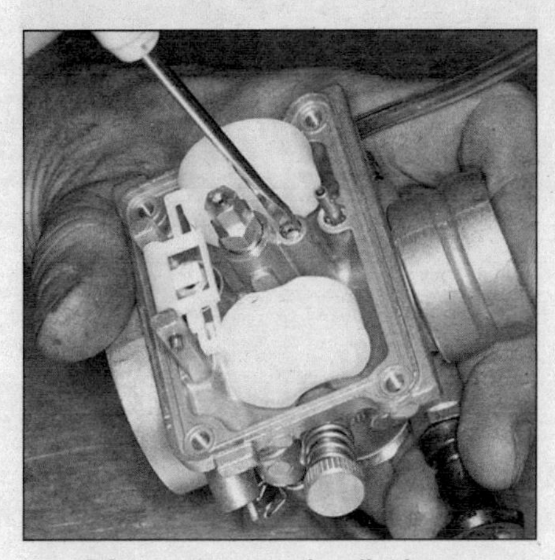

5.3c . . . unscrew the pilot jet . . .

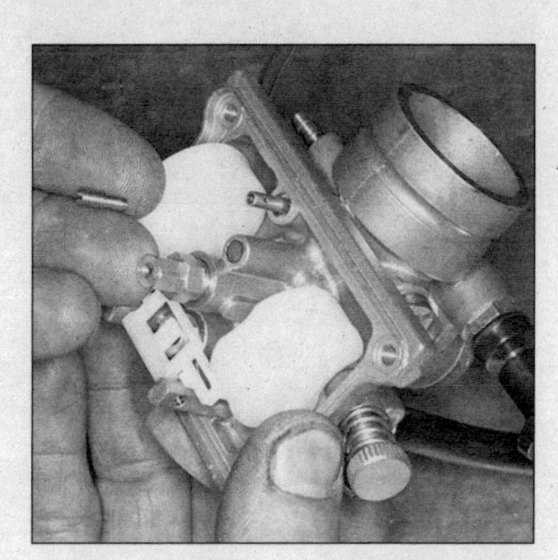

5.3d . . . and lift it out; note which end goes in first . . .

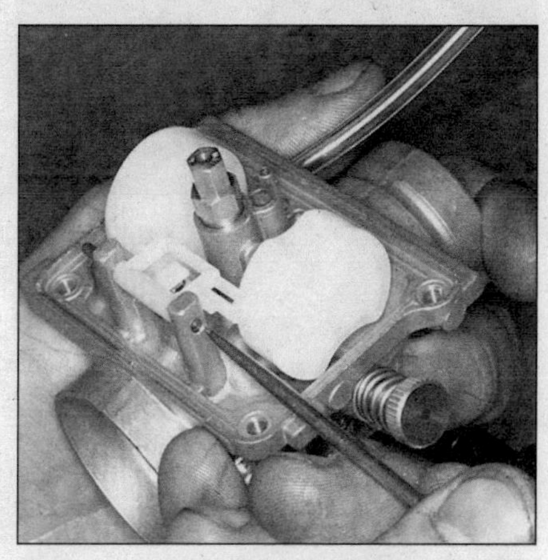

5.3e . . . push out the float pivot pin and remove the float . . .

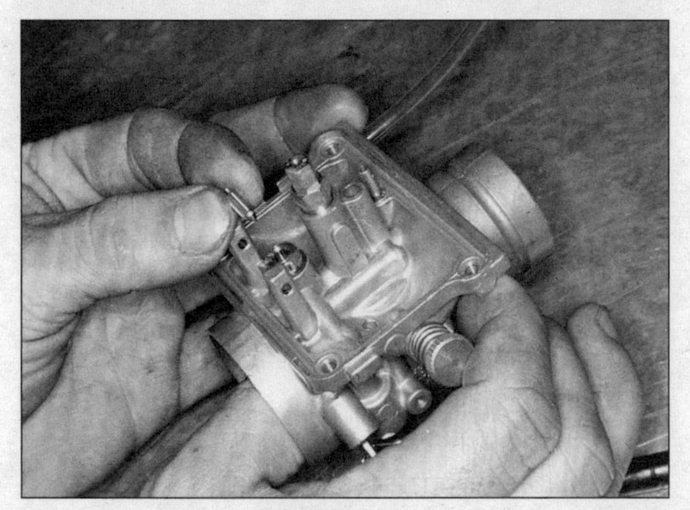

5.3f . . . remove the needle valve . . .

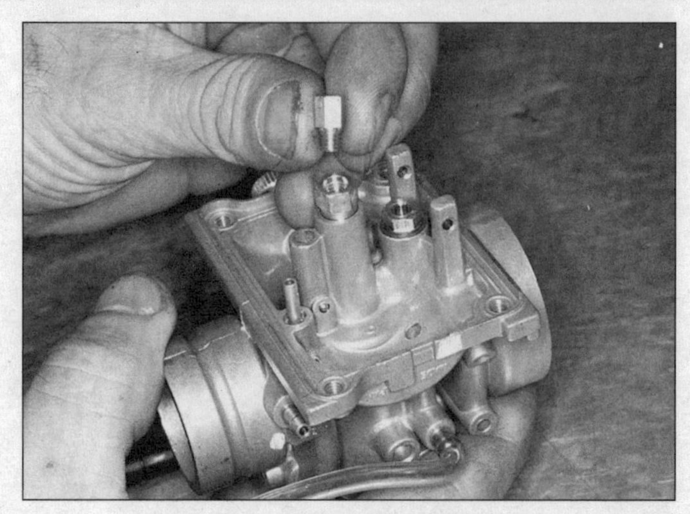

5.3g . . . unscrew the main jet . . .

5.3h . . . remove the needle jet, noting which end goes in first . . .

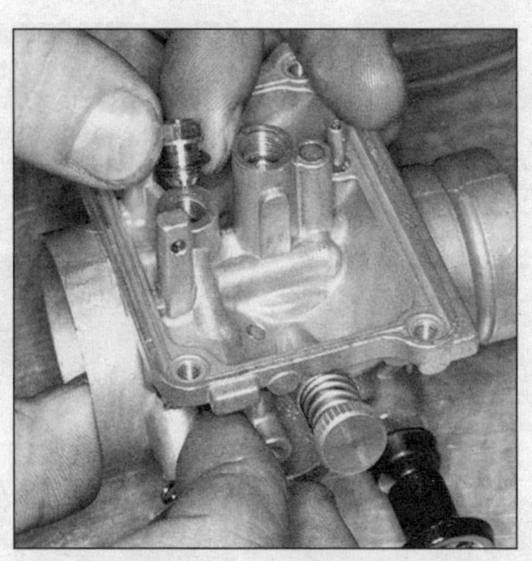

5.3i . . . unscrew the needle valve and remove its gasket . . .

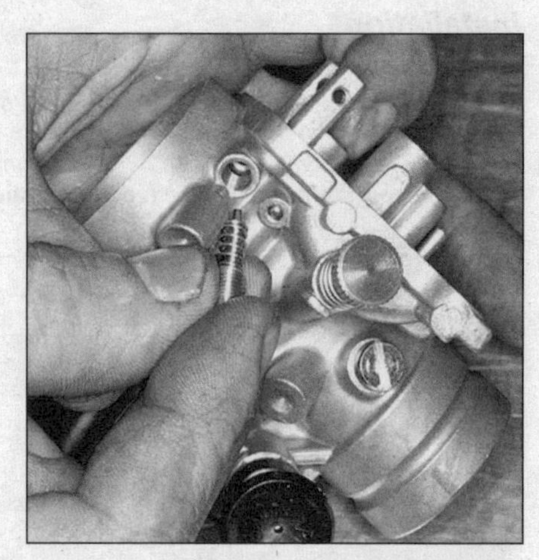

5.3j . . . unscrew the air screw (YZ80 shown; the YZ250 air screw is on the opposite side) . . .

5.3k . . . peel back the choke plunger boot . . .

5.3l . . . and unscrew the choke plunger from the carburetor body . . .

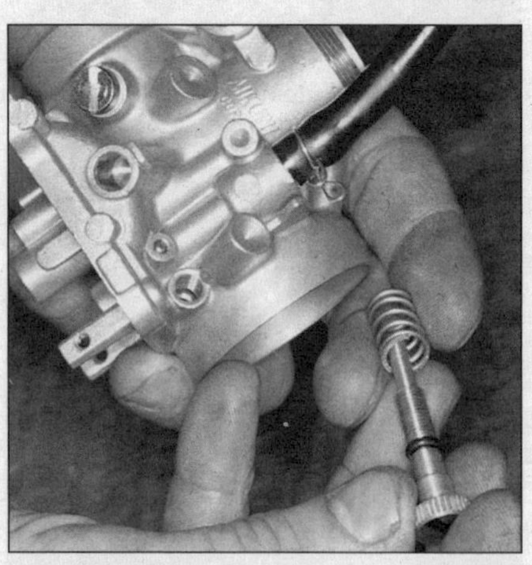

5.3m . . . unscrew the throttle stop screw (YZ80 shown)

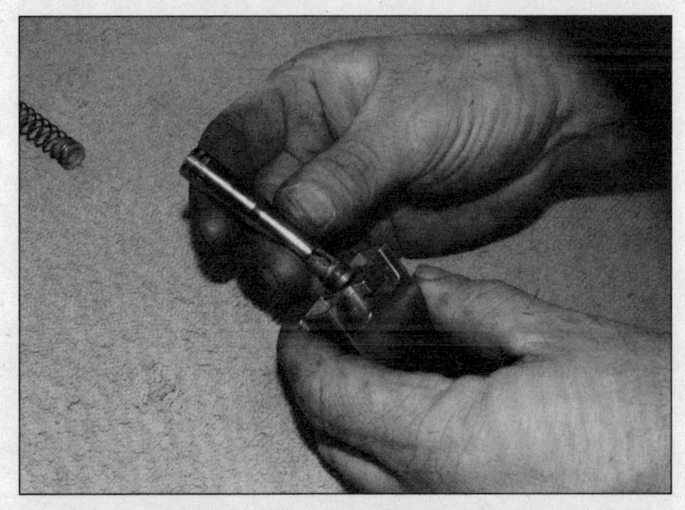

5.5a Unscrew the jet needle holder with a socket and pull it out . . .

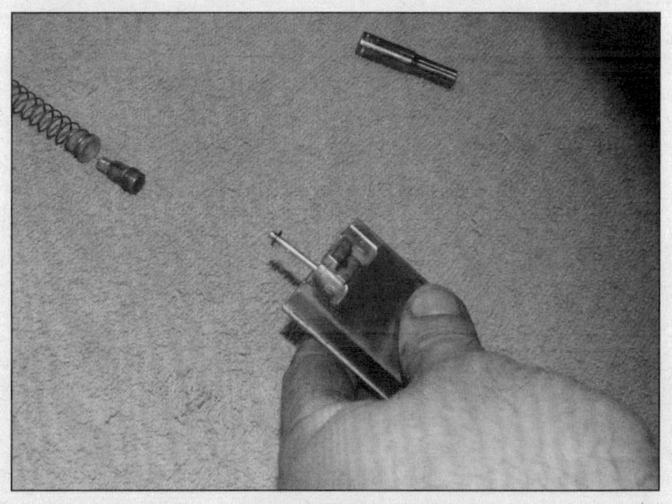

5.5b . . . and pull out the jet needle . . .

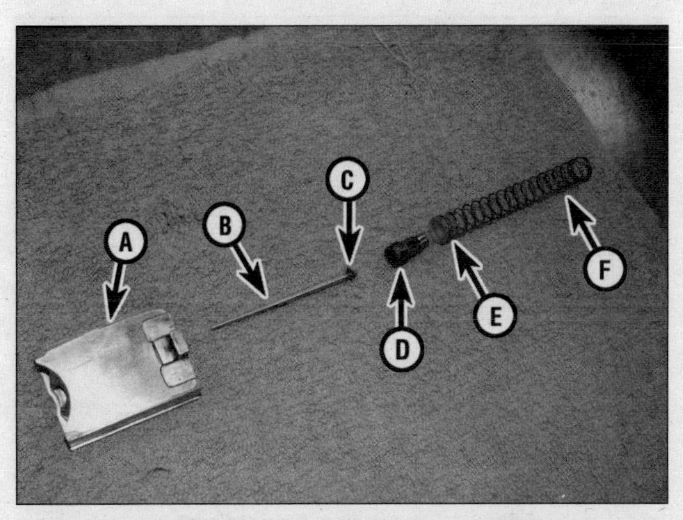

5.5c Throttle valve and jet needle details - TXM36SS carburetor

A	*Throttle piston (slide)*	*D*	*Needle holder*
B	*Jet needle*	*E*	*Spring seat*
C	*Clip*	*F*	*Spring*

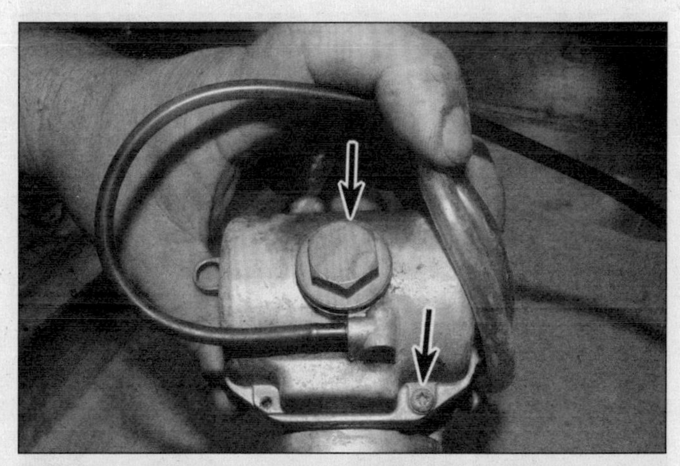

5.5d The float bowl is secured by the jet plug (upper arrow) and a screw (lower arrow) . . .

Mikuni TMX36SS

Refer to illustrations 5.5a through 5.5s

5 To disassemble the carburetor, refer to the accompanying illustrations **(see illustrations)**.

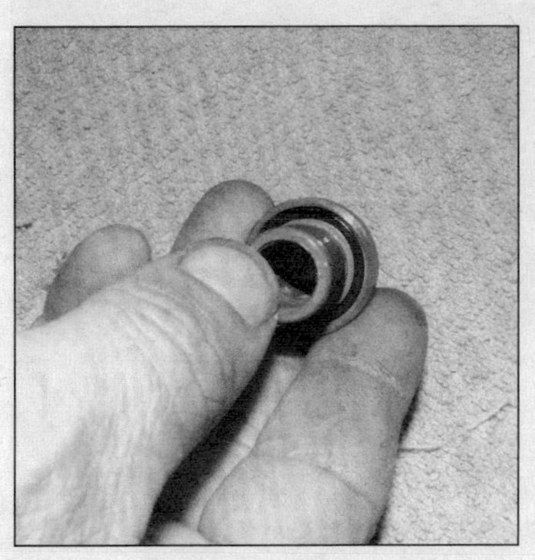

5.5e . . . unscrew the jet plug and remove its O-ring . . .

5.5f . . . remove the O-ring from the float chamber . . .

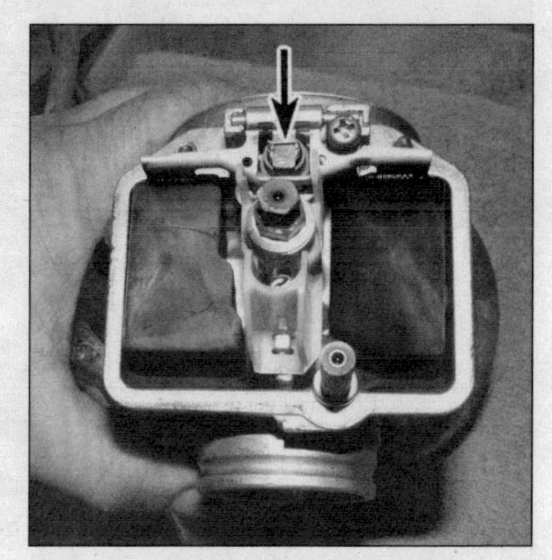

5.5g . . . note how the float clip fits over the tang (arrow) . . .

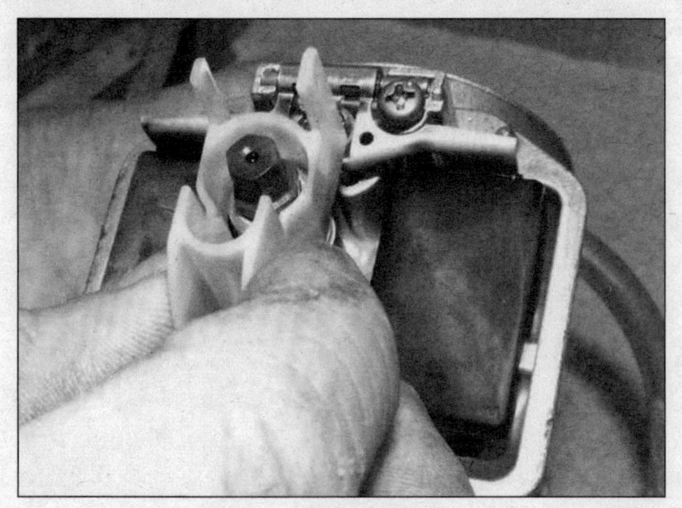

5.5h . . . lift the baffle off . . .

5.5i . . . unscrew the slow jet with a screwdriver . . .

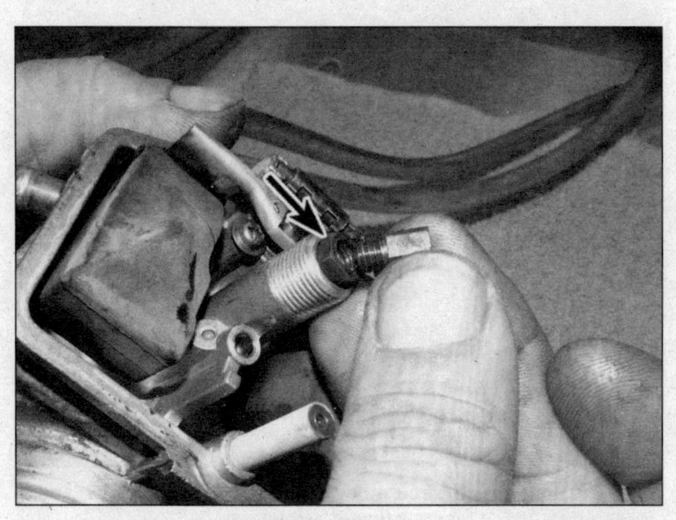

5.5j . . . hold the needle jet (arrow) with a wrench and unscrew the main jet with another wrench . . .

5.5k . . . then unscrew the needle jet . . .

5.5l . . . pull out the float pin and lift out the floats . . .

5.5m . . . together with the needle valve (arrow) . . .

5.5n . . . remove the screw that secures the needle valve seat (arrow) . . .

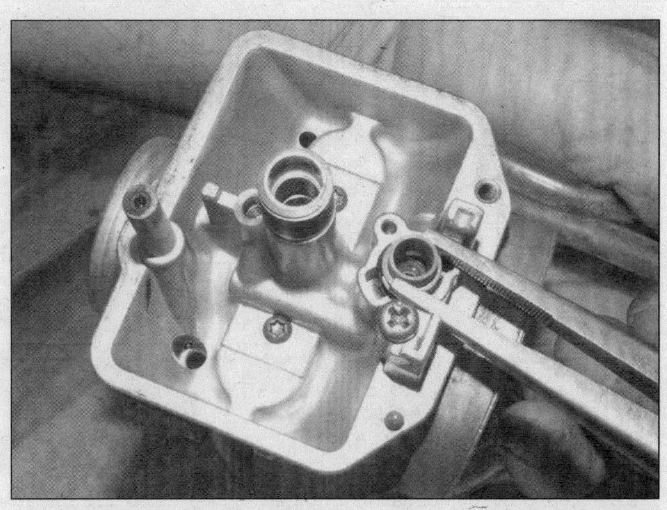

5.5o . . . and remove the needle valve seat - if you have to grip it on the thin part with pliers like this to remove it, you'll probably need a new one because it will probably be distorted . . .

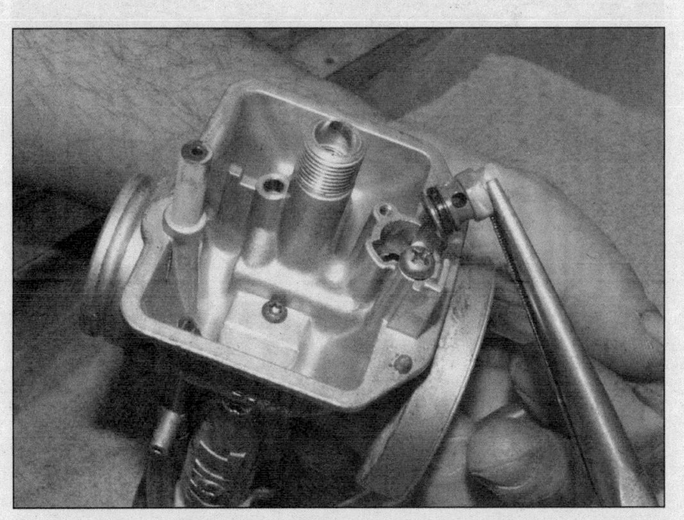

5.5p . . . pull out the seat and remove its O-ring . . .

5.5q . . . unscrew the choke plunger . . .

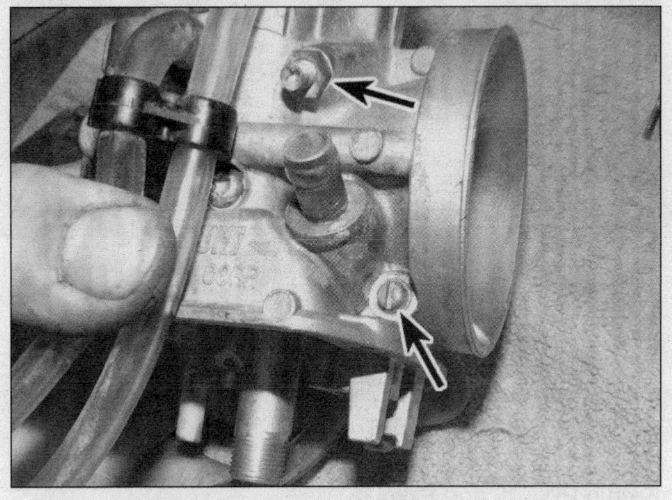

5.5r . . . loosen the locknut on the throttle stop screw (upper arrow) and turn the air screw (lower arrow) in until it bottoms LIGHTLY, counting the turns . . .

5.5s . . . then remove the air screw and spring and the throttle stop screw

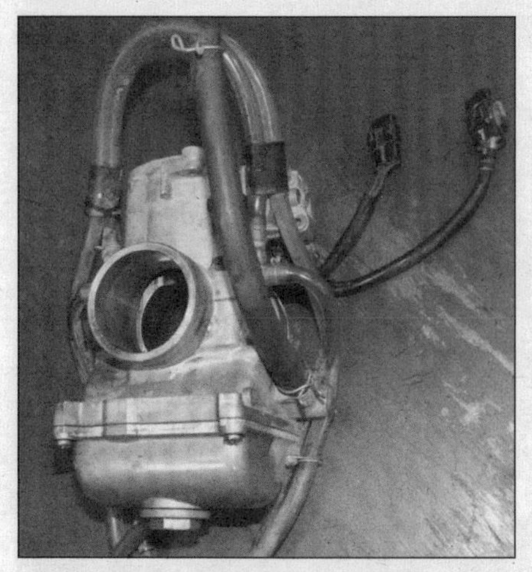

5.6a Note how the hoses are arranged (this is the front side) . . .

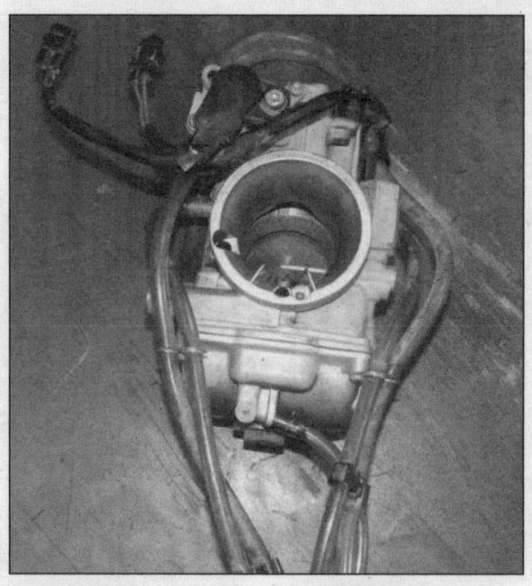

5.6b . . . and this is the back side . . .

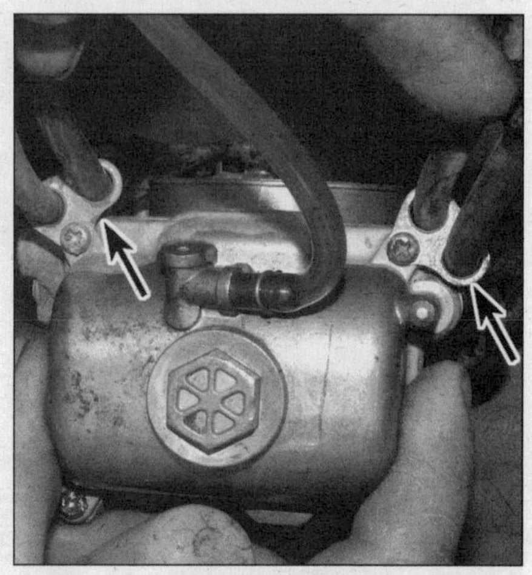

5.6c . . . note the locations of the hose retainers (arrows) . . .

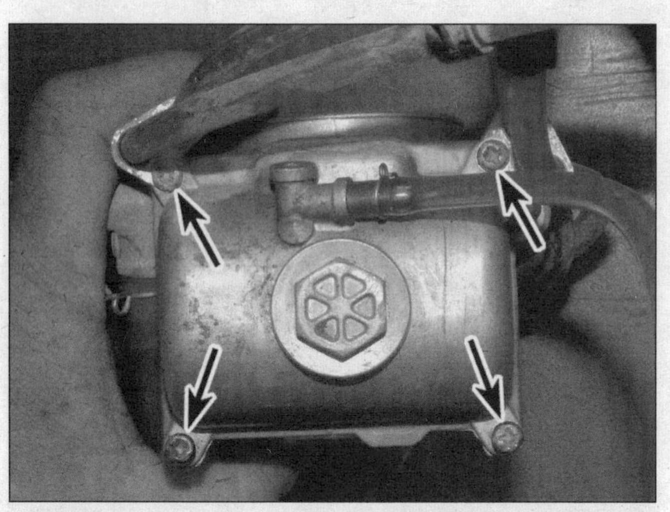

5.6d . . . then remove the float chamber screws (arrows) . . .

5.6e . . . remove the float chamber and its o-ring . . .

5.6f . . . note how the needle valve clip engages the float tang (arrow) . . .

5.6g . . . pull out the float pin . . .

Keihin PWK38 and PWM38

Refer to illustrations 5.6a through 5.6n

6 To disassemble the carburetor, refer to the accompanying illustrations **(see illustrations)**.

5.6h ... lift out the floats, together with the needle valve (arrow) ...

5.6i ... remove the slow jet with a screwdriver ...

5.6j ... and remove the main jet with a wrench - the needle valve seat (arrow) isn't available separately ...

5.6k ... on 1999 and later models, unscrew the power jet ...

5.6l ... and unscrew the solenoid ...

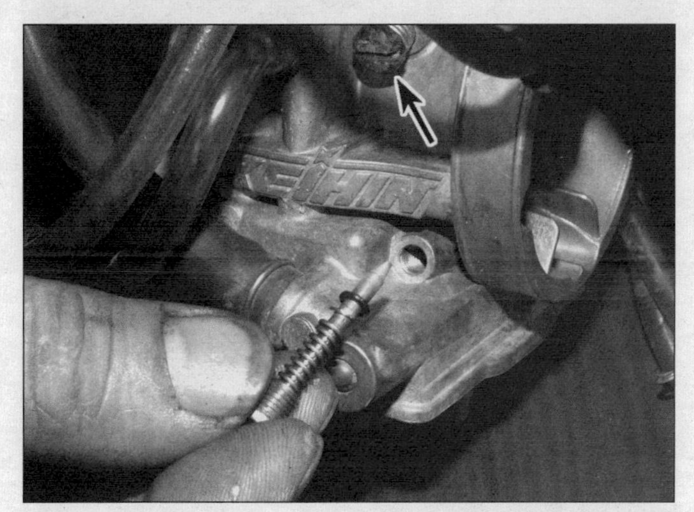

5.6m ... Turn the air screw in until it bottoms LIGHTLY, counting the turns, then remove it, together with its spring, washer and O-ring, then remove the throttle stop screw and spring (arrow) ...

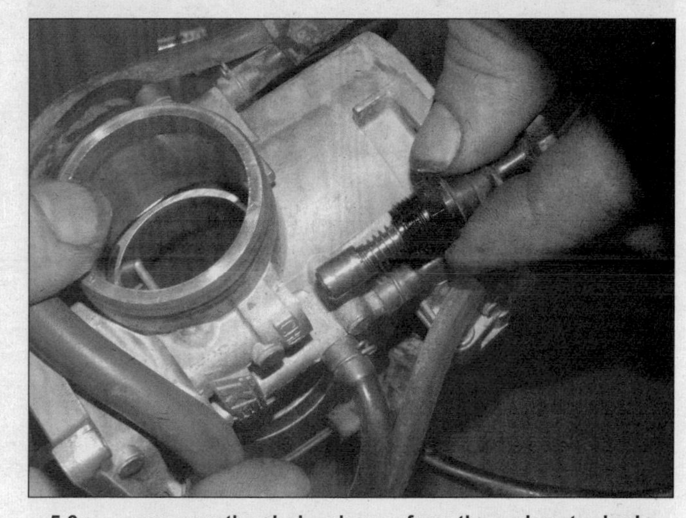

5.6n ... unscrew the choke plunger from the carburetor body

5.7a Before beginning disassembly, note how the hoses are connected . . .

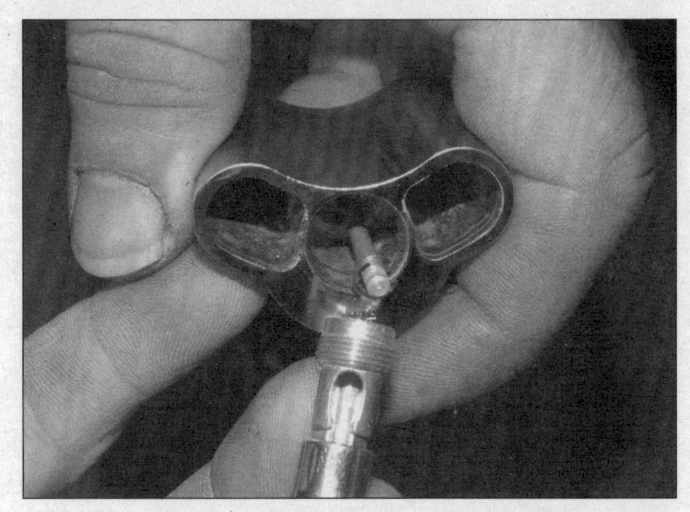

5.7b . . . unscrew the jet needle holder and remove the jet needle with its clip . . .

5.7c . . . remove the float chamber screws (arrows) . . .

5.7d . . . unscrew the main jet access plug and remove its O-ring . . .

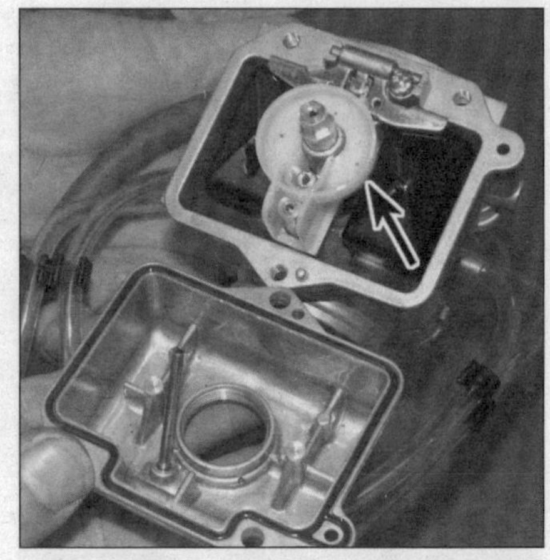

5.7e . . . lift off the float chamber, remove its O-ring and lift out the baffle (arrow) . . .

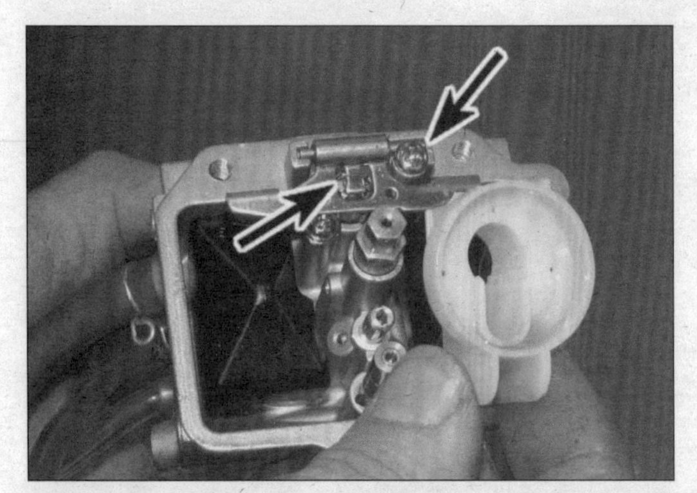

5.7f . . . note how the clip engages the float tang (left arrow), then remove the retaining screw (right arrow) . . .

Mikuni TMXX38S

Refer to illustrations 5.7 a through 5.7m

7 To disassemble the carburetor, refer to the accompanying illustrations **(see illustrations)**.

5.7g . . . and lift out the floats, together with the needle valve (arrow) . . .

5.7h ... remove the needle valve seat retaining screw ...

5.7i ... work the seat out of its bore, taking care not to distort it, then unscrew the main jet (upper arrow) and slow jet (lower arrow) ...

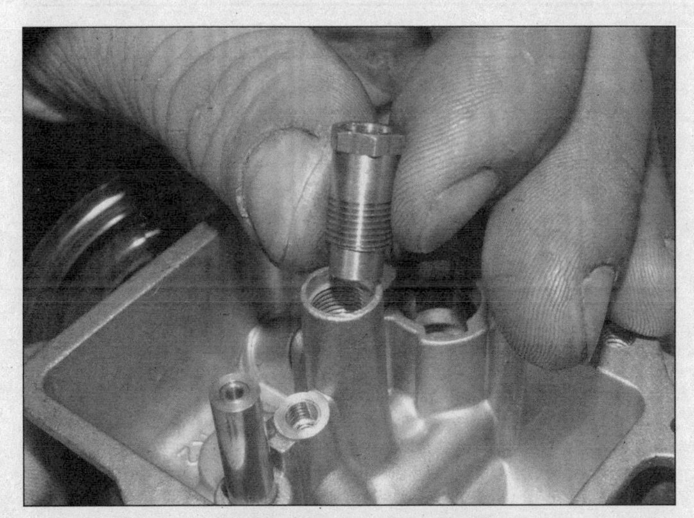

5.7j ... unscrew the needle jet and lift it out ...

5.7k ... remove the Allen bolt and take out the air passage screen ...

5.7l ... unscrew the choke plunger and take it out of its bore ...

5.7m ... turn the air screw in until it bottoms LIGHTLY, counting the turns, then remove the air screw and spring; loosen the locknut on the throttle stop screw and remove it

5.9 Blow out the jets and passages with compressed air - don't use wire or drill bits to clean them

5.10 Check the choke plunger seat for wear or deterioration

5.17 If the plating has worn off the throttle piston like this, it's time for a new one

Cleaning

Refer to illustration 5.9

Caution: *Use only a carburetor cleaning solution that is safe for use with plastic parts (be sure to read the label on the container).*

8 Submerge the metal components in the carburetor cleaner for approximately thirty minutes (or longer, if the directions recommend it).

9 After the carburetor has soaked long enough for the cleaner to loosen and dissolve most of the varnish and other deposits, use a brush to remove the stubborn deposits. Rinse it again, then dry it with compressed air. Blow out all of the fuel and air passages in the carburetor body **(see illustration)**. **Caution:** *Never clean the jets or passages with a piece of wire or a drill bit, as they will be enlarged, causing the fuel and air metering rates to be upset.*

Inspection

Refer to illustrations 5.10 and 5.17

10 Check the operation of the choke plunger. If it doesn't move smoothly, replace it. Check the plunger seat for wear or damage **(see illustration)**. and replace it if problems are found.

11 Check the tapered portion of the air screw for wear or damage. Replace the screw if necessary.

12 Check the carburetor body, float chamber and carburetor top for cracks, distorted sealing surfaces and other damage. If any defects are found, replace the faulty component, although replacement of the entire carburetor will probably be necessary (check with your parts supplier for the availability of separate components).

13 Check the jet needle for straightness by rolling it on a flat surface (such as a piece of glass). Replace it if it's bent or if the tip is worn.

14 Check the tip of the fuel inlet valve needle. If it has grooves or scratches in it, it must be replaced. Push in on the rod in the other end of the needle, then release it - if it doesn't spring back, replace the valve needle.

15 Check the O-rings on the float chamber and the main jet access plug (in the float chamber). Replace them if they're damaged.

16 Check the floats for damage. This will usually be apparent by the presence of fuel inside one of the floats. If the floats are damaged, they must be replaced.

17 Insert the throttle valve in the carburetor body and see that it moves up-and-down smoothly. Check the surface of the throttle valve for wear **(see illustration)**. If it's worn excessively or doesn't move smoothly in the bore, replace the carburetor.

6 Carburetor - reassembly and float check

Caution: *When installing the jets, be careful not to over-tighten them - they're made of soft material and can strip or shear easily.*

Note: *When reassembling the carburetor, be sure to use new O-rings.*

1 Install the clip on the jet needle if it was removed. Place it in the needle groove listed in this Chapter's Specifications. Install the needle and clip in the throttle valve.

2 Install the air screw along with its spring, washer and O-ring, turning it in until it seats lightly. Now, turn the screw out the number of turns listed in this Chapter's Specifications.

3 Reverse the disassembly steps to install the jets.

4 Invert the carburetor. Attach the fuel inlet valve needle to the float. Set the float into position in the carburetor, making sure the valve needle seats correctly. Install the float pivot pin

5 Three different measurements of float level are taken, depending on model (see this Chapter's Specifications for the measurement that applies to your bike). These are float height, float arm height and fuel level. Float height and float arm height are measured before the float chamber is installed; fuel level is measure afterwards.

6 Install the float chamber gasket or O-ring. Place the float chamber on the carburetor and install the screws, tightening them securely. Install the main jet access plug in the bottom of the float chamber, using a new O-ring, and tighten it securely.

Float height

7 To check, hold the carburetor so the float hangs down, then tilt it back until the valve needle is just seated. Measure the distance from the float chamber gasket surface to the top of the float and compare your measurement to the float height listed in this Chapter's Specifications. Bend the float tang as necessary to change the adjustment.

Float arm height

8 This measurement is from the float chamber gasket surface to the metal arms that support the floats. Bend the arms if necessary to change the adjustment. Make sure both arms are at the height listed in this Chapter's Specifications.

Fuel level

Warning: *Gasoline is extremely flammable, so take extra precautions when you work on any part of the fuel system. See the* **Warning** *in Section 2.*

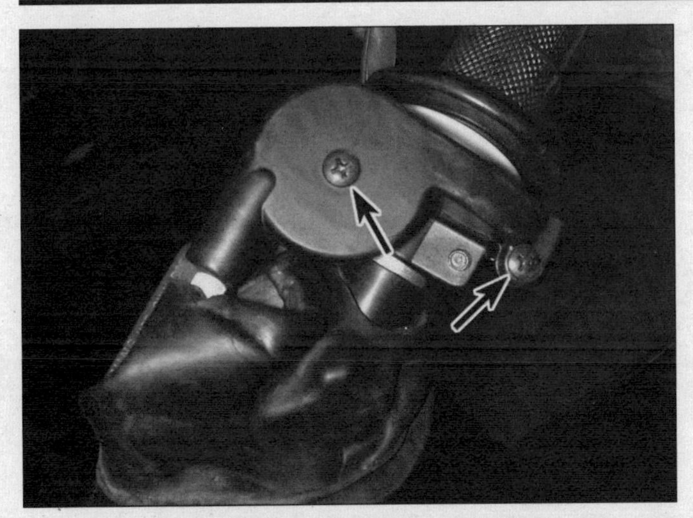

7.4 Remove the screws (arrows) and lift off the cover

9 This procedure measures the fuel level in the float bowl. Since you can't see inside the bowl, a piece of clear plastic tubing is attached to the float chamber drain fitting and held vertically next to the carburetor. The fuel in the tube will rise to the same level as the fuel inside the bowl so you can see what the level is. The level is within a specified distance of the float chamber gasket surface (see this Chapter's Specifications for the measurement).

10 On some models, this is the only procedure used to measure fuel level in the bowl. On others, it is used in addition to the float level setting described above.

11 On 1987 models, this procedure is done with the carburetor mounted on the engine and the engine warmed to normal operating temperature. Connect the clear plastic tube to the float chamber drain fitting and hold it in a vertical position alongside the carburetor. The fuel level should be within the specified distance of the point on the float chamber gasket surface where the hose retainer is attached.

12 On all other models, the procedure is done with the carburetor off the engine and held so that the float chamber gasket surface is horizontal. The fuel level in the clear plastic tube should be within the specified distance of the float chamber gasket surface.

7 Throttle cable - removal and installation

Refer to illustration 7.4

1 Remove the fuel tank (see Section 2).

2 At the handlebar, loosen the throttle cable adjuster all the way (see Chapter 1).

3 Look for a punch mark on the handlebar next to the split in the throttle housing. If you don't see a mark, make one so the throttle housing can be installed in the correct position.

4 Later models are equipped with a throttle roller **(see illustration)**. If the roller has a removable cover, undo its screws and lift off the cover and gasket.

5 Remove the throttle housing screws. If the bike has a throttle roller, lift the cable out of the roller groove. Rotate the cable to align it with the slot in the throttle pulley, then slide the cable end out of the pulley.

6 To detach the cable from the carburetor, refer to Section 4.

7 Route the cable into place. Make sure it doesn't interfere with any other components and isn't kinked or bent sharply.

8 Lubricate the throttle pulley end of the cable with multi-purpose grease. Reverse the disconnection steps to connect the throttle cable to the throttle grip pulley. If the bike has a throttle roller, install it, then install its gasket and cover (if equipped).

9 Coat the twistgrip area of the handlebar with lightweight lithium-based multi-purpose grease and slide the throttle housing and grip on. Align the punch marks on the throttle housing and handlebar.

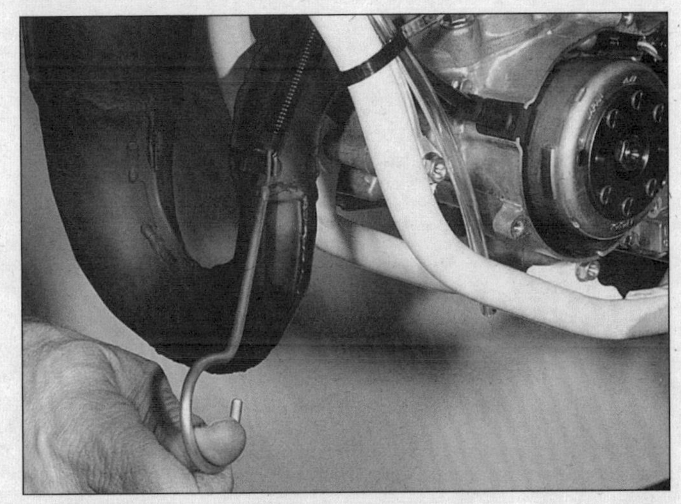

8.1 A tool like this one makes it easy to unhook the expansion chamber springs

10 Reverse the removal steps in Section 4 to connect the cable to the carburetor.

11 Operate the throttle and make sure it returns to the idle position by itself under spring pressure. **Warning:** *If the throttle doesn't return by itself, find and solve the problem before continuing with installation. A stuck throttle can lead to loss of control of the motorcycle.*

12 Follow the procedure outlined in Chapter 1, *Throttle and choke operation/grip freeplay - check and adjustment*, to adjust the cable.

13 Turn the handlebars back and forth to make sure the cable does not cause the steering to bind.

14 Once you're sure the cable operates properly, install the fuel tank.

15 With the engine idling, turn the handlebars through their full travel (full left lock to full right lock) and note whether idle speed increases. If it does, the cable is routed incorrectly. Correct this dangerous condition before riding the bike.

8 Exhaust system - removal and installation

Refer to illustrations 8.1. 8.2 and 8.4

1 Unhook the springs that secure the expansion chamber to the cylinder head or head pipe **(see illustration)**.

2 Remove the expansion chamber and muffler mounting bolts **(see illustration)**.

8.2 Offset insulating mounts are used on the expansion chamber - note the direction of offset before removing them

8.4 **Check the rubber connecting tube for deterioration or damage**

9.2b **. . . and disengage the fork shaft from the governor groove (arrow)**

3 Separate the expansion chamber from the engine and muffler and remove the system from the machine.

9.3b **. . . take the ball retainer off the shaft and remove the balls**

9.2a **Remove the Allen bolts (arrows) . . .**

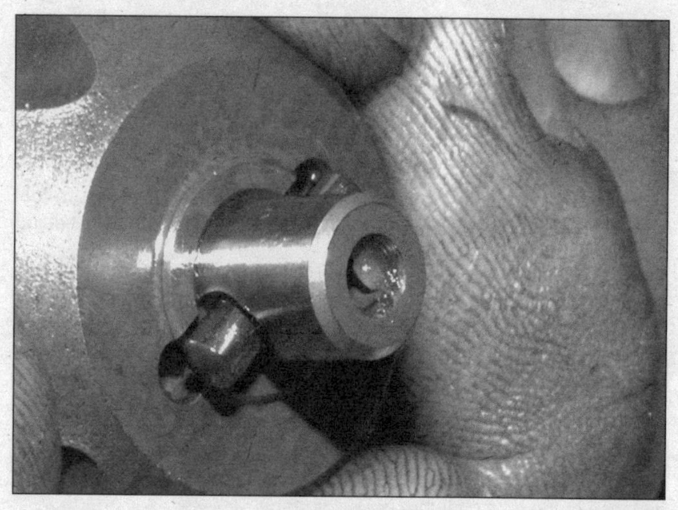

9.3a **Compress the ball retainer against spring tension to expose the retaining pin and pull the pin out . . .**

4 Check the rubber connecting tube (if equipped) for deterioration or damage and replace as needed **(see illustration)**.

5 To replace the glass wool in the muffler, refer to Chapter 1.

6 Installation is the reverse of removal.

9 Power valve governor - removal, inspection and installation

Removal

Refer to illustrations 9.2a and 9.2b

1 Remove the right crankcase cover (see Chapter 2, Section 12).

2 Unbolt the linkage lever from the cover **(see illustration)**. Disengage the governor from the shaft on the linkage fork and remove it from the cover **(see illustration)**.

Disassembly

Refer to illustrations 9.3a through 9.3f

3 Refer to the following illustrations to disassemble the governor **(see illustrations)**.

9.3c The components fit on the shaft like this

A Collar
B Washers and bearing
C Collar
D Washer and bearing (two washers on YZ250)
E Spring seat
F Spring
G Gear

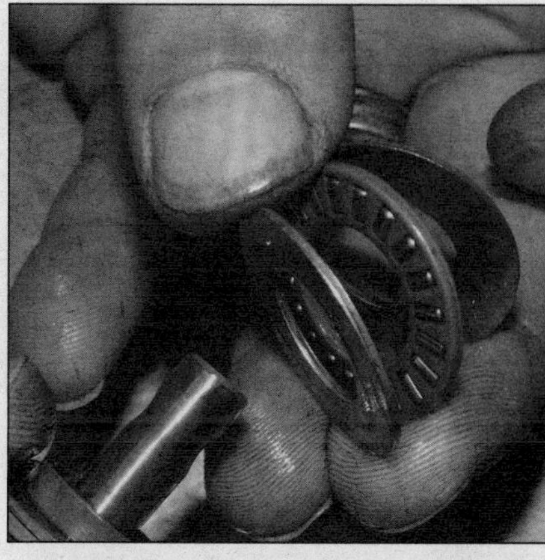

9.3d The outer bearing is sandwiched between a pair of washers; the inner bearing is sandwiched between a washer and collar (YZ125) or two washers (YZ250)

9.3e The narrow part of the spring seat fits inside the spring

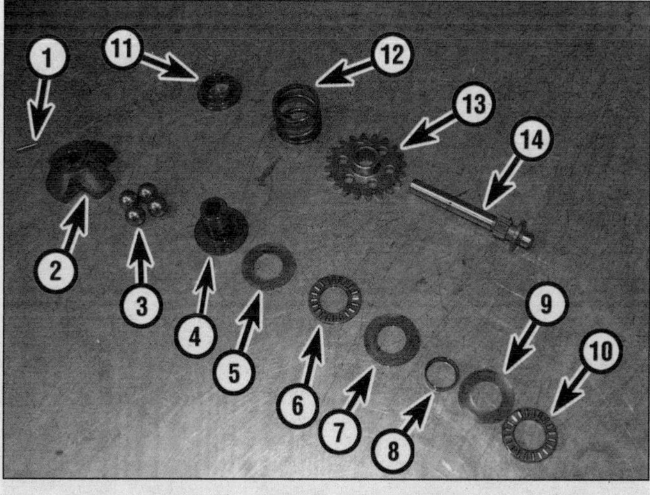

9.3f Power valve governor details

1 Retaining pin
2 Ball retainer
3 Centrifugal weight balls
4 Collar
5 Washer
6 Bearing
7 Washer
8 Collar
9 Washer
10 Bearing (and second washer on YZ250 models)
11 Spring seat
12 Spring
13 Gear
14 Shaft

Inspection

4 Check the gear teeth for wear or breakage and replace the gear if problems are found.

5 Check the spring for weakness and breakage and replace it if problems are found.

6 Inspect the bearings closely. If the rollers are pitted or worn, replace the bearings. It's a good idea to replace them if there's any doubt about their condition.

Assembly

7 Assembly is the reverse of the disassembly steps. Lubricate the bearings with multi-purpose lithium grease. Be sure the dowel pin seats securely in the groove of the ball retainer.

Installation

8 Installation is the reverse of the removal steps. Engage the fork shaft with the groove in the governor **(see illustration 9.2b)**. Tighten the fork Allen bolts securely.

10 Power valve - removal, inspection and installation

1 This system is used on YZ125/250 models. 1987 through 1989 models use a rotary valve mounted in a chamber attached to the cylinder head. Later models use a single or dual sliding gate design. Later YZ250 models also use a secondary power valve, mounted above and behind the main power valve.

2 Opening and closing of the valve is controlled by a centrifugal governor mounted inside the right crankcase cover next to the water pump (see Section 9 for details).

Removal

Refer to illustration 10.3

3 Remove the power valve linkage cover from the right side of the

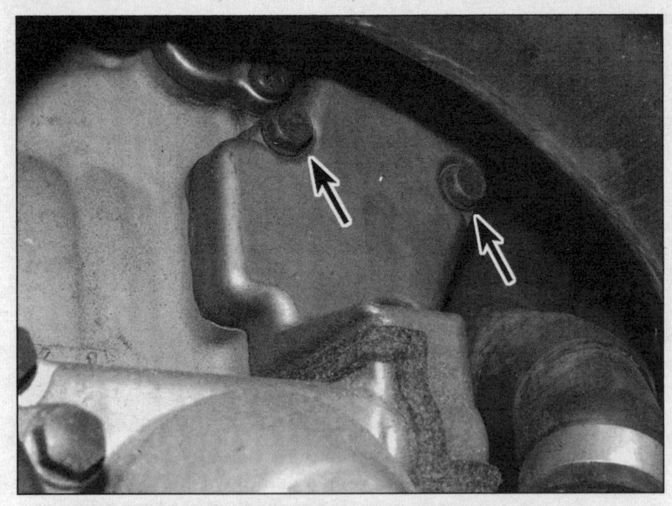

10.3 Remove the bolts (arrows) and take off the linkage cover and gasket

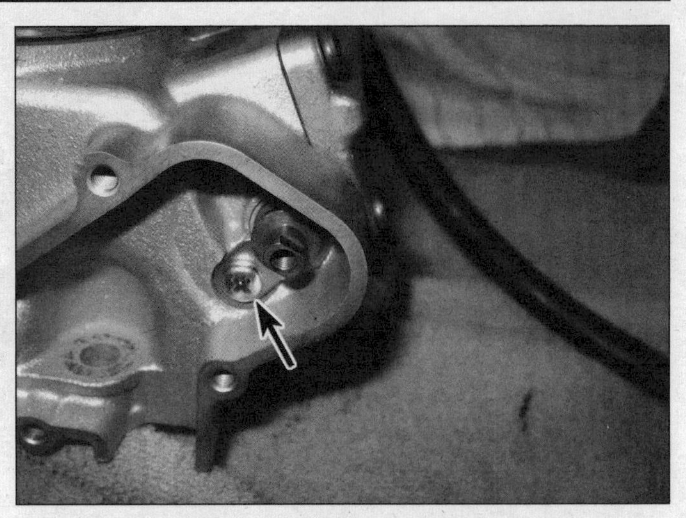

10.9 Remove the screw (arrow) and thrust plate

10.10a Remove the screws and take off the cover - the UP mark must be upright on installation

cylinder **(see illustration)**. Disconnect the linkage rod from the power valve.

Rotary valve

4 Remove the lever boss, thrust plate screw, thrust plate and collar from the power valve holder in the right side of the cylinder.

5 Remove two screws that secure the power valve cover to the left side of the cylinder, then remove the cover and gasket.

6 Remove the Allen bolt from the left side of the power valve. Pull the left half of the power valve out.

7 Push the right half of the power valve out, together with the holder and its O-ring. Locate the two dowel pins that hold the valve halves together.

8 Installation is the reverse of the removal steps. Use new O-rings and a new cover gasket. Lubricate the O-rings with molybdenum disulfide grease.

Slide valve

Refer to illustrations 10.9, 10.10a, 10.10b, 10.11, 10.12a, 10.12b, 10.14a, 10.14b, 10.15, 10.17a, 10.17b and 10.17c

9 Remove the screw and retainer that secure the power valve shaft **(see illustration)**.

10.10b Remove the gasket

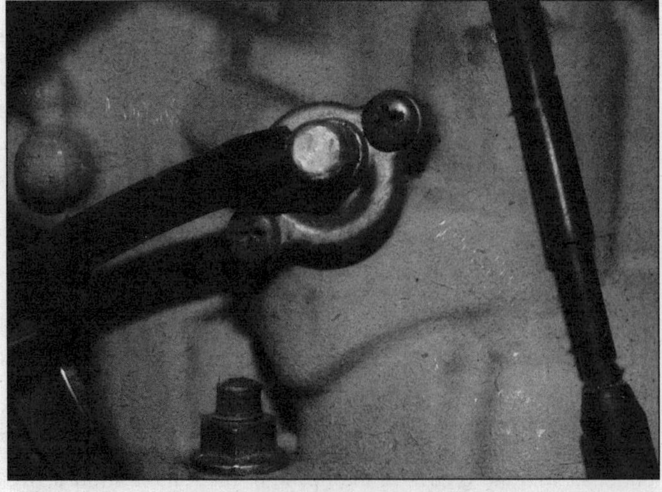

10.11 On later YZ250 models, remove the secondary power valve cover from each side of the cylinder

10.12a Remove the valve holder Allen bolt . . .

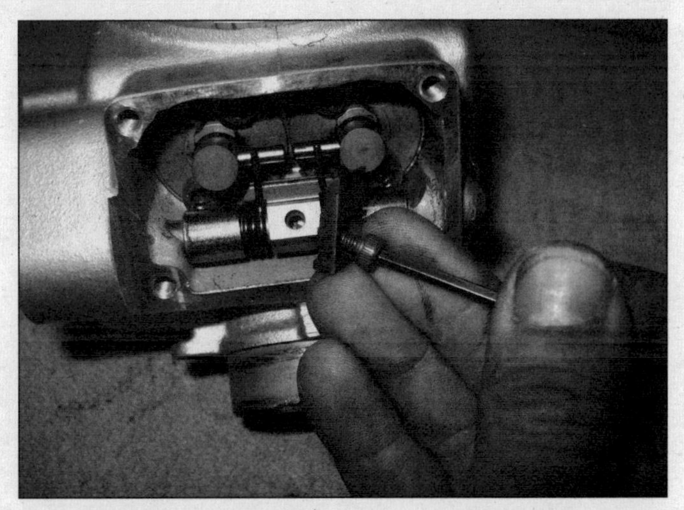

10.12b . . . and take the valve holder off the shaft

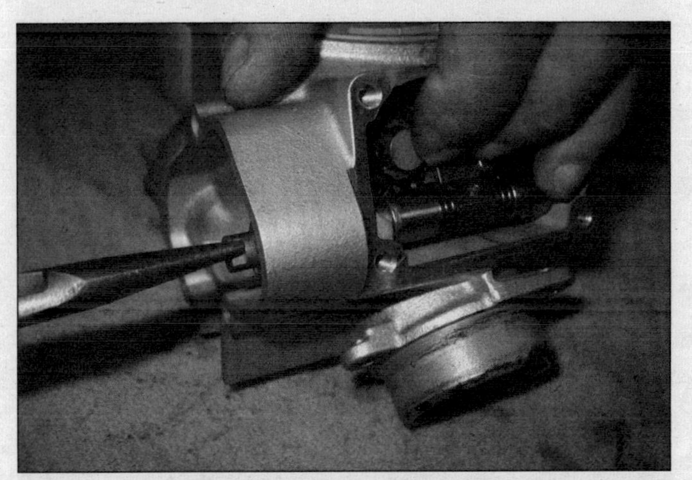

10.14a Pull the shaft out of the cylinder

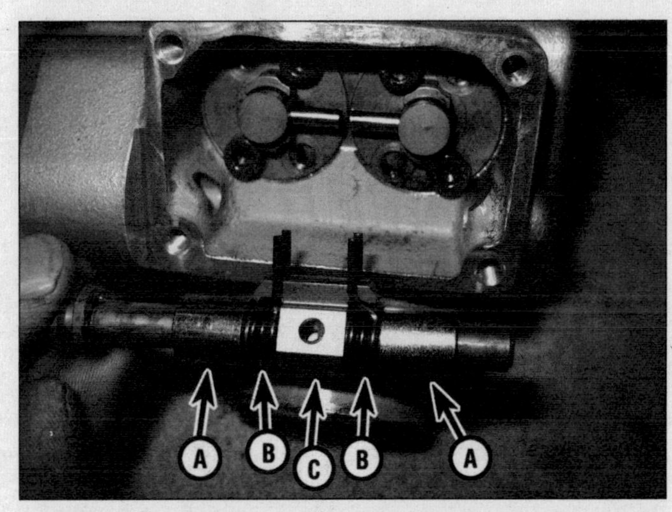

10.14b Shaft component details

A Collar (washer, coil spring and pulley on YZ250 models)
B Valve spring
C Link lever

10.15 Remove the Allen screws that secure the sliding gate(s) (YZ125 shown) . . .

10 Remove the cover and gasket from the front of the cylinder **(see illustrations)**.

11 If you're working on a YZ250 with secondary power valves, remove the secondary cover and O-ring from each side of the cylinder **(see illustration)**.

12 Note how the spring ends fit over the sliding gate pins, then remove the Allen bolt that secures the valve holder to the shaft **(see illustrations)**.

13 If you're working on a YZ250, remove the Allen bolts that secure the pulleys (there's one at each end of the shaft). Remove the pulleys and the link rod.

14 Grip the shaft end with pliers and pull it out of the cylinder **(see illustrations)**.

15 If you're working on a YZ125, unscrew the Allen bolts that secure the sliding gates **(see illustration)**.

16 If you're working on a YZ250, remove the Allen bolts that secure the link rod and secondary power valve retainer. Remove the secondary power valves from the sides of the cylinder.

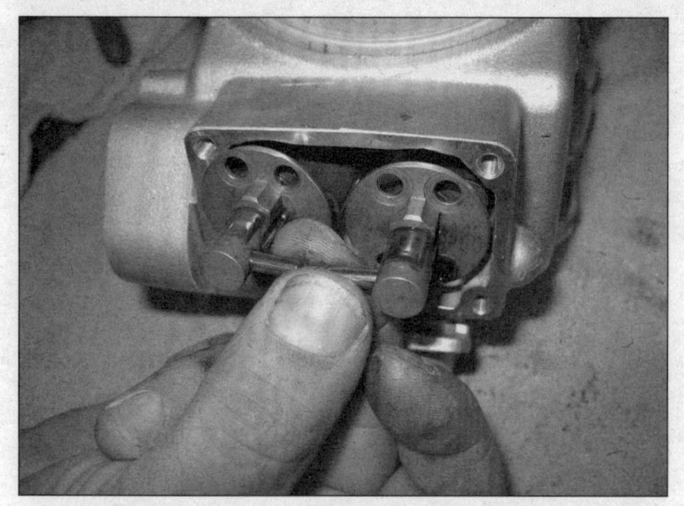

10.17a . . . and pull the gates out of the cylinder . . .

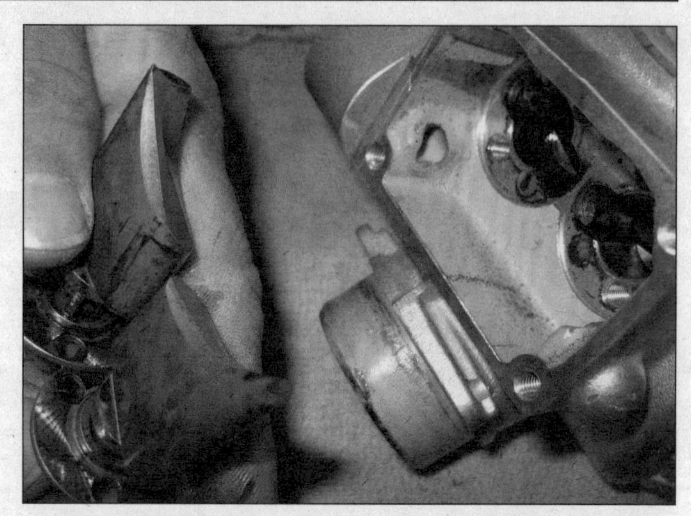

10.17b . . . noting carefully which sides of the gate(s) are upward - it's possible to install some gates upside down

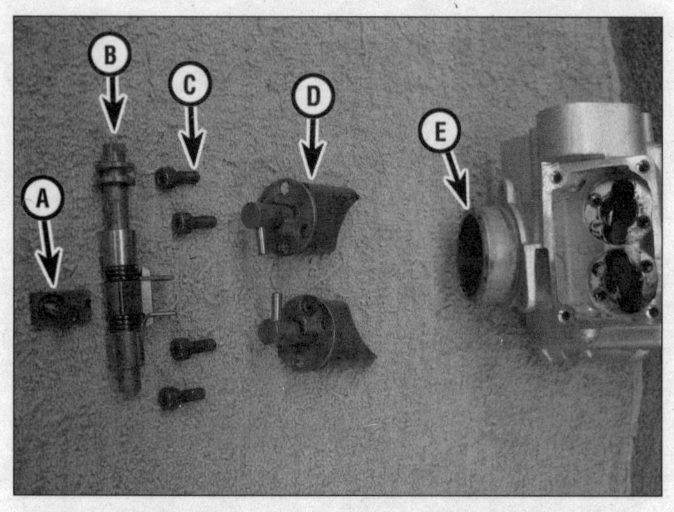

10.17c Sliding gate details (dual gate shown)

A *Valve holder*
B *Shaft and components*
C *Allen screws*
D *Gates*
E *Cylinder*

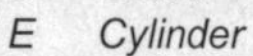

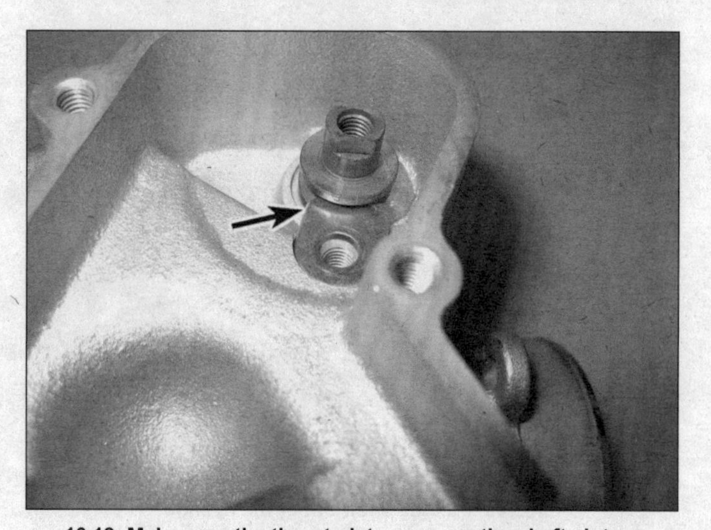

10.19 Make sure the thrust plate engages the shaft slot on assembly

17 Pull the sliding gate(s) out of the cylinder **(see illustrations)**. Be sure to note which side of the gate(s) goes upward **(see illustration)**.

Inspection

18 Thoroughly clean all carbon from the valves and their slots in the cylinder. Check all parts for wear or damage and replace any parts that have problems.

Installation

Refer to illustration 10.19

19 Installation is the reverse of the removal steps. Be sure the thrust plate engages the slot in the shaft **(see illustration)**. Tighten the Allen bolts securely.

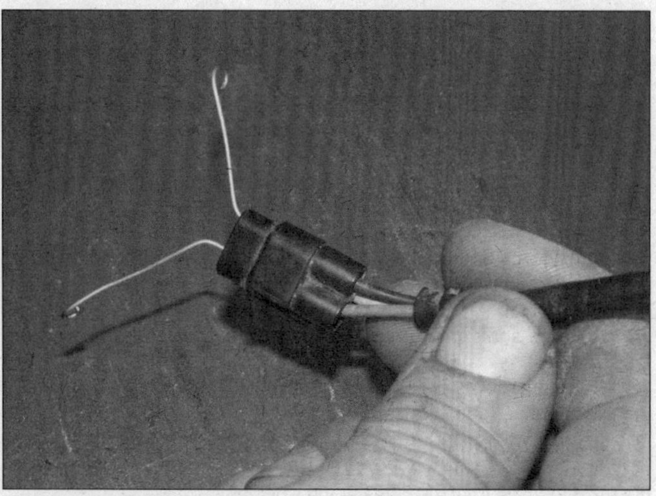

11.2 Make probes of thin wire and place them in the terminals for the blue and black wires

11 Throttle position sensor - check and replacement

Check

Refer to illustrations 11.2, 11.3a and 11.3b

1 Remove the carburetor from the engine (see Section 4). Remove the cover from the top of the carburetor **(see illustration 4.6b)**.

2 Place two wire probes in the blue and black terminals of the sensor **(see illustration)**. Connect an ohmmeter between the terminals

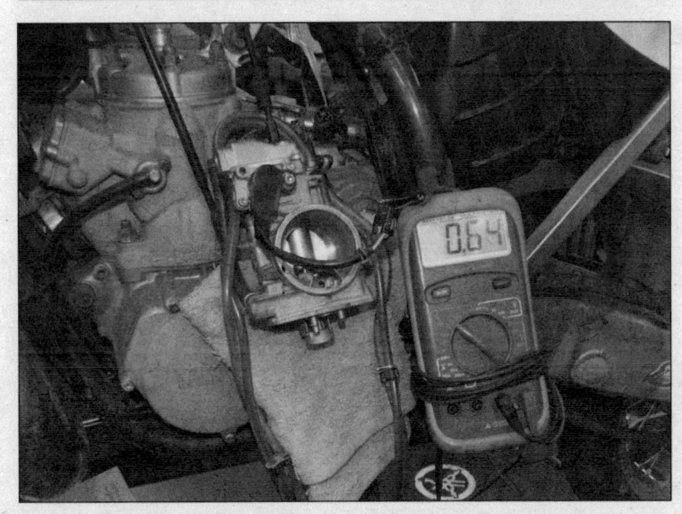

11.3a Check the resistance with the throttle closed . . .

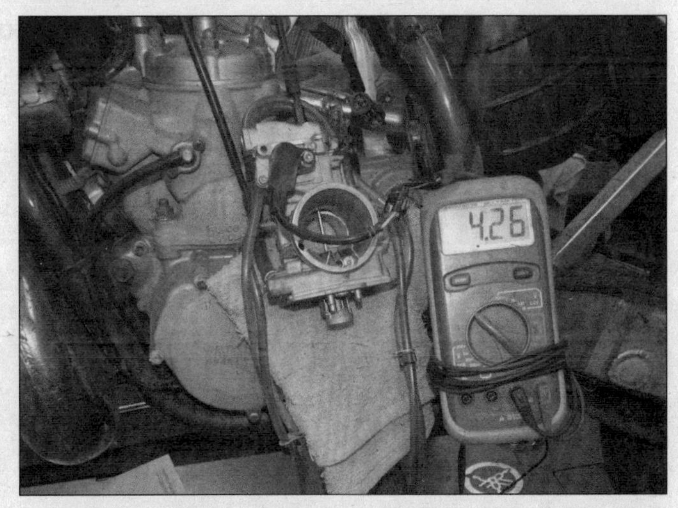

11.3b . . . and with it all the way open

(positive to blue wire; negative to black wire). **Note:** *On some models the black wire may have a blue tracer (stripe).* The ohmmeter should indicate 4000 to 6000 ohms.

3 Now connect the positive lead of the ohmmeter to the yellow wire terminal and the negative lead to the black wire terminal. Operate the throttle roller to raise and lower the throttle piston **(see illustration 4.8)**. With the throttle all the way closed, the ohmmeter should indicate between zero and 2000 ohms **(see illustration)**. With the throttle all the way open, it should indicate 4000 to 6000 ohms **(see illustration)**.

4 If the readings are incorrect, replace and adjust the sensor as described below. Do not remove the sensor unless it needs to be replaced, or performance will be impaired.

Replacement

Refer to illustration 11.5

Note: *Before condemning the TPS as faulty, make sure it is receiving the proper input voltage from the CDI unit (see Chapter 5).*

5 This procedure requires a normal T25 Torx bit and a T20 Torx bit designed for tamper-resistant screws.

6 Remove the mounting screw with a T25 Torx bit **(see illustration)**. Take the sensor off.

7 Install the sensor while holding the throttle roller down **(see illustration 4.8)**, making sure its slot aligns with the tab in the carburetor, and tighten the mounting screw slightly.

8 Loosen the adjusting screws just enough that the sensor can be rotated.

9 Install the carburetor top cover, tightening the screws securely. Install the carburetor on the engine and connect the sensor electrical connector. Backprobe the yellow and black wire terminals of the electrical connector using two thin straight pins inserted between the wires and the connector housing. Connect a voltmeter to the probes, positive to yellow and negative to black. **Caution:** *Don't allow the pins to contact each other, as a short circuit could damage the CDI unit. Also, don't push the straight pins into the electrical connector any farther than necessary, as the waterproof properties of the connector could be compromised.*

11.5 The adjusting screws (left and right arrows) are T20 tamper-resistant Torx; the mounting screw (center) is a normal T25 Torx

10 Start the engine and warm it to normal operating temperature. Connect a tune-up tachometer to the engine and set idle speed to 1700 to 1900 rpm.

11 Check the reading on the voltmeter. It should be 0.5 to 0.7 volts. If not, carefully rotate the sensor to get the correct reading. **Note:** *If the proper reading can't be obtained (or if no voltage is measured at all), check the CDI unit as described in Chapter 5.*

12 Once the correct reading is obtained, mark the sensor position on the carburetor with a felt pen. Shut off the engine.

13 Remove the carburetor and tighten the adjustment screws with a T20 Torx bit designed for tamper-resistant screws, then tighten the mounting screw with a T25 Torx bit.

14 Reinstall the carburetor.

15 Refer to Chapter 1 and reset idle speed and mixture.

Notes

Chapter 5
Ignition system

Contents

Specifications

YZ80/85

Ignition coil resistance

1986	
Primary	0.29 ohms +/- 15 per cent
Secondary	4,000 ohms +/- 15 per cent
1987 through 1992	
Primary	0.2 to 0.3 ohms
Secondary	
1987 through 1991	3400 to 4600 ohms
1992	3500 to 4700 ohms
1993 through 1996	
Primary	0.26 to 0.36 ohms
Secondary	3500 to 4700 ohms
1997	
Primary	0.32 to 0.48 ohms
Secondary	5700 to 8500 ohms
1998 and later	
Primary	0.18 to 0.28 ohms
Secondary	6300 to 9500 ohms

Spark plug cap resistance

1986 through 1992	5000 ohms
1993 through 2003	Not specified
2004 and later	4000 to 6000 ohms

Alternator exciter coil resistance

1986	505 ohms +/- 10 per cent (black to brown)
1987 through 1992	454.5 to 555.5 ohms (brown to black)
1993	324 to 396 ohms (brown to black)
1994 through 1996	198 to 242 ohms (brown to black)
1997 through 2001	257 to 314 ohms (brown to black)
2002 and later	
Coil no. 1	720 to 1080 ohms (green-white to black-red)
Coil no. 2	44 to 66 ohms (black to green-blue)

Alternator pulse generator resistance

1986	10.4 ohms +/- 10 per cent (white-green to white-red)
1987 through 1992	9.4 to 11.5 ohms (white-green to white-red)
1993 through 1996	9.4 to 11.4 ohms (white-green to white-red)
1997 through 2001	15.8 to 19.4 ohms (white-green to white-red)
2002 and later	248 to 372 ohms (white-blue to white-red)

Torque specifications

Alternator rotor nut	
1986 through 1992	35 Nm (25 ft-lbs)
1993 through 2001	40 Nm (29 ft-lbs)
2002 and later	33 Nm (24 ft-lbs)

YZ125

Ignition coil resistance

1986	
Primary	0.22 ohms +/- 10 per cent
Secondary	4400 ohms +/- 20 per cent
1987 through 1989	
Primary	0.20 to 0.24 ohms
Secondary	4000 to 4800 ohms
1990	
Primary	0.26 to 0.36 ohms
Secondary	3480 to 4720 ohms
1991 through 1993	
Primary	0.26 to 0.36 ohms
Secondary	3500 to 4700 ohms
1994	
Primary	0.45 to 0.61 ohms
Secondary	10,700 to 14,500 ohms
1995	
Primary	0.20 to 0.28 ohms
Secondary	7100 to 9500 ohms
1996 through 2003	
Primary	0.14 to 0.20 ohms
Secondary	6700 to 10,100 ohms
2004 and later	
Primary	0.24 to 0.36 ohms
Secondary	5700 to 8500 ohms

Spark plug cap resistance

1986 through 2002	Not specified
2002 and later	4000 to 6000 ohms

Alternator exciter coil resistance

1986	1437 ohms +/- 10 per cent (brown to red)
1987	149 to 201 ohms (brown to red)
1988	9300 to 12,600 ohms (brown to black)
1989	360 to 480 ohms (brown to black)
1990	454.5 to 555.5 ohms (brown to black)
1991	455 to 556 ohms (brown to black)
1992	
Coil no. 1	324 to 396 ohms (brown to red)
Coil no. 2	22 to 26 ohms (white to green)
1993 through 1995	
Coil no. 1	324 to 396 ohms (brown to red)
Coil no. 2	16 to 19 ohms (white to green)
1996 and later	
Coil no. 1	720 to 1080 ohms (green-white to black-red)
Coil no. 2	44 to 66 ohms (black to green-blue)

Alternator pulse generator resistance

1986	433 ohms +/- 10 per cent (red-white to red)
1987	85 to 115 ohms (white-green to green)
1988	360 to 480 ohms (white to red-black)
1989	9300 to 12,600 ohms (white to red-black)
1990 and 1991	4.5 to 5.5 ohms (white-green to white-red)
1992 through 1995	446 to 545 ohms (white-green to white-red)
1996 and later	248 to 372 ohms (white-blue to white-red)

Torque specifications

Alternator rotor nut	
1986 through 2001	38 Nm (27 ft-lbs)
2002 through 2004	33 Nm (24 ft-lbs)
2005 and later	56 Nm (40 ft-lbs)

YZ250

Ignition coil resistance

1986	
Primary	0.22 ohms +/- 10 per cent
Secondary	4400 ohms +/- 20 per cent
1987 through 1989	
Primary	0.20 to 0.24 ohms
Secondary	4000 to 4800 ohms
1990 through 1993	
Primary	0.26 to 0.36 ohms
Secondary	3500 to 4700 ohms
1994	
Primary	0.43 to 0.58 ohms
Secondary	10,800 to 16,200 ohms
1995 and later	
Primary	0.20 to 0.30 ohms
Secondary	9500 to 14,300 ohms

Spark plug cap resistance

1986 through 2003	Not specified
2004 and later	4000 to 6000 ohms

Alternator exciter coil resistance

1986	175 ohms +/- 15 per cent (red to brown)
1987 through 1989	131 to 178 ohms (brown to black)
1990 through 1992	
Coil no. 1	256 to 348 ohms (black to brown)
Coil no. 2	36 to 54 ohms (black to black-red)
1993 through 1995	
Coil no. 1	440 to 660 ohms (black to brown)
Coil no. 2	36 to 54 ohms (black to black-red)
1996 through 1998	
Coil no. 1	720 to 1080 ohms (green-white to black-red)
Coil no. 2	44 to 66 ohms (black to green-blue)
1999 and later	
Coil no. 1	720 to 1080 ohms (black to black-red)
Coil no. 2	44 to 66 ohms (green-blue to green-white)

Alternator pulse generator resistance

1986	100 ohms +/- 15 per cent (white to white-green)
1987 through 1989	170 to 230 ohms (white to red-black)
1993 through 1995	104 to 156 ohms (black to green-white)
1996 and later	248 to 372 ohms (white-blue to white-red)

Torque specifications

Alternator rotor nut	
1986 through 1989	38 Nm (27 ft-lbs)
1990 through 2000	48 Nm (35 ft-lbs)
2001 and 2002	41 Nm (30 ft-lbs)
2003 and later	56 Nm (40 ft-lbs)

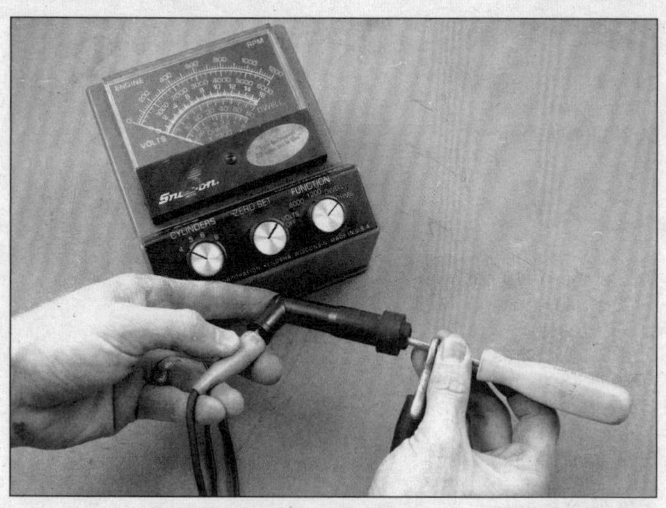

3.4 Unscrew the spark plug cap from the plug wire and measure its resistance with an ohmmeter

1 General information

The only electrical circuit on these models is the ignition system. It consists of an alternator that generates the current, a capacitive discharge ignition (CDI) unit that receives and stores it, and a pulse generator that triggers the CDI unit to discharge its current into the ignition coil, where it is stepped up to a voltage high enough to jump the spark plug gap. To aid in locating a problem in the ignition circuit, wiring diagrams are included at the end of this manual.

The CDI ignition system functions on the same principle as a breaker point ignition system, with the pulse generator and CDI unit performing the tasks previously associated with the breaker points and mechanical advance system. As a result, adjustment and maintenance of breakerless ignition components is eliminated (with the exception of spark plug replacement).

Because these models are intended for motocross competition, they do not have a battery, ignition switch, fuses, turn signals or lights. The engine is started with a kickstarter and turned off with a kill button on the left handlebar. **Note:** *Keep in mind that electrical parts, once purchased, can't be returned. To avoid unnecessary expense, make very sure the faulty component has been positively identified before buying a replacement part.*

2 Electrical troubleshooting

Electrical problems often stem from simple causes, such as loose or corroded connections. Prior to any electrical troubleshooting, always visually check the condition of the wires and connections in the circuit.

If testing instruments are going to be utilized, use the diagrams to plan where you will make the necessary connections in order to accurately pinpoint the trouble spot.

The basic tools needed for electrical troubleshooting include a test light or voltmeter, an ohmmeter or a continuity tester (which includes a bulb, battery and set of test leads) and a jumper wire, preferably with a circuit breaker incorporated, which can be used to bypass electrical components.

A continuity check is performed to see if a circuit, section of circuit or individual component is capable of passing electricity through it. Connect one lead of a self-powered test light or ohmmeter to one end of the circuit being tested and the other lead to the other end of the circuit. If the bulb lights (or the ohmmeter indicates little or no resistance), there is continuity, which means the circuit is passing electricity through it properly. The kill switch can be checked in the same way.

Remember that the electrical circuit on these motorcycles is designed to conduct electricity through the wires, kill switch, etc. to the electrical component (CDI unit, etc.). From there it is directed to the frame (ground) where it is passed back to the alternator. Electrical problems are basically an interruption in the flow of electricity.

Because of their nature, the individual ignition system components can be checked but not repaired. If ignition system troubles occur, and the faulty component can be isolated, the only cure for the problem is to replace the part with a new one. Keep in mind that most electrical parts, once purchased, can't be returned. To avoid unnecessary expense, make very sure the faulty component has been positively identified before buying a replacement part.

3 Ignition system - check

Refer to illustrations 3.4 and 3.10

Warning: *Because of the very high voltage generated by the ignition system, extreme care should be taken when these checks are performed.*

1 If the ignition system is the suspected cause of poor engine performance or failure to start, a number of checks can be made to isolate the problem.

Engine will not start

2 Refer to Chapter 1 and disconnect the spark plug wire. Connect the wire to a spare spark plug and lay the plug on the engine with the threads contacting the engine. If necessary, hold the spark plug with an insulated tool. Crank the engine over and make sure a well-defined, blue spark occurs between the spark plug electrodes. **Warning:** *Don't remove the spark plug from the engine to perform this check - atomized fuel being pumped out of the open spark plug hole could ignite, causing severe injury!*

3 If no spark occurs, the following checks should be made:

4 If a spark plug cap resistance value for your bike is listed in this Chapter's Specifications, unscrew the spark plug cap from the plug wire and check the cap resistance with an ohmmeter **(see illustration)**. If the resistance is higher than specified, replace the cap with a new one. If there's no specification listed, perform the spark test described in Step 2, but with the plug cap removed from the plug wire (lay the end of the wire on the cylinder head). If there's spark with the cap removed, but no spark with the cap installed, replace the cap with a new one.

5 Make sure all electrical connectors are clean and tight. Check all wires for shorts, opens and correct installation.

6 Check the pulse generator and exciter coil (see Section 6).

7 Refer to Section 4 and check the ignition coil primary and secondary resistance.

8 If the preceding checks produce positive results but there is still no spark at the plug, refer to Section 5 and check the CDI unit.

Engine starts but misfires

9 If the engine starts but misfires, make the following checks before deciding that the ignition system is at fault.

10 The ignition system must be able to produce a spark across a six-millimeter (1/4-inch) gap (minimum). A simple test fixture **(see illustration)** can be constructed to make sure the minimum spark gap can be jumped. Make sure the fixture electrodes are positioned seven millimeters apart.

11 Connect the spark plug wire to the protruding test fixture electrode, then attach the fixture's alligator clip to a good engine ground.

12 Crank the engine over with the kickstarter and see if well-defined, blue sparks occur between the test fixture electrodes. If the minimum spark gap test is positive, the ignition coil is functioning properly. If the spark will not jump the gap, or if it is weak (orange colored), refer to Steps 4 through 7 of this Section and perform the component checks described.

3.10 **A simple spark gap testing fixture can be made from a block of wood, two nails, a large alligator clip, a screw and a piece of wire**

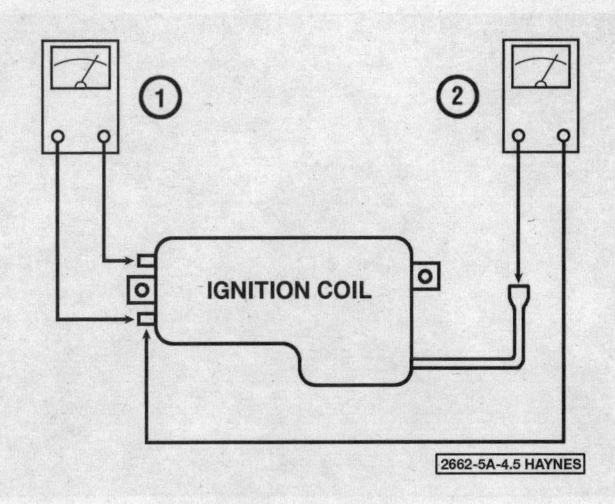

4.5 Ignition coil test

1 Measure primary winding resistance
2 Measure secondary winding resistance

4 Ignition coil - check, removal and installation

Check

1 In order to determine conclusively that the ignition coil is defective, it should be tested by an authorized Yamaha dealer service department which is equipped with the special electrical tester required for this check.

2 However, the coil can be checked visually (for cracks and other damage) and the primary and secondary coil resistances can be measured with an ohmmeter. If the coil is undamaged, and if the resistances are as specified, it is probably capable of proper operation.

3 To check the coil for physical damage, it must be removed (see Steps 8 and 9). To check the resistance, remove the fuel tank (see Chapter 4), unplug the primary circuit electrical connector(s) from the coil and remove the spark plug wire from the spark plug. Mark the locations of all wires before disconnecting them.

4 Label the primary wires, then disconnect them. Unscrew the spark plug cap from the plug wire.

5 Connect an ohmmeter between the primary (small) terminals. Set the ohmmeter selector switch in the Rx1 position and compare the measured resistance to the primary resistance values listed in this Chapter's Specifications.

6 Connect the ohmmeter between the coil primary terminal and the spark plug wire. Place the ohmmeter selector switch in the Rx100 position and compare the measured resistance to the secondary resistance values listed in this Chapter's Specifications.

7 If the resistances are not as specified, unscrew the spark plug cap from the plug wire and check the resistance between the ground wire's primary terminal and the end of the spark plug wire. If it's now within specifications, the spark plug cap is bad. If it's still not as specified, the coil is probably defective and should be replaced with a new one.

Removal and installation

Refer to illustration 4.8

8 To remove the coil, refer to Chapter 4 and remove the fuel tank, then disconnect the spark plug wire from the plug. Unplug the coil primary circuit electrical connector(s). Some models have a single primary circuit connector and another wire that connects to one of the coil mounting bolts to provide ground **(see illustration)**.

9 Remove the coil mounting bolt(s), then lift the coil out.

10 Installation is the reverse of removal.

5 CDI unit - check, removal and installation

Check

Ignition function

1 The CDI unit is tested by process of elimination (when all other possible causes of ignition problems have been checked and eliminated, the CDI unit is at fault).

2 Check the ignition coil, alternator exciter coil, pulse generator and kill switch as described elsewhere in this Chapter.

3 Carefully check the wiring harnesses for breaks or bad connections.

4 If the harness and all other system components tested good, the CDI unit may be defective. Before buying a new one, it's a good idea to substitute a known good CDI unit, if possible.

TPS input voltage check

5 Later model YZ250 models are equipped with a throttle position sensor (TPS). The CDI unit uses the signal from this sensor to fine-tune the ignition curve to the throttle demand from the rider. If the bike exhibits sluggish acceleration or a stumble, and the carburetor has been ruled out as the source of the problem, the TPS may be at fault, or the CDI unit might not be providing the proper input voltage to the TPS.

4.8 Disconnect the primary terminals (left arrows) - if a mounting bolt secures a ground wire (right arrow) be sure to reconnect it on installation

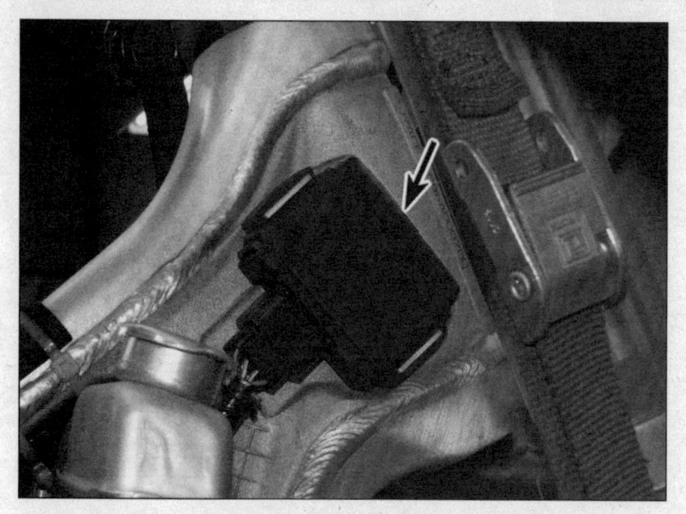

5.10 The CDI unit (arrow) is mounted on the frame - unplug the connector and slide it off the tabs to remove it

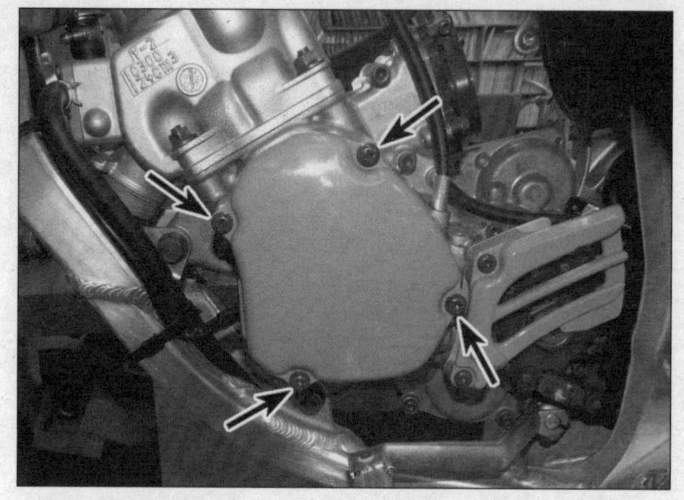

6.4a The left engine cover is secured by screws (arrows) . . .

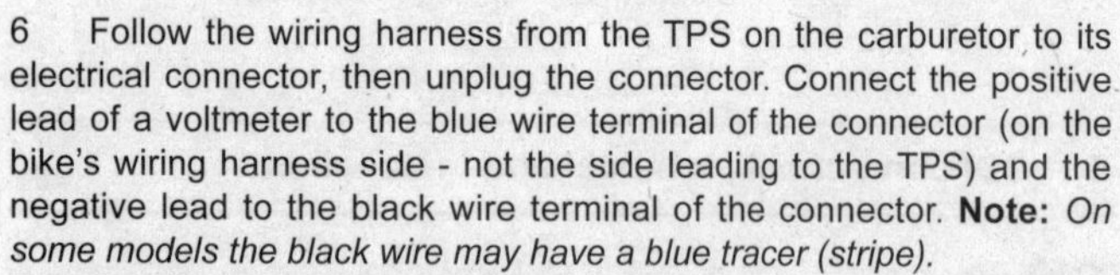

6 Follow the wiring harness from the TPS on the carburetor to its electrical connector, then unplug the connector. Connect the positive lead of a voltmeter to the blue wire terminal of the connector (on the bike's wiring harness side - not the side leading to the TPS) and the negative lead to the black wire terminal of the connector. **Note:** *On some models the black wire may have a blue tracer (stripe).*

7 Start the engine and check the reading on the voltmeter; four to six volts should be present.

8 If the voltage is not as specified, replace the CDI unit (see Chapter 5).

Removal and installation

Refer to illustration 5.10

9 Remove the fuel tank if you haven't already done so (see Chapter 4).

10 Locate the CDI unit **(see illustration)**. Unplug its connector and work the unit out of its mounting band.

11 Installation is the reverse of the removal steps.

6 Alternator and pulse generator - check and replacement

Check

1 Locate and disconnect the alternator coil connector on the left side of the vehicle frame.

2 To check the exciter coil, connect an ohmmeter between the specified terminals in the side of the connector that runs back to the exciter coil on the left side of the engine (refer to this Chapter's Specifications for wire colors and resistance values). If the readings are much outside the value listed, replace the exciter coil as described below.

3 To check the pulse generator, connect the ohmmeter between the specified terminals in the side of the connector that runs back to the pulse generator (refer to this Chapter's Specifications for wire colors and resistance values). If the readings are much outside the value listed in this Chapter's Specifications, replace the pulse generator as described below.

Rotor replacement

Removal

Refer to illustrations 6.4a, 6.4b, 6.5a, 6.5b, 6.6a, 6.6b, 6.7a and 6.7b

Note: *To remove the alternator rotor, the special Yamaha puller or an aftermarket equivalent will be required. Don't try to remove the rotor without the proper puller, as it's almost sure to be damaged. Pullers are readily available from motorcycle dealers and aftermarket tool suppliers.*

4 Remove the left engine cover **(see illustrations)**.

5 Hold the alternator rotor with a universal holder. You can also use a strap wrench. If you don't have one of these tools and the engine is in the frame, the rotor can be locked by placing the transmission in gear and holding the rear brake on. Unscrew the rotor nut and remove the washer **(see illustrations)**.

6 Thread an alternator puller into the center of the rotor and use it to remove the rotor **(see illustrations)**. If the rotor doesn't come off easily, tap sharply on the end of the puller to release the rotor's grip on the tapered crankshaft end.

7 Pull the rotor off **(see illustration)**. Check the Woodruff key; if it's not secure in its slot, pull it out and set it aside for safekeeping. A convenient method is to stick the Woodruff key to the magnets inside the rotor **(see illustration)**, but be certain not to forget it's there, as serious damage to the rotor and stator coils will occur if the engine is run with anything stuck to the magnets.

Installation

8 Take a look to make sure there isn't anything stuck to the inside of the rotor **(see illustration 6.7b)**.

9 Degrease the center of the rotor and the end of the crankshaft.

10 Make sure the Woodruff key is positioned securely in its slot **(see illustration 6.7a)**.

11 Align the rotor slot with the Woodruff key. Place the rotor on the crankshaft.

12 Install the rotor washer and nut. Hold the rotor from turning with

6.4b . . . take the cover off and remove the gasket

6.5a Unscrew the rotor nut . . .

6.5b . . . and remove the washer - you may need to pry it out

6.6a Thread the puller onto the rotor and tighten the puller screw against the crankshaft . . .

6.6b . . . then hold the puller body with a wrench and tighten the puller screw to push the rotor off

6.7a Locate the Woodruff key (arrow); be sure it's in its slot on installation

6.7b Be sure there aren't any small metal objects stuck to the rotor magnets; an item like this Woodruff key (arrow) can ruin the rotor and stator (exciter coil) if the engine is run

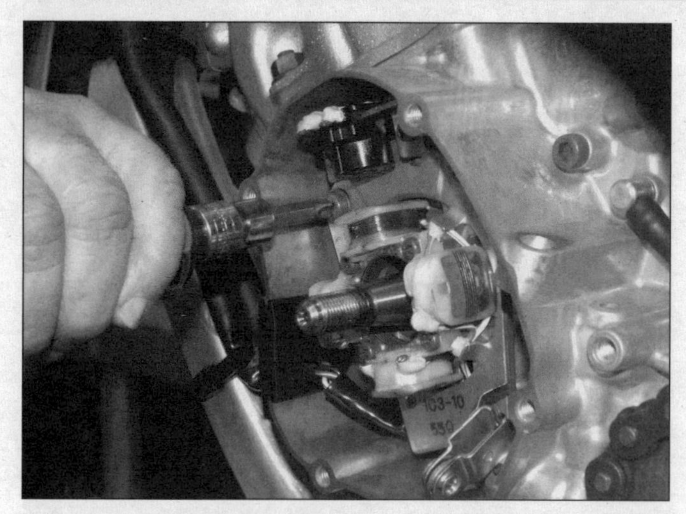

6.16a Remove the stator plate (exciter coil) mounting screws with an impact driver - there are two or three screws, depending on model

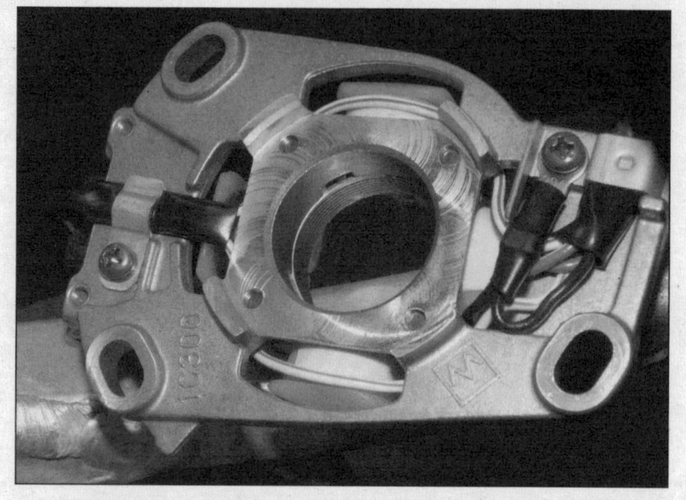

6.16b Make sure wiring connections on the back side of the plate are clean and tight, and retainers are securely fastened

one of the methods described in Step 5 and tighten the nut to the torque listed in this Chapter's Specifications.

13 The remainder of installation is the reverse of the removal steps.

Exciter coil and pulse generator replacement

Refer to illustrations 6.16a, 6.16b, 6.17 and 6.18

14 The exciter coil and pulse generator are replaced as a unit.

15 Remove the left engine cover and alternator rotor as described above.

16 Remove the screws that secure the exciter coil base plate and take it off the engine, together with the exciter coils and pulse generator **(see illustrations)**. **Note:** *On early models, the pulse generator and coil(s) are available separately from the base plate. On later models, the base plate, exciter coil and pulse generator are sold as a unit. Check availability with your parts supplier before removing the coil(s) from the base plate.*

17 Check the crankshaft seal behind the base plate for signs of leakage **(see illustration)**. Crankshaft seals have a major effect on 2-stroke engine performance, so replace the seal if its condition is in doubt.

18 Installation is the reverse of the removal steps. Align the timing marks on the base plate and crankcase **(see illustration)**. Tighten the base plate screws securely, but don't overtighten them and strip the threads.

7 Kill switch - check, removal and installation

1 The kill switch, mounted on the left handlebar, shorts the ignition circuit to ground when its button is pressed.

Check

2 Follow the wires from the switch to their connectors and unplug them.

3 Connect an ohmmeter between the wire terminals in the switch side of the connectors (not the side that leads back to the wiring harness). With the switch in the released position, the ohmmeter should show no continuity (infinite resistance); with the button pushed, the ohmmeter should show continuity (little or no resistance).

4 Repeat the test several times. The ohmmeter should move from continuity to no continuity each time the button is released. If it continues to show continuity after it's released, the ignition system is being shorted out constantly and won't produce a spark.

Removal and installation

5 To remove the switch, remove its mounting screw, separate the clamp and take it off the handlebar. Remove the wiring harness retainers and unplug the switch electrical connector.

6 Installation is the reverse of removal. Note that the clamp screw secures the switch ground wire.

6.17 The crankshaft seal should be replaced if it has been leaking

6.18 Align the timing marks on base plate and crankcase (arrows) (late YZ125 shown)

Chapter 6
Steering, suspension and final drive

Contents

Specifications

YZ80/85

Front forks

Oil type
- 1986 through 1992 ... 10-weight fork oil
- 1993 and later ... Yamaha suspension oil "01" or equivalent

Oil capacity
- 1986 through 1992 ... 272cc (9.2 US fl oz, 9.57 Imp oz)
- 1993 and 1994 ... 329 cc (11.1 US fl oz, 11.5 Imp oz)
- 1995
  - YZ80 ... 329 cc (11.1 US fl oz, 11.5 Imp oz)
  - YZ80LW ... 325 cc (11.0 US fl oz, 11.4 Imp oz)
- 1996
  - YZ80 ... 323 cc (10.9 US fl oz, 11.4 Imp oz)
  - YZ80LW ... 319 cc (10.8 US fl oz, 11.2 Imp oz)
- 1997 through 2001 ... 323 cc (10.9 US fl oz, 11.4 Imp oz)
- 2002 and later ... 318 cc (10.8 US fl oz, 11.2 Impoz0

Oil level*
- 1986 through 1992 ... 157 mm (6.18 inches)
- 1993 and 1994
  - Standard ... 90 mm (3.54 inches)
  - Minimum ... 80 mm (3.15 inches)
  - Maximum ... 120 mm (4.72 inches)
- 1995 and 1996
  - Standard
    - YZ80 ... 90 mm (3.54 inches)
    - YZ80LW ... 95 mm (3.74 inches)
  - Minimum ... 80 mm (3.15 inches)
  - Maximum ... 120 mm (4.72 inches)
- 1997 and later
  - Standard ... 90 mm (3.54 inches)
  - Minimum ... 80 mm (3.15 inches)
  - Maximum ... 120 mm (4.72 inches)

**From top of fork tube, with spring removed and damper rod compressed all the way.*

Fork spring free length
- 1986 through 1992
  - Standard ... 461 mm (18.1 inches)
  - Limit ... 457 mm (18.0 inches)
- 1993 through 2001 ... 430 mm (16.93 inches)
- 2002 and later
  - Standard ... 430 mm (16.93 inches)
  - Limit ... 425 mm (16.7 inches)

Air pressure ... See Chapter 1

Front forks (continued)

Protrusion from upper triple clamp	
1986	7 mm (0.28 inch)
1987 through 1992	12 mm (0.47 inch)
1993 and 1994	24 mm (0.94 inch)
1995 through 2001	
YZ80	24 mm (0.94 inch)
YZ80LW	Zero
2002 and 2003	Zero
2004	24 mm (0.94 inch)
2005 and later	Zero

Drive chain

Length limit (10 links)	
1986 through 1992	123 mm (4.84 inches)
1993 through 1999	122.1 mm (4.81 inches)
2000 and 2001	121.4 mm (4.78 inches)
2002 through 2004	122.1 mm (4.81 inches)
2005 and later	194.3 mm (7.65 inches)

Torque specifications

Handlebar bracket bolts	27 Nm (19 ft-lbs)
Handlebar bracket nuts	Not applicable
Triple clamp bolts	
1986 through 1992	
Lower	23 Nm (16 ft-lbs)
Upper	18 Nm (13 ft-lbs)
1993 through 2001	
Lower	24 Nm (17 ft-lbs)
Upper	22 Nm (16 ft-lbs)
2002 and later	
Lower	20 Nm (14 ft-lbs)
Upper	22 Nm (16 ft-lbs)
Fork cap to fork	
1986 through 1992	23 Nm (16 ft-lbs)
1993 and later	28 Nm (20 ft-lbs)
Fork Allen bolt (damper rod fork)	
1986	23 Nm (16 ft-lbs)
1987 through 1992	30 Nm (22 ft-lbs)
Fork base valve (cartridge fork)	
1993, 4, 5, 01, 02, 03	55 Nm (40 ft-lbs)
Steering stem bearing adjusting nut	See Chapter 1
Steering stem bolt	
1986	85 Nm (61 ft-lbs)
1987 through 1992	60 Nm (43 ft-lbs)
Steering stem nut	
1993 through 2001	110 Nm (80 ft-lbs)
2002	115 Nm (85 ft-lbs)
2003 and later	125 Nm (90 ft-lbs)
Rear shock absorber mounting bolts	
1986 through 1992	32 Nm (23 ft-lbs)
1993 through 2000	
Upper	38 Nm (27 ft-lbs)
Lower	32 Nm (23 ft-lbs)
2001 and 2002	
Upper	36 Nm (25 ft-lbs)
Lower	32 Nm (23 ft-lbs)
2003 and later (upper and lower)	36 Nm (25 ft-lbs)
Shock linkage	
1986 through 1992	
Relay arm to swingarm	32 Nm (23 ft-lbs)
Relay arm to connecting rod	32 Nm (23 ft-lbs)
Connecting rod to frame	32 Nm (23 ft-lbs)
1993 and later	
Connecting rod to swingarm	53 Nm (38 ft-lbs)
Connecting rod to relay arm	53 Nm (38 ft-lbs)
Relay arm to frame	54 Nm (39 ft-lbs)
Swingarm pivot bolt nut	53 Nm (38 ft-lbs)

Engine sprocket nut	
1986 through 2001	Not applicable
2002 and later	60 Nm (43 ft-lbs)
Rear sprocket bolts/nuts	
1986 through 1992	27 Nm (19 ft-lbs)
1993 through 2001	43 Nm (31 ft-lbs)
2002 and later	42 Nm (30 ft-lbs)

YZ125

Front forks

Oil type	
1986	15-weight fork oil
1987	10-weight fork oil
1988 through 2004	Yamaha suspension oil "01" or equivalent
2005 and later	Yamaha suspension oil "S1" or equivalent
Oil capacity	
1986	564 cc (19.1 US fl oz, 19.9 Imp oz)
1987	559 c (18.9 US fl oz, 19.7 Imp oz)
1988	570 cc (19.3 US fl oz, 20.1 Imp oz)
1989	425 cc (14.4 US fl oz, 15.0 Imp oz)
1990	420 cc (14.2 US fl oz, 14.8 Imp oz)
1991	
All except Europe	564 cc (19.1 US fl oz, 19.9 Imp oz)
Europe	559 cc (18.9 US fl oz, 19.7 Imp oz)
1992	
All except Europe	537 cc (18.2 US fl oz, 18.9 Imp oz)
Europe	542 cc (18.3 US fl oz, 19.1 Imp oz)
1993	
All except Europe	509 cc (17.2 US fl oz, 17.9 Imp oz)
Europe	513 cc (17.3 US fl oz, 18.1 Imp oz)
1994 and 1995	515 cc (17.4 US fl oz, 18.1 Imp oz)
1996 and 1997	612 cc (20.7 US fl oz, 21.5 Imp oz)
1998	
All except Europe	570 cc (19.3 US fl oz, 20.1 Imp oz)
Europe	560 cc (18.9 US fl oz, 19.7 Imp oz)
1999 through 2002	573 cc (19.4 US fl oz, 20.2 Imp oz)
2003	568 cc (19.2 US fl oz, 20.0 Imp oz)
2004	662 cc (22.4 US fl oz, 23.3 Imp oz)
2005 (into cartridge)	195 cc (6.59 US fl oz, 6.86 Imp oz)
2005 (into fork tube)	
Standard	
All except Europe	245 cc (8.28 US fl oz, 8.62 Imp oz)
Europe	250 cc (8.45 US fl oz, 8.80 Imp oz)
Minimum	200 cc (6.76 US fl oz, 7.04 Imp oz)
Maximum	300 cc (10.1 US fl oz, 10.6 Imp oz)
2006 (into cartridge)	195 cc (6.59 US fl oz, 6.86 Imp oz)
2006 (into fork tube)	
Standard	
All except Europe	340 cc (11.5 US fl oz, 12.0 Imp oz)
Europe	335 cc (11.3 US fl oz, 11.8 Imp oz)
Minimum	300 cc (10.1 US fl oz, 10.6 Imp oz)
Maximum	380 cc (12.8 US fl oz, 13.4 Imp oz)
Oil level*	
1986	160 mm (6.30 inches)
1987	
Standard	145 mm (5.71 inches)
Minimum	108 mm (4.25 inches)
Maximum	165 mm (6.50 inches)
1988	
Standard	140 mm (5.51 inches)
Minimum	110 mm (4.33 inches)
Maximum	160 mm (5.51 inches)
1989 and 1990	
Standard	120 mm (4.72 inches)
Minimum	100 mm (3.94 inches)
Maximum	140 mm (5.51 inches)
1991	
All except Europe	95 mm (3.74 inches)
Europe	100 mm (3.94 inches)

Front forks (continued)

1992	
Standard	
All except Europe	115 mm (3.74 inches)
Europe	110 mm (4.33 inches)
Minimum	80 mm (3.15 inches)
Maximum	130 m (5.12 inches)
1993	
Standard	
All except Europe	120 mm (4.72 inches)
Europe	115 mm (4.53 inches)
Minimum	80 mm (3.15 inches)
Maximum	140 mm (5.51 inches)
1994 and 1995	
Standard	105 mm (4.13 inches)
Minimum	90 mm (3.54 inches)
Maximum	140 mm (5.51 inches)
1996 and 1997	
Standard	100 mm (3.94 inches)
Minimum	80 mm (3.15 inches)
Maximum	130 mm (5.12 inches)
1998	
Standard	
All except Europe	135 mm (5.31 inches)
Europe	145 mm (5.71 inches)
Minimum	80 mm (3.15 inches)
Maximum	150 mm (5.91 inches)
1999 through 2003	
Standard	135 mm (5.31 inches)
Minimum	80 mm (3.15 inches)
Maximum	150 mm (5.91 inches)
2004	
Standard	125 mm (4.92 inches)
Minimum	105 mm (4.13 inches)
Maximum	135 mm (5.31 inches)
2005 and later	Not applicable

**From top of fork tube, with spring removed and damper rod compressed all the way.*

Fork spring free length	
1986	493.5 mm (19.43 inches)
1987	492 mm (19.4 inches)
1988	493 mm (19.41 inches)
1989 and 1990	505 mm (19.9 inches)
1991	
Standard	480 mm (18.9 inches)
Limit	475 mm (18.7 inches)
1992 and 1993	
Standard	490 mm (19.3 inches)
Limit	485 mm (19.1 inches)
1994 and 1995	
Standard	480 mm (18.9 inches)
Limit	475 mm (18.7 inches)
1996 through 2003	
Standard	460 mm (18.1 inches)
Limit	455 mm (17.9 inches)
2004	
Standard	479 mm (18.9 inches)
Limit	474 mm (18.7 inches)
2005 and later	
Standard	465 mm (18.3 inches)
Limit	460 mm (18.1 inches)
Air pressure	See Chapter 1
Protrusion from upper triple clamp	
1986	Not specified
1987	5 mm (0.20 inch)
1988	4 mm (0.16 inch)
1989	Zero
1990	3 mm (0.12 inch)
1991 and 1992	Zero
1993 and later	5 mm (0.17 inches)

Drive chain

Item	Specification
Length limit (10 links)	
1986	151.5 mm (5.965 inches)
1987 through 1990	Not specified
1991	153.1 mm (6.028 inches)
1992 through 1998	153.0 mm (6.024 inches)
1999 through 2004	152.5 mm (6.004 inches)
Length limit (15 links)	
2005 and later	242.9 mm (9.563 inches)

Torque specifications

Item	Specification
Handlebar bracket bolts	
1986 through 2000	23 Nm (16 ft-lbs)
2001 and later	28 Nm (20 ft-lbs)
Handlebar bracket nuts	
1986 through 1988	Not applicable
1989 through 1993	40 Nm (29 ft-lbs)
1994 and later	Not applicable
Triple clamp bolts	
1986 and 1987	
Lower	Not specified
Upper	23 Nm (16 ft-lbs)
1988	
Lower	32 Nm (23 ft-lbs)
Upper	23 Nm (17 ft-lbs)
1989 and 1990 (upper and lower)	23 Nm (17 ft-lbs)
1991 and later	
Upper	23 Nm (17 ft-lbs)
Lower	20 Nm (14 ft-lbs)
Fork cap to fork	
1986 and 1987	23 Nm (16 ft-lbs)
1988 and 1989	28 Nm (20 ft-lbs)
1990 through 1992	30 Nm (22 ft-lbs)
1993 through 1995	28 Nm (20 ft-lbs)
1996 and later	30 Nm (22 ft-lbs)
Fork base valve	
1986	72 Nm (52 ft-lbs)
1987 through 2004	55 Nm (40 ft-lbs)
2005 and later	29 Nm (21 ft-lbs)
Fork damping adjuster (2005 and later)	55 Nm (40 ft-lbs)
Steering stem bearing adjusting nut	See Chapter 1
Steering stem nut	
1986 and 1987	85 Nm (61 ft-lbs)
1988	115 Nm (85 ft-lbs)
1989	85 Nm (61 ft-lbs)
1990 through 1992	115 Nm (85 ft-lbs)
1993	170 Nm (125 ft-lbs)
1994 and later	145 Nm (105 ft-lbs)
Rear shock absorber mounting bolts	
1986 through 1989	32 Nm (23 ft-lbs)
1990 through 1992	
Upper	56 Nm (40 ft-lbs)
Lower	32 Nm (23 ft-lbs)
1993 through 1997	
Upper	56 Nm (40 ft-lbs)
Lower	48 Nm (35 ft-lbs)
1998 and later	
Upper	56 Nm (40 ft-lbs)
Lower	53 Nm (38 ft-lbs)
Shock linkage	
1986 through 1988	
Connecting rod to swingarm	60 Nm (43 ft-lbs)
Relay arm to connecting rod	60 Nm (43 ft-lbs)
Connecting rod to frame	60 Nm (43 ft-lbs)
1989	
Connecting rod to swingarm	60 Nm (43 ft-lbs)
Relay arm to connecting rod	60 Nm (43 ft-lbs)
Connecting rod to frame	60 Nm (43 ft-lbs)

Torque specifications (continued)

1990 through 1992	
Connecting rod to swingarm	60 Nm (43 ft-lbs)
Relay arm to connecting rod	60 Nm (43 ft-lbs)
Relay arm to frame	60 Nm (43 ft-lbs)
1993 through 2005	
Relay arm to swingarm	80 Nm (58 ft-lbs)
Relay arm to connecting rod	80 Nm (58 ft-lbs)
Connecting rod to frame	80 Nm (58 ft-lbs)
2006	
Relay arm to swingarm	70 Nm (50 ft-lbs)
Relay arm to connecting rod	80 Nm (58 ft-lbs)
Relay arm to frame	80 Nm (58 ft-lbs)
Swingarm pivot bolt nut	85 Nm (61 ft-lbs)
Engine sprocket nut	
1986 through 1988	60 Nm (43 ft-lbs)
1989	75 Nm (54 ft-lbs)
1990 through 2002	60 Nm (43 ft-lbs)
2003 and 2004	65 Nm (47 ft-lbs)
2005 and later	75 Nm (54 ft-lbs)
Rear sprocket bolts/nuts	
1986 through 1992	30 Nm (22 ft-lbs)
1993 through 1998	34 Nm (24 ft-lbs)
1999 and later	42 Nm (30 ft-lbs)

YZ250

Front forks

Oil type	
1986	15-weight fork oil
1987	10-weight fork oil
1988 through 2004	Yamaha suspension oil "01" or equivalent
2005 and later	Yamaha suspension oil "S1" or equivalent
Oil capacity	
1986	564 cc (19.1 US fl oz, 19.9 Imp oz)
1987	587 c (19.8 US fl oz, 20.7 Imp oz)
1988	570 cc (19.3 US fl oz, 20.1 Imp oz)
1989	404 cc (13.7 US fl oz, 14.2 Imp oz)
1990	420 cc (14.2 US fl oz, 14.8 Imp oz)
1991	Not available
1992	
All except Europe	542 cc (18.3 US fl oz, 19.1 Imp oz)
Europe	546 cc (18.5 US fl oz, 19.2 Imp oz)
1993	
All except Europe	523 cc (17.7 US fl oz, 18.4 Imp oz)
Europe	529 cc (17.9 US fl oz, 18.6 Imp oz)
1994 and 1995	520 cc (17.6 US fl oz, 18.3 Imp oz)
1996 and 1997	612 cc (20.7 US fl oz, 21.5 Imp oz)
1998	
All except Europe	570 cc (19.3 US fl oz, 20.1 Imp oz)
Europe	560 cc (18.9 US fl oz, 19.7 Imp oz)
1999 through 2002	573 cc (19.4 US fl oz, 20.2 Imp oz)
2003	568 cc (19.2 US fl oz, 20.0 Imp oz)
2004	662 cc (22.4 US fl oz, 23.3 Imp oz)
2005 (into cartridge)	195 cc (6.59 US fl oz, 6.86 Imp oz)
2005 (into fork tube)	
Standard	245 cc (8.28 US fl oz, 8.62 Imp oz)
Minimum	200 cc (6.76 US fl oz, 7.04 Imp oz)
Maximum	300 cc (10.1 US fl oz, 10.6 Imp oz)
2006 (into cartridge)	195 cc (6.59 US fl oz, 6.86 Imp oz)
2006 (into fork tube)	
Standard	
All except Europe	340 cc (11.5 US fl oz, 12.0 Imp oz)
Europe	345 cc (11.7 US fl oz, 12.1 Imp oz)
Minimum	300 cc (10.1 US fl oz, 10.6 Imp oz)
Maximum	380 cc (12.8 US fl oz, 13.4 Imp oz)
Oil level*	
1986	160 mm (6.30 inches)
1987	
Standard	120 mm (4.72 inches)

Minimum	108 mm (4.25 inches)
Maximum	165 mm (6.50 inches)
1988	
Standard	140 mm (5.51 inches)
Minimum	115 mm (4.53 inches)
Maximum	160 mm (5.51 inches)
1989	
Standard	145 mm (5.71 inches)
Minimum	125 mm (4.92 inches)
Maximum	165 mm (6.50 inches)
1990	
Standard	120 mm (4.72 inches)
Minimum	110 mm (4.33 inches)
Maximum	150 mm (5.91 inches)
1991	Not available
1992	
Standard	
All except Europe	110 mm (4.33 inches)
Europe	105 mm (4.13 inches)
Minimum	80 mm (3.15 inches)
Maximum	130 m (5.12 inches)
1993	
Standard	
All except Europe	105 mm (4.13 inches)
Europe	100 mm (3.94 inches)
Minimum	80 mm (3.15 inches)
Maximum	140 mm (5.51 inches)
1994	
Standard	105 mm (4.13 inches)
Minimum	90 mm (3.54 inches)
Maximum	140 mm (5.51 inches)
1995	
Standard	100 mm (3.94 inches)
Minimum	90 mm (3.54 inches)
Maximum	140 mm (5.51 inches)
1996 and 1997	
Standard	100 mm (3.94 inches)
Minimum	80 mm (3.15 inches)
Maximum	130 mm (5.12 inches)
1998	
Standard	
All except Europe	135 mm (5.31 inches)
Europe	145 mm (5.71 inches)
Minimum	80 mm (3.15 inches)
Maximum	150 mm (5.91 inches)
1999 through 2003	
Standard	135 mm (5.31 inches)
Minimum	80 mm (3.15 inches)
Maximum	150 mm (5.91 inches)
2004	
Standard	125 mm (4.92 inches)
Minimum	105 mm (4.13 inches)
Maximum	135 mm (5.31 inches)
2005 and later	Not applicable

**From top of fork tube, with spring removed and damper rod compressed all the way.*

Fork spring free length	
1986	543.5 mm (19.43 inches)
1987	532 mm (20.9 inches)
1988	493 mm (19.41 inches)
1989	505 mm (19.9 inches)
1990	518 mm (20.4 inches)
1991	Not available
1992 and 1993	490 mm (19.3 inches)
1994 and 1995	
Standard	480 mm (18.9 inches)
Limit	475 mm (18.7 inches)
1996 through 2003	
Standard	460 mm (18.1 inches)
Limit	455 mm (17.9 inches)

Front forks (continued)

2004	
Standard	479 mm (18.9 inches)
Limit	474 mm (18.7 inches)
2005	
Standard	465 mm (18.3 inches)
Limit	460 mm (18.1 inches)
2006	
Standard	454 mm (17.9 inches)
Limit	449 mm (17.7 inches)
Air pressure	See Chapter 1
Protrusion from upper triple clamp	
1986	Not specified
1987 through 1992	Zero
1993 and 1994	5 mm (0.17 inches)
1995 and later	Zero

Drive chain

Length limit (10 links)	
1986 through 1988	151.5 mm (5.965 inches)
1989 through 1991	Not specified
1992 through 1998	153.0 mm (6.024 inches)
1999 through 2004	152.5 mm (6.004 inches)
Length limit (15 links)	
2005 and later	242.9 mm (9.563 inches)

Torque specifications

Handlebar bracket bolts	
1986 through 2000	23 Nm (16 ft-lbs)
2001 and later	28 Nm (20 ft-lbs)
Handlebar bracket nuts	
1986 through 1988	Not applicable
1989 through 1993	40 Nm (29 ft-lbs)
1994 and later	Not applicable
Triple clamp bolts	
1986	
Lower	Not specified
Upper	23 Nm (16 ft-lbs)
1987 and 1988	
Lower	32 Nm (23 ft-lbs)
Upper	23 Nm (16 ft-lbs)
1989 (upper and lower)	23 Nm (17 ft-lbs)
1990 and later	
Lower	20 Nm (14 ft-lbs)
Upper	23 Nm (17 ft-lbs)
Fork cap to fork	
1986 and 1987	23 Nm (16 ft-lbs)
1988 and 1989	28 Nm (20 ft-lbs)
1990 through 1992	30 Nm (22 ft-lbs)
1993 through 1995	28 Nm (20 ft-lbs)
1996 through 2004	30 Nm (22 ft-lbs)
Fork cartridge to fork (2005 and later)	30 Nm (22 ft-lbs)
Fork base valve	
1986 and 1987	72 Nm (52 ft-lbs)
1988 through 2004	55 Nm (40 ft-lbs)
2005 and later (top mount base valve)	29 Nm (21 ft-lbs)
Fork damping adjuster (2005 and later)	55 Nm (40 ft-lbs)
Steering stem bearing adjusting nut	See Chapter 1
Steering stem nut	
1986 and 1987	85 Nm (61 ft-lbs)
1988	115 Nm (85 ft-lbs)
1989	85 Nm (61 ft-lbs)
1990 through 1992	115 Nm (85 ft-lbs)
1993	170 Nm (125 ft-lbs)
1994 and later	145 Nm (105 ft-lbs)
Rear shock absorber mounting bolts	
1986 through 1989	32 Nm (23 ft-lbs)
1990 through 1992	
Upper	56 Nm (40 ft-lbs)
Lower	32 Nm (23 ft-lbs)

1993 through 1997	
Upper	56 Nm (40 ft-lbs)
Lower	48 Nm (35 ft-lbs)
1998 and later	
Upper	56 Nm (40 ft-lbs)
Lower	53 Nm (38 ft-lbs)
Shock linkage to swingarm and frame	
1986 through 1992	60 Nm (43 ft-lbs)
1993 through 2005	80 Nm (58 ft-lbs)
2006	
Relay arm to swingarm	70 Nm (50 ft-lbs)
Relay arm to connecting rod	80 Nm (58 ft-lbs)
Relay arm to frame	80 Nm (58 ft-lbs)
Swingarm pivot bolt nut	85 Nm (61 ft-lbs)
Engine sprocket nut	75 Nm (54 ft-lbs)
Rear sprocket bolts/nuts	
1986 through 1992	30 Nm (22 ft-lbs)
1993 through 1998	34 Nm (24 ft-lbs)
1999 and later	42 Nm (30 ft-lbs)

1 General information

The steering system on these models consists of a one-piece braced handlebar and a steering head attached to the front portion of the frame. The steering stem rides in upper ball bearings and lower tapered roller bearings (early YZ80 models) or tapered roller bearings (all other models).

The front suspension uses one of three basic designs; damper rod, bottom cartridge, or top cartridge.

The rear suspension consists of a single shock absorber with concentric coil spring, a swingarm and progressive rising rate suspension linkage. The suspension linkage causes the suspension to stiffen as its travel increases. This allows a softer ride over small bumps in the terrain, together with firmer suspension control over large irregularities.

2 Handlebars - removal, inspection and installation

Refer to illustrations 2.3a and 2.3b

1 The handlebars rest in brackets on top of the upper triple clamp. If the handlebars must be removed for access to other components, such as the steering head bearings, simply remove the bolts and take the handlebars off the bracket. It's not necessary to disconnect the throttle or clutch cables, brake hose or the kill switch wires, but it is a good idea to support the assembly with a piece of wire or rope, to avoid unnecessary strain on the cables.

2 If the handlebars are to be removed completely, refer to Chapter 2 for the clutch lever removal procedure, Chapter 4 for the throttle housing removal procedure, Chapter 5 for the kill switch removal procedure and Chapter 7 for the brake master cylinder removal procedure.

3 Remove the upper bracket bolts, lift off the brackets and remove the handlebars **(see illustration)**. On 1989 through 1993 YZ125 and YZ250 models, the lower brackets can be removed from the triple clamp if necessary. To do this, remove the bracket nuts from below and lift the brackets out **(see illustration)**.

4 Check the handlebars and brackets for cracks and distortion and replace them if any problems are found.

5 Place the handlebars in the lower brackets. Line up the punch mark on the handlebar with the parting line of the upper and lower brackets.

6 Install the upper brackets with their punch marks facing forward. Tighten the front bolts, then the rear bolts, to the torque listed in this Chapter's Specifications. **Caution:** *If there's a gap between the upper and lower brackets at the rear after tightening the bolts, don't try to close it by tightening beyond the recommended torque. You'll only crack the brackets.*

2.3a Remove the bolts and lift off the upper brackets; on installation, tighten the front bolts first, then the rear bolts, and don't try to close up the gap by overtightening

2.3b On models with removable handlebar brackets, unscrew the nuts from below (arrows)

3.4a Note the position of the fork in the upper triple clamp, then loosen the pinch bolts

3.4b Loosen the lower triple clamp bolts and remove the fork

3 Front forks - removal and installation

Removal

Refer to illustrations 3.4a and 3.4b

1 Support the bike securely upright with its front wheel off the ground so it can't fall over during this procedure. If you're working on a bike with fork air valve caps, use the valves to relieve any accumulated fork air pressure.

2 Remove the front wheel, unbolt the brake caliper and detach the brake hose retainer from the left fork leg (see Chapter 7).

3 If you plan to disassemble the forks, loosen the fork cap bolts now (see Section 4). This can be done later, but it will be easier while the forks are securely held in the triple clamps. Also, set the damping adjuster (if equipped) to its softest setting to prevent damage to the adjuster when the fork is reassembled. Count the number of turns and write this down so you can return it to its original setting after the fork is installed.

4 Loosen the upper and lower triple clamp bolts **(see illustrations)**.

5 Lower the fork leg out of the triple clamps, twisting it if necessary.

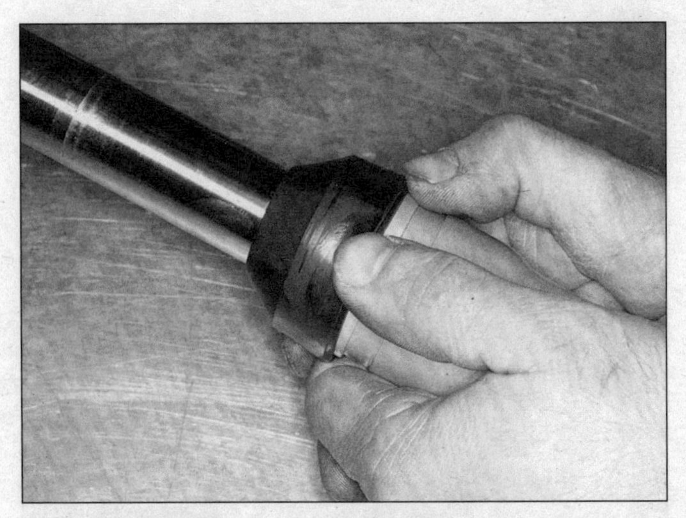

4.4 Push the dust seal off the fork slider)

Installation

6 Slide each fork leg into the lower triple clamp.

7 Slide the fork legs up, installing the tops of the tubes into the upper triple clamp. Position the upper end of each fork tube at the distance from the upper triple clamp listed in this Chapter's Specifications. Make sure the forks protrude an equal amount above each triple clamp.

8 Tighten the triple clamp bolts to the torque listed in this Chapter's Specifications.

9 Make sure the damping adjusters (if equipped) are at the same setting for both forks.

10 The remainder of installation is the reverse of the removal steps.

4 Damper rod forks - disassembly, inspection and reassembly

1 Damper rod forks are used on 1986 through 1992 YZ80 models, as well as 1986 and 1987 YZ125/250 models. The 1987 YZ125/250 forks include a variable damper, located inside the inner fork tube.

2 Remove the forks following the procedure in Section 3. Work on one fork at a time to prevent mixing up the parts.

Disassembly

Refer to illustrations 4.4, 4.6a through 4.6e, 4.8, 4.9a, 4.9b and 4.10

3 Unscrew the air valve from the top of the fork. Remove the valve and its O-ring.

4 Push the dust seal out of its groove and remove it from the fork **(see illustration)**.

5 Remove the fork spring from the top of the fork. On 1987 YZ125/250 models, remove the variable damper from the top of the fork. Turn the fork upside down and pour out the oil.

6 If you're working on a YZ80, unscrew the damper rod bolt from the bottom of the fork tube **(see illustrations)**. This will cause the damper rod to spin inside the fork tube, so you'll need to hold the damper rod from turning while you unscrew the bolt. This can be done with a special tool **(see illustration)**. If you don't have one, you can make one with a bolt, two nuts, some tape, a long extension and a socket **(see illustrations)**.

7 If you're working on a YZ125/250, unscrew the damping adjuster from the bottom of the fork.

8 Remove the damper rod from the fork tube **(see illustration)**.

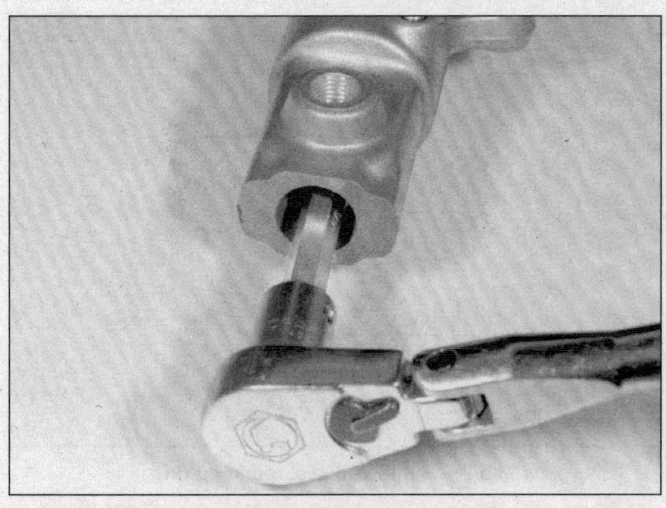

4.6a On YZ80 models, loosen the damper rod bolt with an Allen wrench (on YZ125/250 models, unscrew the base valve with a socket) . . .

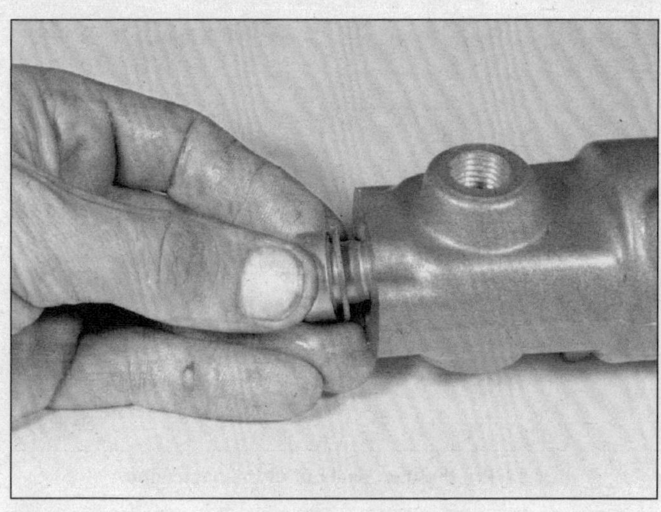

4.6b . . . and remove the bolt or base valve and its washer; use a new washer during assembly

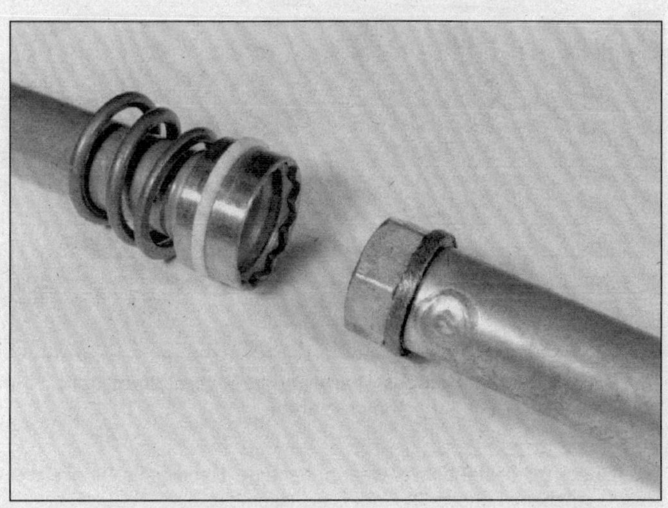

4.6c This is a special tool that's used to hold the damper rod from turning

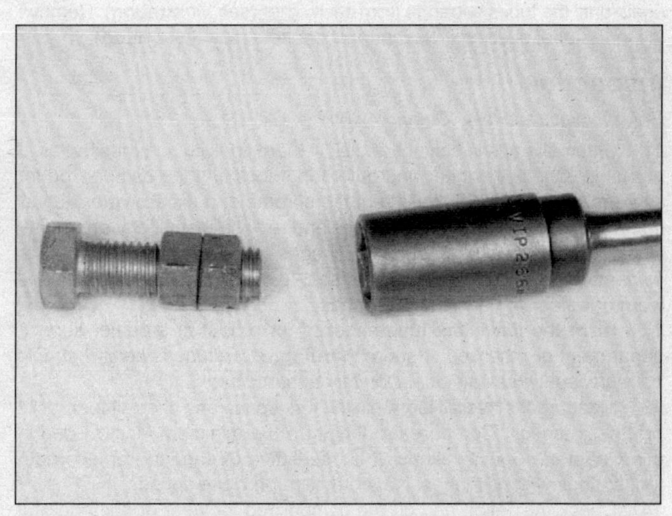

4.6d To make a damper rod holder, thread two nuts onto a bolt with a head that fits inside the damper rod and tighten the nuts against each other . . .

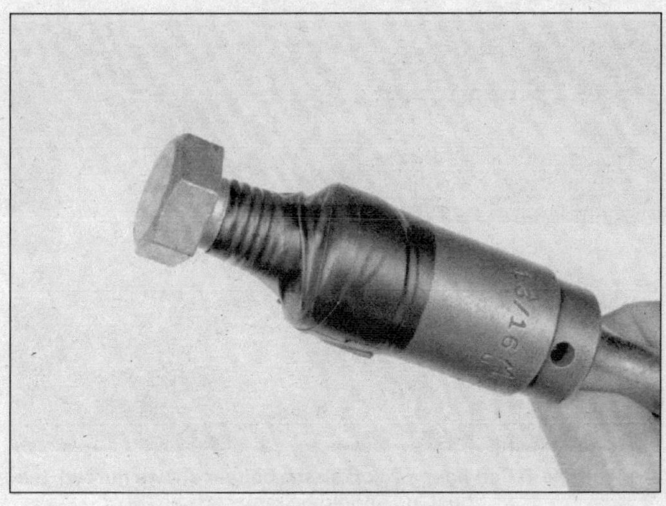

4.6e . . . then install the nut-end into a socket (connected to a long extension) and tape it into place

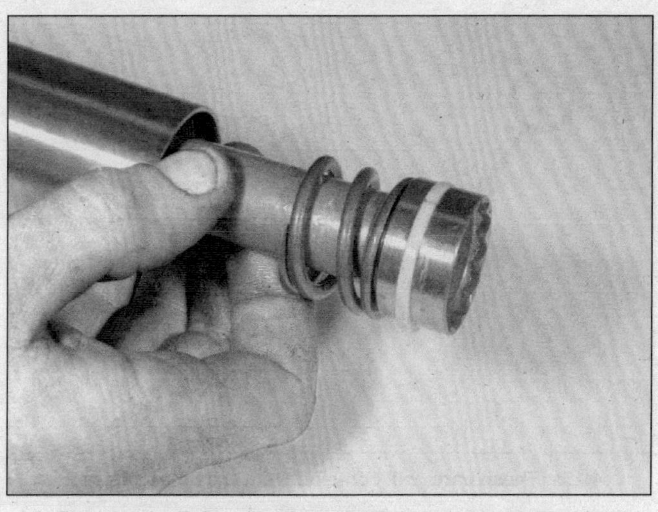

4.8 Remove the Teflon ring from the damper rod only if you plan to replace it

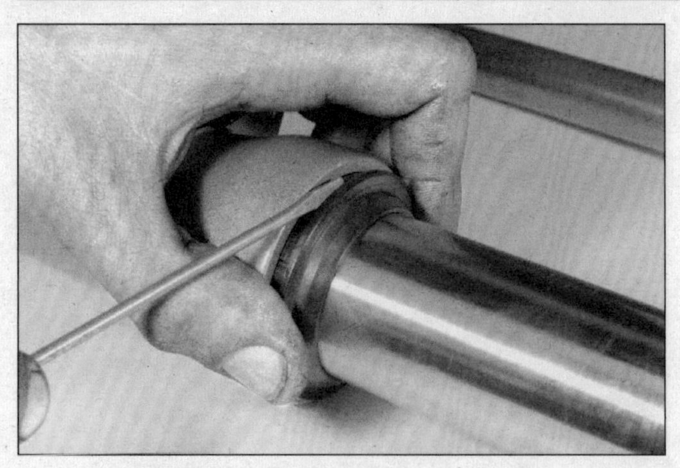

4.9a Pry the dust seal out of the outer tube

4.9b Pry out the oil seal retaining ring

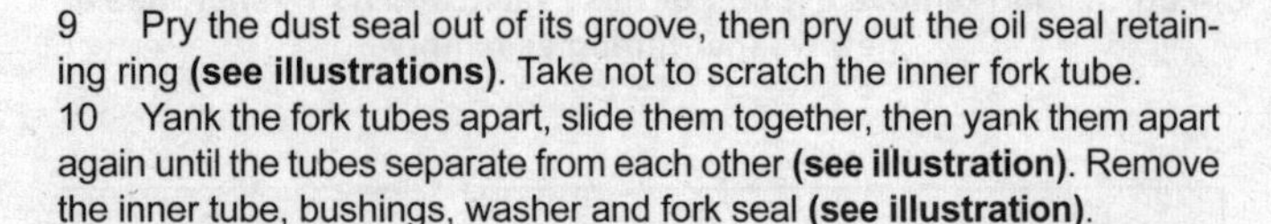

9 Pry the dust seal out of its groove, then pry out the oil seal retaining ring **(see illustrations)**. Take not to scratch the inner fork tube.
10 Yank the fork tubes apart, slide them together, then yank them apart again until the tubes separate from each other **(see illustration)**. Remove the inner tube, bushings, washer and fork seal **(see illustration)**.

Inspection

Refer to illustrations 4.15a and 4.15b

11 Clean all parts in solvent and blow them dry with compressed air, if available. Check the inner and outer fork tubes and the damper rod for score marks, scratches, flaking of the chrome and excessive or abnormal wear. Look for dents in the tubes and replace them if any are found. Check the fork seal seat for nicks, gouges and scratches. If damage is evident, leaks will occur around the seal-to-outer tube junction. Replace worn or defective parts with new ones.
12 Have the inner fork tube checked for runout at a dealer service department or other repair shop. **Warning:** *If the tube is bent, it should be replaced with a new one. Don't try to straighten it.*
13 Measure the overall length of the fork spring and check it for cracks or other damage. Compare the length to the minimum length listed in this Chapter's Specifications. If it's defective or sagged, replace both fork springs with new ones. Never replace only one spring.
14 Check the Teflon ring on the damper rod for wear or damage and replace it if problems are found **(see illustration 4.8)**. **Note:** *Don't remove the ring from the damper rod unless you plan to replace it.*
15 Check the fork tube bushing and fork slider bushing for wear **(see illustrations)** and replace them if their condition is in doubt.

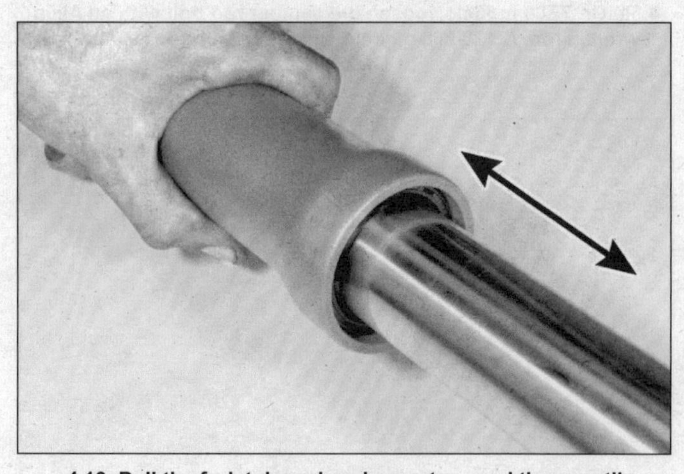

4.10 Pull the fork tubes sharply apart several times until they separate

16 Check the center bolt for wear or damage. Replace its O-rings and sealing washer whenever the fork is disassembled.
17 Check the Teflon ring on the damper rod for wear or damage and replace it if any problems are found **(see illustration 4.8)**.
18 Check the inner circumference of the back-up ring for distortion and replace it if any problems are found.

4.15a These parts will come out with the inner fork tube

1 *Seal*
2 *Washer*
3 *Outer tube bushing*
4 *Inner tube bushing*

4.15b If the Teflon has worn off so the copper shows (arrow), the bushing should be replaced

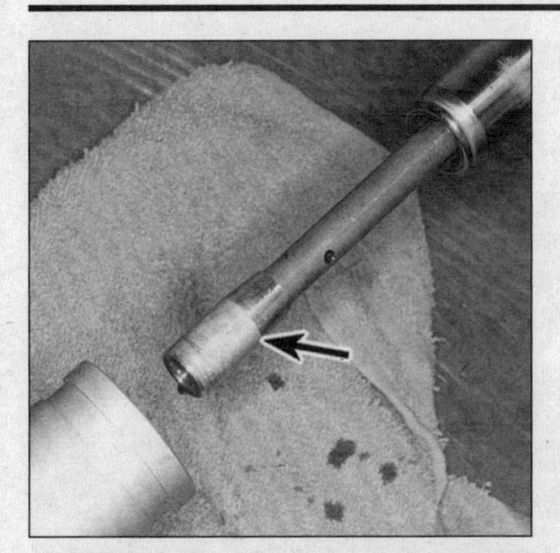

4.20 Place the oil lock piece (arrow) on the bottom of the damper piston

4.23 Drive the bushing into position with a tool like this one if you have it (use the tool like a slide hammer) . . .

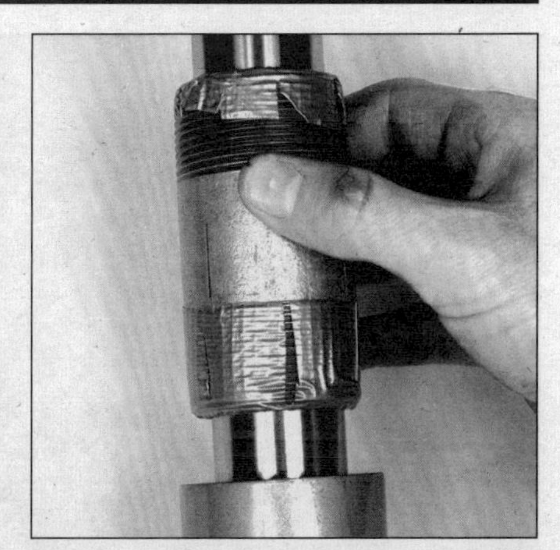

4.24 . . . if you don't have the special tool, drive the bushing with a section of pipe, but tape the ends so they won't scratch the fork tube

Reassembly

Refer to illustrations 4.20, 4.23 and 4.24

19 If the Teflon ring was removed from the damper, install it.

20 Install the damper rod and damper in the inner fork tube. Install the oil lock piece on the end of the damper **(see illustration)**, then install the inner fork tube in the outer fork tube.

21 Place a new sealing washer on the damping adjuster bolt. Coat the bolt threads with non-permanent thread locking agent, then install the bolt in the bottom of the fork and tighten it to the torque listed in this Chapter's Specifications.

22 Smear a coat of the fork oil listed in this Chapter's Specifications onto the inner circumference of the dust seal, the oil seal and the outer fork tube's bushing.

23 Slide the outer tube bushing onto the inner tube. Position the bushing at the edge of its bore, then use a fork seal driver or equivalent to drive the bushing into its bore **(see illustrations)**. Install the backup ring on top of the bushing.

24 Slide the oil seal onto the inner fork tube with its marked side facing up. Drive the oil seal, using the same seal driver, just past the retaining ring groove **(see illustration)**. If you're very careful, the seal can be driven in with a hammer and drift punch. Work around the circumference of the seal, tapping gently on the outer edge of the seal until it's seated. Be careful - if you distort the seal, you'll have to disassemble the fork and end up taking it to a dealer anyway! Compress the seal retaining ring into the groove, making sure it seats securely.

25 Install the dust seal, making sure it seats completely.

26 Fill the fork with oil, referring to this Chapter's Specifications and the fork oil change procedures in Chapter 1.

5 Bottom-mount cartridge forks - disassembly, inspection and reassembly

Refer to illustrations 5.2a, 5.2b, 5.3, 5.4a, 5.4b, 5.4c, 5.5a, 5.5b, 5.6, 5.7, 5.8, 5.9a, 5.9b, 5.9c, 5.10a through 5.10e and 5.11

Warning: *Do not disassemble the cartridge. This is a highly specialized job that even professional mechanics will send out to suspension modification shops. Incorrect assembly can cause erratic handling.*

Note: *Overhaul of the forks on these models requires special tools for which there are no good substitutes. An air compressor and air tools are also very helpful. The tools can be ordered from your local Yamaha dealer, or you may be able to buy equivalent tools from aftermarket suppliers. Read through the procedure and arrange to get the special tools or substitutes before starting. If you don't disassemble the forks on a regular basis, it may be more practical to have the job done by a Yamaha dealer or other motorcycle repair shop.*

1 This fork design is used on 1993 and later YZ80/85 models and on 1988 through 2006 YZ125/250 models.

2 Turn the damping adjuster in until it bottoms, counting the turns, and write this number down so the damping adjuster can be returned to its original setting **(see illustration)**. Now back it out until it's loose. Unscrew the cap bolt from the fork tube (it was loosened while the fork was still in the triple clamps) **(see illustration)**. If you forget to loosen

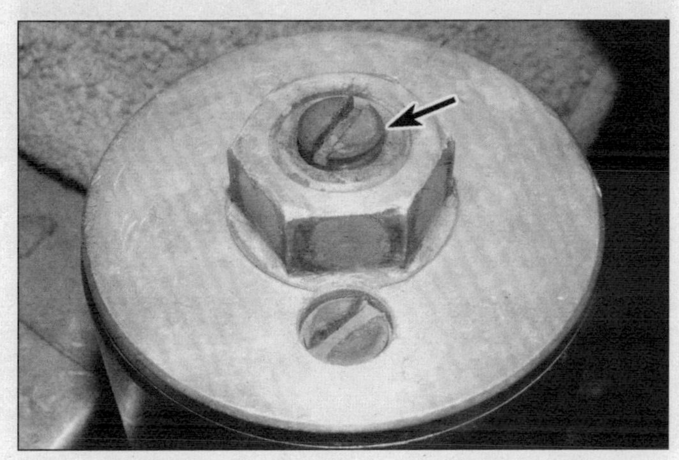

5.2a Counting the turns, turn the damping adjuster (arrow) in until it bottoms, then back it out until it's loose

5.2b Unscrew the fork cap from the tube

5.3 Pour the oil out of the fork

5.4a Hold the locknut with a wrench . . .

5.4b . . . and unscrew the fork cap from the damper rod - this is the 1997 and earlier design . . .

5.4c . . . and this is the 1998 and later design

the cap bolt, temporarily put the fork back into the upper triple clamp and tighten it, then loosen the clamp bolt. Don't use a vise or the inner fork tube may be distorted.

3 Turn the fork upside down and pour the oil into a container **(see illustration)**.

4 Compress the spring far enough to expose the locknut below the fork cap. Hold the locknut with an open-end wrench and unscrew the fork cap from the damper rod **(see illustrations)**.

5 On 1993 through 1997 YZ125/250 models, lift the rod cap out of the cartridge rod **(see illustration)**. On 1993 through 2004 models, remove the pushrod from the cartridge rod **(see illustration)**.

6 Remove the spring seat and spring from the inner fork tube **(see illustration)**.

7 Pry the dust seal away from the outer fork tube and slide it off the

5.5a Remove the rod cap, noting that its oil holes are downward . . .

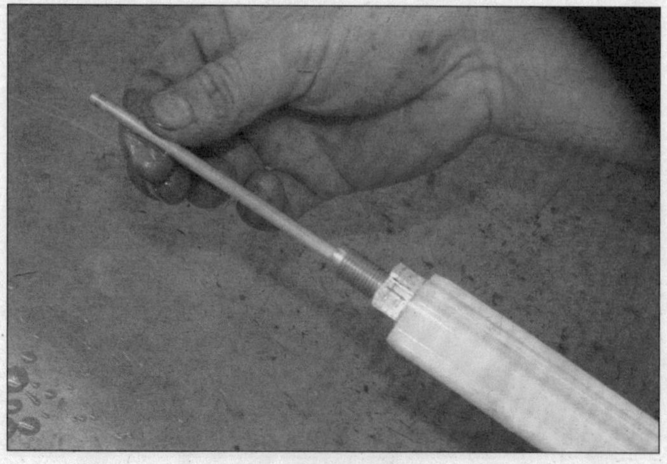

5.5b . . . and remove the pushrod (if equipped) from the damper rod

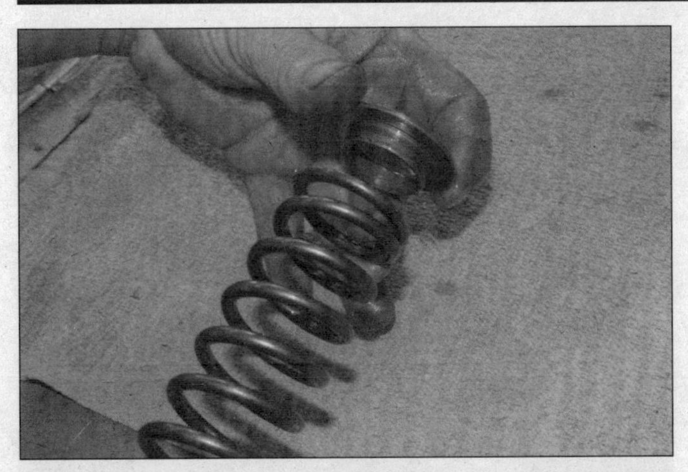

5.6 Remove the spring seat from the spring and pull the spring out of the tube

5.7 Pry the dust seal out of the fork tube . . .

end of the inner fork tube **(see illustration)**.

8 Pry the oil seal retainer out of its groove, taking care not to scratch the inner fork tube **(see illustration)**.

9 Grasp one fork tube in each hand, compress them together, then yank them apart sharply as far as they'll go. Do this several times until the tubes separate; the slide hammer-like motion is necessary to pull the slider bushing out of its bore in the outer fork tube **(see illustration)**. Remove the inner tube, bushings, back-up ring and oil seal **(see illustrations)**.

10 Check for built-up dirt or corrosion in the hex of the base valve at

5.8 . . . and pry out the oil seal retainer, taking care not to scratch the fork tube

5.9a Yank the tubes sharply apart several times to separate them, then remove the inner tube from the outer tube . . .

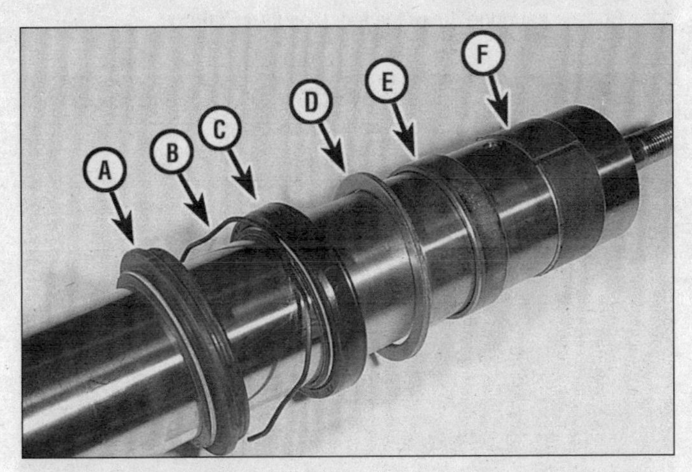

5.9b . . . which will provide access to the bushings and seals

A Dust seal
B Retainer
C Oil seal
D Back-up ring
E Outer tube bushing
F Inner tube bushing

5.9c Note which way the back-up ring faces

5.10a Clean all dirt from the base valve . . .

5.10b . . . and unscrew it from the fork leg

5.10c An air compressor with a hex bit is a convenient way to do this

5.10d If you don't have a compressor, use a damper rod tool . . .

the bottom of the fork **(see illustration)**. Clean as needed. Hold the cartridge from turning and unscrew the base valve from the bottom of the fork **(see illustrations)**. If you don't have the special tool, you can spin the base valve loose with an air wrench **(see illustration)**. However, you'll still need a way to hold the damper rod during assembly so you can tighten the center bolt to the correct torque. The ideal way to do this is with a damper rod holder **(see illustrations)**.You can order the Yamaha tool or an aftermarket equivalent from a Yamaha dealer. Another alternative is to install the fork spring and screw on the cap. The spring tension may be enough to keep the cartridge from turning as you loosen the base valve.

11 Pull the cartridge out of the fork **(see illustration)**.

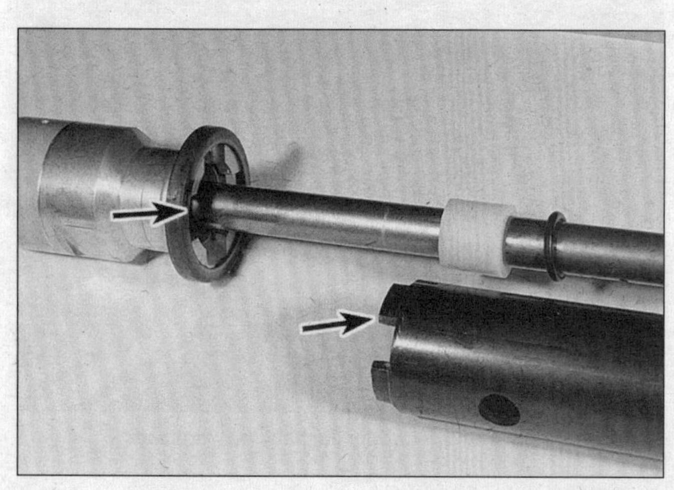

5.10e . . . the tabs on the tool engage the slots in the damper rod (arrows) (damper rod removed for clarity)

5.11 Bottom-mount cartridge fork details

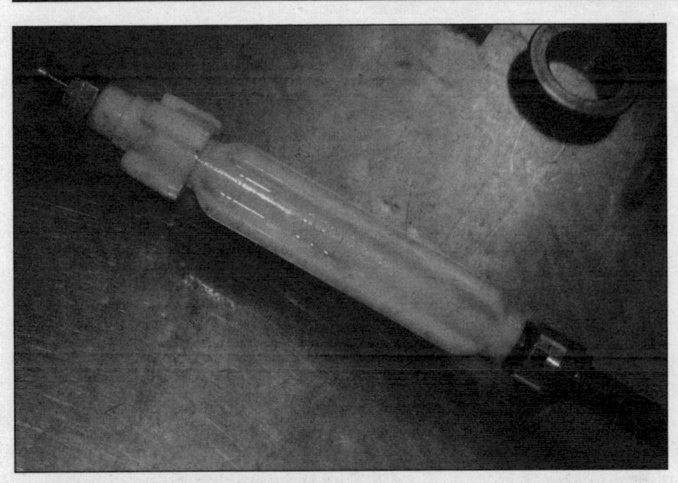

5.15 Don't remove the spring guides and other components from the damper rod unless they need to be replaced

5.16 Tape the end of the fork tube so the sharp edges won't cut the seals

Inspection

Refer to illustration 5.15

12 Refer to Steps 11 through 18 of Section 4 to inspect the fork.
13 Check the damper rod (and the pushrod that fits inside it on 1993 and later models) for bending. Replace either component if it's bent; do not try to straighten them.
14 Check the base valve for wear or damage and replace it if problems are found. Replace the base valve O-rings with new ones whenever the base valve is removed.
15 Check the spring guides, O-rings and other components on the cartridge rod for wear or damage **(see illustration)**. If necessary, remove them from the rod and install new ones. Count the number of turns as you remove the locknut from the top of the pushrod so it can be returned to its original position.

Assembly

Refer to illustration 5.16, 5.17, 5.26 and 5.31

16 Wrap the end of the inner fork tube with electrical tape to protect the new oil seal on installation **(see illustration)**. Coat the lip of the new oil seal with the recommended fork oil. Install the bushings (if removed), backup ring and oil seal on the inner fork tube **(see illustration 5.9b)**.
17 Install the inner tube in the outer tube. Slide the outer tube's bushing all the way down the inner fork tube until it rests against its bore in the outer fork tube. Install the back-up ring on top of the bushing. With a seal driver or equivalent tool **(see illustration 4.24 and the accompanying illustration)**, tap against the backup ring to drive the new bushing into its bore. Once the bushing is seated, use the same tool to seat the oil seal in the case just below the retainer ring groove.
18 Install the retainer ring and make sure it seats securely in its groove, then install the dust seal.
19 Install the cartridge in the outer fork tube.
20 Place new O-ring(s) on the base valve.
21 Coat the threads of the base valve with a non-permanent thread locking agent. Hold the cartridge with the tool mentioned in Step 10, then tighten the base valve to the torque listed in this Chapter's Specifications.
22 Compress the fork all the way, then slowly add the recommended fork oil until it's even with the top of the outer fork tube.
23 Pump the damper rod slowly up-and-down at least ten times, then push it all the way down.
24 Add fork oil to bring the level up to the top of the fork tube again.
25 Slowly pump the outer fork tube another ten times. **Note:** *Do not pump the fork more than eight inches, or air will be sucked into the oil and he procedure will have to be done over.*
26 Wait ten minutes for any air bubbles to flow out. **Note:** *The oil level won't be accurate if it's checked too soon.* With the fork vertical, measure the oil level in the fork **(see illustration)** and compare it to the value listed in this Chapter's Specifications. Add or drain oil as necessary to correct the level. **Note:** *Minimum oil level will make the suspension slightly softer near full compression; maximum oil level will make the suspension slightly stiffer near full compression.* **Warning:** *To prevent unstable handling, make sure the oil level is exactly the same in both forks.*

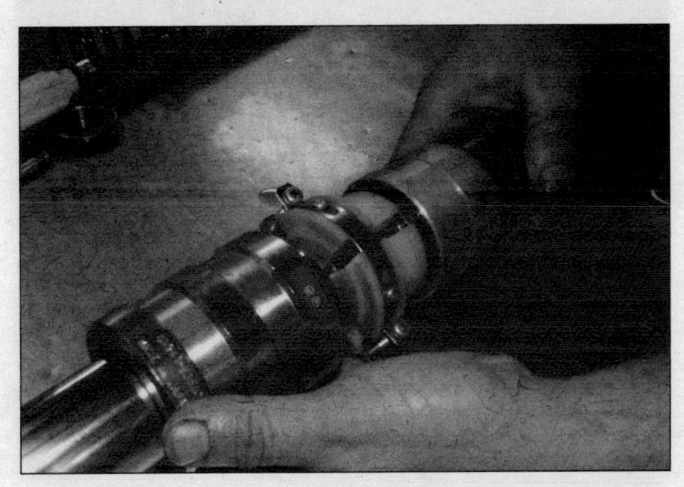

5.17 This is the factory tool used to install bushings and seals

5.26 Measure oil level with the fork fully compressed and the spring removed

5.31 Hold the locknut with a wrench and tighten the cap

6.4 Unscrew the damping adjuster from the bottom of the fork leg (the hex portion, not the adjusting screw in the center)

6.5 Pull the damping adjuster out to expose the locknut and slip a support tool under it

27 Check the size of the hole in the spring seat. If it's too small for the locknut to fit through it, install the spring and spring seat in the fork now. If it's large enough for the locknut to fit through it, don't install it yet.
28 If the locknut was removed from the damper rod, thread it back on to the distance listed in this Chapter's Specifications.
29 If the spring seat will fit over the locknut, install it at this point.
30 Install the pushrod (and pushrod cap if equipped) in the damper rod **(see illustrations 5.5b and 5.5a)**.
31 Thread the fork cap onto the damper rod until it reaches the locknut, then hold the locknut with a wrench and tighten the cap against the locknut to the torque listed in this Chapter's Specifications **(see illustration)**.
32 Extend the outer fork tube and thread the fork cap into it (tighten it to the specified torque later, when the fork leg is held in the triple clamps).
33 Return the damping to its original setting.

6 Top-mount cartridge forks - disassembly, inspection and reassembly

1 This fork design is used on 2005 and later YZ125/250 models. **Note:** *This procedure requires special tools. Read through the procedure before starting to see what's needed. The Yamaha special tools can be ordered from a Yamaha dealer, and aftermarket substitutes may be available.*

Disassembly

Refer to illustrations 6.4, 6.5, 6.6a, 6.6b, 6.7, 6.8, 6.9, 6.10, 6.11, 6.12a, 6.12b, 6.13a, 6.13b, 6.13c, 6.14a, 6.14b, 6.14c, 6.15, 6.16a, 6.16b, 6.17a and 6.17b

2 Remove the plastic protectors from the fork legs if you haven't already done so.
3 Thoroughly clean the outside of the fork, paying special attention to the surface of the inner fork tube and the cavity around the center bolt on the bottom of the fork.
4 Unscrew the adjuster from the bottom of the fork leg **(see illustration)**.
5 Pull the adjuster out and slip a support tool under the locknut to keep it from sliding back into the fork leg **(see illustration)**.
6 Place a wrench on the flats of the locknut and unscrew the adjuster **(see illustrations)**. **Caution:** *DO NOT unscrew the locknut from the damper rod. If you do, the damper rod may fall into the cartridge and be impossible to remove; if this happens, the cartridge will have to be replaced.*
7 Lift the pushrod out of the damper rod **(see illustration)**.
8 Pour the oil out of the fork into a container **(see illustration)**.
9 Remove the support tool **(see illustration)**.
10 Pry the dust seal away from the outer fork tube, taking care not to scratch the inner fork tube **(see illustration)**.
11 Pry the oil seal retainer out of its groove **(see illustration)**.

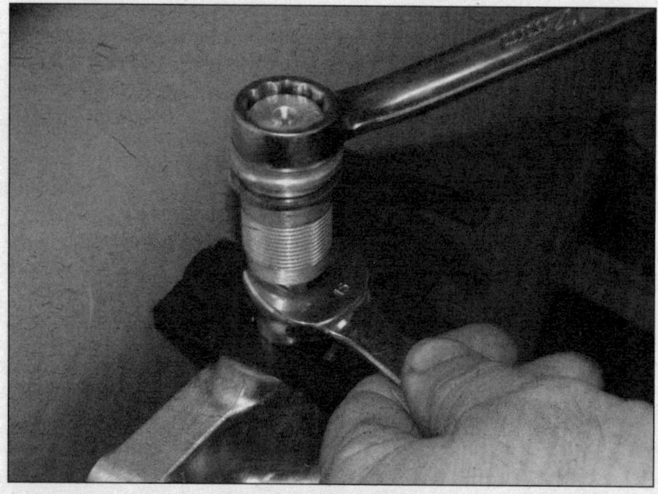
6.6a Hold the locknut with a wrench and unscrew the damping adjuster . . .

6.6b . . . and take it off the damper rod

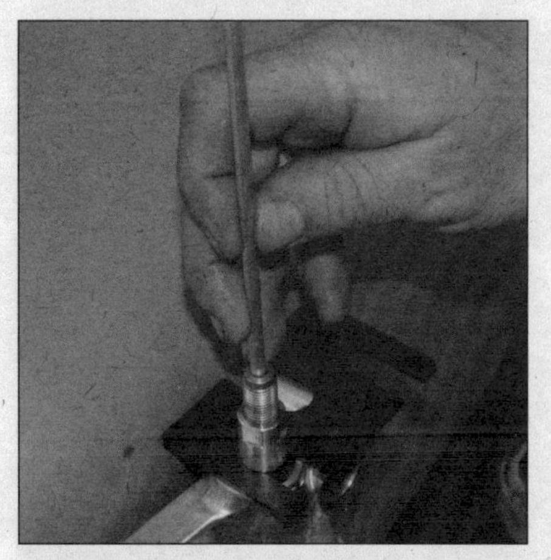

6.7 Pull the pushrod out of the damper rod - inspect the O-ring and replace the copper washer (arrows)

6.8 Pour the oil out of the fork into a container

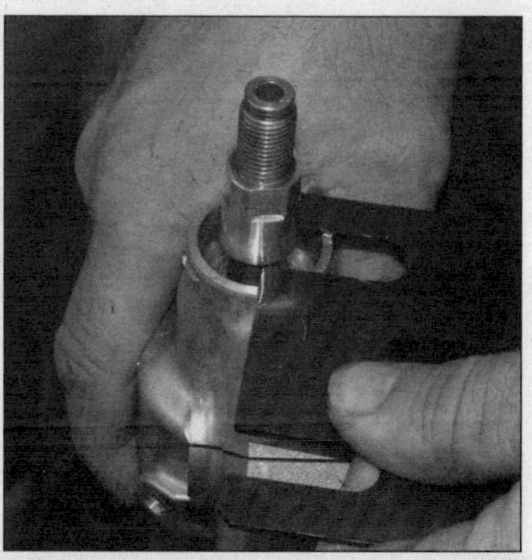

6.9 Remove the support tool; DO NOT remove the locknut or the damper rod may fall into the cartridge and be impossible to get out

6.10 Pry the dust seal out of its bore

6.11 Pry the oil seal retainer out, taking care not to scratch the fork tube

12 Slide the dust seal and retainer down to the bottom of the fork leg, taking care not to scratch the tube **(see illustrations)**. This is necessary to get them out of the way for the next step.

13 Compress the fork tubes together, then yank them sharply apart.

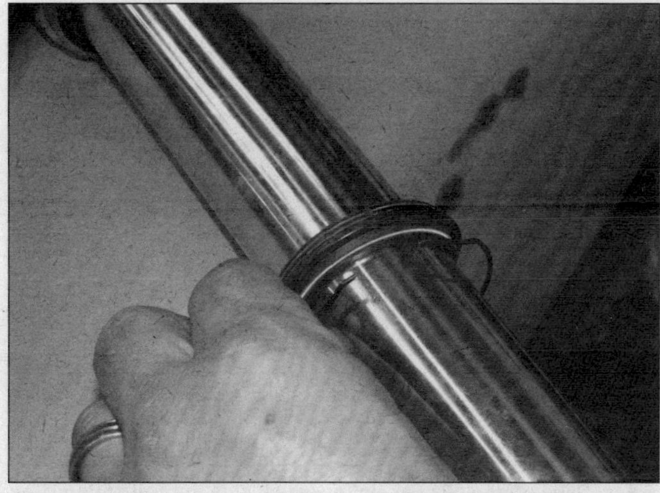

6.12a Slide the retainer and dust seal down the fork tube, taking care not to let the retainer ends scratch the tube . . .

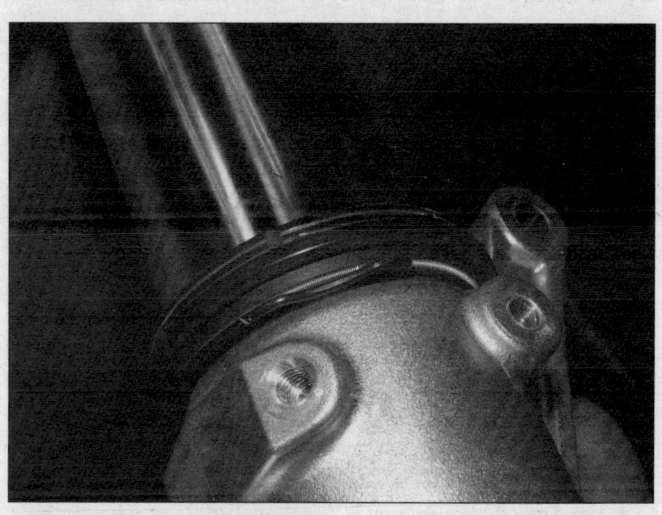

6.12b . . . position the retainer and dust seal against the bracket at the bottom of the tube

6.13a Yank the tubes apart to expose the bushings and oil seal . . .

6.13b . . . then separate the inner and outer tubes . . .

6.13c . . . and remove the fork spring and collar (arrow) from the damper rod

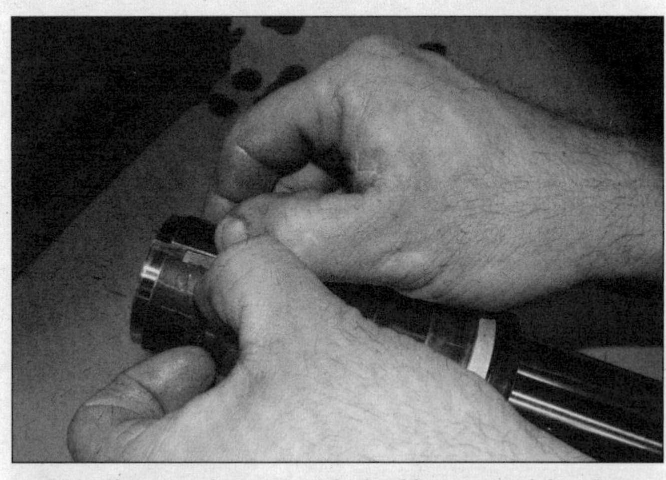

6.14a If you need to remove the bushings, spread them just enough to slip off the fork tube

Do this several times to separate the fork tubes and expose the bushings **(see illustrations)**. Remove the spring from the damper rod, then take the collar out of the fork tube **(see illustration)**.

14 Spread the bushings just enough to remove them from the fork leg, then slide them off, followed by the back-up ring, oil seal, dust seal and retaining ring **(see illustrations)**.

15 Unscrew the damper rod from the fork tube, using a cap ring bolt wrench (tool no. YM-01501-90890-0501, shown and described in the following step). Lift the damper rod out of the fork tube **(see illustration)**.

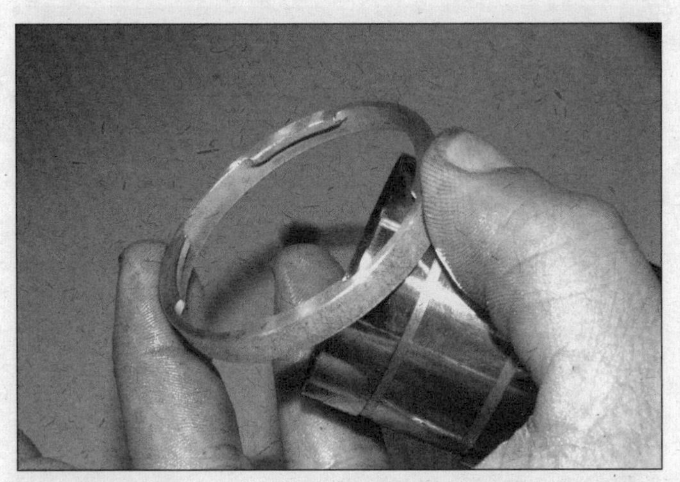

6.14b The oil back-up ring is directional - note which way the tabs face

6.14c Slide off the oil seal, noting which side the coil spring is on

6.15 Unscrew the cartridge and lift it out of the fork tube, together with the damper rod

6.16a Secure the cartridge in a padded vise . . .

6.16b . . . and unscrew the base valve, using special tools

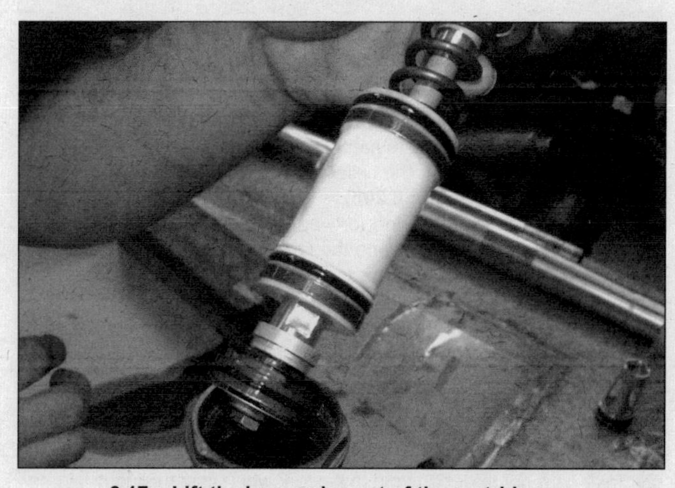
6.17a Lift the base valve out of the cartridge . . .

16 Secure the damper in a padded vise **(see illustration)**. Hold the damper from turning with a cap bolt ring wrench (tool no. YM-01501-90890-0501) and unscrew the base valve with a cap bolt wrench (tool no. YM-01500-90890-0500 **(see illustration)**. These are both eight-sided (not hex). The ring wrench is 49 mm (1.928 inches) across the flats. The cap bolt wrench is 35.6 mm (1.405 inches) across the flats.

17 Once the base valve is unscrewed, lift it out of the cartridge **(see illustration)**. Pour the oil out of the cartridge **(see illustration)**.

Inspection

Refer to illustrations 6.19, 6.20a and 6.20b

18 Check the bushings for wear or damage **(see illustration 4.15b)**. Replace them if problems are found.

19 Check the O-rings and bushings on the base valve for wear or damage **(see illustration)**. Replace them if problems are found. It's a good idea to replace the O-rings whenever the fork is disassembled.

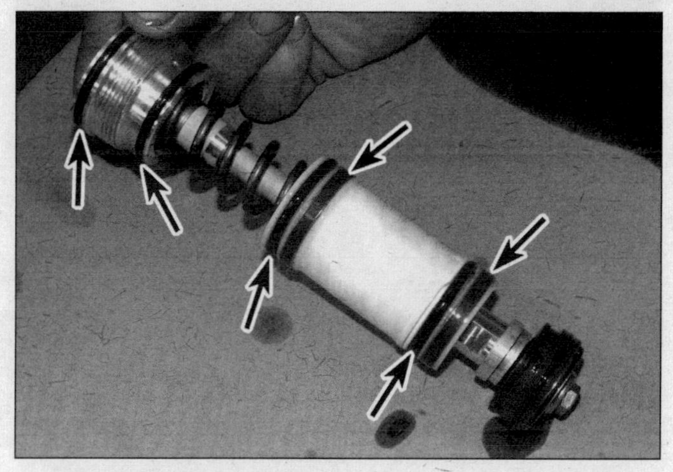
6.19 Inspect the base valve O-rings and bushings (arrows)

6.17b . . . and pour the oil out of the cartridge

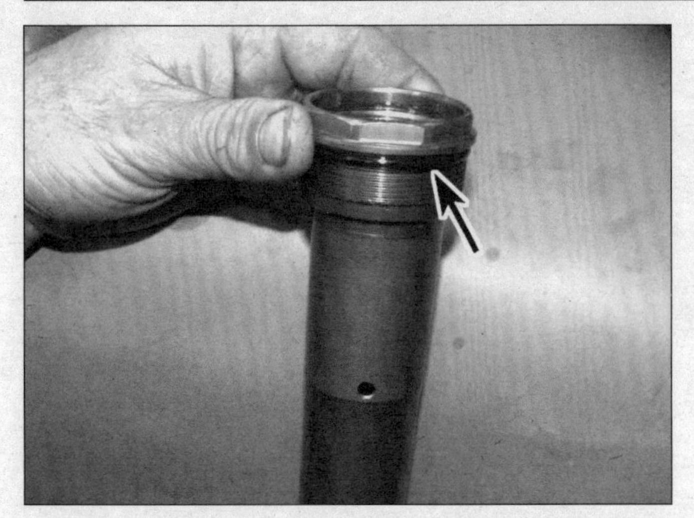

6.20a Inspect the O-ring at the top of the cartridge . . .

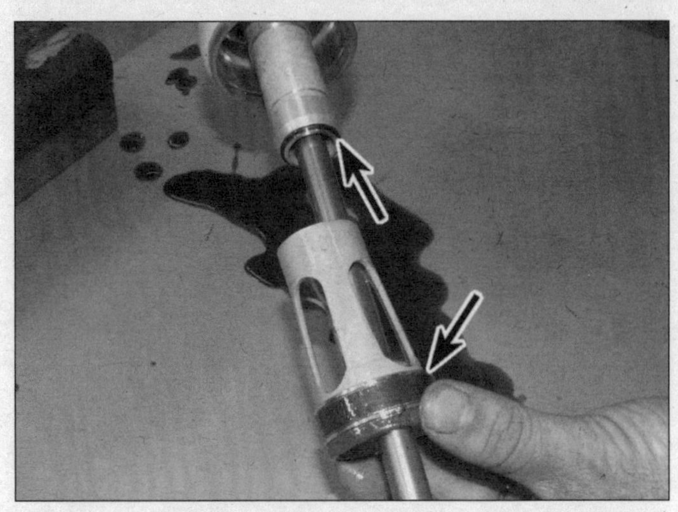

6.20b . . . and at the bottom (upper arrow) - also check the bushing on the collar (lower arrow)

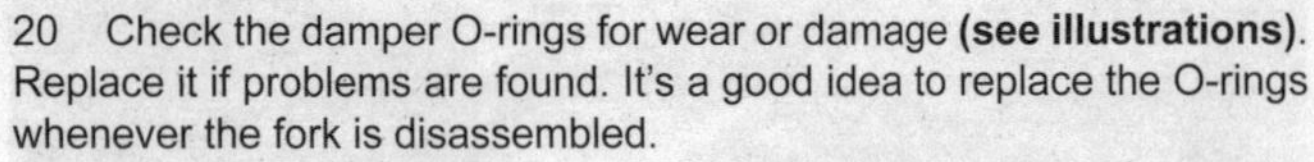

20 Check the damper O-rings for wear or damage **(see illustrations)**. Replace it if problems are found. It's a good idea to replace the O-rings whenever the fork is disassembled.

21 Check the bushing on the collar for wear and damage and replace as needed **(see illustration 6.20b)**.

22 Check the adjuster O-ring for wear or damage **(see illustration 6.6b)**. It's a good idea to replace the O-ring whenever the fork is disassembled. Always replace the copper washer when the adjuster is removed.

23 Check the plated surface of the inner fork tube for scratches or other damage. Check it for bending (ideally with a dial indicator, but you can also roll it on a flat surface such as a piece of glass). If it's bent more than the limit listed in this Chapter's Specifications, replace it. Do not try to straighten a bent fork tube.

24 Make sure all parts are spotlessly clean before beginning assembly. Take care not to get any dirt in the fork when assembling it.

Assembly

Refer to illustrations 6.25, 6.26, 6.28a, 6.28b, 6.28c, 6.32a, 6.32b, 6.36, 6.38a, 6.38b, 6.44 and 6.49

25 Pull the damper rod all the way out of the cartridge **(see illustration)**.

26 Hold the cartridge vertical and pour the specified amount of oil into the top **(see illustration)**.

27 With the cartridge held vertical, slowly compress the damper rod into the cartridge, then pull it back down, several times to bleed air out of the oil. **Note:** *Do not extend the damper rod more than 200 mm (8 inches) or air will be pulled into the oil and the bleeding procedure will have to be done over.*

28 Measure the oil level in the cartridge and add or remove oil to bring to the correct level. This can be done with a measuring tool made of a baster, some hose and a piece of tape **(see illustrations)**.

29 Once you've got the oil level correct in the cartridge, check the position of the locknut. Thread it all the way onto the damper rod, using fingers only (don't tighten it with a wrench).

30 Loosen the adjuster screw in the top of the base valve, counting the turns for use later.

31 Mount the cartridge in a vise with padded jaws, taking care not to damage the cartridge **(see illustration 6.16a)**.

32 Push up on the damper rod, then place the base valve into position, push it into the cartridge and tighten it **(see illustrations)**. As you do this, let the damper rod extend.

33 Check to make sure the damper rod is extended. If it isn't, repeat Step 32.

34 Finish tightening the base valve in the cartridge to the specified

6.25 Extend the damper rod all the way . . .

6.26 . . . and pour the specified amount of oil into the top of the cartridge . . .

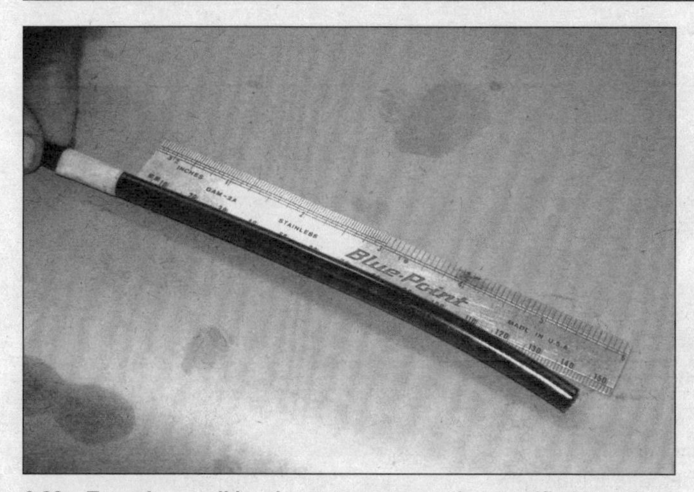

6.28a To make an oil level gauge, measure the specified length on a piece of rubber tubing and wrap it with tape . . .

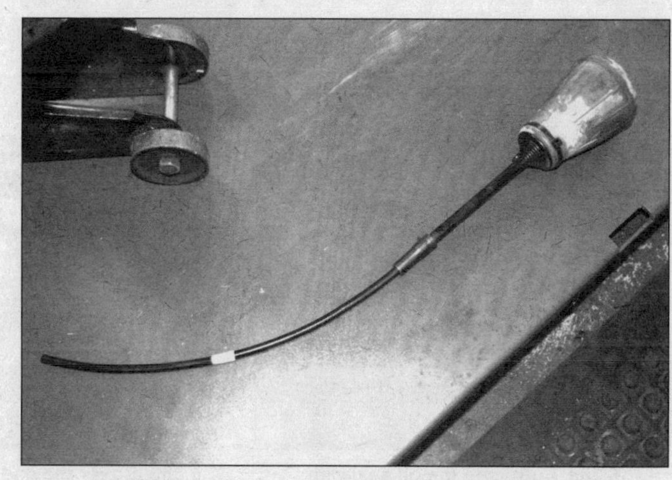

6.28b . . . then attach the tubing to a baster . . .

torque, using the tools described in Step 16.

35 With the cartridge held vertical, slowly extend and compress the damper rod at least 10 times to distribute the oil in the cartridge.

36 Place the end of the damper rod on a pile of rags on the floor (to protect the damper rod from damage). Push the cartridge down to compress the damper all the way, allowing any excess oil to flow out of the oil hole in the cartridge **(see illustration)**.

37 Once this is done, extend and compress the damper rod by hand, checking for smooth movement. If movement is tight or uneven, repeat the oil filling procedure.

6.28c . . . and insert the marked tube into the cartridge - if oil level is too high, the baster can be used to suck some out

6.32a Push the base valve into the cartridge . . .

6.32b . . . and tighten it temporarily

6.36 Excess oil will run out this hole in the cartridge

6.38a Lubricate the oil seal with suspension grease or fork oil applied to the seal lip so it will slip onto the fork tube easily

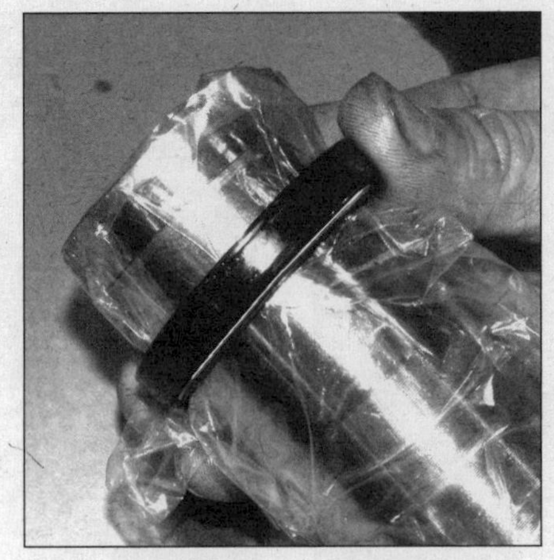

6.38b Cover the end of the fork tube with a plastic bag to protect the seal

6.44 Slip the support tool under the locknut

38 Note how the oil seals and bushings are installed **(see illustration 6.13a)**. Lubricate the oil seal with suspension grease or fork oil **(see illustration)**, then install the seals and bushings on the inner fork tube. Protect the oil seal by covering the end of the tube with a plastic bag **(see illustration)**. Note the direction of the oil seal and the back-up ring **(see illustration 6.14b)**.

39 Assemble the fork tubes to each other. Drive the outer bushing and oil seal into position using a seal driver **(see illustration 5.17)**. Once the bushings and oil seals are in place, install the retaining ring and make sure it seats securely in its groove.

40 Lubricate the inner fork tube with multipurpose grease where the dust seal fits into it, then install the dust seal.

41 Extend and compress the fork tubes, checking for rough or uneven movement. If this is found, find out what the problem is before continuing.

42 Measure the length of the exposed threads between the damper rod locknut and the end of the damper rod. Here should be at least 19 mm (0.75 inch) of exposed threads.

43 Install the collar and fork spring on the damper. The larger end of the collar faces the spring **(see illustration 6.13c)**.

44 Hold the fork leg at an angle, with its open end (top end) facing down. Install the damper rod in the fork tube. Pull the damper rod end out of the bottom of the fork tube and secure it with a holding tool **(see illustration)**.

45 Install the pushrod in the damper rod **(see illustration 6.7)**.

46 Loosen the screw in the center of the rebound damping adjuster until it's finger-tight, counting the turns. Thread the damping adjuster onto the damper rod, using fingers only **(see illustration 6.6b)**. Check the gap between the adjuster and the locknut on the damper rod - it should be 0.5 to 1.0 mm (0.02 to 0.04 inch).

6.49 Pour the specified amount of oil into the outer fork tube

47 Hold the locknut with a wrench and tighten the damping adjuster against it to the torque listed in this Chapter's Specifications.

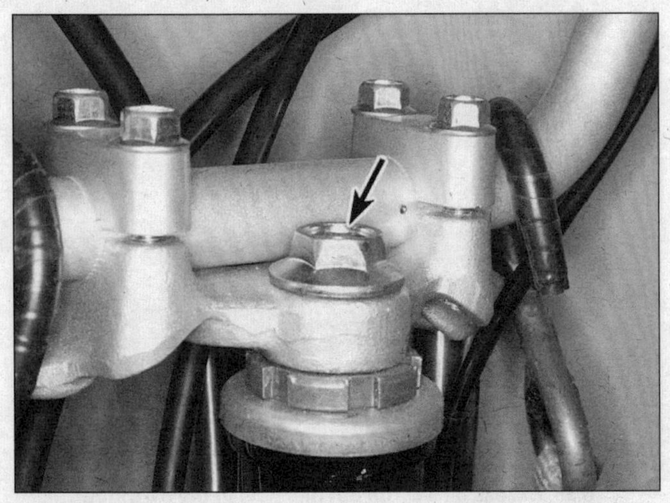

7.3a Loosen the steering stem bolt (1992 and earlier YZ80) . . .

7.3b . . . or nut (all other models) . . .

7.3c . . . and unscrew it from the steering stem

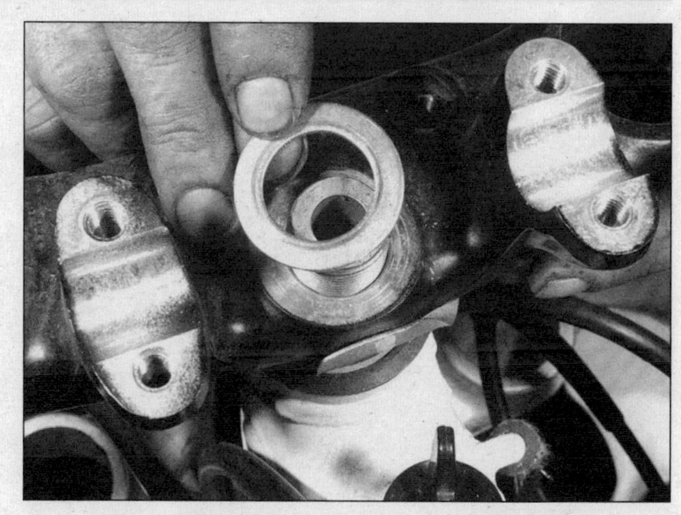

7.3d . . . lift off the washer and upper triple clamp

7.4a Remove the bearing adjusting nut(s) . . .

7.4b . . . and lift off the bearing cover

48 Thread the damping adjuster into the bottom of the fork, then tighten it to the torque listed in this Chapter's Specifications.
49 Pour the recommended amount of fork oil into the top of the fork **(see illustration)**.
50 Thread the cartridge into the upper end of the fork leg and tighten it temporarily. Tighten it to the torque listed in this Chapter's Specifications after securing it in the triple clamps.
51 If you removed the guide for the fork leg protector, slip it onto the fork tube with its wider ring downward.

7 Steering head bearings - replacement

Refer to illustrations 7.3a, 7.3b, 7.3c, 7.3d, 7.4a, 7.4b, 7.5, 7.6a, 7.6b, 7.7, 7.9, 7.11 and 7.14

1 If the steering head bearing check/adjustment (see Chapter 1) does not remedy excessive play or roughness in the steering head bearings, the entire front end must be disassembled and the bearings and races replaced with new ones.
2 Remove the handlebars (see Section 2), the front wheel and brake caliper (see Chapter 7), the front fender (see Chapter 8) and the forks (see Section 3).
3 Loosen the steering stem bolt or nut with a socket **(see illustrations)**. Remove the nut, washer and upper triple clamp **(see illustrations)**.
4 Using a spanner wrench of the type described in Chapter 1, remove the stem locknut(s) and bearing cover **(see illustrations)** while supporting the steering head from the bottom.
5 Remove the steering stem and lower triple clamp assembly **(see illustration)**. If it's stuck, gently tap on the top of the steering stem with a plastic mallet or a hammer and a wood block.

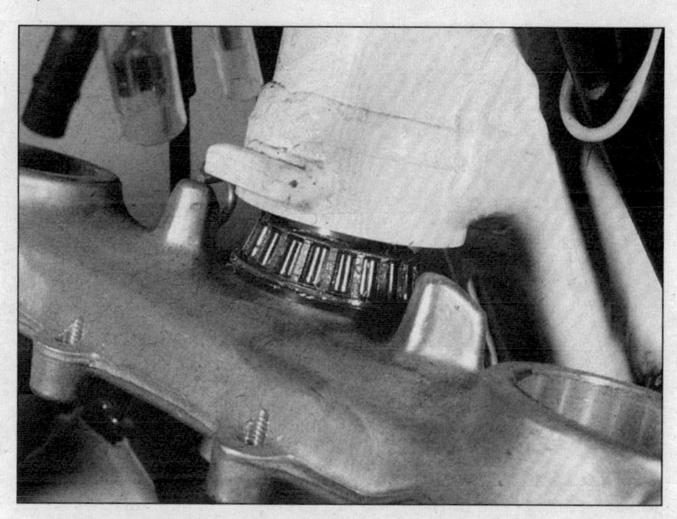

7.5 Lower the steering stem out of the steering head

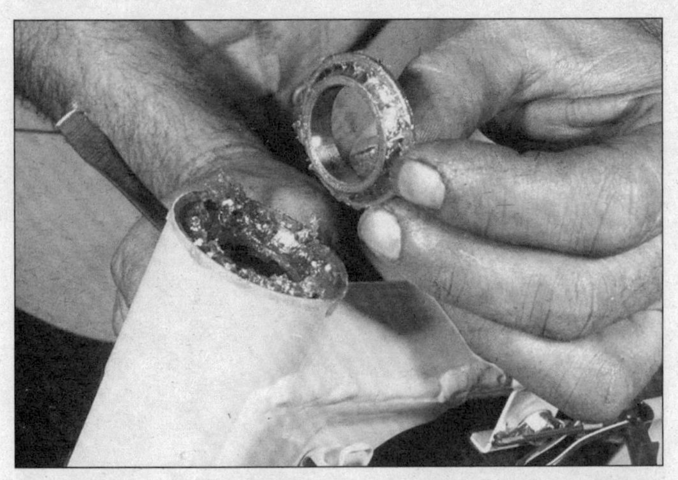

7.6a If the bike has upper ball bearings (1992 and earlier YZ80), lift out the top race and ball cage

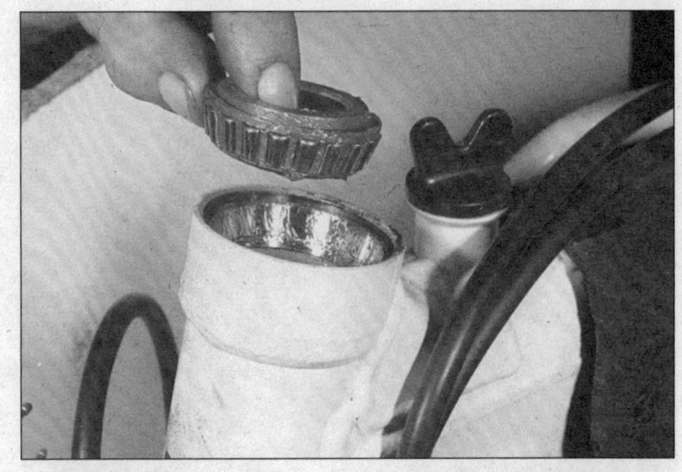

7.6b If the bike has upper roller bearings (all except 1992 and earlier YZ80), lift the upper bearing out of the steering head

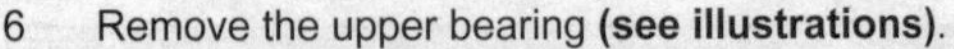

6 Remove the upper bearing **(see illustrations)**.

7 Clean all the parts with solvent and dry them thoroughly, using compressed air, if available **(see illustration)**. If you do use compressed air, don't let the bearings spin as they're dried - it could ruin them. Wipe the old grease out of the frame steering head and bearing races.

8 Examine the races in the steering head for cracks, dents, and pits. If even the slightest amount of wear or damage is evident, the races should be replaced with new ones.

9 To remove the races, drive them out of the steering head with a bearing driver or a hammer and drift punch **(see illustration)**. A slide hammer with the proper internal-jaw puller will also work. Since the races are an interference fit in the frame, installation will be easier if the new races are left overnight in a refrigerator. This will cause them to contract and slip into place in the frame with very little effort. When installing the races, use a bearing driver the same diameter as the outer race, or tap them gently into place with a hammer and punch or a large socket. Do not strike the bearing surface or the race will be damaged.

10 Check the bearings for wear. Look for cracks, dents, and pits in the races and flat spots on the bearings. Replace any defective parts with new ones. If a new bearing is required, replace both of them as a set.

11 Check the grease seal under the lower bearing and replace it with a new one if necessary **(see illustration)**.

12 To remove the lower bearing and grease seal from the steering stem, you may need to use a bearing puller, which can be rented. Don't remove this bearing unless it, or the grease seal underneath, must be replaced. Removal will damage the grease seal, so replace it whenever the bearing is removed.

7.7 Steering stem and bearing details (tapered roller bearings)

13 Inspect the steering stem/lower triple clamp for cracks and other damage. Do not attempt to repair any steering components. Replace them with new parts if defects are found.

14 Pack the bearings with high-quality grease (preferably a moly-based grease) **(see illustration)**. Coat the outer races with grease also.

15 Install the grease seal and lower bearing onto the steering stem.

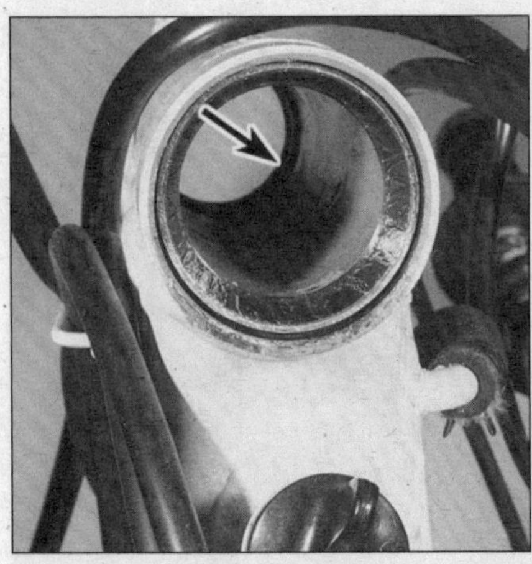

7.9 Place the drift against the edge of the lower bearing race (arrow) and tap evenly around it to drive the bearing out

7.11 Leave the lower bearing and grease seal (arrow) on the steering stem unless you plan to replace them

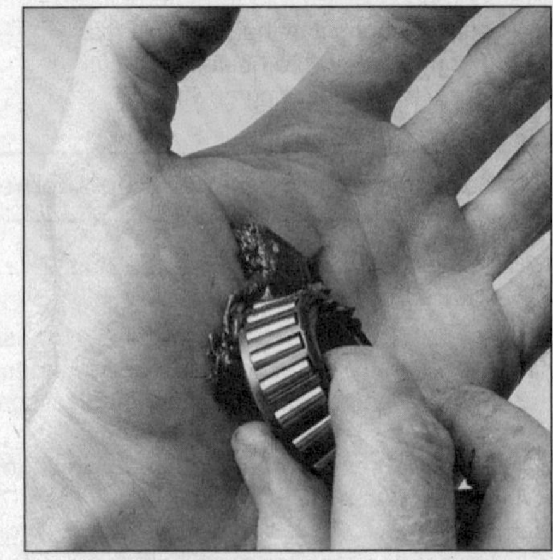

7.14 Work the grease completely into the bearing

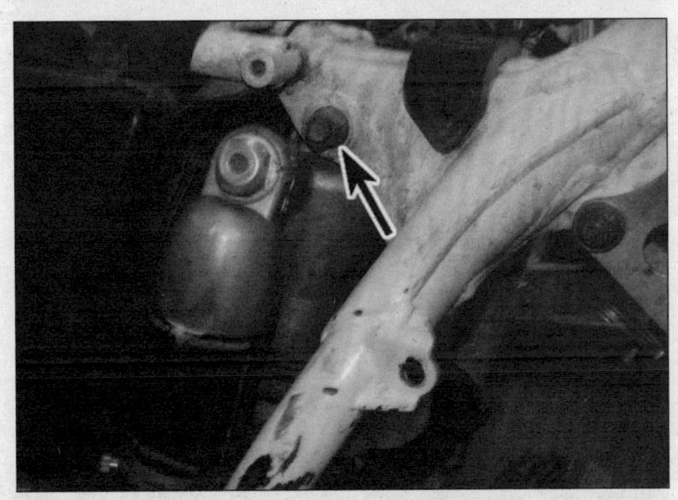

8.4a Unbolt the upper end of the shock absorber from the frame and the lower end from the shock linkage

Drive the lower bearing onto the steering stem using a pipe the same diameter as the bearing inner race. Drive the bearing on until it's fully seated.

16 Insert the steering stem/lower triple clamp into the frame head. Install the upper bearing, bearing cover and locknut. Refer to the adjustment procedure in Chapter 1 and tighten the locknut to the torque listed in the Chapter 1 Specifications.

17 Make sure the steering head turns smoothly and that there's no play in the bearings.

18 Install the upper triple clamp, then install the washer and nut, but don't tighten the nut yet.

19 Slide the forks through the lower triple clamp and into the upper triple clamp, then install the front wheel (this is to align the upper triple clamp). Tighten the lower triple clamp bolts securely, then install the steering stem washer and nut or bolt. Tighten the nut or bolt to approximately half the torque listed in this Chapter's Specifications to seat the upper triple clamp on the steering stem.

20 Loosen the lower triple clamp bolts and install the forks to their proper height (see Section 3 and this Chapter's Specifications), then tighten the upper and lower triple clamp bolts to the torque listed in this Chapter's Specifications.

21 Tighten the steering stem nut or bolt to its full torque.

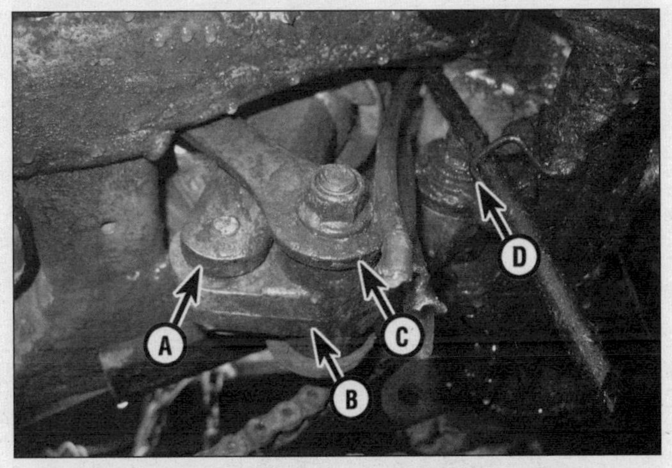

8.4b Shock linkage details (1993 and later YZ80/85)

A Shock absorber lower end
B Relay arm
C Connecting rod
D Relay arm-to-frame attaching point

22 Install the handlebars (see Section 2).

23 The remainder of installation is the reverse of removal.

8 Rear shock absorber - removal, inspection and installation

Removal

Refer to illustrations 8.4a, 8.4b, 8.4c and 8.4d

1 Support the bike securely so it can't be knocked over during this procedure. Support the swingarm with a jack so the suspension can be raised or lowered as needed for access.

2 Remove the muffler (see Chapter 4).

3 Remove the seat and sub-frame (see Chapter 8).

4 Remove the upper and lower mounting bolts **(see illustrations)**. **Note:** *On early models, the bolts have hex heads; on later models, they have round heads with a flat on one side, which fits into a matching flat in the component it attaches to.*

5 Remove the shock from the bike.

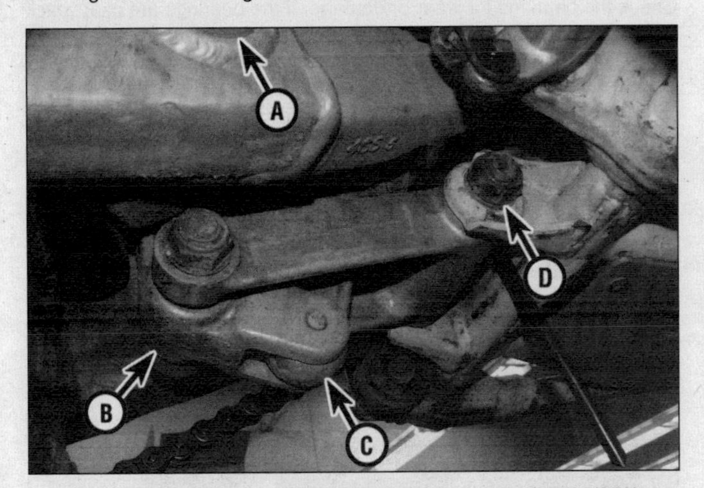

8.4c Shock linkage details (1996 through 2001 YZ125/250)

A Access hole plug - relay arm-to-swingarm bolt
B Relay arm
C Shock absorber lower end
D Connecting rod-to-frame attaching point

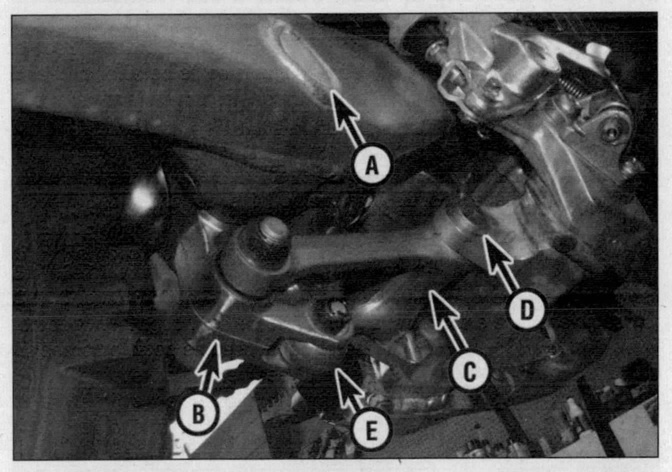

8.4d Shock linkage details (2002 and later YZ125/250)

A Access hole plug - relay arm-to-swingarm bolt
B Relay arm
C Connecting rod
D Connecting rod-to-frame attaching point
E Shock absorber lower end

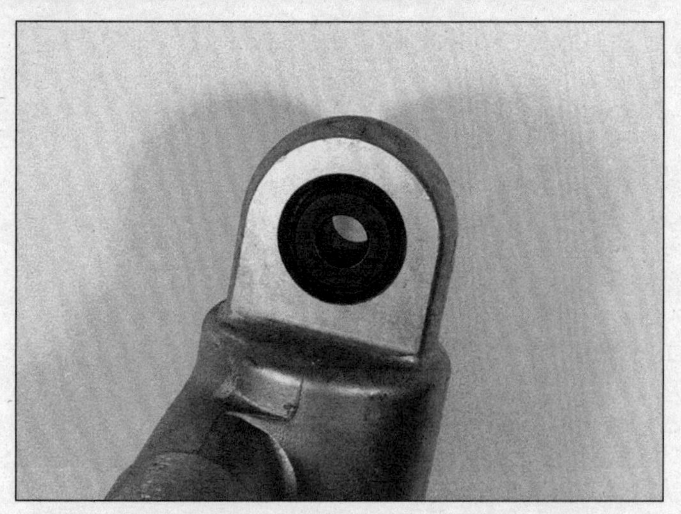

8.8 Check the shock absorber bearings or bushings for wear or damage

9.2 Here's the connecting rod-to-swingarm attachment on 1993 and later YZ80/85 models

Inspection

Refer to illustration 8.8

6 The shock absorber can be overhauled, but it's a complicated procedure that requires special tools not readily available to the typical owner. If inspection reveals problems, have the shock rebuilt by a dealer or motorcycle repair shop.

7 Check the shock absorber for damage and oil leaks. If these can be seen, have the shock overhauled.

8 Check the spherical bearing at the upper end of the shock for leaking grease, looseness or signs of damage **(see illustration)**. If any of these problems can be seen, have the bearing pressed out and a new one pressed in by a dealer or motorcycle repair shop.

9 Clean all parts thoroughly with solvent and dry them with compressed air, if available. Check all parts for scoring, damage or heavy corrosion and replace them as necessary.

Installation

10 Installation is the reverse of the removal steps. Tighten the bolts to the torques listed in this Chapter's Specifications.

9 Shock linkage - removal, inspection and installation

1 The shock linkage consists of two parts, a relay arm and a connecting rod. The shock absorber lower end is attached to the relay arm, which in turn is attached to the connecting rod. The connecting rod is connected to the swingarm and frame.

2 The connecting rod on 1986 through 1992 YZ125/250 models is made up of two side pieces and a spacer that holds them together. The connecting rod on all other models is made in one piece.

Removal

Refer to illustration 9.2

1 Support the bike securely so it can't be knocked over during this procedure. Support the swingarm with a jack so the suspension can be raised or lowered as needed for access.

2 Remove the shock absorber lower mounting bolt. Unbolt the linkage from the swingarm and frame **(see illustrations 8.4b, 8.4c and 8.4d and the accompanying illustration)**.

3 Take the linkage out of the bike, then separate the relay arm from the connecting rod.

Inspection

Refer to illustrations 9.4a and 9.4b

4 Slip the collars out of the needle bearings **(see illustrations)**. Check the bearings for wear or damage. If the bearings are okay, pack them with molybdenum disulfide grease and reinstall the collars.

5 If the dust seals are worn or appear to have been leaking, pry

9.4a Pull the covers off the shock link pivots and inspect the seals and needle bearings

9.4b . . . Pull out the collar to inspect the needle roller bearings

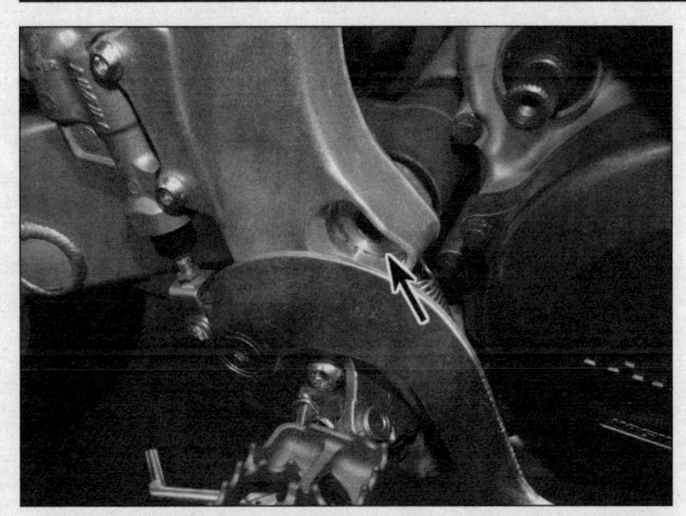

11.4a The swingarm pivot bolt head on later models fits into a shaped recess in the frame (arrow)

11.4b With the engine supported, unscrew the pivot bolt nut (arrow) and pull out the bolt

them out and press in new ones with a seal driver or socket the same diameter as the seals.

6 If the bearings need to be replaced, press them out and press new ones in. To prevent damage to the new bearings, you'll need a shouldered drift with a narrow diameter the same size as the inside diameter of the bearings. If you don't have the proper tool, have the bearings replaced by a Yamaha dealer or other motorcycle repair shop. A well-equipped automotive machine shop should also be able to do the job.

Installation

7 Installation is the reverse of the removal steps. Lubricate the bearings and thrust washers with molybdenum disulfide grease. Tighten the nuts and bolts to the torques listed in this Chapter's Specifications. Connections are as follows:

1986 through 1992 YZ80

a) Upper (rear) relay arm hole to shock absorber
b) Lower (rear) relay arm hole to swingarm
c) Front relay arm hole to connecting rod upper end (separate arms)
d) Connecting rod lower end to frame

1993 and later YZ80/85

a) Connecting rod upper end to swingarm **(see illustration 9.2)**.
b) Connecting rod lower end (separate arms) to relay arm center hole (relay arm center hole downward)
c) Relay arm rear hole to shock absorber lower end
d) Relay arm front hole to frame

1986 through 1992 YZ125/250

a) Connecting rod upper ends to swingarm
b) Connecting rod lower ends (offset toward each other) to relay arm center hole (relay arm center hole downward)
c) Relay arm rear hole to shock absorber bottom end
d) Relay arm front hole to frame

1993 through 1995 YZ125/250

a) Relay arm rear hole to swingarm (rear hole upward)
b) Relay arm center hole to connecting rod rear ends (without offsets)
c) Relay arm front hole to shock absorber
d) Connecting rod front ends to frame (offsets toward each other)

1996 and later YZ125/250

a) Relay arm rear hole to swingarm (rear hole upward) **(see illustration 8.4c or 8.4d)**
b) Relay arm center hole to connecting rod rear ends (separate ends)
c) Relay arm front hole to shock absorber
d) Connecting rod front end to frame

10 Swingarm bearings - check

1 Refer to Chapter 7 and remove the rear wheel, then refer to Section 8 and remove the rear shock absorber.

2 Grasp the rear of the swingarm with one hand and place your other hand at the junction of the swingarm and frame. Try to move the rear of the swingarm from side-to-side. Any wear (play) in the bushings should be felt as movement between the swingarm and the frame at the front. The swingarm will actually be felt to move forward and backward at the front (not from side-to-side). If any play is noted, the bearings should be replaced with new ones (see Section 12).

3 Next, move the swingarm up and down through its full travel. It should move freely, without any binding or rough spots. If it doesn't move freely, refer to Section 11 and 12 for servicing procedures.

11 Swingarm - removal and installation

Refer to illustrations 11.4a and 11.4b

1 Refer to Section 13 and disconnect the drive chain.

2 Remove the rear wheel (see Chapter 7). If you're working on a bike with a rear disc brake, remove the caliper (without disconnecting the hose), detach the brake hose from the retainers on the swingarm and support the caliper so it doesn't hang by the hose. **Note:** *If the brake pedal interferes with the pivot bolt, remove the pedal (see Chapter 7).*

3 Unbolt the shock absorber and shock linkage from the swingarm (Sections 8 and 9).

4 Support the swingarm from below, then unscrew its pivot bolt nut and pull the bolt out **(see illustrations)**.

5 Check the chain slider, chain adjuster plates and brake disc guard for wear or damage. Replace them as necessary.

6 Installation is the reverse of the removal steps, with the following additions:

a) Lubricate the swingarm bearings and thrust washers with molybdenum disulfide grease (see Section 12).
b) Tighten the swingarm pivot bolt and nut to the torque listed in this Chapter's Specifications.
c) Refer to Chapter 1 and adjust the drive chain and rear brake pedal (drum brake models).

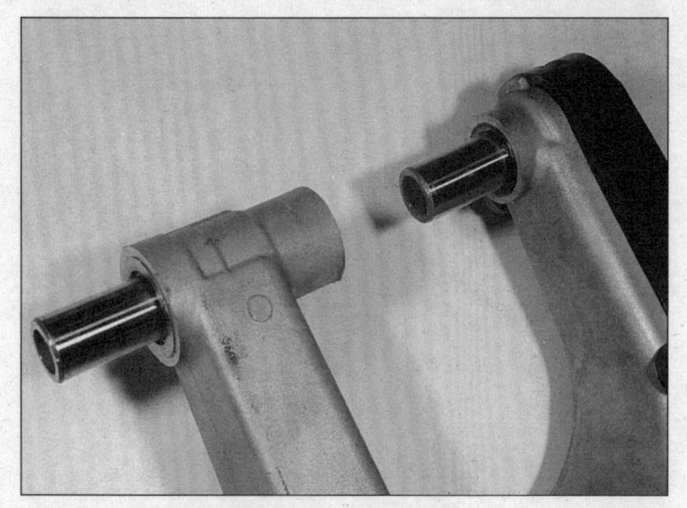

12.2 Slide the pivot collars out

13.1 Remove the clip from the master link; its open end (arrow) faces rearward when the chain is on the top run and forward when the chain is on the bottom run

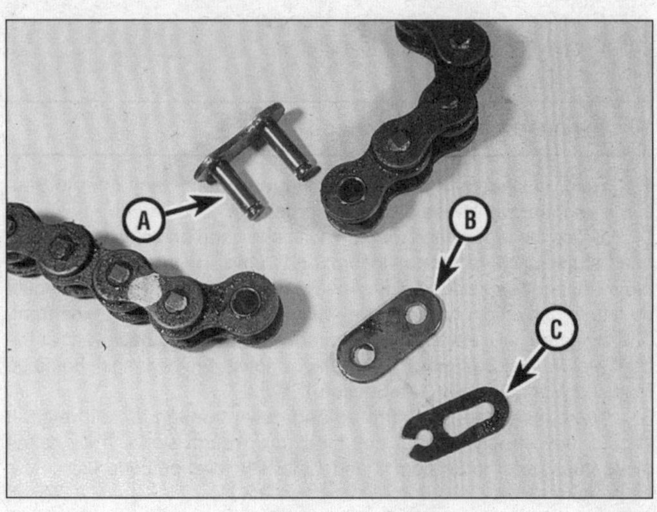

13.2 Master link details

A Link
B Plate
C Clip

13.3 Remove the screws and take off the sprocket cover

12 Swingarm bearings - replacement

Refer to illustration 12.2

1 Refer to Section 11 and remove the swingarm.

2 Pull the pivot collars out of the swingarm bearings, then inspect the bearings and seals **(see illustration)**.

3 If the dust seals are worn or appear to have been leaking, pry them out and press in new ones with a seal driver or socket the same diameter as the seals.

4 Check the needle bearings for wear or damage. Needle bearing replacement requires a special puller, a press and a shouldered drift the same diameter as the inside of the bearings. If you don't have these, have the bearings replaced by a Yamaha dealer or other motorcycle repair shop.

5 Coat the bearings and pivot collars with moly-based grease and slip the collar into the swingarm. Install the dust covers.

13 Drive chain - removal, cleaning, inspection and installation

Removal

Refer to illustrations 13.1, 13.2 and 13.3

1 Turn the rear wheel to place the drive chain master link where it's easily accessible **(see illustration)**.

2 Remove the clip and plate and pull the master link out of the chain **(see illustration)**.

3 Remove the engine sprocket cover **(see illustration)**.

4 Lift the chain off the sprockets and remove it from the bike.

5 Check the chain guards and rollers on the swingarm and frame for wear or damage and replace them as necessary.

Cleaning and inspection

6 Soak the chain in a high flash point solvent for approximately five or six minutes. Use a brush to work the solvent into the spaces between the links and plates.

7 Wipe the chain dry, then check it carefully for worn or damaged links. Replace the chain if wear or damage is found at any point.

8 Stretch the chain taut and measure its length between the number of pins listed in this Chapter's Specifications. Compare the measured length to the specified value replace the chain if it's beyond the limit. If the chain needs to be replaced, refer to Section 14 and check the

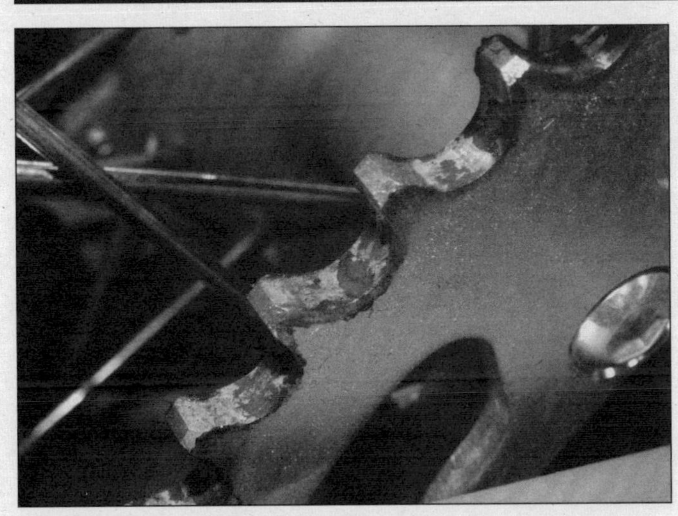

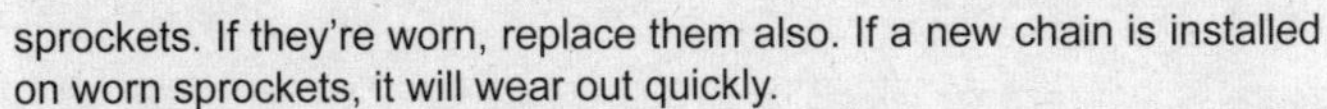

14.3 Inspect the sprocket teeth for excessive or uneven wear

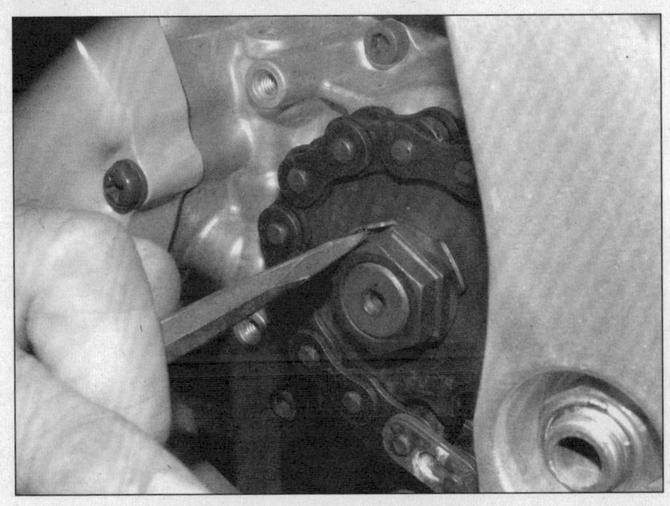

14.6a Bend back the lockwasher tabs . . .

sprockets. If they're worn, replace them also. If a new chain is installed on worn sprockets, it will wear out quickly.

9 Lubricate the chain with the type of lubricant listed in the Chapter 1 Specifications.

Installation

10 Installation is the reverse of the removal steps, with the following additions:

a) *Install the master link clip so its opening faces the back of the motorcycle when the master link is in the upper chain run* **(see illustration 13.1)**

b) *Refer to Chapter 1 and adjust the chain.*

14 Sprockets - check and replacement

Refer to illustrations 14.3, 14.6a, 14.6b and 14.6c

1 Support the bike securely so it can't be knocked over during this procedure.

2 Whenever the sprockets are inspected, the chain should be inspected also and replaced if it's worn. Installing a worn chain on new sprockets will cause them to wear quickly.

3 Check the teeth on the engine sprocket and rear sprocket for wear **(see illustration)**. The engine sprocket is visible through the cover slots.

4 If the sprockets are worn, remove the chain (see Section 13) and the rear wheel (see Chapter 7).

5 Remove the sprocket from the rear wheel hub.

6 If you're working on a YZ80, remove the sprocket snap-ring and take the sprocket off the transmission shaft. To remove the engine sprocket on all other models, bend back the tabs on the lockwasher **(see illustration)**. Unscrew the nut, remove the lockwasher and take the sprocket off the transmission shaft **(see illustrations)**.

7 Inspect the seal behind the engine sprocket. If it has been leaking, remove the collar and O-ring (see Chapter 2). Pry the seal out (taking care not to scratch the seal bore) and tap in a new seal with a socket the same diameter as the seal.

8 Installation is the reverse of the removal steps, with the following additions:

a) *Use a new snap-ring to secure the engine sprocket onYZ80 models.*

b) *Tighten the engine sprocket nut to the torque listed in this Chapter's Specifications.*

c) *Tighten the driven sprocket bolts to the torque listed in this Chapter's Specifications.*

d) *Install the master link clip so its opening faces the back of the motorcycle when the master link is in the upper chain run* **(see illustration 13.1)**.

e) *Refer to Chapter 1 and adjust the chain.*

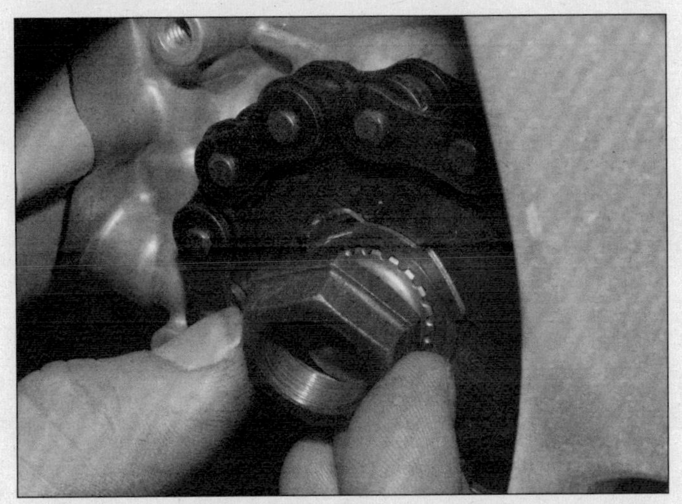

14.6b . . . unscrew the nut and remove the lockwasher . . .

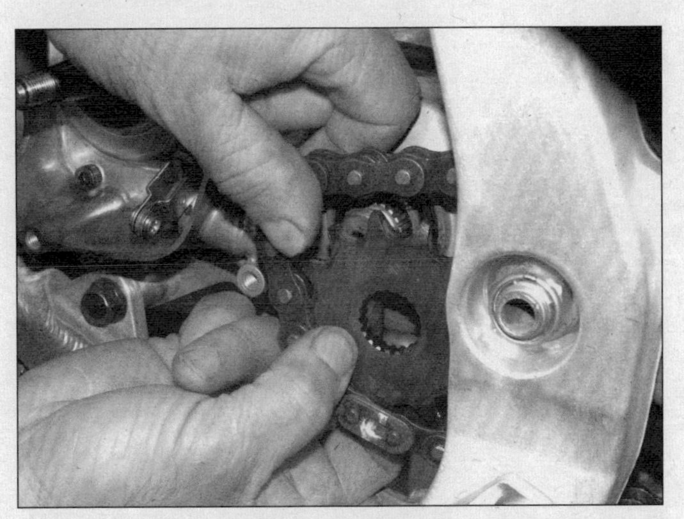

14.6c . . . and slip the sprocket off the transmission shaft

Notes

Chapter 7
Brakes, wheels and tires

Contents

Specifications

YZ80/85

Disc brakes

Brake fluid type	See Chapter 1
Brake pad minimum thickness	See Chapter 1
Disc thickness (front and rear)	
Standard	3.0 mm (0.12 inch)
Limit*	2.5 mm (0.10 inch)
Disc runout limit	0.15 mm (0.006 inch)

** Refer to marks stamped into the disc (they supersede information printed here)*

Drum brakes

Brake lining minimum thickness	See Chapter 1
Brake pedal height	See Chapter 1
Drum diameter	
Standard	95.0 mm (3.74 inches)
Wear limit	96.0 mm (3.78 inches)*

** Refer to marks cast into the drum (they supersede information printed here)*

Wheels and tires

Tire pressures	See Chapter 1
Tire tread depth	See Chapter 1
Axle runout limit (front and rear)	
1986 through 2001	No visible bending
2002 and later	0.5 mm (0.020 inch)
Wheel out-of-round and lateral runout limit (front and rear)	2.0 mm (0.08 inch)

Torque specifications

Front axle	
1986 and 1987	74 Nm (53 ft-lbs)
1988 and later	70 Nm (50 ft-lbs)
Rear axle nut	
1986 through 1992	85 Nm (61 ft-lbs)
1993 through 2002	110 Nm (80 ft-lbs)
2003 and later	90 Nm (65 ft-lbs)
Front caliper	
Caliper bracket to fork bolts	30 Nm (22 ft-lbs)
Pad retaining pins/bolts	
1986	23 Nm (17 ft-lbs)
1987 through 1992	30 Nm (22 ft-lbs)
1993 and later	23 Nm (17 ft-lbs)
Rear caliper	
Caliper mounting bolts	23 Nm (17 ft-lbs)
Pad retaining pins	18 Nm (156 in-lbs)
Brake hose union bolts	26 Nm (19 ft-lbs)
Brake disc-to-wheel bolts	12 Nm (104 inch-lbs)*
Rear drum brake arm pinch bolt	10 Nm (86 in-lbs)
Front master cylinder	
Mounting bolts	
1986	Not specified
1987 and later	9 Nm (78 inch-lbs)
Brake lever pivot bolt	
1986 through 1996	Not specified
1997 through 2000	7 Nm (61 inch-lbs)
2001 and later	6 Nm (52 inch-lbs)
Brake lever pivot bolt locknut	
1986 through 1996	Not specified
1997 through 2000	7 Nm (61 inch-lbs)
2001 and later	6 Nm (52 inch-lbs)
Rear master cylinder mounting bolts	10 Nm (86 inch-lbs)
Rear brake fluid reservoir bolts	10 Nm (86 inch-lbs)

**Apply non-permanent thread locking agent to the threads.*

YZ125

Disc brakes

Brake fluid type	See Chapter 1
Brake pad minimum thickness	See Chapter 1
Front disc thickness	
Standard	3.0 mm (0.12 inch)
Limit*	2.5 mm (0.10 inch)
Rear disc thickness	
1988 through 1997	
Standard	4.5 mm (0.18 inch)
Limit*	4.0 mm (0.16 inch)
1998 and later	
Standard	4.0 mm (0.16 inch)
Limit	3.5 mm (0.14 inch)
Disc runout limit	0.15 mm (0.006 inch)

** Refer to marks stamped into the disc (they supersede information printed here)*

Drum brakes

Brake lining minimum thickness	See Chapter 1
Brake pedal height	See Chapter 1
Drum diameter	
Standard	130 mm (5.12 inches)
Wear limit*	131 mm (5.16 inches)

** Refer to marks cast into the drum (they supersede information printed here)*

Wheels and tires

Tire pressures	See Chapter 1
Tire tread depth	See Chapter 1
Axle runout limit (front and rear)	
1986 through 1994	No visible bending
1995 and later	0.5 mm (0.020 inch)
Wheel out-of-round and lateral runout limit (front and rear)	2.0 mm (0.08 inch)

Torque specifications

Front axle	
1986 through 1995	60 Nm (43 ft-lbs)
1996 and later	105 Nm (75 ft-lbs)
Front axle holder nuts (1986 through 1995)	
1986 through 1992	10 Nm (86 inch-lbs)
1993 through 1995	9 Nm (78 inch-lbs)
Front axle pinch bolts (1996 on)	23 Nm (17 ft-lbs)
Rear axle nut	
1986 and 1987	100 Nm (72 ft-lbs)
1988 through 1998	115 Nm (85 ft-lbs)
1999 and later	125 Nm (90 ft-lbs)
Front caliper	
Caliper bracket bolts	
1986 through 1988	30 Nm (22 ft-lbs)
1989 and later	23 Nm (173 ft-lbs)
Pad retaining pins	
1986 through 1988	23 Nm (17 ft-lbs)
1989 and later	18 Nm (13 ft-lbs)
Rear caliper	
Mounting bolt(s)	
1988 through 1992	23 Nm (17 ft-lbs)
1993 and later	Not applicable
Pad retaining pin(s)	
1988	Not applicable
1989 and later	18 Nm (156 in-lbs)
Pad pin plugs	3 Nm (26 inch-lbs)
Brake hose union bolts	
1986 through 1999	26 Nm (19 ft-lbs)
2000 and later	30 Nm (22 ft-lbs)
Brake hose fitting to master cylinder (1990 through 1995)	26 Nm (19 ft-lbs)
Front brake disc-to-wheel bolts*	
1986 through 1988	12 Nm (108 inch-lbs)
1989	14 Nm (120 inch-lbs)
1990 through 1992	12 Nm (108 inch-lbs)
1993 and later	
Front	12 Nm (108 inch-lbs)
Rear	14 Nm (120 inch-lbs)
Rear drum brake arm pinch bolt	10 Nm (86 inch-lbs)
Front master cylinder	
Mounting bolts	
1986 through 1988	Not specified
1989	10 Nm (86 inch-lbs)
1990 and later	9 Nm (78 inch-lbs)
Brake lever pivot bolt	
1986 through 1995	Not specified
1996 through 2000	7 Nm (61 inch-lbs)
Brake lever pivot bolt locknut	
1986 through 1995	Not specified
1996 through 2000	7 Nm (61 inch-lbs)
Rear master cylinder mounting bolts	10 Nm (86 in-lbs)
Pedal pivot bolt	
1986 and 1987	Not specified
1988 through 1991	16 Nm (132 inch-lbs)
1992	18 Nm (156 in-lbs)
1993	26 Nm (19 ft-lbs)
1994 through 2000	18 Nm (156 in-lbs)
2001 and later	26 Nm (19 ft-lbs)

Apply non-permanent thread locking agent to the threads.

YZ250

Disc brakes

Brake fluid type	See Chapter 1
Brake pad minimum thickness	See Chapter 1
Front disc thickness	
Standard	3.0 mm (0.12 inch)
Limit*	2.5 mm (0.10 inch)

YZ250 (continued)

Rear disc thickness	
1988 through 1997	
Standard	4.5 mm (0.18 inch)
Limit*	4.0 mm (0.16 inch)
1998 and later	
Standard	4.0 mm (0.16 inch)
Limit	3.5 mm (0.14 inch)
Disc runout limit	0.15 mm (0.006 inch)

** Refer to marks stamped into the disc (they supersede information printed here)*

Drum brakes

Brake lining minimum thickness	See Chapter 1
Brake pedal height	See Chapter 1
Drum diameter	
Standard	130 mm (5.12 inches)
Wear limit*	131 mm (5.16 inches)

** Refer to marks cast into the drum (they supersede information printed here)*

Wheels and tires

Tire pressures	See Chapter 1
Tire tread depth	See Chapter 1
Axle runout limit (front and rear)	
1986 through 1994	No visible bending
1995 and later	0.5 mm (0.020 inch)
Wheel out-of-round and lateral runout limit (front and rear)	2.0 mm (0.08 inch)

Torque specifications

Front axle	
1986 through 1995	60 Nm (43 ft-lbs)
1996 and later	105 Nm (75 ft-lbs)
Front axle holder nuts (1986 through 1995)	
1986 and 1987	10 Nm (84 inch-lbs)
1988 through 1995	9 Nm (78 inch-lbs)
Front axle pinch bolts (1996 on)	23 Nm (17 ft-lbs)
Rear axle nut	
1986 and 1987	100 Nm (72 ft-lbs)
1988 through 1998	115 Nm (85 ft-lbs)
1999 and later	125 Nm (90 ft-lbs)
Front caliper	
Caliper bracket bolts	
1986 through 1988	30 Nm (22 ft-lbs)
1989 and later	23 Nm (17 ft-lbs)
Pad retaining pins	
1986 through 1988	23 Nm (17 ft-lbs)
1989 and later	18 Nm (156 in-lbs)
Rear caliper	
Mounting bolt(s)	
1988 through 1992	23 Nm (17 ft-lbs)
1993 and later	Not applicable
Pad retaining pin(s)	
1988	Not applicable
1989 and later	18 Nm (156 in-lbs)
Pad pin plugs	3 Nm (26 inch-lbs)
Brake hose union bolts	
1986 through 1999	26 Nm (19 ft-lbs)
2000 and later	30 Nm (22 ft-lbs)
Brake hose fitting to master cylinder (1990 through 1995)	26 Nm (19 ft-lbs)
Front brake disc-to-wheel bolts*	
1986 through 1988	12 Nm (108 inch-lbs)
1989	14 Nm (120 inch-lbs)
1990 and later	
Front	12 Nm (108 inch-lbs)
Rear	14 Nm (120 inch-lbs)
Rear drum brake arm pinch bolt	10 Nm (86 inch-lbs)
Front master cylinder	
Mounting bolts	
1986 through 1988	Not specified
1989	10 Nm (86 inch-lbs)
1990 and later	9 Nm (78 inch-lbs)

Brake lever pivot bolt	
1986 through 1995	Not specified
1996 through 2000	7 Nm (61 inch-lbs)
2001 and later	6 Nm (52 inch-lbs)
Brake lever pivot bolt locknut	
1986 through 1995	Not specified
1996 through 2000	7 Nm (61 inch-lbs)
2001 and later	6 Nm (52 inch-lbs)
Rear master cylinder mounting bolts	10 Nm (86 in-lbs)
Pedal pivot bolt	
1986 and 1987	Not specified
1988 through 1991	16 Nm (132 inch-lbs)
1992	18 Nm (156 in-lbs)
1993 and 1994	26 Nm (19 ft-lbs)
1995 through 2000	18 Nm (156 in-lbs)
2001 and later	26 Nm (19 ft-lbs)

**Apply non-permanent thread locking agent to the threads.*

1 General information

The front wheel on all motorcycles covered by this manual is equipped with a hydraulic disc brake using a pin slider caliper. The front caliper has dual pistons. The rear wheel on 1986 through 1992 YZ80 models, as well as 1986 and 1987 YZ125/YZ250 models, is equipped with a drum brake. The rear wheel on all other models is equipped with a hydraulic disc brake using a pin slider caliper. **Caution:** *Disc brake components rarely require disassembly. Do not disassemble components unless absolutely necessary. If any hydraulic brake line connection in the system is loosened, the entire system should be disassembled, drained, cleaned and then properly filled and bled upon reassembly. Do not use solvents on internal brake components. Solvents will cause seals to swell and distort. Use only clean brake fluid, brake system cleaner or denatured (rubbing) alcohol for cleaning. Use care when working with brake fluid as it can injure your eyes and it will damage painted surfaces and plastic parts.*

2 Front brake pads - replacement

Warning: *The dust created by the brake system may contain asbestos, which is harmful to your health. Yamaha hasn't used asbestos in brake parts for a number of years, but aftermarket parts may contain it. Never blow it out with compressed air and don't inhale any of it. An approved filtering mask should be worn when working on the brakes.*

Removal

1 Support the bike securely upright.

All YZ80/85 and 1986 through 1988 YZ125/250

2 The caliper doesn't need to be removed for pad replacement.
3 Unscrew the lower caliper bolt.

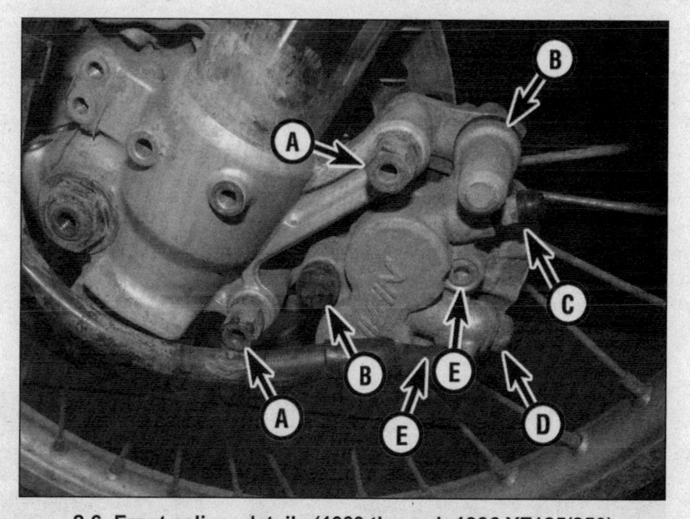

2.6 Front caliper details (1989 through 1996 YZ125/250)

A Caliper mounting bolts
B Slide pins
C Bleed valve
D Brake hose banjo bolt
E Pad pins (lower pin hidden)

4 Pivot the caliper up off the pads and remove the pads from the caliper bracket.
5 Check the pad spring for wear, damage or corrosion and replace it if necessary.

1989 through 1996 YZ125/250

Refer to illustration 2.6

6 Loosen the pad pins while the caliper is still bolted to the bracket **(see illustration)**.

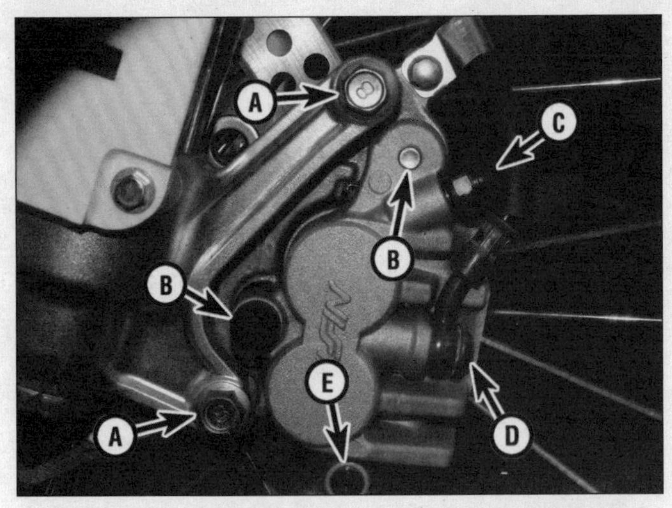

2.9a Front caliper details (1989 through 1996 YZ125/250)

A Caliper mounting bolts
B Slide pins
C Bleed valve
D Brake hose banjo bolt
E Pad pin plug

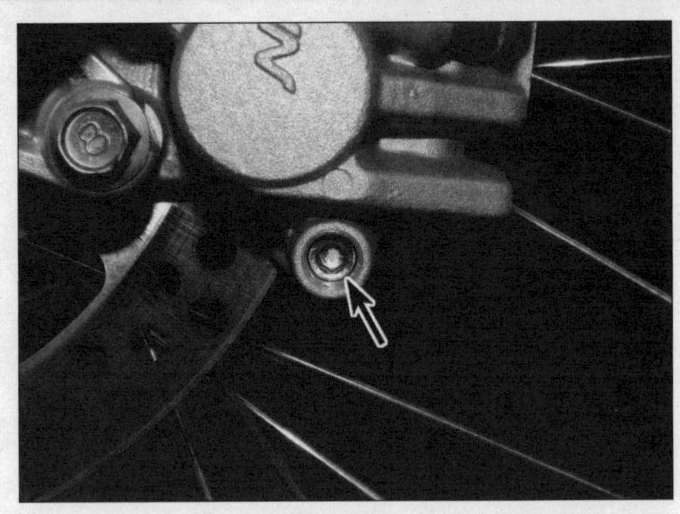

2.9b Loosen the pad pin (arrow) while the caliper is still bolted to the bracket . . .

7 Remove the caliper mounting bolts and lift the caliper off **(see illustration 2.6)**. Leave the brake hose connected and support the caliper so the hose won't be strained.

8 Unscrew the pad pins and pull the pads out of the caliper, noting how the forked end of the inner pad fits over the post on the caliper.

1997 and later YZ125/250

Refer to illustrations 2.9a, 2.9b, 2.11a, 2.11b and 2.11c

9 Unscrew the plug from the pad pin **(see illustration)**. Loosen the pad pin while the caliper is still bolted to the bracket **(see illustration)**.

10 Remove the caliper mounting bolts and lift the caliper off **(see illustration 2.9a)**. Leave the brake hose connected and support the caliper so the hose won't be strained.

11 Take the pads out of the caliper **(see illustrations)**.

Inspection

12 Inspect the pad spring and the steel shield that protects the caliper bracket. Replace the spring or shield it if it's rusted or damaged.

13 Refer to Chapter 1 and inspect the pads.

14 Look for signs of fluid leakage past the pistons. If this has occurred, overhaul the caliper (see Section 4).

15 Check the condition of the brake disc (see Section 5). If it's in need of replacement, follow the procedure in that Section to remove it. If it's okay, deglaze it with sandpaper or emery cloth, using a swirling motion.

Installation

16 Remove the cover from the master cylinder reservoir and drain out some fluid. Push the piston(s) into the caliper as far as possible, while checking the master cylinder reservoir to make sure it doesn't overflow. If you can't depress the pistons with thumb pressure, try using a C-clamp. If the pistons stick, remove the caliper and overhaul it as described in Section 4.

17 Install the spring, caliper shield and new pads. Coat the threads of the retaining pin(s) with non-permanent thread locking agent and install the retaining pins. Tighten the retaining pins to the torque listed in this Chapter's Specifications.

18 Install the plug over the retaining pin and tighten it to the torque listed in this Chapter's Specifications.

19 Operate the brake lever several times to bring the pads into contact with the disc, then check the brake fluid level in the master cylinder reservoir, adding the proper type of fluid as necessary (see Chapter 1).

20 Check the operation of the brake carefully before riding the motorcycle.

2.11a . . . and unscrew the pin with an Allen wrench after lifting the caliper off

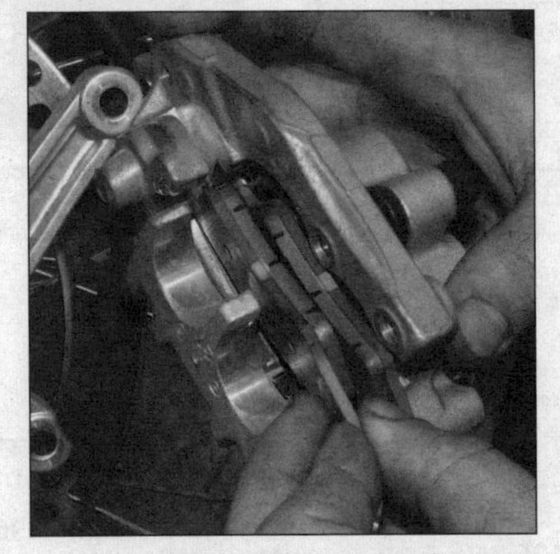

2.11b Slide out the outer pad . . .

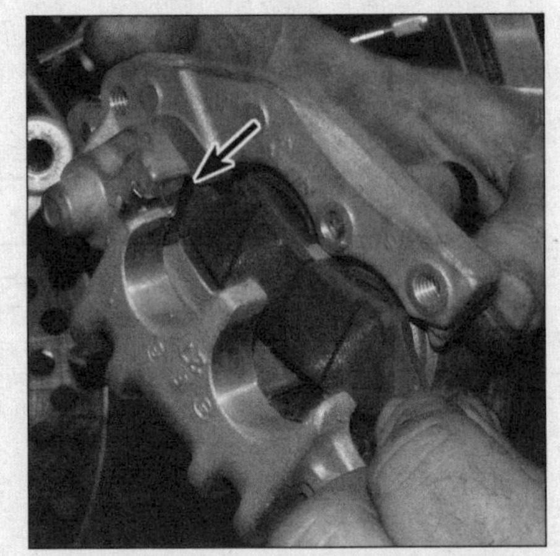

2.11c . . . then slide out the inner pad, noting how the pad ends engage the caliper (arrow)

3.3 Rear caliper details (YZ80/85)

A Caliper shield bolts (right bolt hidden)
B Pad pins (right pin hidden)
C Caliper mounting bolts (right bolt hidden)
D Bleed valve
E Brake hose banjo bolt

3.11 Unbolt the caliper shield and lift it off

3 Rear brake pads - replacement

Removal

1988 YZ125/250

1 Unbolt the caliper shield and lift it off.

2 Remove the caliper mounting bolt. Pivot the caliper forward and take the pads out.

1993 and later YZ80/85, 1989 through 1993 YZ125/250

Refer to illustration 3.3

3 Unbolt the caliper shield and lift it off **(see illustration)**.

4 Loosen the pad pins while the caliper is still bolted to the bracket.

5 Remove the caliper mounting bolts and lift the caliper off **(see illustration 3.3)**. Leave the brake hose connected and support the caliper so the hose won't be strained.

6 Unscrew the pad pins and pull the pads out of the caliper.

1994 through 1998 YZ125/250

7 Unbolt the caliper shield and lift it off.

8 Loosen the pad pins while the caliper is still bolted to the bracket.

9 Remove the rear wheel (see Chapter 7). Slide the caliper rearward off its rail on the swingarm. Leave the brake hose connected and support the caliper so the hose won't be strained.

10 Unscrew the pad pins and pull the pads out of the caliper.

1999 and later YZ125/250

Refer to illustrations 3.11, 3.12a, 3.12b, 3.13a, 3.13b, 3.14a and 3.14b

11 Remove the caliper shield **(see illustration)**.

12 Unscrew the plug that covers the pad retaining pin **(see illustrations)**.

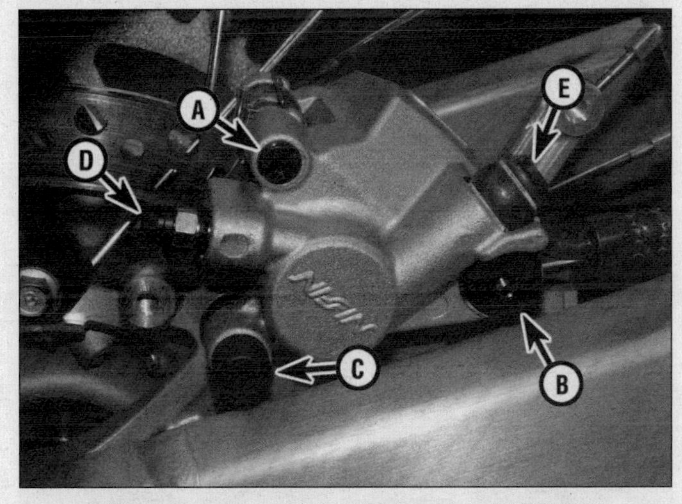

3.12a Rear caliper details (1999 and later YZ125/250)

A Pad pin plug
B Caliper mounting bolt
C Slide pin
D Bleed valve
E Brake hose union bolt

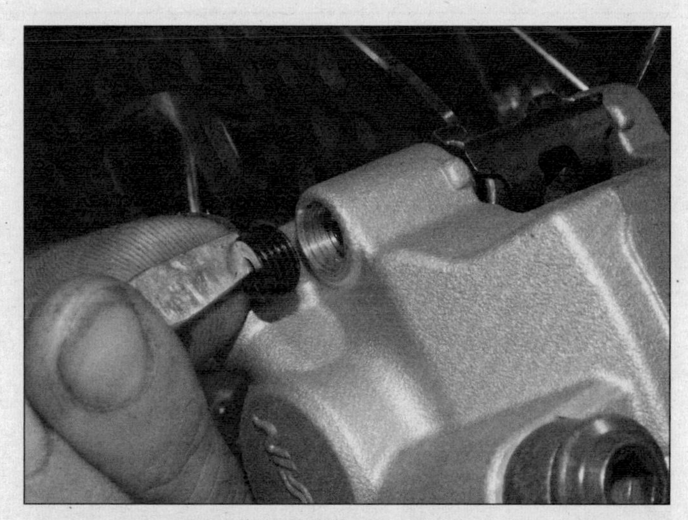

3.12b Unscrew the pad pin plug . . .

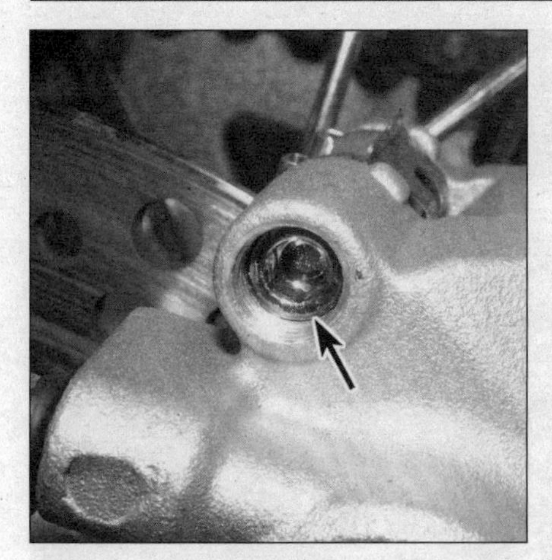
3.13a . . . and loosen the pad pin (arrow) with an Allen wrench

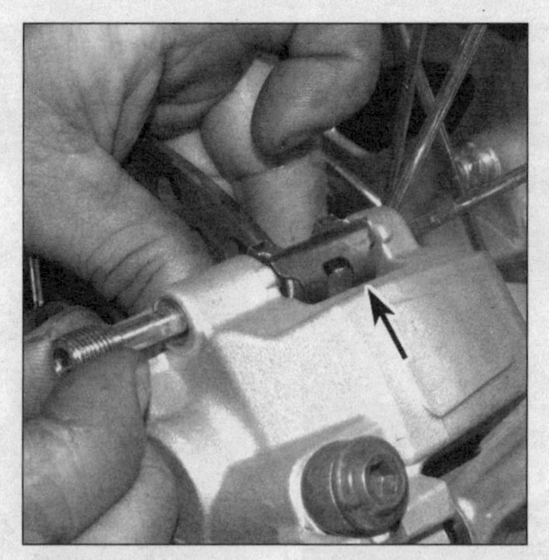
3.13b Push back the pad spring to relieve pressure on the pin and pull out the pin

3.14a Lift the inner pad up and out . . .

13 Unscrew the pad retaining pin with an Allen wrench **(see illustrations)**.
14 Pull the pads and shim out of the caliper **(see illustrations)**.

Inspection

Refer to illustration 3.15

15 Inspection is the same as for front pads (see Section 2). Look inside the caliper to inspect the pad spring **(see illustration)**. If it's worn, corroded or damaged, replace it (on some models, you'll need to remove the caliper for access).

Installation

16 Installation is the reverse of the removal steps. Lubricate the pad pin(s) with high temperature grease before installing them **(see illustration)**.
17 Operate the brake pedal several times to bring the pads into contact with the disc, then check the brake fluid level in the master cylinder reservoir, adding the proper type of fluid as necessary (see Chapter 1).
18 Check the operation of the brakes carefully before riding the motorcycle.

4 Brake caliper - removal, overhaul and installation

Warning: *If a caliper indicates the need for an overhaul (usually due to leaking fluid or sticky operation), all old brake fluid must be flushed from the system. Also, the dust created by the brake system may contain asbestos, which is harmful to your health. Never blow it out with compressed air and don't inhale any of it. An approved filtering mask should be worn when working on the brakes. Do not, under any circumstances, use petroleum-based solvents to clean brake parts. Use brake system cleaner, clean brake fluid or denatured alcohol only!*
Note: *If you are removing the caliper only to remove the front forks or rear swingarm, don't disconnect the hose from the caliper.*

3.15 Check the pad spring (arrow) and replace it if it's worn, damaged or corroded

3.16 Lubricate the pad pin before you install it

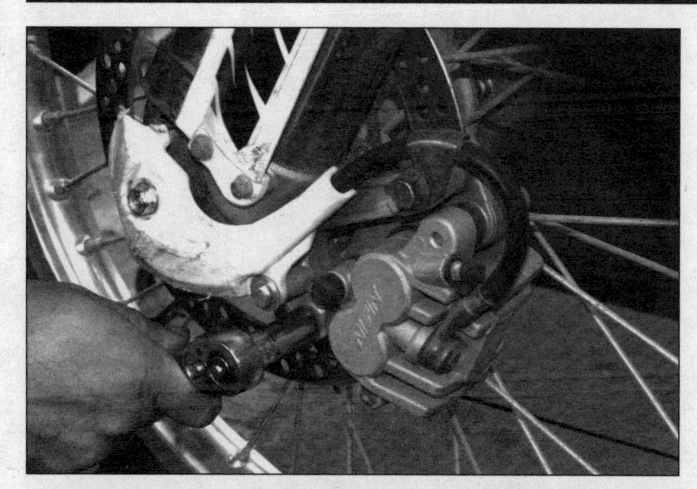

4.2 Unbolt the caliper from the bracket (late YZ250 shown) . . .

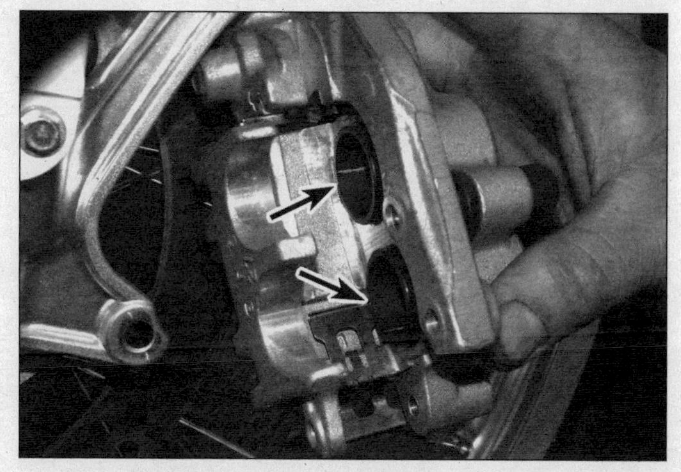

4.3 . . . and lift it off - check for signs of fluid leakage from the pistons (arrows)

Removal

1 Support the bike securely upright. **Note:** *If you're planning to disassemble the caliper, read through the overhaul procedure, paying particular attention to the steps involved in removing the pistons with compressed air. If you don't have access to an air compressor, you can use the bike's hydraulic system to force the pistons out instead. To do this, remove the pads and pump the brake lever or pedal. If one piston in a dual-piston caliper comes out before the other, push it back into its bore and hold it in with a C-clamp while pumping the brake lever to remove the remaining piston.*

Front caliper

Refer to illustrations 4.2 and 4.3

2 **Note:** *Remember, if you're just removing the caliper to remove the forks, ignore this step.* Disconnect the brake hose from the caliper. Remove the brake hose banjo fitting bolt and separate the hose from the caliper **(see illustration)**. Discard the sealing washers. Plug the end of the hose or wrap a plastic bag tightly around it to prevent excessive fluid loss and contamination.

3 Unscrew the caliper mounting bolts and lift it off the fork leg, being careful not to strain or twist the brake hose if it's still connected **(see illustration)**.

Rear caliper

Refer to illustration 4.7

4 If you're planning to overhaul the caliper, remove its protective bracket and loosen the brake hose union bolt (it's easier to loosen the bolts while the caliper is mounted on the bike) **(see illustrations 3.3, 3.11 and 3.12a)**.

5 If you're working on a 1988 YZ125/250, remove the mounting bolt (see Section 3). Pivot the caliper up and slide it off the bracket pin.

6 If you're working on a YZ80/85 or a 1989 through 1998 YZ125/250, caliper removal is part of the pad removal procedure (see Section 3).

7 If you're working on a 1999 or later YZ125/250, refer to Section 12 and remove the rear wheel. Slide the caliper bracket backward off its rail **(see illustration)**. Support the caliper so it doesn't hang by the brake hose.

8 Disconnect the brake hose from the caliper if you haven't already done so. Remove the brake hose banjo fitting bolt and separate the hose from the caliper. Discard the sealing washers. Plug the end of the hose or wrap a plastic bag tightly around it to prevent excessive fluid loss and contamination.

Overhaul

Refer to illustrations 4.10,4.12, 4.15 and 4.18

9 Remove the brake pads and anti-rattle spring from the caliper (see Section 2 or 3, if necessary). Clean the exterior of the caliper with denatured alcohol or brake system cleaner.

10 Slide the caliper off the bracket **(see illustration)**.

11 Pack a shop rag into the space that holds the brake pads. Use compressed air, directed into the caliper fluid inlet, to remove the piston(s). Use only enough air pressure to ease the piston(s) out of the bore. If a piston is blown out forcefully, even with the rag in place, it may

4.7 Slide the caliper backward off its rail on the swingarm, then slide the caliper off the bracket

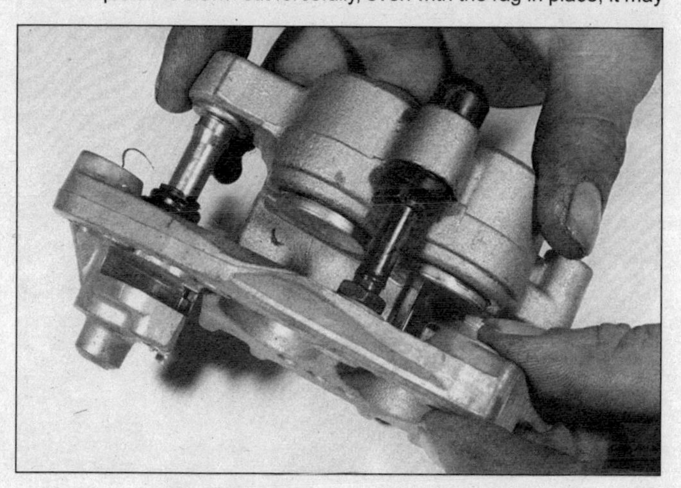

4.10 Slide the caliper off the bracket

4.12 Brake caliper details (typical rear shown, front similar but with an additional piston)

1 *Pin boot*
2 *Caliper body*
3 *Pad spring*
4 *Piston seal*
5 *Dust seal*
6 *Piston*

be damaged. **Warning:** *Never place your fingers in front of the piston in an attempt to catch or protect it when applying compressed air, as serious injury could occur.*

12 Using a wood or plastic tool, remove the piston seals **(see illustration)**. Metal tools may cause bore damage.

13 Clean the pistons and the bores with denatured alcohol, clean brake fluid or brake system cleaner and blow dry them with filtered, unlubricated compressed air. Inspect the surfaces of the pistons for nicks and burrs and loss of plating. Check the caliper bores, too. If surface defects are present, the caliper must be replaced.

14 If the caliper is in bad shape, the master cylinder should also be checked.

15 Lubricate the piston seals with clean brake fluid and install them in their grooves in the caliper bore **(see illustration)**. Make sure they seat completely and aren't twisted.

16 Lubricate the dust seals with clean brake fluid and install them in their grooves, making sure they seat correctly.

17 Lubricate the piston (both pistons on front calipers) with clean brake fluid and install it into the caliper bore. Using your thumbs, push the piston all the way in, making sure it doesn't get cocked in the bore.

4.18 Install the boot in the front caliper with its wide end facing the same direction as the piston(s)

4.15 Fit the seals all the way into their grooves

18 Pull the old pin boots out of the caliper and bracket. Coat new ones with silicone grease and install them, making sure they seat completely **(see illustrations)**.

19 Make sure the shields are in position on the caliper brackets.

Installation

20 Installation is the reverse of the removal steps, with the following additions:

a) *Apply silicone grease to the slider pins on the caliper bracket and caliper.*
b) *If you're installing the pads and caliper together, space the pads apart so the disc will fit between them (on later YZ125/250 models, the pads are installed after the caliper is installed).*
c) *Use new sealing washers on the brake hose fitting. Position the brake hose fitting in the caliper notch or against the stop.*
d) *Tighten the caliper mounting bolts (if equipped), rear caliper shield bolts and brake line union bolt to the torque listed in this Chapter's Specifications.*
e) *If you're working on a 1999 or later YZ125/250 rear caliper, adjust chain slack (see Chapter 1).*

23 Fill the master cylinder with the recommended brake fluid (see Chapter 1) and bleed the system (see Section 11). Check for leaks.

24 Check the operation of the brakes carefully before riding the motorcycle.

5 Brake disc(s) - inspection, removal and installation

Inspection

Refer to illustrations 5.3 and 5.4

1 Support the bike securely upright. Place a jack beneath the bike and raise the wheel being checked off the ground. Be sure the bike is securely supported so it can't be knocked over.

2 Visually inspect the surface of the disc(s) for score marks and other damage. Light scratches are normal after use and won't affect brake operation, but deep grooves and heavy score marks will reduce braking efficiency and accelerate pad wear. If the discs are badly grooved they must be replaced (machining is not recommended).

3 To check disc runout, mount a dial indicator to a fork leg or the swingarm, with the plunger on the indicator touching the surface of the disc **(see illustration)**. Slowly turn the wheel and watch the indicator needle, comparing your reading with the limit listed in this Chapter's Specifications. If the runout is greater than allowed, check the hub bearings for play (see Chapter 1). If the bearings are worn, replace them and repeat this check. If the disc runout is still excessive, the disc will have to be replaced.

5.3 **Set up a dial indicator against the brake disc and turn the wheel in its normal direction of rotation to measure runout**

5.4 **Marks on the disc indicate the minimum thickness and direction of rotation (typical)**

4 The disc must not be allowed to wear down to a thickness less than the minimum allowable thickness, listed in this Chapter's Specifications. The thickness of the disc can be checked with a micrometer. If the thickness of the disc is less than the minimum allowable, it must be replaced. The minimum thickness is also stamped into the disc **(see illustrations)**.

Removal

Refer to illustration 5.6

5 Remove the wheel (see Section 12). **Caution**: *Don't lay the wheel down and allow it to rest on the disc - the disc could become warped.* Set the wheel on wood blocks so the disc doesn't support the weight of the wheel.

6 Mark the relationship of the disc to the wheel, so it can be installed in the same position. Remove the bolts that retain the disc to the wheel **(see illustration)**. Loosen the bolts a little at a time, in a criss-cross pattern, to avoid distorting the disc.

Installation

Refer to illustration 5.7

7 Position the disc on the wheel, aligning the previously applied matchmarks (if you're reinstalling the original disc). On models so equipped, make sure the arrow (stamped on the disc) marking the direction of rotation is pointing in the proper direction **(see illustration)**.

8 Install the bolts, tightening them a little at a time in a criss-cross pattern, until the torque listed in this Chapter's Specifications is reached. Clean off all grease from the brake disc using acetone or brake system cleaner.

9 Install the wheel.

10 Operate the brake lever or pedal several times to bring the pads into contact with the disc. Check the operation of the brakes carefully before riding the motorcycle.

6 Brake drum and shoes - removal, inspection and installation

Warning: *The dust created by the brake system may contain asbestos, which is harmful to your health (Yamaha hasn't used asbestos in brake parts for a number of years, but aftermarket parts may contain it). Never blow it out with compressed air and don't inhale any of it. An approved filtering mask should be worn when working on the brakes.*

5.6 **The rear brake disc is secured to the hub by four or six bolts (arrows); late YZ80/85 front discs have three bolts and all other front discs have six bolts**

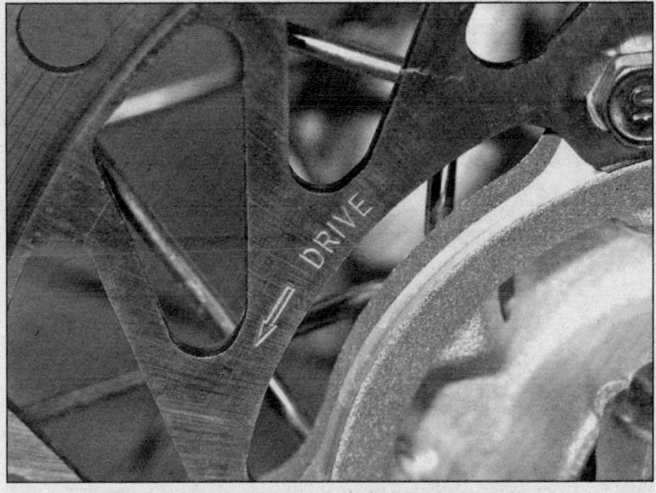

5.7 **When installing the disc, pay attention to the direction of rotation marking**

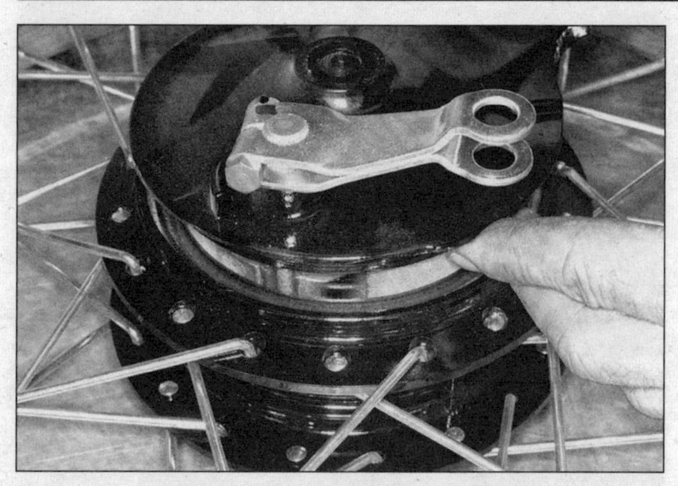

6.2 Lift the brake panel out of the drum

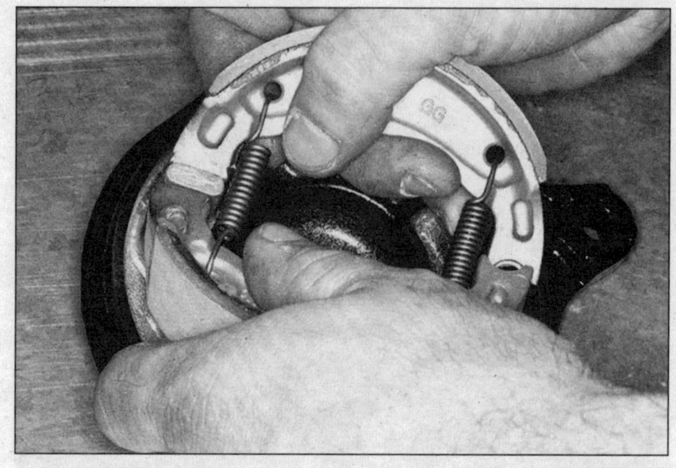

6.6 Spread the shoes and fold them into a V to release the spring tension

Removal

Refer to illustration 6.2

1 Remove the wheel (see Section 12).
2 Lift the brake panel out of the wheel **(see illustration)**.

Inspection

Refer to illustrations 6.6, 6.9, 6.10 and 6.11

3 Check the brake drum for wear or damage. Measure the diameter at several points with a drum micrometer (or have this done by a Yamaha dealer or other qualified repair shop). If the measurements are uneven (indicating that the drum is out-of-round) or if there are scratches deep enough to snag a fingernail, replace the drum. The drum must also be replaced if the diameter is greater than that cast inside the drum. Yamaha recommends against machining the brake drums. The drum is an integral part of the wheel hub. Replacement should be done by a Yamaha dealer service department or other qualified shop.
4 Check the linings for wear, damage and signs of contamination from road dirt or water. If the linings are visibly defective, replace them.
5 Measure the thickness of the lining material (just the lining material, not the metal backing) and compare with the value listed in the Chapter 1 Specifications. Replace the shoes if the material is worn to the minimum or less.
6 To remove the shoes, fold them toward each other to release the spring tension and lift them off the brake panel **(see illustration)**.
7 Check the ends of the shoes where they contact the brake cam and anchor pin. Replace the shoes if there's visible wear.
8 Check the brake cam and anchor pin for wear and damage.

6.9 Look for alignment marks on the brake arm and cam (arrows); make your own marks if you can't see any

The brake cam can be replaced separately; the brake panel must be replaced if the anchor pin is unserviceable.
9 Look for alignment marks on the brake arm and anchor pin **(see illustration)**. Make your own if they aren't visible.
10 Remove the pinch bolt and nut and pull the brake arm off the cam **(see illustration)**.
11 Remove the brake cam shaft from the panel **(see illustration)**.

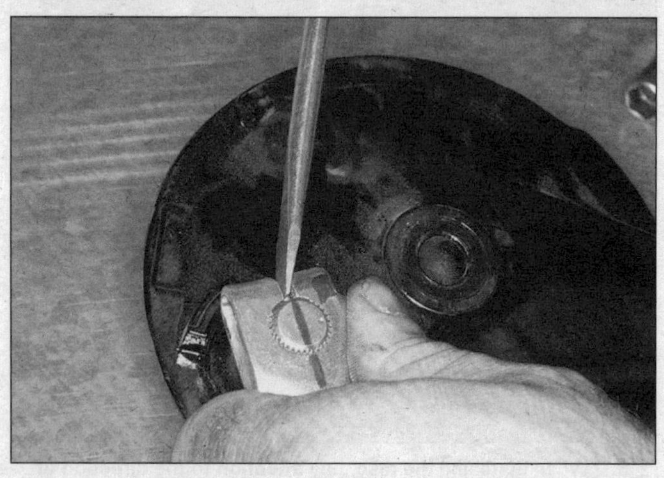

6.10 Remove the pinch bolt and nut and take the brake arm off the camshaft . . .

6.11 . . . and twist and pull the cam shaft out of the brake panel

6.15 The assembled brakes should look like this

Installation

Refer to illustration 6.15

12 Apply high temperature brake grease to the brake cam, the anchor pin and the ends of the springs.

13 Install the cam through the dust seal.

14 Install the brake arm on the cam, aligning the punch marks. Tighten the nut and bolt to the torque listed in this Chapter's Specifications.

15 Hook the ends of the springs to the shoes. Position the shoes in a V on the brake panel, then fold them down into position. Make sure the ends of the shoes fit correctly on the cam and the anchor pin **(see illustration)**.

16 The remainder of installation is the reverse of the removal steps.

17 After installing the wheel, adjust the drive chain slack and the rear brake (see Chapter 1).

7 Front brake master cylinder - removal, overhaul and installation

1 If the master cylinder is leaking fluid, or if the lever doesn't produce a firm feel when the brake is applied, and bleeding the brakes doesn't help, master cylinder overhaul is recommended. Before disassembling the master cylinder, read through the entire procedure and make sure that you have the correct rebuild kit. Also, you will need some new, clean brake fluid of the recommended type, some clean rags and internal snap-ring pliers. **Note:** *To prevent damage to the paint, plastic or graphics from spilled brake fluid, always cover the surrounding areas when working on the master cylinder.*

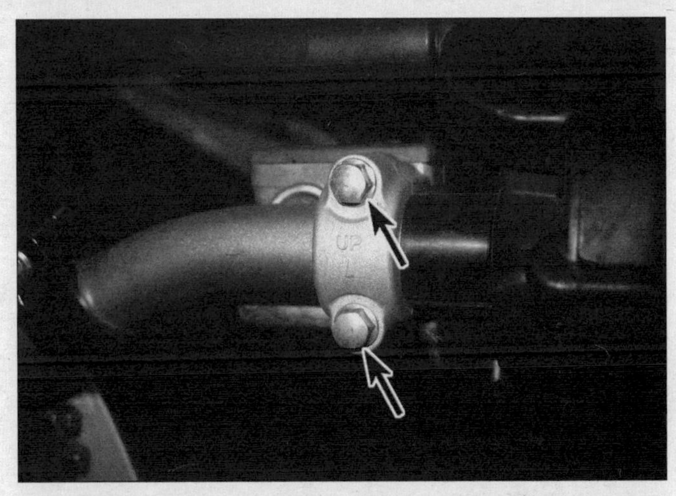

7.6 Make an alignment mark for the clamp if there isn't one, then remove the bolts (arrows) - the UP mark and arrow face upward on installation

2 **Caution:** *Disassembly, overhaul and reassembly of the brake master cylinder must be done in a spotlessly clean work area to avoid contamination and possible failure of the brake hydraulic system components.*

Removal

Refer to illustration 7.6

3 Place rags beneath the master cylinder to protect surrounding areas in case of brake fluid spills.

4 Brake fluid will run out of the upper brake hose during this step, so either have a container handy to place the end of the hose in, or have a plastic bag and rubber band handy to cover the end of the hose. The objective is to prevent excess loss of brake fluid, fluid spills and system contamination.

5 Remove the banjo fitting bolt and sealing washers from the master cylinder.

6 Remove the master cylinder mounting bolts **(see illustration)**. Take the master cylinder off the handlebar.

Overhaul

Refer to illustrations 7.8a, 7.8b, 7.9, 7.10, 7.11a, 7.11b and 7.13

7 Remove the master cylinder cover, retainer (if equipped) and diaphragm (see Chapter 1).

8 Remove the locknut from the underside of the lever pivot bolt, then unscrew the bolt **(see illustrations)**. Remove the lever pivot cover (it's

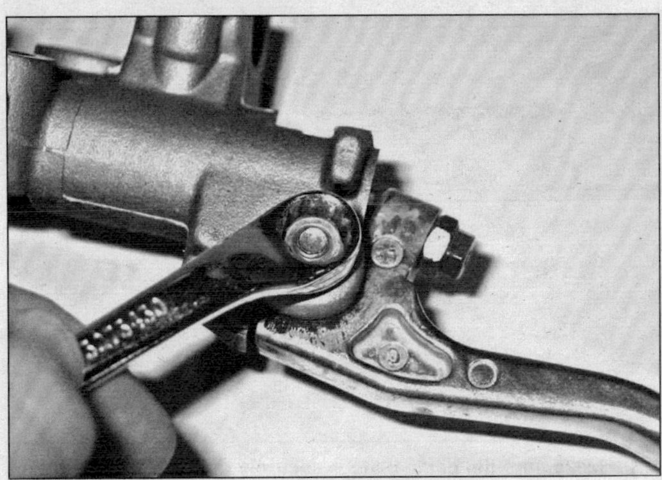

7.8a Remove the locknut . . .

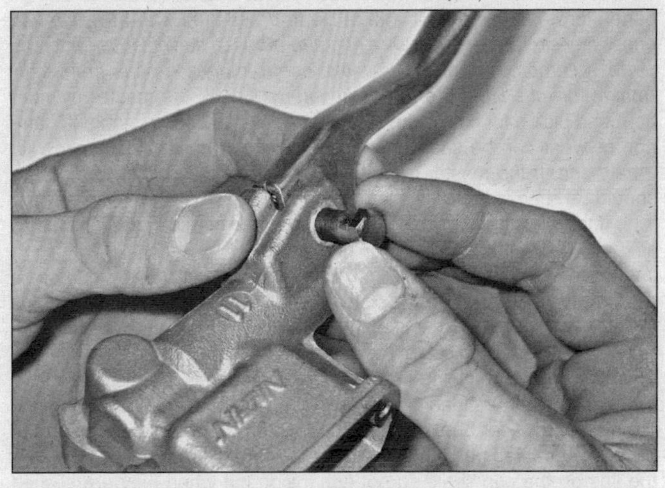

7.8b . . . and unscrew the pivot bolt to detach the lever

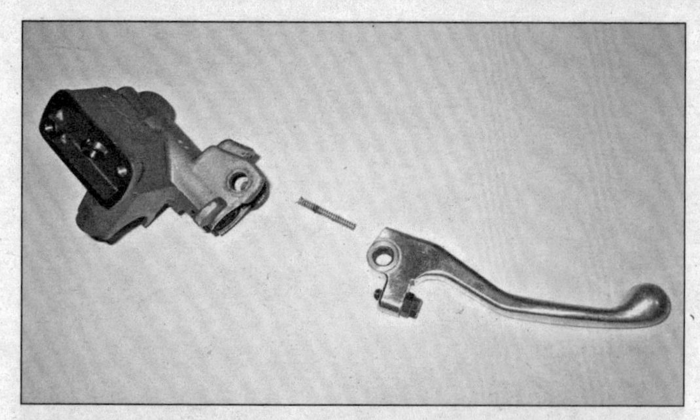

7.9 Remove the lever (and spring on early models) from the master cylinder

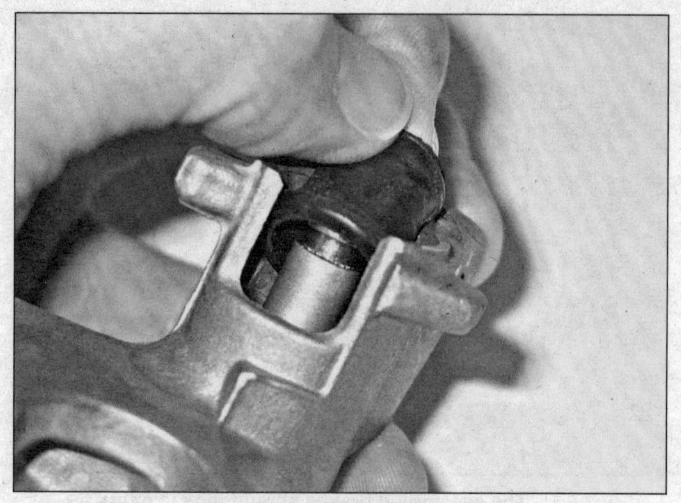

7.10 Remove the dust boot . . .

7.11a . . . then remove the snap-ring from the master cylinder bore

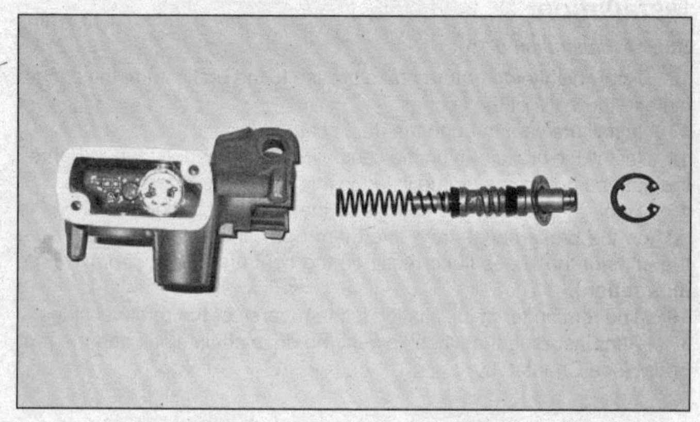

7.11b Remove the piston assembly from the bore

held on by the pivot bolt).

9 On early models, the lever is equipped with a spring **(see illustration)**. This doesn't have to be removed to remove the hydraulic components, but make sure it doesn't get lost.

10 Remove the dust boot **(see illustration)**.

11 Using snap-ring pliers, remove the snap-ring and slide out the piston assembly and the spring **(see illustrations)**. Lay the parts out in the proper order to prevent confusion during reassembly.

12 Clean all of the parts with brake system cleaner (available at auto parts stores), isopropyl alcohol or clean brake fluid. **Caution:** *Do not, under any circumstances, use a petroleum-based solvent to clean brake parts. If compressed air is available, use it to dry the parts thoroughly (make sure it's filtered and unlubricated).* Check the master cylinder bore and piston for corrosion, scratches, nicks and score marks. If damage or wear can be seen, the master cylinder must be replaced with a new one. If the master cylinder is in poor condition, then the caliper should be checked as well.

13 If there's a baffle plate in the bottom of the reservoir, make sure it's securely held by its retainer **(see illustration)**.

14 Yamaha supplies a new piston in its rebuild kits. If the cup seals are not installed on the new piston, install them, making sure the lips face away from the lever end of the piston **(see illustration 6.11b)**. Use the new piston regardless of the condition of the old one.

15 Before reassembling the master cylinder, soak the piston and the rubber cup seals in clean brake fluid for ten or fifteen minutes. Lubricate the master cylinder bore with clean brake fluid, then carefully insert the piston and related parts in the reverse order of disassembly. Make sure the lips on the cup seals do not turn inside out when they are slipped into the bore.

16 Depress the piston, then install the snap-ring (make sure the snap-ring is properly seated in the groove with the sharp edge facing out). Install the rubber dust boot (make sure the lip is seated properly in the piston groove).

17 Install the brake lever, pivot cover and pivot bolt. Tighten the pivot bolt locknut.

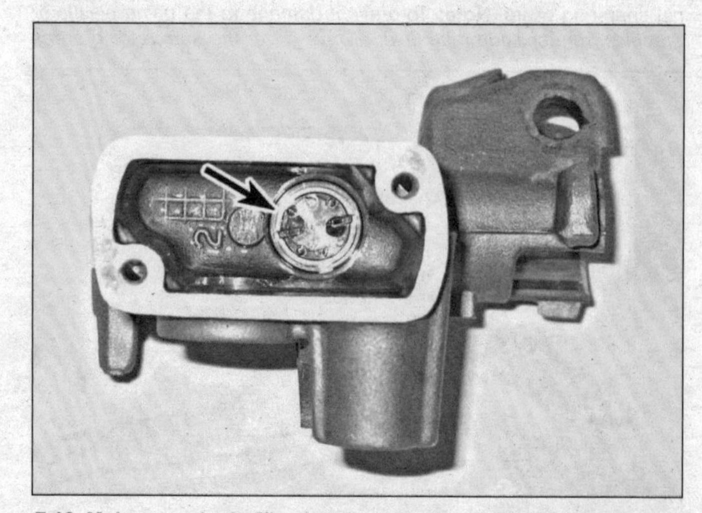

7.13 Make sure the baffle plate is securely retained in the bottom of the reservoir

7.18 The pivot cover fits like this, with the drain hole downward (arrow)

Installation

Refer to illustration 7.18

18 Installation is the reverse of the removal steps, with the following additions:

a) *Attach the master cylinder to the handlebar. Align the upper gap between the master cylinder and clamp with the punch mark on the handlebar.*

b) *Make sure the arrow and the word UP on the master cylinder clamp are pointing up* **(see illustration 7.6)**, *then tighten the bolts to the torque listed in this Chapter's Specifications.*

c) *Use new sealing washers at the brake hose banjo fitting. Tighten the union bolt to the torque listed in this Chapter's Specifications.*

d) *Install the dust cover over the lever and pivot with its drain hole downward* **(see illustration)**.

19 Refer to Section 11 and bleed the air from the system.

8 Rear brake master cylinder - removal, overhaul and installation

1 If the master cylinder is leaking fluid, or if the pedal does not produce a firm feel when the brake is applied, and bleeding the brake does not help, master cylinder overhaul is recommended. Before disassembling the master cylinder, read through the entire procedure and make sure that you have the correct rebuild kit. Also, you will need some new, clean brake fluid of the recommended type, some clean rags and internal snap-ring pliers.

2 **Caution:** *Disassembly, overhaul and reassembly of the brake master cylinder must be done in a spotlessly clean work area to avoid contamination and possible failure of the brake hydraulic system components.*

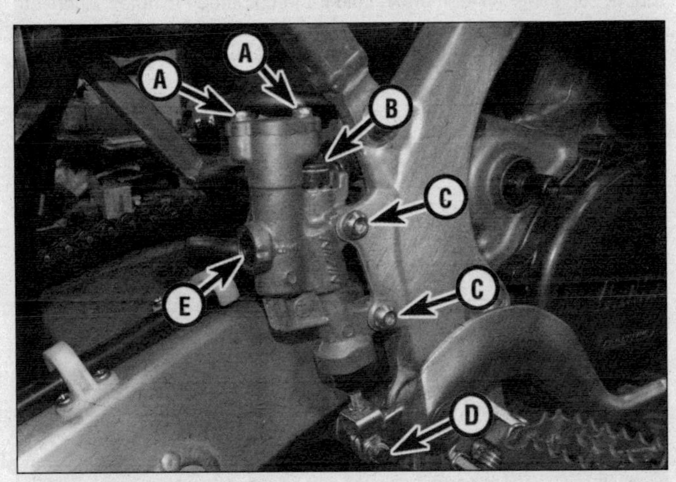

8.4b Rear master cylinder details (integral reservoir type)

A *Cover screws*
B *Brake hose union bolt*
C *Mounting bolts*
D *Clevis pin*
E *Fluid level window*

8.4a Rear master cylinder details (separate reservoir type)

A *Clevis pin*
B *Mounting bolts*
C *Brake hose banjo bolt*

Removal

Refer to illustrations 8.4a, 8.4b and 8.6

3 Support the bike securely upright.

4 Remove the cotter pin from the clevis pin on the master cylinder pushrod **(see illustrations)**. Remove the clevis pin.

5 Have a container and some rags ready to catch spilling brake fluid. Using a six-point box wrench, unscrew the banjo fitting bolt from the top of the master cylinder. Discard the sealing washers on either side of the fitting.

6 On early models with a separate reservoir, squeeze the fluid feed hose clamp with pliers and slide the clamp up the hose **(see illustration)**. Disconnect the hose from the fitting on the master cylinder. If necessary, unbolt the reservoir from the frame and take it out.

7 Remove the two master cylinder mounting bolts and detach the cylinder from the frame **(see illustration 8.4a or 8.4b)**.

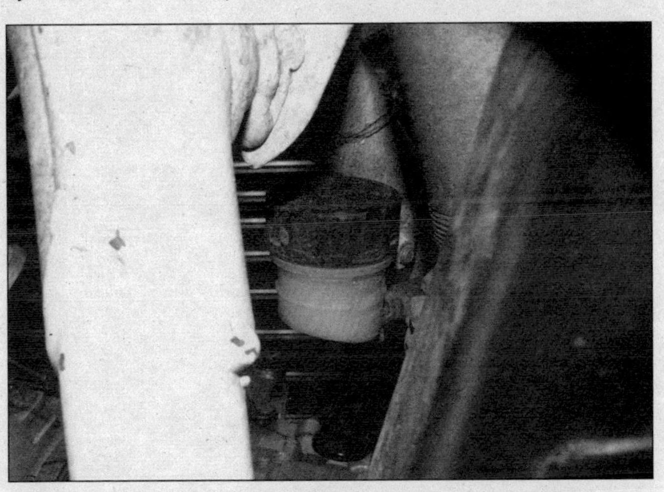

8.6 Early models use a separate reservoir for the rear master cylinder

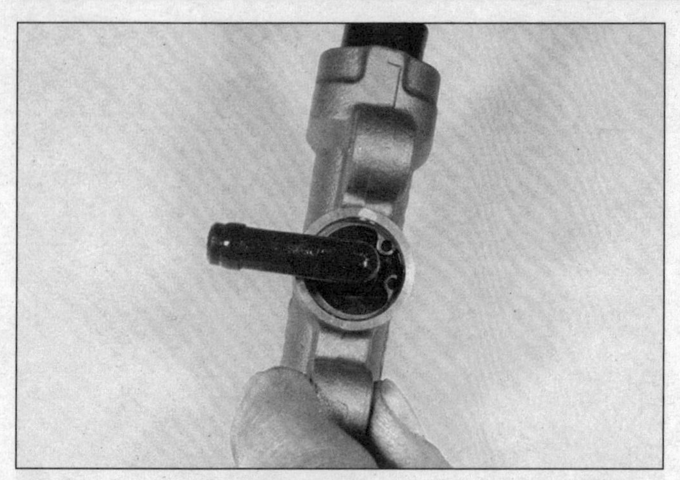

8.8a Remove the snap-ring . . .

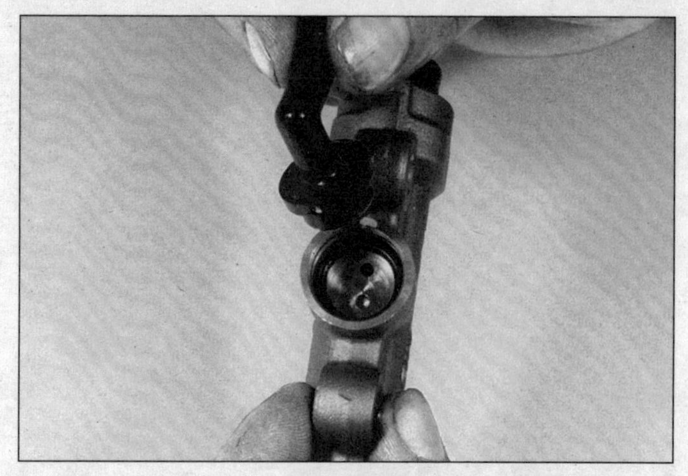

8.8b . . . then work the fluid feed fitting free of its bore and remove the O-ring

Overhaul

Refer to illustrations 8.8a, 8.8b, 8.9, 8.10a, 8.10b, 8.11a, 8.11b, 8.11c, 8.11d and 8.15

8 On early models, use a pair of snap-ring pliers to remove the snap-ring from the fluid inlet fitting and detach the fitting from the master cylinder. Remove the O-ring from the bore **(see illustrations)**.

9 On later models, remove the cover, gasket and diaphragm from the master cylinder **(see illustration)**.

10 Count the number of exposed threads on the end of the pushrod inside the clevis, or measure the distance between the centerline of the lower mounting bolt hole and the clevis pin hole **(see illustration)**. Write this number down for use on assembly. Hold the clevis with a pair of pliers and loosen the locknut, then unscrew the clevis and locknut from the pushrod **(see illustration)**.

11 Remove the rubber dust boot from the master cylinder bore **(see illustration)**. Depress the pushrod and, using snap-ring pliers, remove the snap-ring **(see illustration)**. Slide out the piston, the cup seal and spring. Lay the parts out in the proper order to prevent confusion during reassembly **(see illustrations)**.

12 Clean all of the parts with brake system cleaner, isopropyl alcohol or clean brake fluid. **Caution:** *Do not, under any circumstances, use a petroleum-based solvent to clean brake parts.* If compressed air is available, use it to dry the parts thoroughly (make sure it's filtered and unlubricated). Check the master cylinder bore for corrosion, scratches, nicks and score marks. If damage is evident, the master cylinder must be replaced with a new one. If the master cylinder is in poor condition, then the caliper should be checked as well.

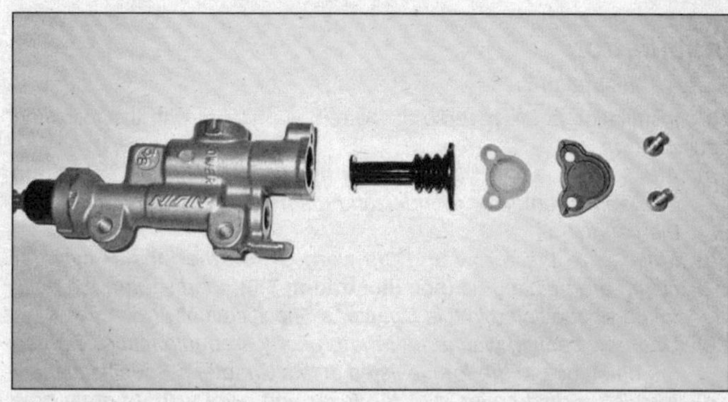

8.9 Rear master cylinder cover, gasket and diaphragm (integral reservoir type)

13 Yamaha supplies a new piston in its rebuild kits. If the cup seals are not installed on the new piston, install them, making sure the lips face away from the lever end of the piston. Use the new piston regardless of the condition of the old one.

14 Before reassembling the master cylinder, soak the piston and the rubber cup seals in clean brake fluid for ten or fifteen minutes. Lubricate the master cylinder bore with clean brake fluid, then carefully insert the parts in the reverse order of disassembly. Make sure the lips on the cup

8.10a Measure the length of the pushrod

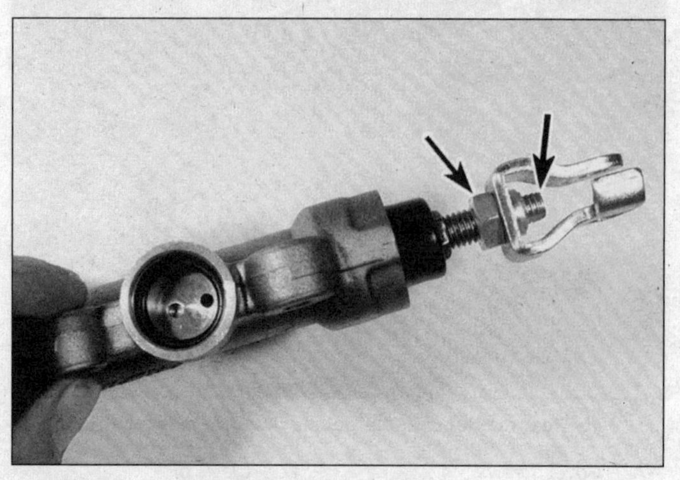

8.10b Loosen the locknut (left arrow) and unscrew the locknut and clevis from the pushrod

8.11a Take the dust boot off the pushrod

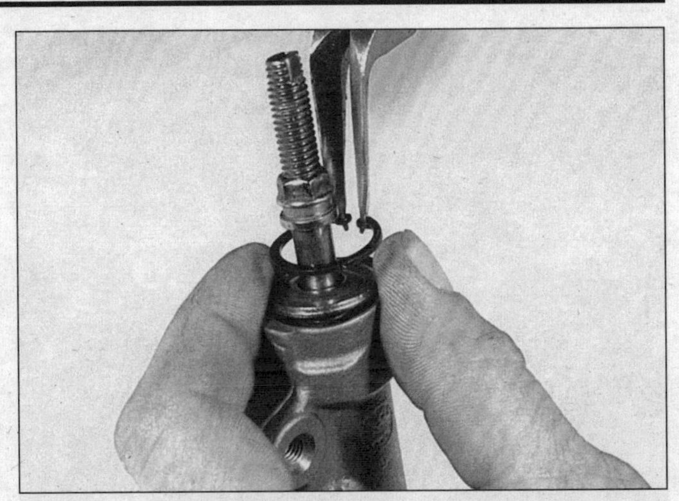

8.11b Remove the snap-ring from the master cylinder bore and withdraw the piston assembly and spring

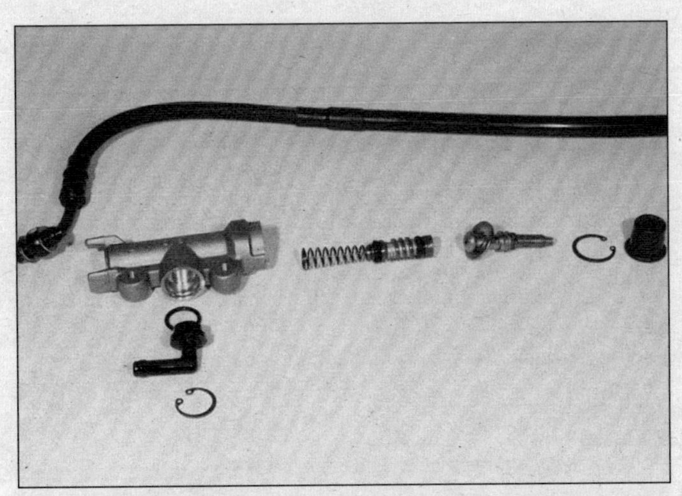

8.11c Rear master cylinder details (separate reservoir type)

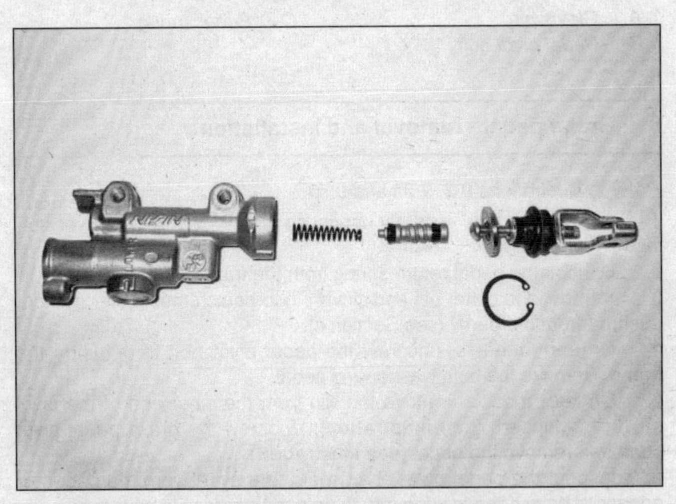

8.11d Rear master cylinder details (integral reservoir type)

seals do not turn inside out when they are slipped into the bore.

15 Lubricate the end of the pushrod with PBC (poly butyl cuprysil) grease, or silicone grease designed for brake applications, and install the pushrod and stop washer into the cylinder bore. Depress the pushrod, then install the snap-ring (make sure the snap-ring is properly seated in the groove with the sharp edge facing out) **(see illustration)**. Install the rubber dust boot (make sure the lip is seated properly in the groove in the piston stop nut).

16 Install the locknut and clevis to the end of the pushrod, making sure the dimension between the master cylinder lower mounting hole and clevis pin hole is the same as before disassembly, or leaving the same number of exposed threads inside the clevis as was written down during removal. This will ensure the brake pedal will be positioned correctly. Tighten the locknut securely.

17 Install the feed hose fitting, using a new O-ring. Install the snap-ring, making sure it seats properly in its groove.

Installation

18 On early models, install the fluid reservoir if it was removed. Connect the fluid feed hose to the fitting on the master cylinder and secure it with the clamp.

19 Position the master cylinder on the frame and install the bolts, tightening them to the torque listed in this Chapter's Specifications.

20 Connect the banjo fitting to the top of the master cylinder, using new sealing washers on each side of the fitting. Tighten the banjo fitting bolt to the torque listed in this Chapter's Specifications.

21 Connect the clevis to the brake pedal and secure the clevis pin with a new cotter pin.

22 Fill the fluid reservoir with the specified fluid (see Chapter 1) and bleed the system following the procedure in Section 11.

23 Check the position of the brake pedal (see Chapter 1) and adjust it if necessary. Check the operation of the brakes carefully before riding the motorcycle.

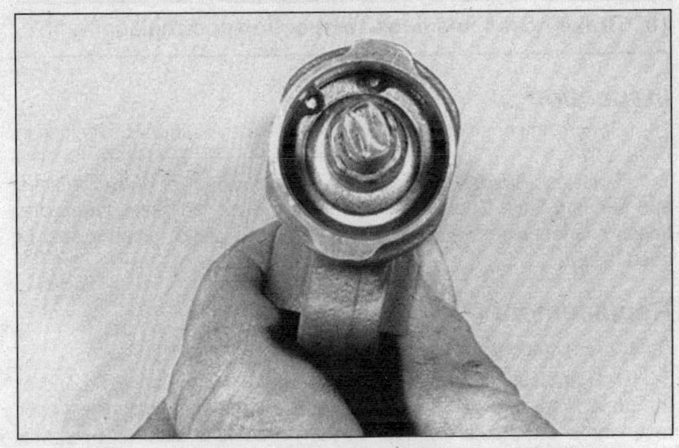

8.15 Make sure the snap-ring is securely seated in its groove

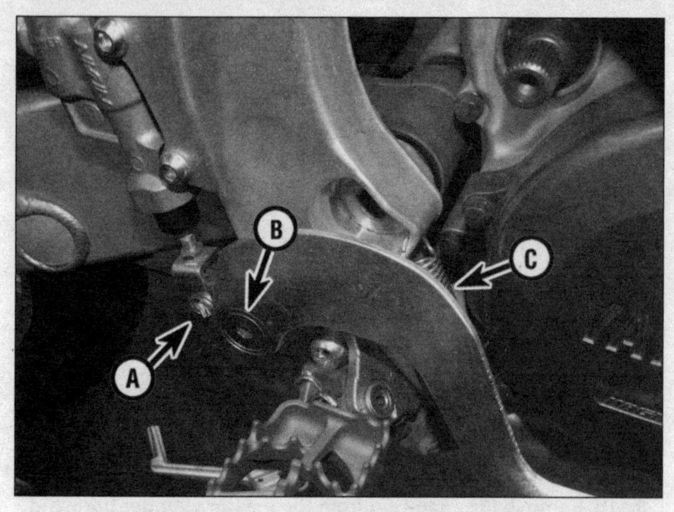

9.2 Brake pedal details (disc brake pedal shown)

A Clevis pin
B Pedal pivot bolt
C Pedal spring

9 Brake pedal - removal and installation

Refer to illustrations 9.2, 9.5a and 9.5b

1 Support the bike securely upright so it can't be knocked over during this procedure.

2 Unhook the pedal return spring from the frame **(see illustration)**.

3 Remove the cotter pin and clevis pin to detach the master cylinder pushrod from the pedal (see Section 8).

4 On early models, unscrew the pedal pivot bolt from inside the frame. Remove the bolt, washer and pedal.

5 On later models, remove the clip from the inner end of the pivot shaft (if equipped) **(see illustration)**. Unscrew the brake pedal pivot shaft and remove the pedal **(see illustration)**.

6 Inspect the pedal pivot shaft seals. If they're worn, damaged or appear to have been leaking, pry them out and press in new ones.

7 Installation is the reverse of the removal steps, with the following additions:

a) *Lubricate the pedal shaft or pivot bolt O-rings and the pivot hole with multi-purpose grease.*
b) *Tighten the pedal pivot shaft to the torque listed in this Chapter's Specifications.*
c) *Use a new cotter pin.*
d) *Refer to Chapter 1 and adjust brake pedal height.*

10 Brake hoses and lines - inspection and replacement

Inspection

1 Check the condition of the brake hoses at the intervals specified in Chapter 1.

2 Twist and flex the rubber hoses while looking for cracks, bulges and seeping fluid. Check extra carefully around the areas where the hoses connect with the metal fittings, as these are common areas for hose failure.

Replacement

Refer to illustrations 10.4a, 10.4b and 10.4c

3 The pressurized brake hoses have banjo fittings on each end of the hose. The fluid feed hose that connects the rear master cylinder reservoir to the master cylinder on early models is secured by spring clamps.

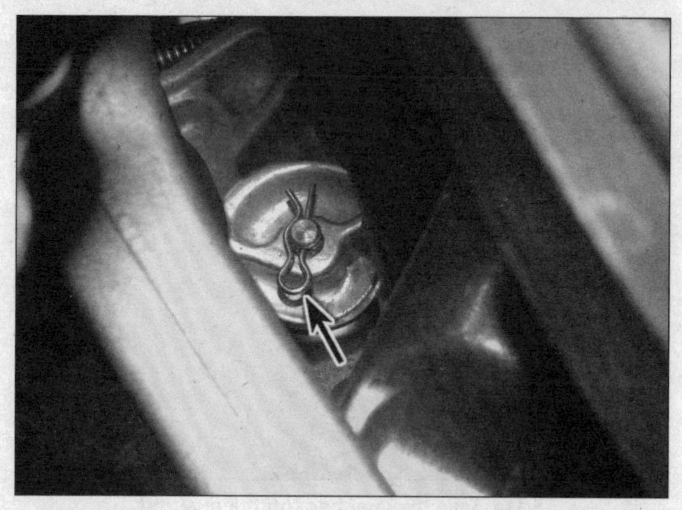

9.5a Remove the clip (if equipped) from the inner end of the pedal shaft

9.5b Unscrew the pedal shaft - use new O-rings on installation

4 Cover the surrounding area with plenty of rags and unscrew the banjo bolt on either end of the hose. Detach the hose or line from any clips that may be present and remove the hose **(see illustrations)**.

5 Position the new hose or line, making sure it isn't twisted or otherwise strained. On hoses equipped with banjo fittings, make sure the metal tube portion of the banjo fitting is located against the stop on the component it's connected to, if equipped. Install the banjo bolts, using new sealing washers on both sides of the fittings, and tighten them to the torque listed in this Chapter's Specifications.

6 Flush the old brake fluid from the system, refill the system with the recommended fluid (see Chapter 1) and bleed the air from the system (see Section 11). Check the operation of the brakes carefully before riding the motorcycle.

11 Brake system bleeding

1 Bleeding the brake is simply the process of removing all the air bubbles from the brake fluid reservoir, the lines and the brake caliper. Bleeding is necessary whenever a brake system hydraulic connection is loosened, when a component or hose is replaced, or when the master cylinder or caliper is overhauled. Leaks in the system may also allow air to enter, but leaking brake fluid will reveal their presence and warn you of the need for repair.

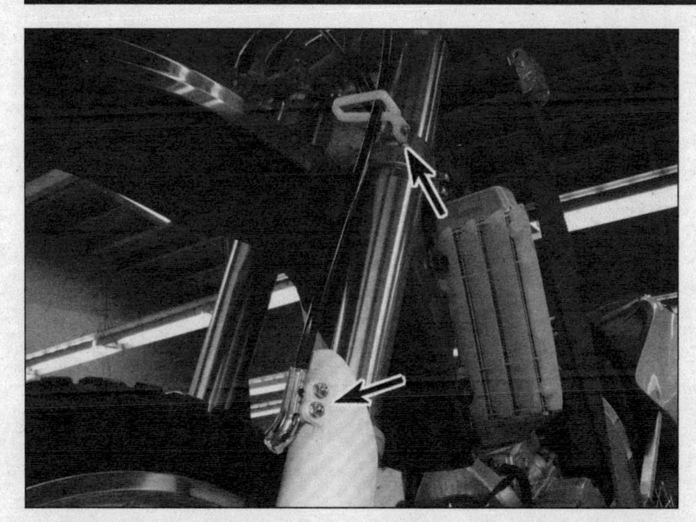

10.4a Make sure the front brake hose retainers (arrows) are securely attached

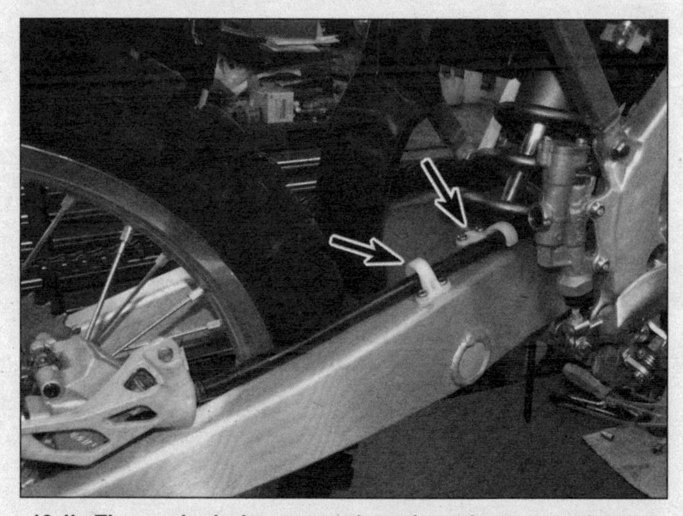

10.4b The rear brake hose runs along the swingarm - make sure it's retainers are securely attached

2 To bleed the brake, you will need some new, clean brake fluid of the recommended type (see Chapter 1), a length of clear vinyl or plastic tubing, a small container partially filled with clean brake fluid, some rags and a wrench to fit the brake caliper bleeder valve.
3 Cover the fuel tank and other painted components to prevent damage in the event that brake fluid is spilled.
4 Remove the reservoir cover or cap and slowly pump the brake lever or pedal a few times, until no air bubbles can be seen floating up from the holes at the bottom of the reservoir. Doing this bleeds the air from the master cylinder end of the line. Reinstall the reservoir cover or cap.
5 Attach one end of the clear vinyl or plastic tubing to the brake caliper bleeder valve and submerge the other end in the brake fluid in the container **(see illustrations 2.9a and 3.12a)**.
6 Check the fluid level in the reservoir. Do not allow the fluid level to drop below the lower mark during the bleeding process.
7 Carefully pump the brake lever or pedal three or four times and hold it while opening the caliper bleeder valve. When the valve is opened, brake fluid will flow out of the caliper into the clear tubing and the lever will move toward the handlebar or the pedal will move down.
8 Retighten the bleeder valve, then release the brake lever or pedal gradually. Repeat the process until no air bubbles are visible in the brake fluid leaving the caliper and the lever or pedal is firm when applied. Remember to add fluid to the reservoir as the level drops. Use only new, clean brake fluid of the recommended type. Never reuse the fluid lost during bleeding.
9 Be sure to check the fluid level in the master cylinder reservoir frequently.
10 Replace the reservoir cover or cap, wipe up any spilled brake fluid and check the entire system for leaks. **Note:** *If bleeding is difficult, it may be necessary to let the brake fluid in the system stabilize for a few hours (it may be aerated). Repeat the bleeding procedure when the tiny bubbles in the system have settled out.*

12 Wheels - inspection, removal and installation

Inspection

1 Clean the wheels thoroughly to remove mud and dirt that may interfere with the inspection procedure or mask defects. Make a general check of the wheels and tires as described in Chapter 1.
2 Support the motorcycle securely upright with the wheel to be checked in the air, then attach a dial indicator to the fork slider or the swingarm and position the stem against the side of the rim. Spin the wheel slowly and check the side-to-side (axial) runout of the rim, then compare your readings with the value listed in this Chapter's Specifications. In order to accurately check radial runout with the dial indicator, the wheel would have to be removed from the machine and the tire removed from the wheel. With the axle clamped in a vise, the wheel can be rotated to check the runout.
3 An easier, though slightly less accurate, method is to attach a stiff wire pointer to the outer fork tube or the swingarm and position the end a fraction of an inch from the wheel (where the wheel and tire join). If the wheel is true, the distance from the pointer to the rim will be constant as the wheel is rotated. Repeat the procedure to check the runout of the rear wheel. **Note:** *If wheel runout is excessive, refer to the appropriate Section in this Chapter and check the wheel bearings very carefully before replacing the wheel.*
4 The wheels should also be visually inspected for cracks, flat spots on the rim and other damage. Individual spokes can be replaced. If other damage is evident, the wheel will have to be replaced with a new one. Never attempt to repair a damaged wheel.

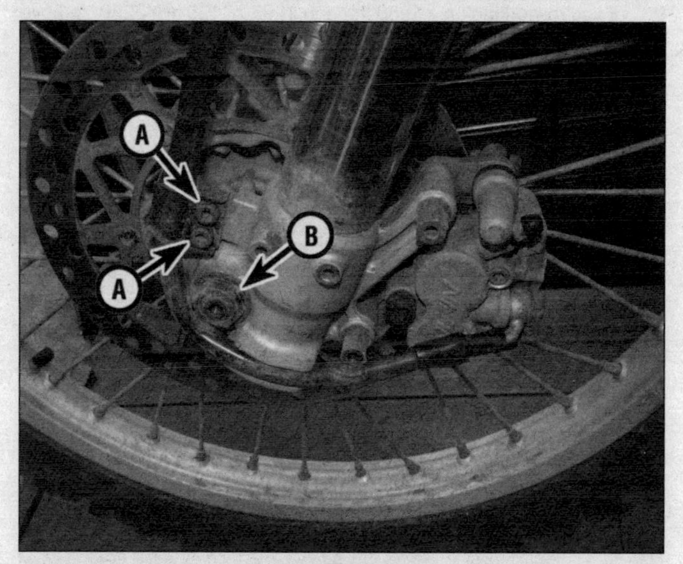

10.4c On 1996 through 2004 YZ125/250 models, the brake hose runs under the axle, through a groove in the bottom of the fork, to the caliper

A Brake hose retainer bolts *B Axle nut*

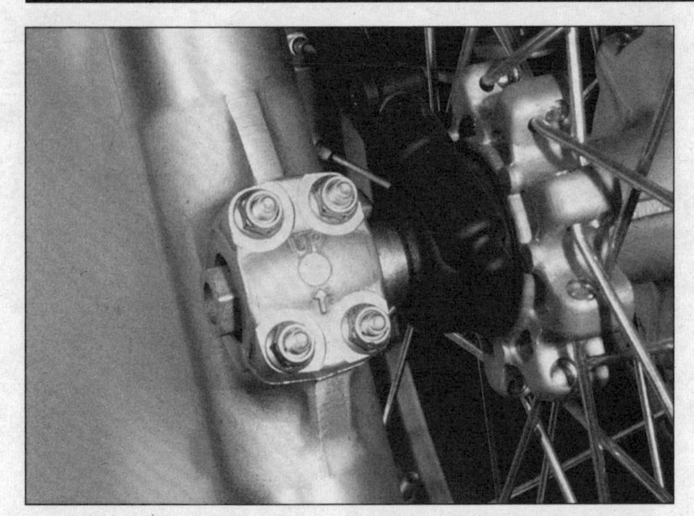

12.9 On 1986 through 1995 YZ125/250 models, remove the axle holder; be sure its arrow points upward on installation

12.10a On 1996 and later YZ125/250 models, the axle is secured by pinch bolts and has an external hex head . . .

5 Before installing the wheel, check the axle for straightness. If the axle is corroded, first remove the corrosion with fine emery cloth. Set the axle on V-blocks and check it for runout with a dial indicator. If the axle exceeds the maximum allowable runout limit listed in this Chapter's Specifications, it must be replaced.

Removal

Front wheel

Refer to illustrations 12.9, 12.10a, 12.10b, 12.10c, 12.12a and 12.12b

6 Support the bike from below with a jack beneath the engine. Securely prop the bike upright so it can't fall over when the wheel is removed.

7 If you're working on a YZ80/85, hold the axle with a wrench on the head and remove the nut from the left side.

8 If you're working on a 1996 through 2004 YZ125/250, remove the brake hose cover from the left fork leg, then loosen the brake hose retainer bolts **(see illustration 10.4c)**.

9 If you're working on a 1986 through 1995 YZ125 or YZ250, remove the axle holder from the right fork leg **(see illustration)**.

10 On 1996 and later YZ125/250 models, unscrew the axle pinch bolts **(see illustrations)**.

11 If you're working on a 1986 through 1995 YZ125/250, unscrew the axle from the left fork leg. On 1996 and later YZ125/250 models, hold the axle from turning by placing a socket on the hex (external hex) or a hex bit in the hex (internal hex), then remove the axle nut from the left side **(see illustrations 12.8 and 12.10c)**.

12 Remove the axle from the right fork leg. Support the wheel and pull the axle out. Lower the wheel away from the motorcycle, sliding the brake disc out from between the pads. Collect the wheel bearing spacers **(see illustrations)**.

Rear wheel

13 Support the bike from below with a jack beneath the swingarm. Securely prop the bike upright so it can't fall over when the wheel is removed.

14 If you're working on a drum brake model, remove the rear brake adjuster wingnut from the brake rod (see Chapter 1). Pull the rod out of its pivot and remove the pivot from the brake drum arm. Unbolt the torque link from the brake panel.

15 Loosen the rear axle nut and back off the chain adjusters all the way (see Chapter 1). Disengage the drive chain from the rear sprocket.

16 Hold the axle with a wrench or socket and remove the axle nut and chain adjusters (see Chapter 1).

12.10b . . . or an internal hex head . . .

12.10c . . . the left side of the axle is secured by pinch bolts and a nut

12.12a If the wheel spacers are corroded like this, they should be cleaned up or replaced to prevent damage to the wheel bearing seals

12.12b This spacer is covered with sand, which should be removed to protect the seal

17 Support the wheel and pull the axle out. Slide the wheel back until the axle clears the swingarm, then lower the wheel away from the motorcycle.

Installation

18 Installation is the reverse of the removal steps, with the following additions:

a) If you're installing a rear wheel on a drum brake model, connect the brake rod to the arm and the torque rod to the brake panel.

b) If you're working on a front wheel, tighten the axle nut to the torque listed in this Chapter's Specifications, then tighten the holder nuts or pinch bolts to the torque listed in this Chapter's Specifications. **Note 1:** *If you're working on a 1996 or later YZ125/250, move the bottom of the right fork leg to make sure it's floating in its "neutral" position on the axle (not binding towards or away from the wheel), then tighten the right-side pinch bolts to the torque listed in this Chapter's Specifications.* **Note 2:** *If you can't move the axle holder on the axle, wedge a small screwdriver into the gap in the holder to spread it, then try again.*

c) If you're working on a rear wheel, adjust the drive chain slack (see Chapter 1), then tighten the axle nut to the torque listed in this Chapter's Specifications.

d) If you're working on a model with a drum brake, adjust the brake as described in Chapter 1.

13 Wheels - alignment check

1 Misalignment of the wheels, which may be due to a cocked rear wheel or a bent frame or triple clamps, can cause strange and possibly serious handling problems. If the frame or triple clamps are at fault, repair by a frame specialist or replacement with new parts are the only alternatives.

2 To check the alignment you will need an assistant, a length of string or a perfectly straight piece of wood and a ruler graduated in 1/64 inch increments. A plumb bob or other suitable weight will also be required.

3 Support the motorcycle securely upright, then measure the width of both tires at their widest points. Subtract the smaller measurement from the larger measurement, then divide the difference by two. The result is the amount of offset that should exist between the front and rear tires on both sides.

4 If a string is used, have your assistant hold one end of it about half way between the floor and the rear axle, touching the rear sidewall of the tire.

5 Run the other end of the string forward and pull it tight so that it is roughly parallel to the floor. Slowly bring the string into contact with the front sidewall of the rear tire, then turn the front wheel until it is parallel with the string. Measure the distance from the front tire sidewall to the string.

6 Repeat the procedure on the other side of the motorcycle. The distance from the front tire sidewall to the string should be equal on both sides.

7 As was previously pointed out, a perfectly straight length of wood may be substituted for the string. The procedure is the same.

8 If the distance between the string and tire is greater on one side, or if the rear wheel appears to be cocked, refer to *Swingarm bearings - check,* Chapter 6, and make sure the swingarm is tight.

9 If the front-to-back alignment is correct, the wheels still may be out of alignment vertically.

10 Using the plumb bob, or other suitable weight, and a length of string, check the rear wheel to make sure it is vertical. To do this, hold the string against the tire upper sidewall and allow the weight to settle just off the floor. When the string touches both the upper and lower tire sidewalls and is perfectly straight, the wheel is vertical. If it is not, place thin spacers under one leg of the centerstand.

11 Once the rear wheel is vertical, check the front wheel in the same manner. If both wheels are not perfectly vertical, the frame and/or major suspension components are bent.

14 Wheel bearings - inspection and maintenance

Front wheel bearings

Refer to illustrations 14.7a, 14.7b and 14.7c

1 Support the bike securely and remove the front wheel (see Section 12).

2 Set the wheel on blocks so as not to allow the weight of the wheel rest on the brake disc.

3 On 1986 through 1991 models, remove the dust cover from each side of the wheel.

4 Remove the spacers (if you haven't already done so) from the wheel (see Section 12).

5 Remove the seal from the right side of the wheel **(see illustration 12.12a or 12.12b)**.

6 Turn the wheel over. Pry the grease seal out of the left side.

7 A common method of removing front wheel bearings is to insert a metal rod (preferably a brass drift punch) through the center of one hub bearing and tap evenly around the inner race of the opposite bearing to

14.7a If you can't position a metal rod against the bearings, this tool can be used instead - place the split portion inside the bearing and pass the wedged rod through the hub into the split; tapping on the end of the rod will spread the split portion, locking it to the bearing, so the split portion and bearing can be driven out together

14.7b The split portion fits into the bearing like this - if it keeps slipping out when you tap on it, coat it with valve grinding compound

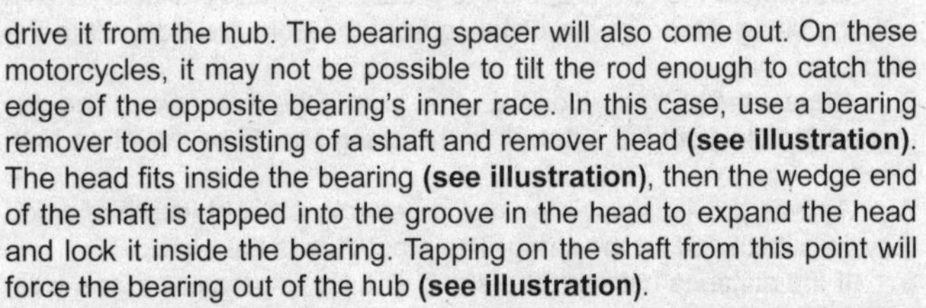

drive it from the hub. The bearing spacer will also come out. On these motorcycles, it may not be possible to tilt the rod enough to catch the edge of the opposite bearing's inner race. In this case, use a bearing remover tool consisting of a shaft and remover head **(see illustration)**. The head fits inside the bearing **(see illustration)**, then the wedge end of the shaft is tapped into the groove in the head to expand the head and lock it inside the bearing. Tapping on the shaft from this point will force the bearing out of the hub **(see illustration)**.

8 Lay the wheel on its other side and remove the remaining bearing using the same technique. **Note:** *The bearings must be replaced with new ones whenever they're removed, as they're almost certain to be damaged during removal.*

9 If you're installing bearings that aren't sealed on both sides, pack the new bearings with grease from the open side. Rotate the bearing to work the grease in between the bearing balls.

10 Thoroughly clean the hub area of the wheel. Install the bearing into the recess in the left side of the hub, with the sealed side facing out. Using a bearing driver or a socket large enough to contact the outer race of the bearing, drive it in until it seats.

11 Turn the wheel over and install the bearing spacer and the other bearing, driving the bearing into place as described in Step 10.

14.7c The tool can be used for front or rear wheel bearings - the wedged rod fits through the hub like this

12 Coat the lip of a new grease seal with grease.

13 Install the grease seal; it should go in with thumb pressure but if not, use a seal driver, large socket or a flat piece of wood to drive it into place. Install the grease seal on the other side in he same way.

14 On 1986 through 1991 models, install the dust cover on each side of the wheel.

15 Clean off all grease from the brake disc using acetone or brake system cleaner. Install the wheel.

Rear wheel bearings

16 Refer to Section 12 and remove the rear wheel.

Drum brake models

Refer to illustration 14.18

17 Drum brake models use three rear wheel bearings. On YZ80 models, there are two bearings on the right side and one on the left. On YZ125/250 models, there are two bearings on the left side and one on the right.

18 Pull the collars out of the seals and pry the seals out **(see illustration)**.

14.18 Pull out the collar and pry the seal out of its bore

14.19 This seal removal tool is convenient, but a screwdriver will also work

14.23 Using a bearing driver or socket slightly smaller in diameter than the bearing OUTER race, tap a new bearing in - do not tap against the inner race or the bearing will be ruined

Disc brake models

Refer to illustration 14.19

19 Pull the collars out of the seals and pry the seals out **(see illustration)**.

20 On 1993 and later YZ80/85 models, the left rear wheel bearing is secured by a snap-ring. On 1999 and YZ125/250 models, the right rear wheel bearing is secured by a snap-ring. A snap-ring is not used on other models. Remove the snap-ring with snap-ring pliers. Use a new one on assembly.

All models

Refer to illustration 14.23

21 Remove the bearings from the hub, using the tools and methods described in Step 7.

22 Thoroughly clean the hub area of the wheel.

23 Pack the single bearing with grease and install it into the recess in the hub, with the sealed side (if equipped) facing out. Using a bearing driver or a socket large enough to contact the outer race of the bearing, drive it in until it seats **(see illustration)**.

24 Turn the wheel over. Apply a coat of multi-purpose grease to the inside of the spacer and install it in the hub.

25 Pack the remaining bearings from the open side with grease, then install them in the hub (one at a time), driving the bearing in with a socket or bearing driver large enough to contact the outer race of the bearing. Drive the bearing in until it seats.

26 Install a new snap-ring on models so equipped.

Install a new grease seal in each side of the hub. It may go in with thumb pressure, but if not, use a seal driver, large socket or a flat piece of wood to drive it into place.

27 Install the collars in the grease seals.

28 Clean off all grease from the brake drum or disc using acetone or brake system cleaner. Install the wheel.

15 Tires - removal and installation

1 To properly remove and install tires, you will need at least two motorcycle tire irons (three is better), some water and a tire pressure gauge.

2 Begin by removing the wheel from the motorcycle. If the tire is going to be re-used, mark it next to the valve stem, wheel balance weight or rim lock.

3 Deflate the tire by removing the valve stem core. When it is fully deflated, push the bead of the tire away from the rim on both sides. In some extreme cases, this can only be accomplished with a bead breaking tool, but most often it can be carried out with tire irons. Riding on a deflated tire to break the bead is not recommended, as damage to the rim and tire will occur.

4 Dismounting a tire is easier when the tire is warm, so an indoor tire change is recommended in cold climates. The rubber gets very stiff and is difficult to manipulate when cold.

5 Place the wheel on a thick pad or old blanket. This will help keep the wheel and tire from slipping around.

6 Once the bead is completely free of the rim, lubricate the inside edge of the rim and the tire bead with water only. Honda recommends against the use of soap or other tire mounting lubricants, as the tire may shift on the rim. Remove the locknut and push the tire valve through the rim.

7 Insert one of the tire irons under the bead of the tire at the valve stem and lift the bead up over the rim. This should be fairly easy. Take care not to pinch the tube as this is done. If it is difficult to pry the bead up, make sure that the rest of the bead opposite the valve stem is in the dropped center section of the rim.

8 Hold the tire iron down with the bead over the rim, then move about 1 or 2 inches to either side and insert the second tire iron. Be careful not to cut or slice the bead or the tire may split when inflated. Also, take care not to catch or pinch the inner tube as the second tire iron is levered over. For this reason, tire irons are recommended over screwdrivers or other implements.

9 With a small section of the bead up over the rim, one of the levers can be removed and reinserted 1 or 2 inches farther around the rim until about 1/4 of the tire bead is above the rim edge. Make sure that the rest of the bead is in the dropped center of the rim. At this point, the bead can usually be pulled up over the rim by hand.

10 Once all of the first bead is over the rim, the inner tube can be withdrawn from the tire and rim. Push in on the valve stem, lift up on the tire next to the stem, reach inside the tire and carefully pull out the tube. It is usually not necessary to completely remove the tire from the rim to repair the inner tube. It is sometimes recommended though, because checking for foreign objects in the tire is difficult while it is still mounted on the rim.

11 To remove the tire completely, make sure the bead is broken all the way around on the remaining edge, then stand the tire and wheel up on the tread and grab the wheel with one hand. Push the tire down over the same edge of the rim while pulling the rim away from the tire. If the bead is correctly positioned in the dropped center of the rim, the tire should roll off and separate from the rim very easily. If tire irons are used to work this last bead over the rim, the outer edge of the rim may be marred. If a tire iron is necessary, be sure to pad the rim as described earlier.

12 Refer to Section 16 for inner tube repair procedures.

13 Mounting a tire is basically the reverse of removal. Some tires have a balance mark and/or directional arrows molded into the tire sidewall. Look for these marks so that the tire can be installed properly. The dot should be aligned with the valve stem.

14 If the tire was not removed completely to repair or replace the inner tube, the tube should be inflated just enough to make it round. Sprinkle it with talcum powder, which acts as a dry lubricant, then carefully lift up the tire edge and install the tube with the valve stem next to the hole in the rim. Once the tube is in place, push the valve stem through the rim and start the locknut on the stem.

15 Lubricate the tire bead, then push it over the rim edge and into the dropped center section opposite the inner tube valve stem. Work around each side of the rim, carefully pushing the bead over the rim. The last section may have to be levered on with tire irons. If so, take care not to pinch the inner tube as this is done.

16 Once the bead is over the rim edge, check to see that the inner tube valve stem and the rim lock are pointing to the center of the hub. If they're angled slightly in either direction, rotate the tire on the rim to straighten it out. Run the locknut the rest of the way onto the stem and rim lock but don't tighten them completely.

17 Inflate the tube to approximately 1-1/2 times the pressure listed in the Chapter 1 Specifications and check to make sure the guidelines on the tire sidewalls are the same distance from the rim around the circumference of the tire. **Warning:** *Do not overinflate the tube or the tire may burst, causing serious injury.*

18 After the tire bead is correctly seated on the rim, allow the tire to deflate. Replace the valve core and inflate the tube to the recommended pressure, then tighten the valve stem locknut securely and tighten the cap. **Note:** *Some riders choose to leave off the valve stem locknut. They feel that installing the nut will make the tube more susceptible to failure at the valve stem if the tire happens to shift on the rim when riding.* Tighten the locknut on the rim locknut to the torque listed in the Chapter 1 Specifications.

16 Tubes - repair

1 Tire tube repair requires a patching kit that's usually available from motorcycle dealers, accessory stores or auto parts stores. Be sure to follow the directions supplied with the kit to ensure a safe repair. Patching should be done only when a new tube is unavailable. Replace the tube as soon as possible. Sudden deflation can cause loss of control and an accident.

2 To repair a tube, remove it from the tire, inflate and immerse it in a sink or tub full of water to pinpoint the leak. Mark the position of the leak, then deflate the tube. Dry it off and thoroughly clean the area around the puncture.

3 Most tire patching kits have a buffer to rough up the area around the hole for proper adhesion of the patch. Roughen an area slightly larger than the patch, then apply a thin coat of the patching cement to the roughened area. Allow the cement to dry until tacky, then apply the patch.

4 It may be necessary to remove a protective covering from the top surface of the patch after it has been attached to the tube. Keep in mind that tubes made from synthetic rubber may require a special patch and adhesive if a satisfactory bond is to be achieved.

5 Before replacing the tube, check the inside of the tire to make sure the object that caused the puncture is not still inside. Also check the outside of the tire, particularly the tread area, to make sure nothing is projecting through the tire that may cause another puncture. Check the rim for sharp edges or damage. Make sure the rubber trim band is in good condition and properly installed before inserting the tube.

TIRE CHANGING SEQUENCE - TUBED TIRES

1 Deflate the tire and loosen the rim lock nut. After pushing the tire beads away from the rim flanges push the tire bead into the well of the rim at the point opposite the valve. Insert the tire lever adjacent to the valve and work the bead over the edge of the rim.

Use two levers to work the bead over the edge of the rim. Note the use of rim protectors

Remove the inner tube from the tire

When the first bead is clear, remove the tire as shown. If the bead isn't too tight, rim protectors won't be necessary

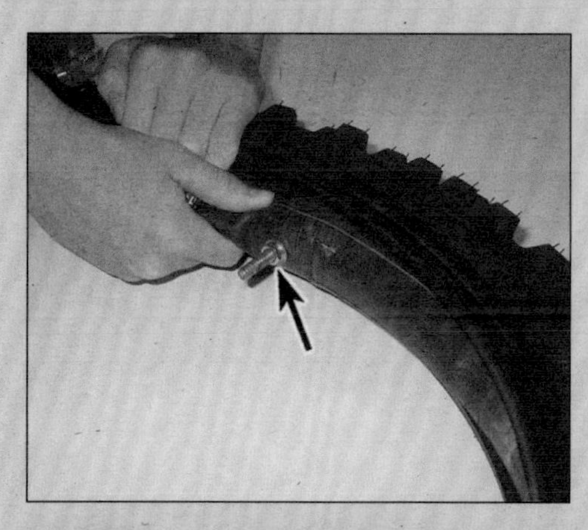

To install, partially inflate the inner tube and insert it in the tire. Make sure there's a nut on the valve stem

Work the first bead over the rim and feed the valve through the hole in the rim. Partially screw on the retaining nut to hold the valve in place. (The nut should be removed after the tire has been inflated)

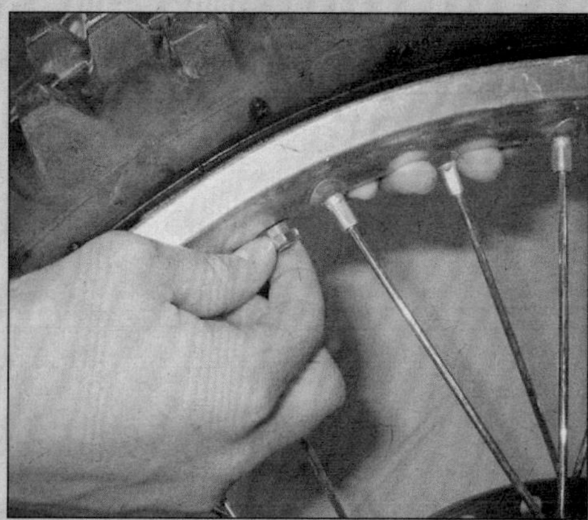

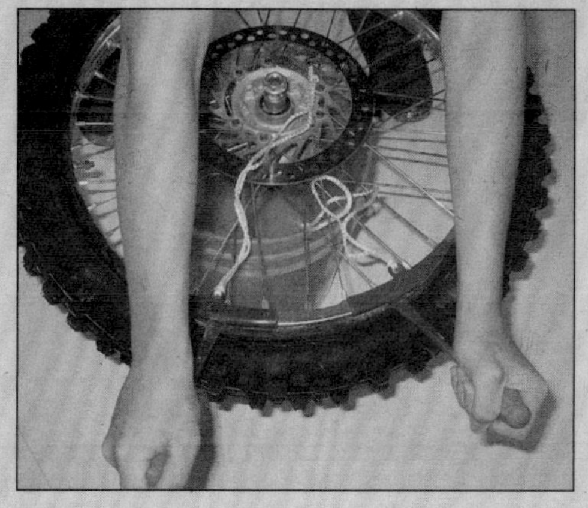

Check that the inner tube is positioned correctly and work the second bead over the rim using the tire levers. Start at a point between the valve stem and the rim lock

8 Work final area of the bead over the rim while pushing the valve inwards to ensure that the inner tube is not trapped. Also push the rim lock inwards and, if necessary, pry the tire bead over the rim lock. After inflating the tire, tighten the rim lock nut securely

Notes

Chapter 8
Frame and bodywork

Contents

1 General information

This Chapter covers the procedures necessary to remove and install the fenders and other body parts. Since many service and repair operations on these motorcycles require removal of the fenders and/or other body parts, the procedures are grouped here and referred to from other Chapters.

In the case of damage to plastic body parts, it is usually necessary to remove the broken component and replace it with a new (or used) one. The material that the fenders and other plastic body parts are composed of doesn't lend itself to conventional repair techniques. There are, however, some shops that specialize in "plastic welding", but in most cases it is more cost effective to just replace the part.

Note: *When attempting to remove any body panel, first study the panel closely, noting any fasteners and associated fittings, to be sure of returning everything to its correct place on installation. In some cases, the aid of an assistant will be required when removing panels, to help avoid damaging the paint. Once the visible fasteners have been removed, try to lift off the panel as described but DO NOT FORCE the panel - if it will not release, check that all fasteners have been removed and try again. Where a panel engages another by means of lugs and grommets, be careful not to break the lugs or damage the bodywork. Remember that a few moments of patience at this stage will save you a lot of money in replacing broken panels!*

2 Seat - removal and installation

Refer to illustrations 2.1a, 2.1b and 2.2

1 Remove one bolt from each side of the seat **(see illustration)**.

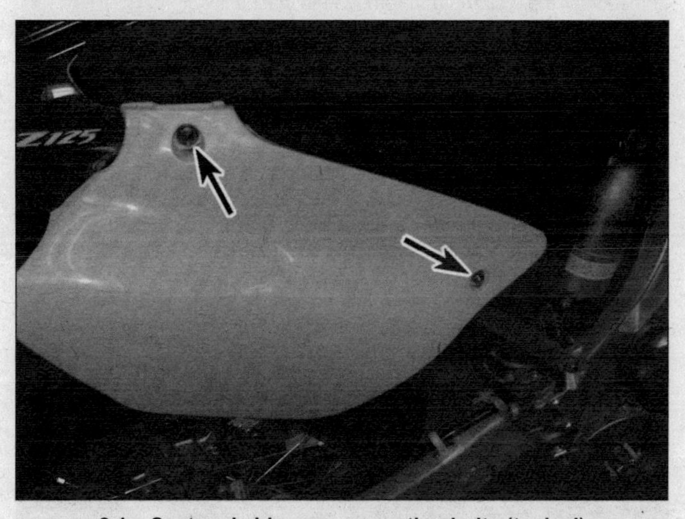

2.1a Seat and side cover mounting bolts (typical)

2.1b Unscrew the seat/side cover bolt on each side (2006 YZ125 shown)

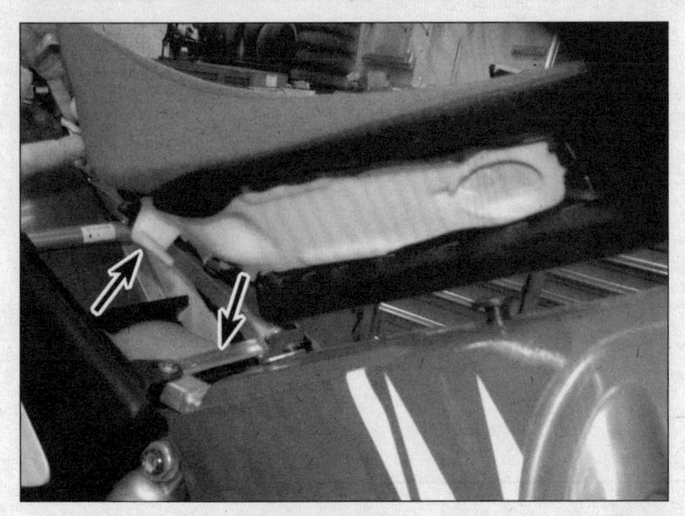

2.2 Detach the hook under the front of the seat from the retainer on the frame (arrows)

5.1a Remove the bolt . . .

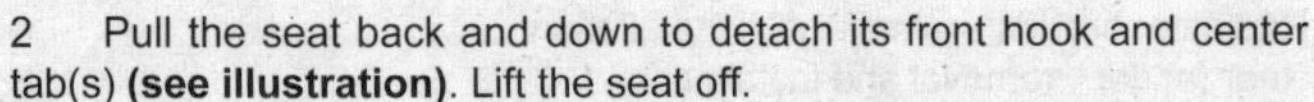

2 Pull the seat back and down to detach its front hook and center tab(s) **(see illustration)**. Lift the seat off.

3 Installation is the reverse of removal. Be sure to engage the front hook.

3 Side covers - removal and installation

1 Remove the seat (see Section 2).

2 Remove the side cover bolt and screw and take it off **(see illustration 2.1a)**.

3 Installation is the reverse of the removal steps.

4 Footpegs - removal and installation

1 Support the bike securely so it can't be knocked over during this procedure.

2 To detach the footpeg from the pivot pin, note how the spring is installed, then remove the cotter pin, washer and pivot pin. Separate the footpeg from the motorcycle.

3 Installation is the reverse of removal, with the following addition: Use a new cotter pin and wrap its ends around the pivot pin.

5 Number plate - removal and installation

Refer to illustrations 5.1a, 5.1b, 5.2 and 5.3

1 Unscrew the number plate bolt and unhook its integral strap **(see illustrations)**.

2 On models so equipped, free the clutch cable from the clip inside the number plate **(see illustration)**.

3 Lift the number plate off its posts **(see illustration)**.

4 Installation is the reverse of the removal steps.

6 Radiator shrouds - removal and installation

Refer to illustration 6.1

1 To remove the shrouds, undo their bolts and screws and remove them from the motorcycle **(see illustration)**.

2 Installation is the reverse of the removal steps.

7 Front fender - removal and installation

Refer to illustration 7.1

1 Remove the fender bolts **(see illustration)**. Lower the fender clear of the lower triple clamp and remove the washers.

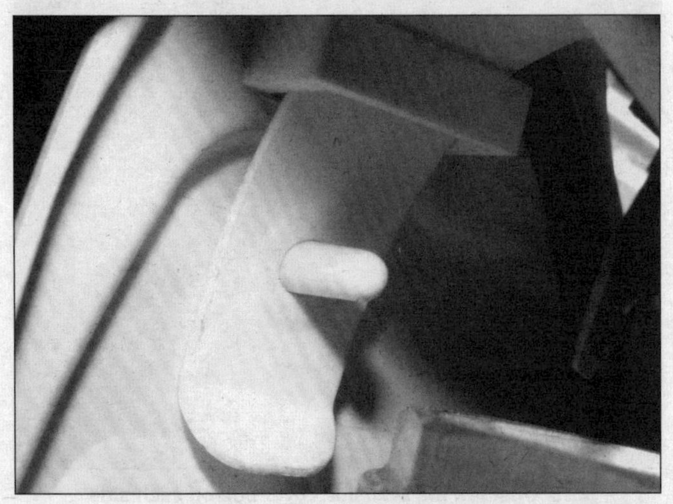

5.1b . . . and unhook the strap to detach the number plate

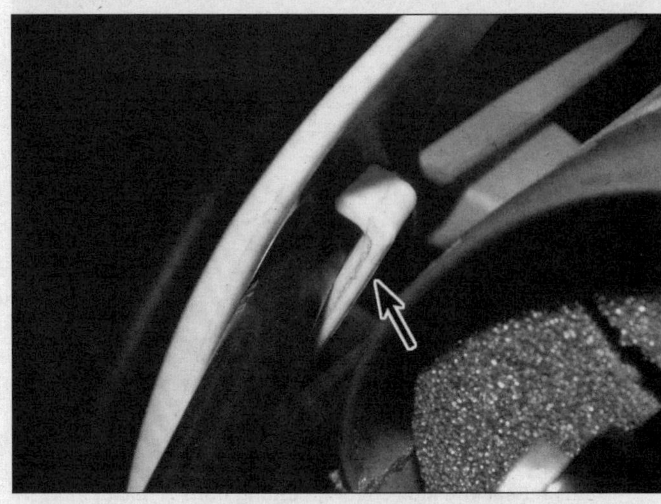

5.2 Free the clutch cable from the clip (arrow) (if equipped)

5.3 Disengage the number plate from its posts (if equipped) (2006 YZ125 shown)

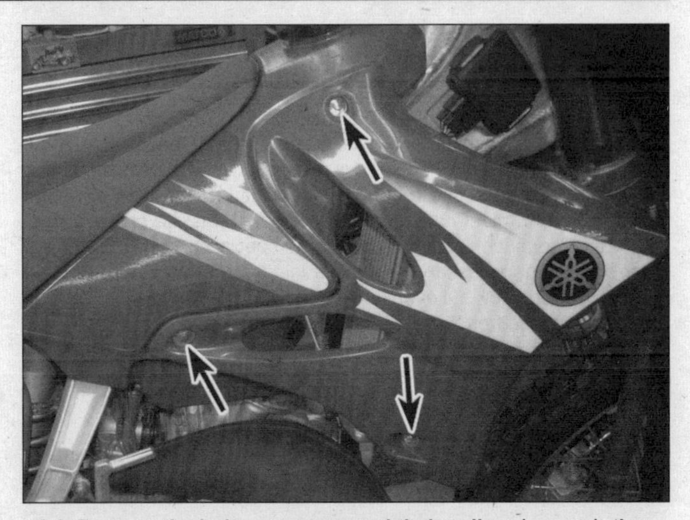

6.1 Remove the bolts or screws and their collars (arrows), then remove the radiator shroud (2006 YZ125 shown)

2 Installation is the reverse of removal. Be sure to reinstall the grommets in their correct locations. Tighten the bolts securely, but don't overtighten them and strip the threads.

8 Rear fender - removal and installation

Refer to illustration 8.2

1 Remove the seat and both side covers (see Sections 2 and 3).
2 Remove the fender mounting bolts (and grommets if equipped) and take the fender off **(see illustration)**.
3 If necessary, unbolt the inner fender from the air cleaner housing and lift it off.
4 Installation is the reverse of removal. Tighten the bolts securely, but don't overtighten them and strip the threads.

9 Sub-frame - removal and installation

Refer to illustration 9.3

1 Remove the seat (Section 2).
2 Loosen the clamping band that secures the carburetor to the air cleaner housing (see Chapter 4).
3 Unbolt the sub-frame from the main frame and lift it off, together with the air cleaner housing and rear fender **(see illustration)**.
4 Installation is the reverse of the removal steps.

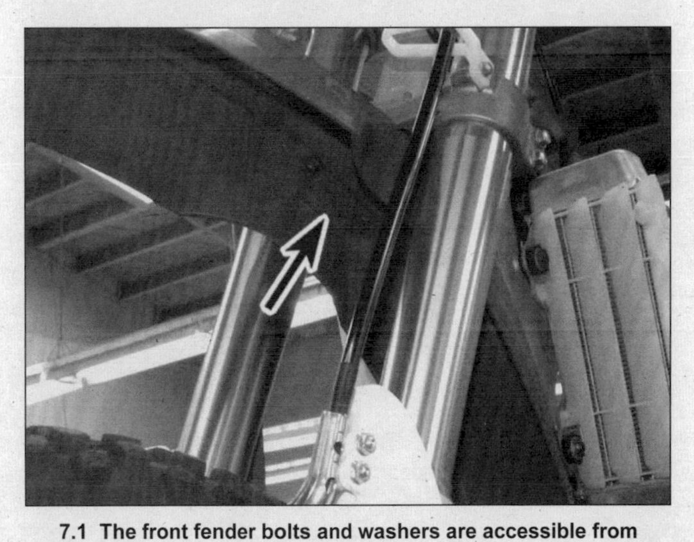

7.1 The front fender bolts and washers are accessible from below (arrow)

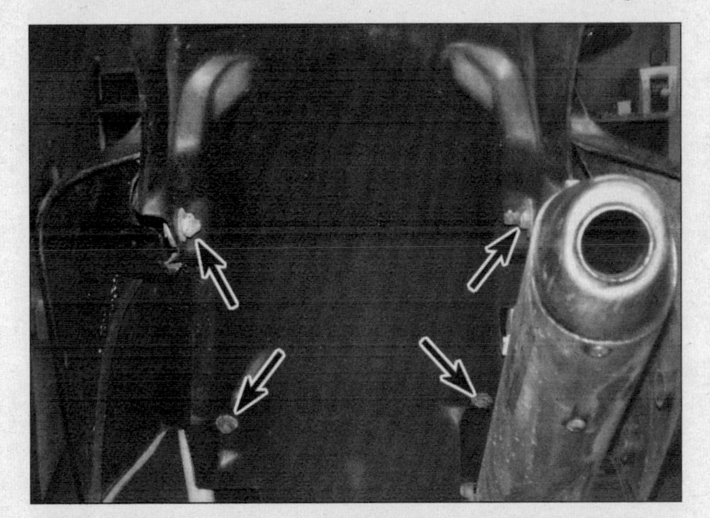

8.2 Typical rear fender mounting bolts (2006 YZ125 shown)

9.3 The sub-frame is secured by upper and lower bolts on each side (arrows)

10 Frame - general information, inspection and repair

1 All models use a semi-double cradle frame. On early models, the frame is made of round-section steel tubing. On later models, the frame uses aluminum spars. All models have a detachable sub-frame at the rear.

2 The frame shouldn't require attention unless accident damage has occurred. In most cases, frame replacement is the only satisfactory remedy for such damage. A few frame specialists have the jigs and other equipment necessary for straightening the frame to the required standard of accuracy, but even then there is no simple way of assessing to what extent the frame may have been overstressed.

3 After the motorcycle has accumulated a lot of running time, the frame should be examined closely for signs of cracking or splitting at the welded joints. Corrosion can also cause weakness at these joints. Loose engine mount bolts can cause ovaling or fracturing to the mounting bolt holes. Minor damage can often be repaired by welding, depending on the nature and extent of the damage.

4 Remember that a frame that is out of alignment will cause handling problems. If misalignment is suspected as the result of an accident, it will be necessary to strip the machine completely so the frame can be thoroughly checked.

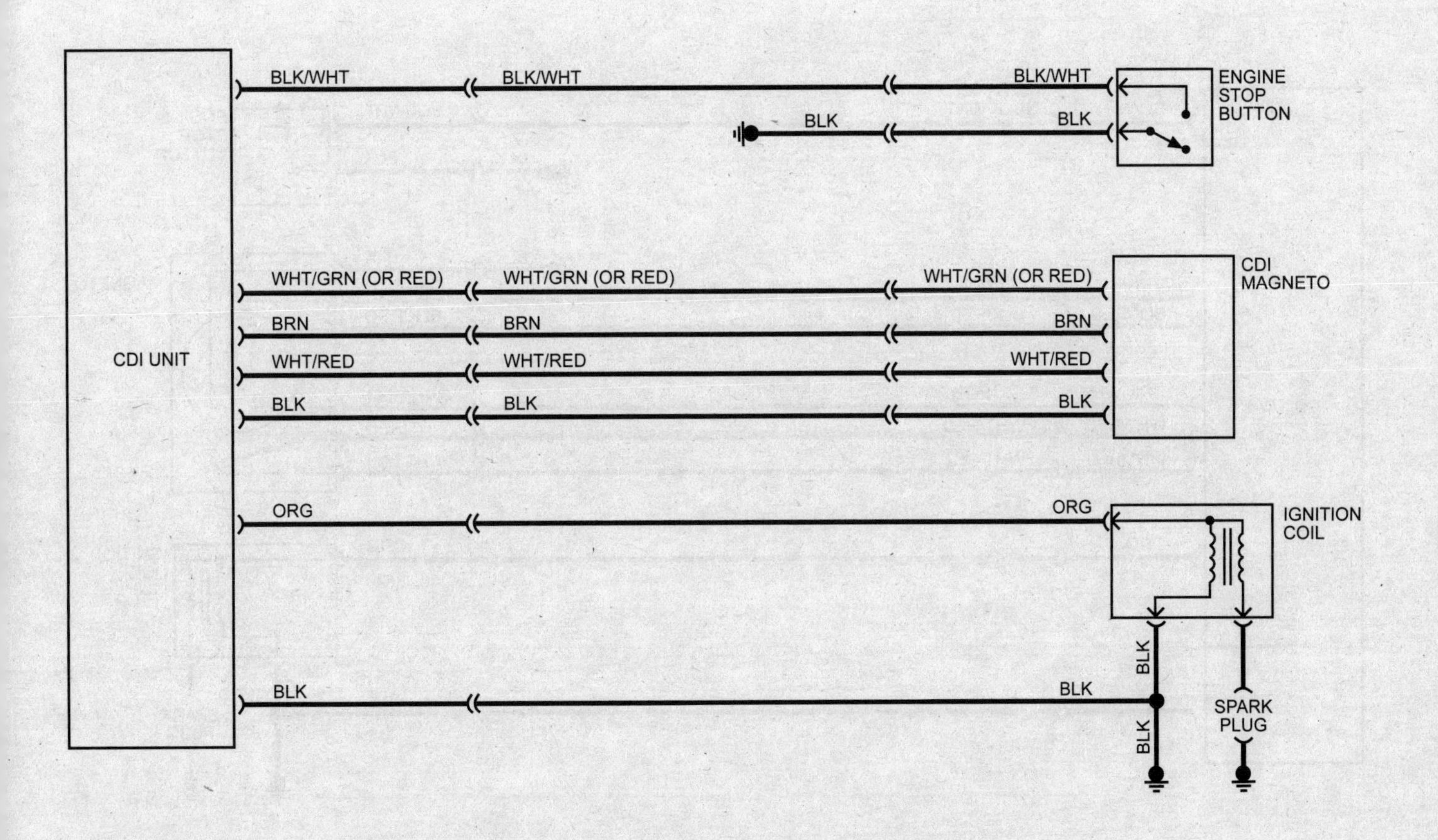

YZ80 1986-2001, YZ125 1986-1987 & 1990-1991, YZ250 1986 & 1990-1995

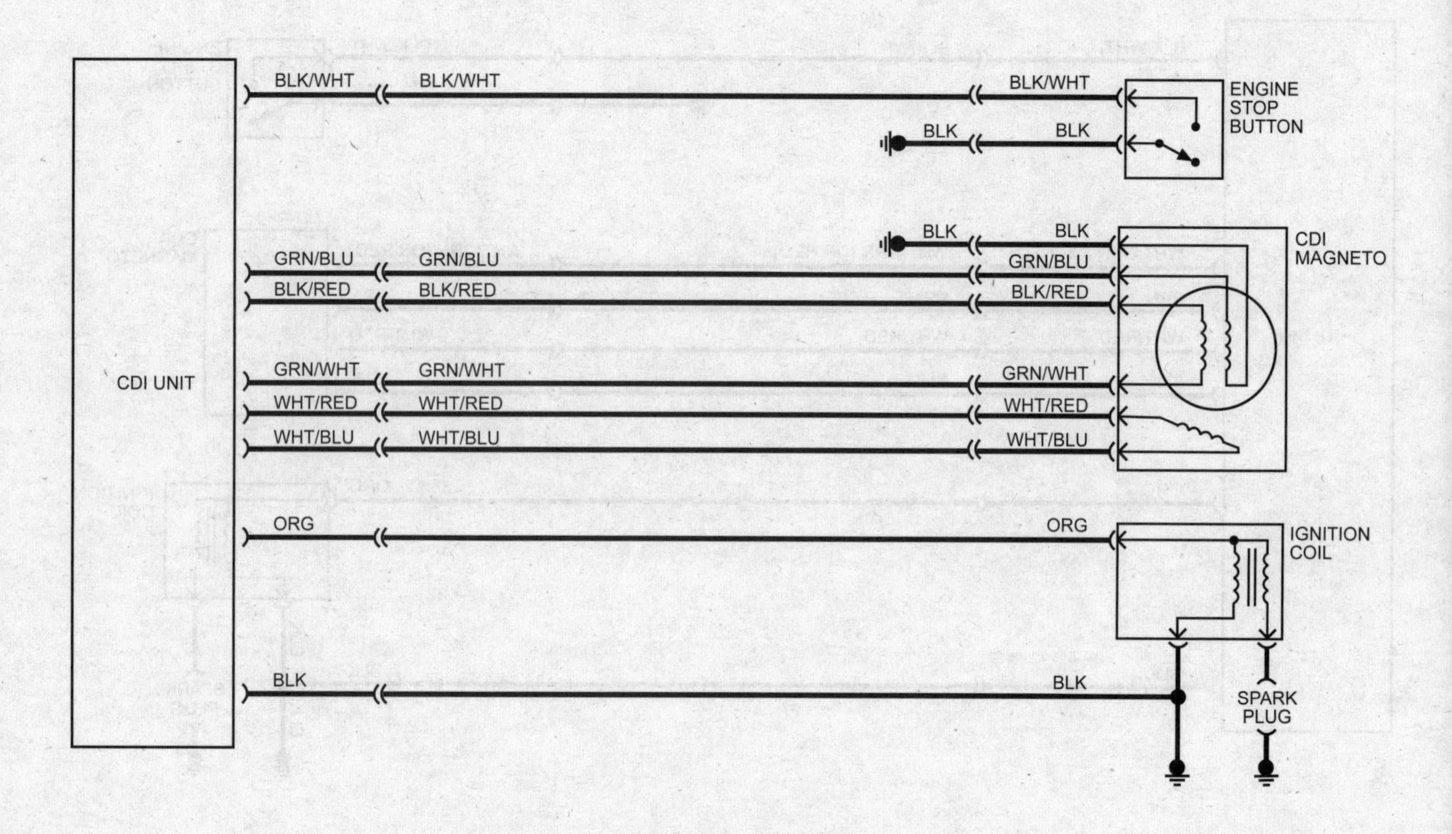

YZ85 2002 and later

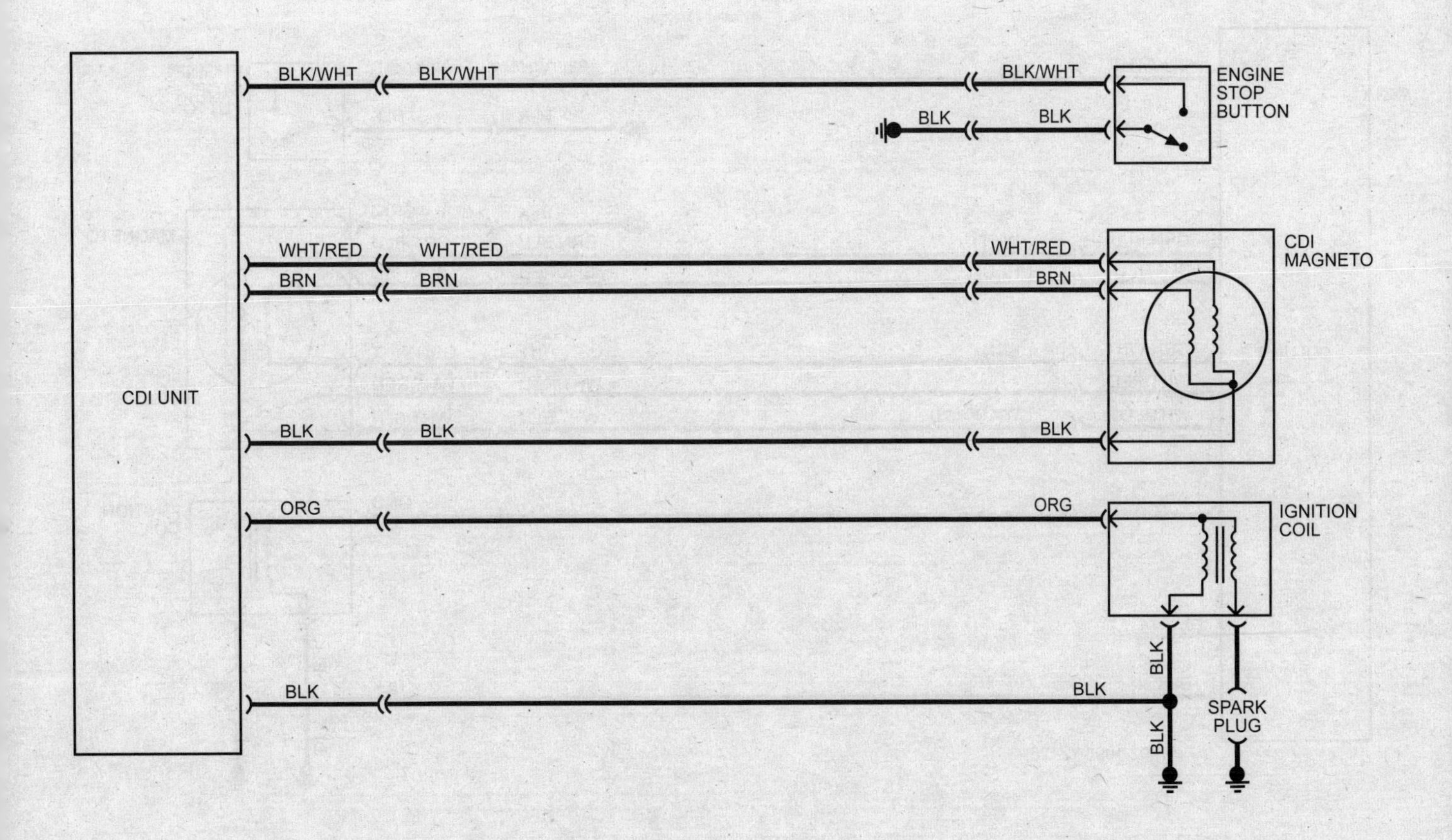

YZ125 1988-1989, YZ250 1987-1989

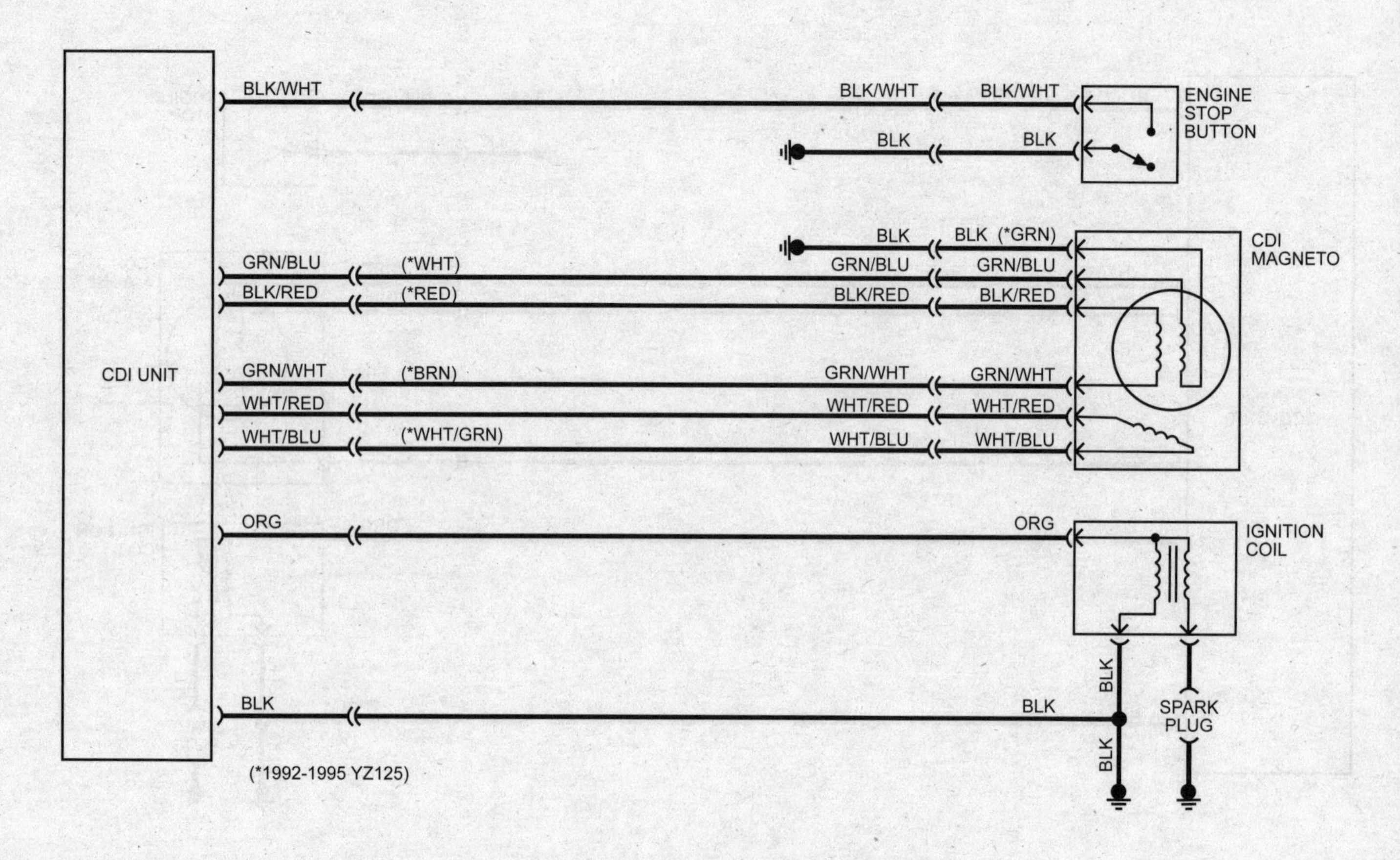

YZ125 1992 and later, YZ250 1996-1998

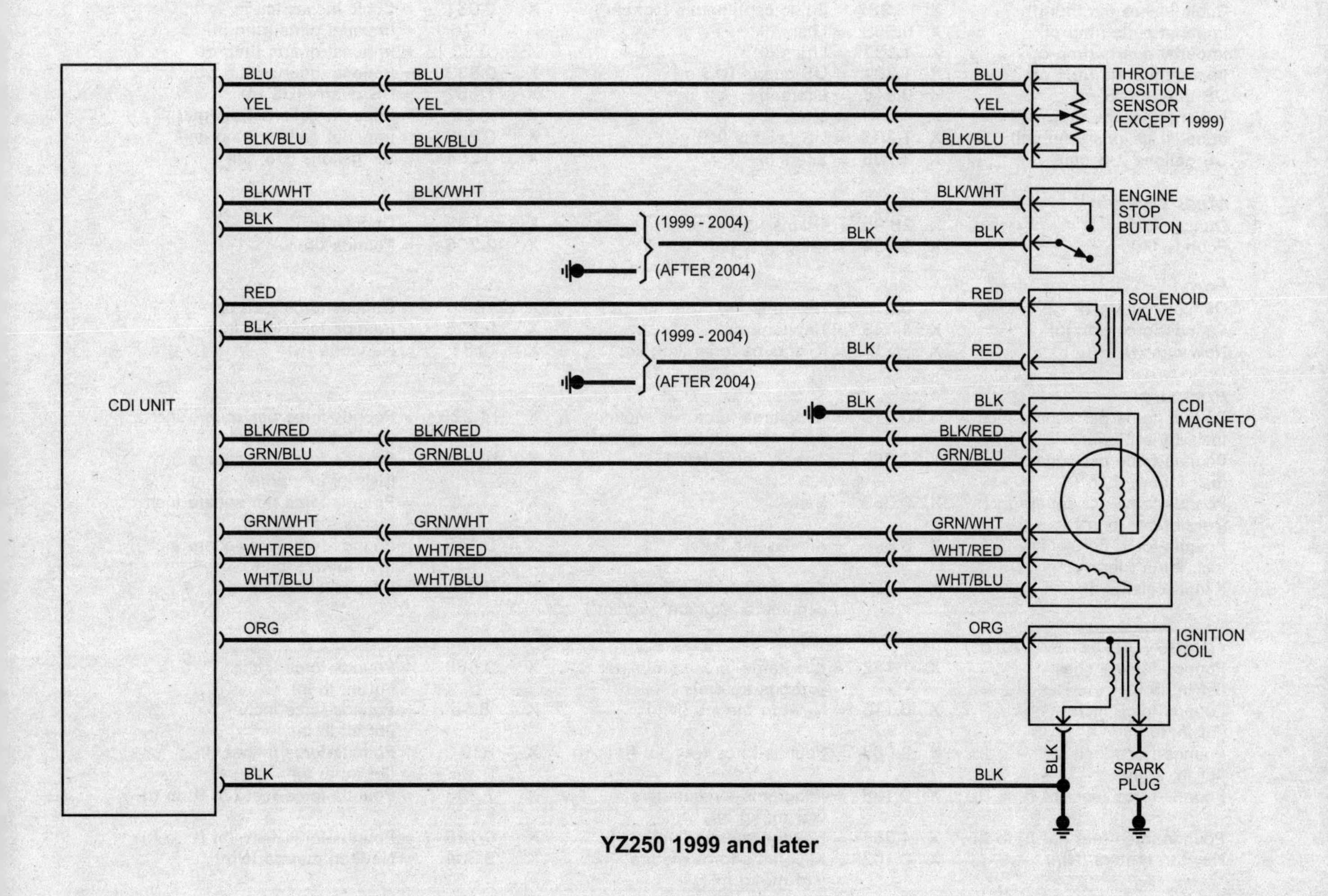

YZ250 1999 and later

Conversion factors

Length (distance)						
Inches (in)	X	25.4	= Millimeters (mm)	X	0.0394	= Inches (in)
Feet (ft)	X	0.305	= Meters (m)	X	3.281	= Feet (ft)
Miles	X	1.609	= Kilometers (km)	X	0.621	= Miles
Volume (capacity)						
Cubic inches (cu in; in^3)	X	16.387	= Cubic centimeters (cc; cm^3)	X	0.061	= Cubic inches (cu in; in^3)
Imperial pints (Imp pt)	X	0.568	= Liters (l)	X	1.76	= Imperial pints (Imp pt)
Imperial quarts (Imp qt)	X	1.137	= Liters (l)	X	0.88	= Imperial quarts (Imp qt)
Imperial quarts (Imp qt)	X	1.201	= US quarts (US qt)	X	0.833	= Imperial quarts (Imp qt)
US quarts (US qt)	X	0.946	= Liters (l)	X	1.057	= US quarts (US qt)
Imperial gallons (Imp gal)	X	4.546	= Liters (l)	X	0.22	= Imperial gallons (Imp gal)
Imperial gallons (Imp gal)	X	1.201	= US gallons (US gal)	X	0.833	= Imperial gallons (Imp gal)
US gallons (US gal)	X	3.785	= Liters (l)	X	0.264	= US gallons (US gal)
Mass (weight)						
Ounces (oz)	X	28.35	= Grams (g)	X	0.035	= Ounces (oz)
Pounds (lb)	X	0.454	= Kilograms (kg)	X	2.205	= Pounds (lb)
Force						
Ounces-force (ozf; oz)	X	0.278	= Newtons (N)	X	3.6	= Ounces-force (ozf; oz)
Pounds-force (lbf; lb)	X	4.448	= Newtons (N)	X	0.225	= Pounds-force (lbf; lb)
Newtons (N)	X	0.1	= Kilograms-force (kgf; kg)	X	9.81	= Newtons (N)
Pressure						
Pounds-force per square inch (psi; lbf/in^2; lb/in^2)	X	0.070	= Kilograms-force per square centimeter (kgf/cm^2; kg/cm^2)	X	14.223	= Pounds-force per square inch (psi; lbf/in^2; lb/in^2)
Pounds-force per square inch (psi; lbf/in^2; lb/in^2)	X	0.068	= Atmospheres (atm)	X	14.696	= Pounds-force per square inch (psi; lbf/in^2; lb/in^2)
Pounds-force per square inch (psi; lbf/in^2; lb/in^2)	X	0.069	= Bars	X	14.5	= Pounds-force per square inch (psi; lbf/in^2; lb/in^2)
Pounds-force per square inch (psi; lbf/in^2; lb/in^2)	X	6.895	= Kilopascals (kPa)	X	0.145	= Pounds-force per square inch (psi; lbf/in^2; lb/in^2)
Kilopascals (kPa)	X	0.01	= Kilograms-force per square centimeter (kgf/cm^2; kg/cm^2)	X	98.1	= Kilopascals (kPa)
Torque (moment of force)						
Pounds-force inches (lbf in; lb in)	X	1.152	= Kilograms-force centimeter (kgf cm; kg cm)	X	0.868	= Pounds-force inches (lbf in; lb in)
Pounds-force inches (lbf in; lb in)	X	0.113	= Newton meters (Nm)	X	8.85	= Pounds-force inches (lbf in; lb in)
Pounds-force inches (lbf in; lb in)	X	0.083	= Pounds-force feet (lbf ft; lb ft)	X	12	= Pounds-force inches (lbf in; lb in)
Pounds-force feet (lbf ft; lb ft)	X	0.138	= Kilograms-force meters (kgf m; kg m)	X	7.233	= Pounds-force feet (lbf ft; lb ft)
Pounds-force feet (lbf ft; lb ft)	X	1.356	= Newton meters (Nm)	X	0.738	= Pounds-force feet (lbf ft; lb ft)
Newton meters (Nm)	X	0.102	= Kilograms-force meters (kgf m; kg m)	X	9.804	= Newton meters (Nm)
Vacuum						
Inches mercury (in. Hg)	X	3.377	= Kilopascals (kPa)	X	0.2961	= Inches mercury
Inches mercury (in. Hg)	X	25.4	= Millimeters mercury (mm Hg)	X	0.0394	= Inches mercury
Power						
Horsepower (hp)	X	745.7	= Watts (W)	X	0.0013	= Horsepower (hp)
Velocity (speed)						
Miles per hour (miles/hr; mph)	X	1.609	= Kilometers per hour (km/hr; kph)	X	0.621	= Miles per hour (miles/hr; mph)
Fuel consumption*						
Miles per gallon, Imperial (mpg)	X	0.354	= Kilometers per liter (km/l)	X	2.825	= Miles per gallon, Imperial (mpg)
Miles per gallon, US (mpg)	X	0.425	= Kilometers per liter (km/l)	X	2.352	= Miles per gallon, US (mpg)

Temperature

Degrees Fahrenheit = (°C x 1.8) + 32

Degrees Celsius (Degrees Centigrade; °C) = (°F - 32) x 0.56

**It is common practice to convert from miles per gallon (mpg) to liters/100 kilometers (l/100km), where mpg (Imperial) x l/100 km = 282 and mpg (US) x l/100 km = 235*

Fraction/Decimal/Millimeter Equivalents

DECIMALS TO MILLIMETERS

Decimal	mm
0.001	0.0254
0.002	0.0508
0.003	0.0762
0.004	0.1016
0.005	0.1270
0.006	0.1524
0.007	0.1778
0.008	0.2032
0.009	0.2286
0.010	0.2540
0.020	0.5080
0.030	0.7620
0.040	1.0160
0.050	1.2700
0.060	1.5240
0.070	1.7780
0.080	2.0320
0.090	2.2860
0.100	2.5400
0.110	2.7940
0.120	3.0480
0.130	3.3020
0.140	3.5560
0.150	3.8100
0.160	4.0640
0.170	4.3180
0.180	4.5720
0.190	4.8260
0.200	5.0800
0.210	5.3340
0.220	5.5880
0.230	5.8420
0.240	6.0960
0.250	6.3500
0.260	6.6040
0.270	6.8580
0.280	7.1120
0.290	7.3660
0.300	7.6200
0.310	7.8740
0.320	8.1280
0.330	8.3820
0.340	8.6360
0.350	8.8900
0.360	9.1440
0.370	9.3980
0.380	9.6520
0.390	9.9060
0.400	10.1600
0.410	10.4140
0.420	10.6680
0.430	10.9220
0.440	11.1760
0.450	11.4300
0.460	11.6840
0.470	11.9380
0.480	12.1920
0.490	12.4460

Decimal	mm
0.500	12.7000
0.510	12.9540
0.520	13.2080
0.530	13.4620
0.540	13.7160
0.550	13.9700
0.560	14.2240
0.570	14.4780
0.580	14.7320
0.590	14.9860
0.600	15.2400
0.610	15.4940
0.620	15.7480
0.630	16.0020
0.640	16.2560
0.650	16.5100
0.660	16.7640
0.670	17.0180
0.680	17.2720
0.690	17.5260
0.700	17.7800
0.710	18.0340
0.720	18.2880
0.730	18.5420
0.740	18.7960
0.750	19.0500
0.760	19.3040
0.770	19.5580
0.780	19.8120
0.790	20.0660
0.800	20.3200
0.810	20.5740
0.820	21.8280
0.830	21.0820
0.840	21.3360
0.850	21.5900
0.860	21.8440
0.870	22.0980
0.880	22.3520
0.890	22.6060
0.900	22.8600
0.910	23.1140
0.920	23.3680
0.930	23.6220
0.940	23.8760
0.950	24.1300
0.960	24.3840
0.970	24.6380
0.980	24.8920
0.990	25.1460
1.000	25.4000

FRACTIONS TO DECIMALS TO MILLIMETERS

Fraction	Decimal	mm	Fraction	Decimal	mm
1/64	0.0156	0.3969	33/64	0.5156	13.0969
1/32	0.0312	0.7938	17/32	0.5312	13.4938
3/64	0.0469	1.1906	35/64	0.5469	13.8906
1/16	0.0625	1.5875	9/16	0.5625	14.2875
5/64	0.0781	1.9844	37/64	0.5781	14.6844
3/32	0.0938	2.3812	19/32	0.5938	15.0812
7/64	0.1094	2.7781	39/64	0.6094	15.4781
1/8	0.1250	3.1750	5/8	0.6250	15.8750
9/64	0.1406	3.5719	41/64	0.6406	16.2719
5/32	0.1562	3.9688	21/32	0.6562	16.6688
11/64	0.1719	4.3656	43/64	0.6719	17.0656
3/16	0.1875	4.7625	11/16	0.6875	17.4625
13/64	0.2031	5.1594	45/64	0.7031	17.8594
7/32	0.2188	5.5562	23/32	0.7188	18.2562
15/64	0.2344	5.9531	47/64	0.7344	18.6531
1/4	0.2500	6.3500	3/4	0.7500	19.0500
17/64	0.2656	6.7469	49/64	0.7656	19.4469
9/32	0.2812	7.1438	25/32	0.7812	19.8438
19/64	0.2969	7.5406	51/64	0.7969	20.2406
5/16	0.3125	7.9375	13/16	0.8125	20.6375
21/64	0.3281	8.3344	53/64	0.8281	21.0344
11/32	0.3438	8.7312	27/32	0.8438	21.4312
23/64	0.3594	9.1281	55/64	0.8594	21.8281
3/8	0.3750	9.5250	7/8	0.8750	22.2250
25/64	0.3906	9.9219	57/64	0.8906	22.6219
13/32	0.4062	10.3188	29/32	0.9062	23.0188
27/64	0.4219	10.7156	59/64	0.9219	23.4156
7/16	0.4375	11.1125	15/16	0.9375	23.8125
29/64	0.4531	11.5094	61/64	0.9531	24.2094
15/32	0.4688	11.9062	31/32	0.9688	24.6062
31/64	0.4844	12.3031	63/64	0.9844	25.0031
1/2	0.5000	12.7000	1	1.0000	25.4000

Service record

Date	Mileage/hours	Work performed

Index

D

E

F

G

H

I

K

L

M

N

O

P

R

S

T

W